INDIA

History, Religion, Vision and Contribution to the World

Volume I

Alexander P. Varghese

ATLANTIC
PUBLISHERS & DISTRIBUTORS (P) LTD

Published by

ATLANTIC

PUBLISHERS & DISTRIBUTORS (P) LTD

B-2, Vishal Enclave, Opp. Rajouri Garden,
New Delhi-110027
Phones : +91-11-25413460, 25429987, 25466842

Sales Office
7/22, Ansari Road, Darya Ganj,
New Delhi-110002
Phones : +91-11-23273880, 23275880, 23280451
Fax : +91-11-23285873
web : www.atlanticbooks.com
e-mail : info@atlanticbooks.com

Branch Office
5, Nallathambi Street, Wallajah Road,
Chennai-600002
Phones : +91-44-64611085, 32413319
e-mail : chennai@atlanticbooks.com

ISBN 978-81-269-0903-2 (Vol. I)
ISBN 978-81-269-0904-9 (Vol. II)
ISBN 978-81-269-0905-6 (Set)

Printed in India
at Nice Printing Press, Delhi

Foreword

I have had occasion to go through the manuscript written by Shri Alexander P. Varghese, as an integral part of his book titled, *India: History, Religion, Vision and Contribution to the World* after elaborate research and collection of data. I am very much delighted to note that the author, a Christian, has taken a lot of pains to prepare and present a compact and authoritative treatise, not only on Hinduism but also on a comparative study on Hinduism and Christianity, two major religions of the world, in the realm of doctrines and practices. He concludes with an exhortation for a dialogue between these religions with a view to create a new era of openness, understanding and cooperation based on the brotherhood of men rather than religious syncretism or amalgamation of religions.

I am glad to congratulate him for this commendable endeavour and wish him all success.

Acharya Narendra Bhushan
First Amrita Keerthi Award Winner,
Chief Editor of *Hindu Encyclopaedia* and
Author of more than fifty books on religion

Dedicated to

The memory of my late beloved parents,
Dr. M.C. Varghese and Ms. Mariam Varghese,
Kallarackal, who inculcated in me certain ideas,
values, principles and strict religious upbringing,
which contributed for what I am today.

Preface

When I was a boy of nine, my parents, along with all children, embraced a religious denomination, different from that of the rest of the members of our extended family tree. This incident naturally incurred the wrath of our friends and relatives that culminated in imposing on our family isolation, a sort of ostracism. Ever since, it was an amusing pastime for many elders in our neighbourhood to confront me with puzzling or mischievous questions on religions, in a playful way, that inevitably led me, an ignoramus on religions, to concede defeat. Repeated defeats at their hands not only wounded my self-esteem but also emboldened me to take it up as a challenge to learn more on religions, preferably to equip myself to counter the arguments of opponents, which developed, in the course of time, into a fascination. Thenceforth, I utilised every opportunity that came across me – sermons, speeches, books, magazines, pamphlets, dialogues, discourses and so on – to enrich my knowledge on religions. But the more I learnt, the more I succumbed to temptations in the form of scruples and scepticism. Resultantly, I had the feeling of an evolutionary transformation from theism to materialism slowly taking roots in me. But I never ventured to forsake my yearning for learning on religions. Concerted efforts to acquire more knowledge, coupled with the growth in maturity in consonance with age, exerted a tremendous impact on me – a full-scale retraction from a sceptic to a monotheist. In the latter half of my thirties, I was fully relieved from scepticism that made my faith in God more deep-rooted and unshakeable. One wise man once said, 'One who is not a socialist before twenty-five and one who is a socialist after twenty-five, both are fools.' These circumstances provided me with the requisite inspiration to put pen to paper aimed at sharing my knowledge on religions with those who aspire for it.

This book is basically an academic endeavour to enlighten students, teachers, religious preachers, educationists, libraries and all English-knowing people, who aspire to enrich their knowledge on one's own or others' religion or both. Eleven world religions, according to UN statistics, are dealt with in the book with emphasis on major religions like Hinduism, Christianity and Islam having adherents crossing 4.2 billion, around two-thirds of today's world population. Two among these eleven religions, Confucianism and Shintoism do not deserve to be treated as world religions in the strict sense of the term, as the former is a socio-ethical system and the latter being a primitive animism, strictly restricted to the Japanese citizens.

The manner of presentation of each religion is matter-of-fact, historical and authentic, supported by authoritative contextual references supplied then and there. Clarity, the hallmark of presentation, is maintained by elucidating matters in comprehensible language and wherever possible, with the help of illustrative charts, pro formas, specially devised formats and statements. Religion, being a sentimental issue for its adherents everywhere, particular care has been taken to avoid ugly insinuations or satire or similar other adverse comments likely to wound the sentiments of the readers. Here, the author wishes to clarify that the attempt in this book is only to factually introduce the religion within the ambit of its theoretical framework and not to present a critique of any religion on any count.

Besides religions, more than thirty philosophies representing various shades of thought, classified into five broad categories, introduced in the book are:

(i) Saddarsanas (Six Visions)

These philosophies, inspired by the *Vedas* (the basic scripture of Hinduism), are independent in approach and arguments, but not fully isolated from each other. Some ideas are seen common to all systems.

(ii) Sramana Philosophies (Sramanas mean Strivers)

These propositions, independent of the Vedas, emerged in the sixth century B.C. that repudiated the conventional value system in Hinduism. The proponents of these systems were generally empiricists appealing to experience and observation as source of knowledge. These systems dominated the Indian philosophy for several centuries.

(iii) Modern Philosophies in Hinduism

Many of these philosophies emanated from the movements for revival of Hinduism initiated by reformist organisations like 'The Hindu Free Thought Union', 'The Hindu Tract Society', 'The Brahma Samaj', 'The Arya Samaj', 'The Theosophical Society' and so on. The struggle for Indian independence provided them with a fertile ground for their growth.

(iv) The Upanishadic Philosophies

These independent thoughts mainly contained secret or esoteric doctrines of a philosophical character that revolve around two main conceptions, the Absolute and the individual Self – the *Brahman* and the *Atman*. In few modern Upanishads, materialist ideas and rational approaches are seen.

(v) The Philosophies of Religions

Each religion has its own exclusive philosophy as basis of its faith and practices propounded either by its founder or by successors, e.g.: Zoroaster, Confucius, Buddha etc.

It is hoped that the book will prove a lasting valuable source for both the students and teachers of History, Philosophy and Religion.

Lastly, I take this opportunity to thank all those persons who have directly or indirectly helped me in bringing out this book. Any suggestions from the readers of the book for the enhancement of its value will by gratefully acknowledged.

Alexander P. Varghese

Introduction

India: History, Religion, Vision and Contribution to the World is an academic endeavour done in all seriousness by an acknowledged administrator who always have had a taste and talent for a study in comparative religions. Basically an assertively academic and enlightened person so firmly convinced of the importance of faith and spirituality, the author has done his research in the subject with a very sharp intellectual exercise in the process of probing the true teachings of religions as also the potential of dialogue leading to a better understanding amongst them.

Shri Alexander P. Varghese through his voluminous book has produced a beautiful piece of literature which contains a content that comprises of a variety of themes – History, Society, Science, Vedas, Upanishads, Epics, Religions, Peace etc. The book touches the Movements led by the various personalities who enjoy places of prominence both in history and religion.

This elaborate study is divided into two Volumes, each one consisting of a number of Parts that include chapters, explaining the various topics, which fall under the umbrella of that theme. The author has made a logical distribution of the topics he wishes to discuss and debate and hence the book has proved itself a very systematically arranged piece, worthy of intelligent reading.

Part I of the Volume I makes a detailed discussion on India, going in-depth into the name, basic characters, geography, history and civilization, contributions to science and literature and world peace. Chapters herein comprehensively deal with the early, middle and modern history of India, emphasising the basic and fundamental unity of India but at the same time throwing enough light on India's unique characteristic, viz. 'Unity in diversity'. This section of the book discusses, besides all these, some of the apparently modern themes like pranic healing, counselling, vegetarianism, music therapy, environment and so on. Part I effectively unveils India's identity as a nation with its historical realities, socio-cultural features, spiritual contributions, India's international interaction down the centuries, besides India's impact and legacies in the field of *Ayurveda*, Agriculture, *Siddha*, Architecture, Sculpture, Textiles, Natyasastra and a score of other topics.

The subsequent divisions of the book somewhat authentically discusses world religions of Indian origin with special reference to Hinduism, making good academic research into highly interesting themes like *Vedas* and *Upanishads*, *Sutras*, *Smritis*, *Sastras* and *Puranas*. It attempts to make an enlightened study of the *Ramayana*, the *Mahabharata* and the sacred *Bhagavad Gita*.

In addition, Volume I contains a detailed discourse on Buddhism, Jainism, Sikhism and Christianity in India. Volume II is totally dedicated to Christianity (with much of its denominational differences), discussing in detail the Catholic Church, the non-Catholic Christians, the Orthodox, and the Jacobite shades. Besides, it studies Jews, Mohammedia, Zoroastrian, Confucian, Shinto and Baha'i faiths.

The concluding Part of Volume II is a concise but self-contained comparative study of Hinduism and Christianity, dealing with doctrinal issues as also other relevant issues which mark the points of accord and possible discords in the cordiality and mutuality of these two great spiritual shades.

Annexures provided at the end constitute an integral part of the Volume. These will undoubtedly prove useful study-aids to the reader of the book as they facilitate the quick access to events and Popes chronologically, Christian denominations, Member Churches in the World Council of Churches, Roman Curia, bibliography for pursuing further study on the subject and glossary of difficult terms for easy understanding. Furthermore, Index that completes the book enables for easy location of the desired and specific terms.

Shri Alexander Varghese deserves our compliments for the pains he has taken in bringing out such a serious academic piece, enriching the intellectual world with his book, indeed, a laborious work on comparative religion. The efforts taken, the data processed and the time spent in putting this book in shape can be well imagined. The author has done a wonderful work.

The book *India: History, Religion, Vision and Contribution to the World* stands separate as a book in volume as also in depth. I congratulate the author for the exemplary intellectual endeavour he has undertaken in writing a book of this stature and dimension, adding to the literature in comparative religion.

May I prayerfully wish the book all the best.

Dr. Cyriac Thomas
Formerly Vice Chancellor
Mahatma Ghandhi University
Kottayam

R.V. House
Palai

Contents

VOLUME - I

PART ONE: **INDIA – A GLIMPSE**

PART TWO: **HINDUISM**

PART FOUR: **CHRISTIANITY IN INDIA**

PART SIX: **JUDAISM (ISRAEL)**

PART SEVEN: **OTHER WORLD RELIGIONS**

PART EIGHT: **HINDUISM VS CHRISTIANITY (ACCORD & DISCORD)**

PART ONE

INDIA – A GLIMPSE

A Prefatory Introduction

1

Introduction

'India', that is 'Bharat' is a vast country, often described as a subcontinent, with a long past and chequered history behind it. But, Indians traditionally had an instinctive aversion to history. Historical writings on India started only in the 18th century after the English East India Company established their rule in India. Early historians on India are Englishmen, Sir William Jones, Charles Wilkins, H.T. Colebrooke and H.H. Wilson, who made significant contributions to arouse interest in the study of Indian culture. Consequently, several scholars in Europe worked on Sanskrit and related subjects. Christian Lassen, E. Eurnouf, Max Mueller, W. Weber, H. Oldenberg, Karl Geldner, A.A. Mc Donnell, M. Bloomfield and Dr. A.B. Keith became great Vedic scholars. German scholars brought out the first printed editions of the *Vedas*, Theodore Benfey of *Samaveda*, Max Mueller of *Rig Veda* and *Atharvaveda* and A. Weber of *Vajasaneyi Samhita*. Max Mueller, Deussen and Frederic Schlegel greatly admired Indian literature and civilization. The names of historians like Fleet, Cunningham, Fergusson, Burgess, Poussin and many others are noteworthy. Among them, the name of James Mill, a utilitarian stands apart from others. He divided Indian history into three periods, Hindu, Muslim and British. He criticised Indian culture as barbarous and anti-rational. According to him, Indian civilization showed no concern for political values and India was ruled by a series of despotic rulers. The Indian Society was opposed to progress and they always remained stagnant, he added.

India, that is Bharat

The *Koormapurana* (an ancient Indian religious literature) enumerates the list of seven islands (continents) called *Saptadweepa* and seven oceans known as *Saptasamudra* in the globe. These islands (continents) are termed Jambudweepa, Plakshadweepa, Sakadweepa, Shalmalidweepa, Kusadweepa, Krounchadweepa and Pushkaradweepa. India is referred to as a part of Jambudweepa, situated in the centre of these seven islands. Jambudweepa consists of nine islands described as Ilavrutham in the middle, Bhadrasyam in the East, Bharathom in the South, Hari in the South-West, Kethumalam in the West, Champaleom in the North-West, Kuruvarsha in the North, and Kimpurushavarsha in the North-East. Among these nine islands, Bharathom is again composed of nine islands, separated by mutually inaccessible oceans, named Indradweepa, Kaseruman, Thamraparnam, Gabasthiman, Nagadweepa, Kataham, Simhalam, Varunam and Kumarom.

The subcontinent of India, stretching from the Himalayas in the North to the Tri Seas in the South, known to the Hindus as Bharatavarsha (the land of Bharata, a famous King according to Hindu religious tradition) was later renamed 'Bharat'. Many Bharatas appear in ancient Indian history. Historians fail to arrive at a consensus to identify the Bharata to whom 'Bharat' is attached. In the *Mahabhaghavatha* (Page 92) it is mentioned that the geographical area known as Aryavarta was renamed 'Bharat' after King Bharata, son of Rishabhan. This theory seems to be more acceptable.

The old as well as the present Indian name for the River 'Indus' is 'Sindhu'. On the banks of this great river flourished an ancient civilization named 'Indus Valley Civilization'. The people of Central and Western Asia used the word 'Hindu' for thousands of years to refer to the people on the banks of 'Sindhu'. In their ancient literature like 'Zend Avesta', the word 'Hindu' is used to denote the people of India. But in India, the word 'Hindu' first appeared only in a tantric literature of 8th century AD. Prior to that, the word does not appear in any ancient Indian literature. Even in the tantric book, the word is used to refer to the people of India and not to any religion. The use of the word to refer to religion is of late occurrence. The old inclusive name for the religion in India was *Arya Dharma*, even though 'Dharma' means something more than a religion. The land of 'Hindu' was called India. Thus the word 'Hindu' is derived from 'Sindhu' and the word 'India' is derived from the word 'Hindu'. Today, both names 'Bharat' and 'India' are in use, 'Bharat' as the historical and religious name and 'India' as the political and international name. In the 'Constitution of India', both these names are mentioned – 'India, that is Bharat'.

Unity in Diversity

India, with a civilization 4000 to 5000 years old, is a land of many diversities – diverse terrain, weather, races, languages, religions, customs, cultural patterns, arts, dresses, food-habits etc. It is an 'ethnological museum' as V.A. Smith calls it, with a variety of races – Negritto, Proto-Australoid, Mongoloid, Mediterranean or Dravidian, Western Brachycephal, Nordic Aryan and others. India has 22 constitutionally approved languages and more than 700 dialects, besides English as link language. Almost all world religions are found in India. In the course of its long history spanning many millennia, considerable intermixture of blood occurred among its people. The Iranians might have come to India during the period of Achaemenian rule in the North-West. The Greeks who accompanied Alexander the Great settled here. The Parthians and the Sakas, who ruled in the North-Western and Western India for a long period, ultimately merged themselves in the Indian populace. After the Sakas came the Kushans. The Huns, who came in the time of the Guptas, also introduced foreign blood into the Indian population. It is believed that some of the *Rajput* clans as well as the *Jats*, *Gujars* and allied tribes descended either from the Huns or from allied tribes. The Muslims, who invaded and settled in India, belonged to various races like the Arabs, Turks, Persians, Afghans and Mongols. Africans, especially Abyssinians, settled in India. The coming of Europeans in India created a considerable population of mixed Indo-European blood, derived from the union of Portuguese, Dutch, French, the British and other Europeans with Indian women of various tribes and castes. On the West coast are to be found some Jews who left their country after the destruction of their great sanctuary by Titus in 70 AD. A large number of Parsis fled from Persia are now inhabited in the coast of Bombay. The Mopalas of Malabar are the product of unions between Muslim merchants from Arabia and women of the West Coast.[1] In spite of the diversities mentioned above, there is a deep underlying fundamental unity in India. Sir Herbert Risley observes, "Beneath the manifold diversity of physical and social type, language, customs and religion which strikes the observer in India, there can still be discerned a certain underlying uniformity of life from the Himalayas to Cape Comorin" (*People of India*, p. 299).

V.A. Smith writes, "India encircled as she is by seas and mountains is indisputably a geographical unit and, as such, is rightly designated by one name. Her type of civilization, too, has many features that differentiate it from that of all other regions of the world. While they are common to the whole country or rather subcontinent, in a degree sufficient to justify its treatment as a unit in the history of the social, religious and intellectual development of mankind" (*Early History of India*, p. 5).

The concept of unity in India has persisted from the ages surviving the onslaught of all manner of political and external changes. Jawaharlal Nehru says "That unity was not conceived as something imposed from outside, a standardisation of externals or even of beliefs. It was something deeper and, within its fold, the widest tolerance of belief and custom was practised and every variety acknowledged and even encouraged."[2] Unity in diversity is the hallmark of Indian nationhood, not only in modern times, but also in the course of its entire history. Geographical compactness, common civilization, a common culture deeply rooted in spirituality, a theology based on faith in one Supreme Being, a philosophy embracing different aspects of human life, natural boundaries, a network of rivers with fertile banks, economic self-reliance – all these have immensely contributed to cement its cohesiveness.

This gifted land attracted many from far and near its frontiers to migrate and settle down in its vast plains to find solace in a life of contentment and harmony with nature, thereby enriching its civilization. Likewise, this country tempted many conquerors like Alexander the Great of Macedonia, Mahmud Ghazni, Muhammad Gory, Kiljis, Tuglaq, Timurlang, Babur and several others to conquer and plunder the wealth of this nation. Trading companies of the Portuguese, the Dutch, the French and the English who came to India exclusively for trade found the situation conducive to establish political authority over some parts of this vast nation. Petty rivalries and feuds among the local chieftains and monarchs paved the way for the foreigners, through dubious means, to hold sway over Indian territory.

The historical boundaries of India have not always coincided with its geographical boundaries. Although Afghanistan and Baluchistan are geographically a part of the great Iranian plateau, they have been closely associated with India for many centuries from the historical point of view. The Mauryan kings ruled over some portions of them. The Bactrians, the Greeks, the Parthians, the Sakas and the Kushans of Indian history ruled over these regions.

Geography

While considering the effect of geography on Indian history, the Himalayas on the North-East ranges acted as the 'great sentinel' in preventing the influence of Northern culture in India to a great extent. The North-Western ranges of the Himalayas called the Sulaiman and Hindukush Mountains are not very high. There are a large number of passes that enabled many foreigners to enter India. The Khyber Pass is 3400 feet above sea level. This pass connects Peshawar with Kabul and most of the foreign invaders came to India through this pass. The Tochi, Kurram and Gomal Passes connect India with Afghanistan. The Bolan Pass is a very wide one and it links India with Kandahar. It is very easy to cross this pass. It was through these passes that the Persians, Greeks, Scythians, Kushans, Huns, Turks, Tartars, the Mughuls and even invaders like Nadir Shah and Ahmad Shah Abdali attacked India. These passes changed the fortunes of India. Whenever the rulers of India failed to take keen interest to prevent the dangers in this respect, the people of India had to pay heavily for it.

There had never been an India in the past with the territories of present India. Once it extended up to the present Pakistan and part of Afghanistan in the West and upto Burma (present Myanmar) in the East. In the early Christian centuries, cultural and religious influence of India spread to South East Asia now known as Champa, Java, Sumatra, Borneo, Bali, Kambuja, Siam (Thailand), Malaya Peninsula, Sailendra Empire, Ceylon, Burma, China and Tibet, together often called 'Greater India'. Modern Indian nation, cut to its present size in 1947 is situated in the Northern hemisphere between 8° and 37° N latitude and 68° and 97° E longitude. The tropic of Cancer passes through the middle with the influence of tropical climate in the North and both tropical and equatorial climates in the South.

Civilizations

Arnold Joseph Toynbee, the world-famous historian, after elaborate investigations and study, published his book 'A Study of History' in twelve volumes, representing the nearest approach to a universal history. Historians, before his period, generally attempted to take up a national state as the unit of historical study. But Toynbee argues that national histories are unintelligible, unless they are linked with the wider field of civilizations. He identified 23 civilizations that flourished during a period covering six thousand years, as enumerated below:

(i) Western, (ii) Orthodox, (iii) Iranic, (iv) Arabic, (v) Islamic, (vi) Hindu, (vii) Far Eastern, (viii) Hellenic, (ix) Syriac, (x) Indic, (xi) Sinic, (xii) Minoan, (xiii) Indus Culture, (xiv) Sumeric, (xv) Hittite, (xvi) Babylonic, (xvii) Egyptian, (xviii) Andean, (xix) Mexic, (xx) Yucatec, (xxi) Mayan, (xxii) Russian, (xxiii) Shang Culture.

Toynbee's study was mainly centred on three aspects: why and how civilizations arise, why and how they grow and why and how they break down. In the course of centuries, eighteen out of the twenty-three civilizations are dead and buried. India is one among the surviving civilizations.

According to Toynbee, a civilization originates when people respond to challenges and adapt their mode of life to confront those challenges. People who live in easy environments and who never work hard cannot advance in the scales of civilizations. Not all civilizations are destined to grow to full maturity. Some break down even in their infancy. The Polynesians, the Eskimos, the Nomads, the Osmanlis (the Ottoman Turks) and the Spartans in the Hellenic world are examples of arrested civilizations. Adversities often play a positive role in the shaping of a civilization. The second-generation civilizations such as the Syriac, the Indic, the Hellenic and the Sinic have provided human beings with spiritual opportunities by giving birth to higher religions. Toynbee views history as shaped by spiritual forces rather than by economic forces as put forward by Karl Marx. Toynbee was a staunch believer in free will.[3]

Three distinct civilizations developed in ancient India in different places and periods of history, the Indus Valley civilization, the Adi Dravida civilization and the Aryan civilization. The Indus Valley civilization discovered at Mohenjodaro in Sind and Harappa in Western Punjab gives us the earliest picture of India's past with an astoundingly high standard of living. There is nothing that we know of the pre-historic Egypt or Mesopotamia or anywhere else in Western Asia to compare with the commodious houses made of baked bricks, well-built baths, two-storeyed private buildings, magnificent temples, tombs of kings, palaces, drainage system etc. found on excavations in the Indus Valley. Cotton used for textiles even at that remote past was restricted to India alone and not extended to the Western world until two thousand or more years later.[4] Though this urban-based civilization was buried in sand due to frequent floods in the Indus, the impact of its culture and living standards lingered for centuries in the Indian mind. Sir John Marshall, the acknowledged authority on Indus Valley civilization, who himself was responsible for the excavation, comments. "One thing that stands out clear and unmistakable both at Mohenjodaro and Harappa is that the civilization hitherto revealed at these two places is not an incipient civilization but one already age-old and stereo-typed on Indian soil with many millennia of human endeavour behind it. Thus, India must henceforth be recognised along with Persia, Mesopotamia and Egypt as one of the most important areas where the civilising processes were initiated and developed."

Many historians are of the view that the architects of the Indus Valley Civilization were the original natives of India, probably Adi Dravidars. After the collapse of Indus Valley civilization, they migrated to the South – the banks of the Narmada River and the valleys of the Western Ghats.

Later excavations on the banks of Narmada and in the valleys of Western Ghats have revealed stone utensils representing the Stone Age (Palaeolithic Man). Subsequent investigations have brought to light metal utensils, cultivation of land, cattle rearing, handicrafts etc. confirming the culture and civilization of the Neolithic Man, the original natives of India (likely to be Adi Dravidars). Carts fitted on wheels, ornaments, toys, an extinct alphabet and other things, which formed the symbols of their civilization, have revolutionised the conceptions of ancient history and civilization of India. Thereafter came the Aryan civilization. The word 'Arya' or 'Airya' means the persons living on agriculture or persons of good family. The Aryans of India came to be known as the Indo-Aryans. They were a nomadic tribe, white in colour, stout in body than the native tribes in India, Sanskrit-speaking and a pastoral race by profession, but not so advanced in civilization as the Dravidians. The exact period of Aryan migration to India is still unknown. It is logical to conclude that they being a nomadic tribe, the migration would not have been a sudden influx or an invasion under a leadership but a long and gradual process, which took hundreds of years.

Dr. Hoernie has put forward his theory of double invasion of India by the Aryans. The first horde of the Aryans came to the Punjab and settled there. They came along with their families. Then came their second invasion. As they found the route by the Kabul Valley blocked, they pushed their way through Gilgit and Chitral and entered like a wedge into the midland country which extended from the Himalayas in the North to the Vindhyas in the South and from Sirhind in Eastern Punjab in the West to the confluence of the *Yamuna* and the *Ganges* in the East. The second group developed its system of sacred rites on the banks of the *Saraswati*, the *Yamuna* and the *Ganges*. The result was that the Punjab which was inhabited by the first group came to be considered an unholy land and the land between the *Saraswati* and *Drishadwati*, i.e., *Brahmavarta*, came to be considered a Holy Land. The theory of Dr. Hoernie is based on a study of the Indian languages. According to him Punjabi, Rajasthani and Eastern Hindi belonged to the first group of invaders and Western Hindi as the language of the second group of invaders. Most historians are of the view that they crossed the Himalayas through Hindukush and settled down in the Northern and Western Punjab, somewhere around 1500 BC. Being a nomadic tribe moving from one place to another in search of pastoral fields, it is only natural that having learnt about the fertile lands on the banks of the *Sindhu* river, they moved into a new area in search of new pastures and better living conditions. After reaching here, they intermingled with the native tribes. This resulted in the emergence of a classical Indian civilization.

Caste System

The coming of the Aryans raised new problems, racial and political. On the basis of colour, the Aryans considered themselves superior to the native non-Aryans (the Dravidians, the aboriginal tribes, the nomads and forest dwellers). Moreover, they were better warriors using advanced weapons. These factors widened the gulf between the Aryans and the non-Aryans just as in the case of the conquerors and the conquered. Out of this conflict and interaction between races emerged the caste system – a division among the people based on race and superiority.

Caste began with a hard and fast division between the Aryans and the non-Aryans, the latter again being divided into the Dravidian race and the aboriginal tribes. The Aryans as a whole were agriculturists and agriculture was considered a noble profession. The tiller of the soil also functioned as priest, soldier and trader. The division originally intended to separate the Aryans from the non-Aryans later boomeranged on the Aryans themselves. As division of functions and specialisation increased, new classes based on functions and specialisation gradually emerged and took the form of castes and growing specialisation resulted in grading of lives in a hierarchical order as below:

From the priests and thinkers who were supposed to guide and maintain the nation emerged the *Brahmins*, the top order in the hierarchy.

From the rulers and warriors evolved the *Kshatriyas* who enjoyed great latitude, the second in the order.

From the mass of agriculturists, traders and artisans evolved the *Vaisyas*, the third in the order.

Below the line came the *Sudras*, the labourers and unskilled workers other than the agriculturists, the last and the fourth order.

Position of Various Castes

The Brahmins as a class were considered the highest in the society. Their duty, according to the *Dharma Sastras*, was to read and teach the Vedic literature and to perform various sacrifices for themselves and for others. They were to live on the charity of the people or on the fees obtained for the performance of various rites. This was the intellectual aristocracy from which were drawn the best brains of the day. They were expected to maintain a very high standard of morality and were to be an ideal for the rest of the society. They were not to covet wealth, power or any worldly gain. Their only job was to make an effort to realise the truth by leading the best of life, an ideal for others. Sometimes they turned out to be the best of soldiers as well. Dronacharya, a teacher by profession, was one of the best soldiers of his time.

The *Kshatriyas* were primarily concerned with the administration of the country, especially defence. As political power was the most important power, the *Kshatriyas* often asserted their superiority over the *Brahmins*. To the *Kshatriyas*, the door of learning was always open. Probably, they produced the *Upanishads*. King Janak was one of the profoundest scholars of *Vedas* in his time.

The *Vaisyas* were connected with the economic life of the country. They were responsible for the production of wealth. As India was and has been an agricultural country, the *Vaisyas* tilled the land and reared cattle. They also carried on trade and commerce. Sometimes, they even became kings and warriors.

The Sudras were the strangest creation of the Indo-Aryans. They were denied the study of the Vedic literature and the wearing of sacred thread. Mixing with them was not permitted to the three upper castes, as they were untouchables. This section of society became the most underdeveloped and their lot was the hardest.

The aboriginals, forest dwellers and all those outside the four castes were treated as outcastes with no rights or privileges. In the preliminary stages, the distinction between castes was flexible, rigidity coming up later only. Any person, who by conquest or otherwise assumed power, if he so willed, could join the hierarchy as a *Kshatria* and get the priests to fabricate an appropriate genealogy connecting him with an ancient hero. According to Sham Sastri, the words *Brahmins*, *Kshatrias*, *Vaisyas* and *Sudras* were names of classes rather than of castes during the pre-historic period. Again "Varna, once a common name for all castes, perhaps taken from the colour of the garments that were different with different classes, as for example, white for the *Brahmins*, red for the *Kshatrias*, yellow for the *Vaisyas* and black for the *Sudras*, which came to mean a caste in post-Buddhistic literature". Thus, 'Chaturvarnya' literally meaning four colours, became an influential factor in the religious, social, economic and political life of the Indians segregating and grading the people rigidly, enclosing each group in separate water-tight compartments.

Brahminism

In India, learning and erudition always stood high in public esteem as learning was supposed to imply superior knowledge and virtue. The rulers and the warriors bowed before the learned man. Even in the twentieth century, Gandhiji enjoyed a very high and enviable position in public esteem not due to any money power or political power but due to his knowledge, virtue and moral standards in life. The general conception was that those who were concerned with the exercise of power could not be completely objective. Their personal prejudices, preferences and inclinations may come in conflict with their public duties and obligations. Hence, the task of determining values and preservation of ethical standards became the prerogative of the learned class, who were supposed to be free from material cares and obligations. The Brahmins alone fulfilled these attributes of learning and detachment, though they have shown all the vices of a privileged and entrenched class.

A large number of them possessed neither learning nor virtue. Yet, they retained the esteem of the public.[5] Therefore, the *Brahmins* occupied the prime place of honour in the durbars or courts of every king or ruler. Being priests, the places of worship were under their control. Even the kings did not dare to do anything against the wishes of the *Brahmins*. Consequently, they enjoyed a vital role in law making in every sphere, religious, political, economic, social, ethical and moral. Being shrewd and intelligent, they could nip in the bud any move to infringe or encroach upon their rights and privileges. The net result was that the *Brahmins* became semi-gods. Inviting their wrath meant dooming one's life forever. They viewed the other castes in the hierarchical order with contempt and distanced themselves from the outcastes (the native races and the aborigines outside the four castes). In fact, *Brahmins* enjoyed an overlordship in every walk of life. They became *de facto* kings, who can do no wrong, the mediators between God and people, the custodians of God's grace, the supreme lawmakers and what else. In this Brahminism, which developed through centuries, we see the elements of apartheid, untouchability, tyranny, oligarchy and the worst exploitation in the name of God.

The Vedic Age and Religions

The vigour and vitality emanated from the spirituality-oriented civilizations led to a spiritual awakening in India in the Vedic Age that transformed the lives of the ancient Indians. *Veda* means knowledge and the Vedic Age represents an era of spiritual knowledge. Despite the inherent vices in the caste system and the brahminical tyranny, the Vedic Age brought forth positive changes in the social and cultural spheres of India. This transformation gradually evolved into a belief in a Supreme Being, revealed to man by that Being. These revelations, transmitted from memory (*Smriti*) to subsequent generations, were later divided and compiled by Sage Vyasa into four texts, together known as the *Vedas*. This facilitated the widespread diffusion of knowledge about *Brahma* (Supreme Being), which served as a catalyst to transform their faith gradually into an unorganised Vedic religion based on individual knowledge and experience.

On the basis of the theological conceptions in the Vedas, several subsidiary books emerged in the long run; (i) the *Brahmanas* (each linked with one of the Vedas) containing the rituals and practices (liturgy) to propitiate the God, which became instrumental in the transition of the Vedic social order to a brahminical social order, (ii) the *Aranyakas* dealing with ascetic life, mysticism and philosophy, (iii) the *Upanishads* containing esoteric doctrines and speculations of a philosophical character that revolved around two conceptions – *Brahman* and *Atman* (God and Man), (iv) the *Ithihasas* like the *Ramayana* and the *Mahabharata* (inclusive of the *Bhagavad Gita*) emphasising intermittent incursions of God into the world for the establishment of *Dharma*, and (v) the *Puranas, Upavedas* etc. dealing with sacred subjects, ancient history, mythological treatises and so on.

We are not sure about the period of the Vedic Age. Many Western philosophers think that the Vedic literature spans about thousand years from 1500 BC onwards. According to them the period of the Vedas is 1500 BC to 1000 BC and that of the Upanishads from 900 BC to 600 BC, allowing the gradual development of ideas. But, the Indian philosophers attribute an earlier origin, even upto 8000 BC.

The Vedic Age immensely contributed to a substantial change in the pattern and perspective of human life. It brought forth a spiritual purpose, aim, norm and orderliness in the life of the Aryans, which gradually evolved into a religion, earlier called *Arya Dharma* and later known as 'Hinduism', the religion of the Hindus. One of the consequential offshoots of this evolution was the change from collective self-government to legalised monarchy enjoying the consent of the people. But, the influence of caste system led to confrontations and tension.

Through generous behaviour and courteous dealings, the *Kshatriyas* earned the respect and commanded the obedience of the common people. On the contrary, the priests (Brahmins) through their vices and tyrannical behaviour more and more distanced themselves from the common man. A few of the Kshatriyas came forward to organise the people against the brahminical oppression. Sidhartha, the founder of Buddhism (563 - 483 BC) and Vardhamana Mahavira of Jainism (540 BC) were Kshatriyas who came forward to rescue the people from the brahminical tyranny supported by the arms of Hinduism. The result was the widespread acceptance of these new religions, especially Buddhism both in ideology and practice through the patronage of Emperor Asoka in the third century BC. (More exhaustive details are given in Part Three.)

Hinduism, which originated as a Revelation-based belief through an evolutionary process extending centuries, developed into a religion surviving all threats and tribulations in its long history and subsists today as a major world religion without a founder or an organisational structure. Buddhism and Jainism emerged from Hinduism as a challenge against the exploitation of the common man by the Brahmins and the excessive and burdensome rituals and practices. Though Buddhism and Jainism were conceived in the womb of Hinduism, these religions stand a long way apart on the fundamental doctrine of theism.

In the 16th century AD Guru Nanak founded Sikhism, a monotheistic religion free from superstitions, casteism, idolatry, rituals, gods and goddesses. This religion acquired fantastic growth in the last five centuries with present membership over twenty-three million.

We do not find a single nation in world history, other than India, having given birth to four world religions of today subsisting in the modern world with adherents crossing one thousand three hundred million, more than one fifth of the world population.

Centralised Government in India

Alexander the Great (356-323 BC), the King of Macedonia in Greece defeated King Darius of Persia, subdued the principal cities of Syria, overran Egypt, crossed the Euphrates and Tigris rivers, swept everything before him, advanced to the East and conquered India in 326 BC. Puru, one of the ablest rulers in North India confronted the Greek army on the banks of the Jhelum (a tributary of the Sindhu River) but failed to withstand the might of Alexander's cavalry. Though Alexander won the battle, he negotiated a truce with Puru and returned to Greece after retaining in India a section of the Greek army under Commander Seleucus. Shortly after returning from India, Alexander died. Greek soldiers who remained in India married Indian women and settled here, merging in the Indian community.

The Maurya Empire (322-185 BC)

For the first time in recorded history, a vast centralized government arose in India under the leadership of Chandragupta Maurya with capital at Pataliputra (present Patna) in 322 BC. Alexander's General Seleucus who inherited from Alexander, the countries from Asia Minor to India, tried to re-establish his authority in North-West India. Chandragupta defeated Seleucus, annexed a part of Afghanistan upto Kabul and Herat and married the daughter of Seleucus. Chandragupta's Empire covered the whole of North India extending from the Arabian Sea to the Bay of Bengal upto Kabul in the North West. Chanakya, also known as Kautilya, the author of *Arthasastra* (literally meaning "Science of wealth" but really a 'Science of polity') was a friend, minister and councillor of Chandragupta Maurya. Chanakya was not only a scholar but also a man who played a pivotal role in the establishment, growth and preservation of the Maurya Empire. A clear picture of Chanakya is given in an old Indian play named *Mudra-Rakshasa*, which reads: "Bold and scheming, proud and revengeful, never forgetting a slight, never forgetting his purpose, availing himself of every device to delude and defeat the enemy, he sat with the reins of Empire in his hands and looked upon the Emperor more as a loved pupil than as a master. He was simple and austere in his life, uninterested in the pomp and pageantry of high position. When he had redeemed his pledge and accomplished his purpose, he wanted to retire Brahmin-like, to a life of contemplation."

Chandragupta Maurya established diplomatic relations with the Greek world, Seleucus, the Ptolemies of Egypt and many other countries. These relations rested on the solid foundation of mutual commercial interests.

Chandragupta's son Bindusara, who succeeded him, maintained these contacts.

Asoka (273 to 232 BC)

Asoka, the famous Emperor in Indian history, the grandson of Chandragupta Maurya, succeeded his father Bindusara in 273 BC. Before becoming Emperor, he was the Viceroy of the North Western Province with headquarters at Taxila, the ancient university centre. The old dream of uniting the whole of India under one supreme government fired his imagination and he undertook the conquest of Kalinga on the East Coast, which corresponds roughly with modern Orissa and part of Andhra State. Although he won the war, the misery, slaughter and bloodbath of the war forced him for introspection on the utility of war. Buddha's gospel of non-violence (Ahimsa) influenced him and he became a strong adherent of Buddhism. In one of his edicts, he said: "Kalinga was conquered by His Sacred and Gracious Majesty when he had been consecrated eight years. One hundred and fifty thousand persons were thence carried away as captives, one hundred thousand were thence slain, and many times that number died. Directly after the annexation of Kalinga began his Sacred Majesty's zealous protection of the Law of Piety, his love of that law and his inculcation of that law (Dharma)." He sent messengers and ambassadors to Syria, Macedonia, Cyrene, Epirus, Burma, Siam etc. conveying his greetings and Buddha's message. He sent his son Mahendra and daughter Sangamitra to Ceylon. Ardent Buddhist as he was, he showed consideration to all other faiths. In one of his edicts, he proclaimed:

> All sects deserve reverence for one reason or other. By thus acting, a man exalts his own sect and at the same time does service to the sects of other people.

Thus, Asoka turned from the conquests of other countries to the conquest of the mind and hearts of others. During his period, Buddhism flourished in India (replacing Hinduism to a very large extent) and the neighbouring countries. Asoka stands unique in world history as model to all rulers in his commitment and hard labour for the welfare of the ruled. His declaration reproduced below gives a lot of insight into his eminent personality. "At all times and at all places, whether I am dining or in the ladies apartments, in my bedroom or in my closet, in my palace or in palace gardens, the official reporters must keep me informed of the people's business..., at any hour and at any place work I must for the commonweal."

He died after ruling strenuously for forty-one years. H.G. Wells says in his *Outline of History*: "Amidst the tens of thousands of names of monarchs that crowd the columns of history, their majesties, graciousness and serenities and royal highnesses and the like, the name of Asoka shines, and shines almost alone, a star. From the Volga to Japan, his name is still honoured. China, Tibet and even India, though it has left his doctrine, preserve the tradition of his greatness. More living men cherish his memory today than have ever heard the names of Constantine or Charlemagne."

After the Kalinga war, we see a King transformed into a 'Philosopher King' of Plato, an unparalleled episode in world history.

After Asoka's period, the Maurya Empire gradually dwindled in size. The Deccan area first seceded. The Satavahanas established an independent kingdom with capital at Nasik. The Oriya people liberated themselves from the Maurya rule. Bruhadrathan, the last King of the Maurya dynasty was assassinated by Pushyamitra, a Brahmin soldier who made himself King. This marked the end of the Maurya rule. The Saka and Kushana tribes who came as conquerors settled in India and embraced Buddhism.

After the breakup of the Maurya Empire, the Sungas and the Kanvas succeeded the Mauryas. But, various dynasties like Satavahanas, Sakas and Kushans ruled over various parts of India. The Greeks, the Parthians, the Sakas and the Kushans ruled North-West India. There were also a good number of indigenous states and republics like Ahichatra, Ayodhya, Kausambi, Kalinga, Malavas and Youdheyas. The centralised Government established by the Mauryas disintegrated.

The Kushana Dynasty

The period of establishment of Kushana rule is not known. There is evidence to show that in the beginning of the Christian era, there was a strong and powerful Empire of Kushans in North India. Historians are not unanimous on the nationality of Kushans. They are described as Turks, Iranians, Mongolians, Bactrians and so on. The Indians named them 'Tusharas'. The fame and glory of Kushans reached its zenith during the period of Kanishka I (78-123 AD) Peshawar was his capital. Kashmir, Punjab and several petty kingdoms in the North accepted his sovereignty. He frequently convened Buddhist Councils for discourses on Buddhist teachings and philosophy. The great schism dividing Buddhism into two schools, Mahayana and Hinayana, occurred during the period of Kanishka. India accepted the Mahayana school. Nagarjuna, the great scholar, scientist and philosopher, was a member of Kanishka's court. Hiuen Tsang, the Chinese traveller referred to Nagarjuna as one of the four lights of the world. The successors of Kanishka I failed to maintain the cohesion and greatness of the Kushana Empire. After Vasudev-II, the sixth successor of Kanishka, the

Empire broke down. The reasons attributed for their downfall are:

(i) Division of power between two Kushana kings, Huvishka and Kanishka II.

(ii) The rise of Nagas into prominence.

(iii) The strengthening of the Sassanian power in Iran.

(iv) The tension between the Hindus and Buddhists consequent on the revival of Hinduism by Sungas and the patronage of Buddhism by Kushanas. and

(v) The inefficiency of the successors of Kanishka I.

After their downfall, sometime after 200 AD, the Kushanas merged in the Indian Society.

The Gupta Age

In the period between the fall of the Kushana Empire and the coming of the Guptas, there existed a number of monarchical states and republics in Northern India like the Ahichatra, Ayodhya, Kausambi, Vakatakas, Maukharis and the Guptas. The Guptas subdued all others and succeeded in establishing the rule of the Gupta dynasty, beginning a golden age in Indian history. A few *Puranas* (ancient religious literature), the *Dharmasastras*, the literary works like *Nitisara* of Saketha, *Kavyanataka*, the writings of Chinese travellers like Fahien and Itsing, inscriptions on caves and pillars and coins minted by various Gupta rulers shed much light on the Gupta period. But, we are still unsure about the founder or year of establishment of the hegemony of the Gupta dynasty. The general consensus among the historians is that Sri Gupta (240-280) is the founder of the Gupta dynasty. Some historians like Fleet conclude that Chandragupta I established the Empire in 319/320. The actual glory of the Guptas was during the period of Chandragupta I (319-335), Samudragupta (335-375), Vikramaditya also known as Chandragupta II (375-414) and Skandagupta (455-467) who defeated the Huns and Pushymitra, even when he was a prince. The Guptas had their capital at Pataliputra on the banks of the Ganges (present Patna). Few historians claim that the capital was later transferred to Magadha.

Chandragupta's son Samudragupta ruled over a vast Empire extending from River Brahmaputra in the East to River Yamuna in the West and River Narmada in the South and a long stretch of territory in the Eastern coast extending as far South as Chingleput and probably even further.

While Chandragupta I and Samudragupta extended and consolidated the Empire, Chandragupta II (Vikramaditya) mainly devoted his attention to maintain peace and tranquility in the nation for promoting literature, art, architecture and science and also to streamline administration and justice to ensure the welfare of the people. He was a benevolent ruler who occupied an enviable position even in myths and later folklores. A calendar named 'Vikram Samvat' is observed in many parts of India even today. The reckoning of this calendar shows its beginning as 57 BC. It is a mystery as to how a calendar began in 57 BC was named after Vikramaditya who ruled four centuries later. We find in Indian history several kings named Vikramaditya in subsequent years, especially among the Chalukyas. It is presumed that the calendar was renamed in later years because of Vikramaditya's popularity among the Indians as the symbol of Indian mind and ideals, a lover of art, music and literature and most of all his generosity and self-sacrifice for others.[6]

Renaissance in Literature, Art and Science in Gupta Age

The names of some of the famous literary works produced during the Gupta period by eminent men like Kalidasa, Bhasa, Sudraka, Vishnukarman and several panegyric authors are given below:

Author	Branch	Name of Work
1. Kalidasa	Drama	Abhijnana – Sakuntala
		Ritusamhara
		Malavikagnimitram
		Kumarasambhava
		Meghaduta
		Raghuvamsa
		Vikrama Urvashiyam

Author	Branch	Name of Work
2. Bhasa	13 Trivandrum Plays (Drama)	1. Madhyamavyayoga
		2. Duta Vakya
		3. Balacharita
		4. Abhisheka
		5. Avimarka
		6. Pratijna
		7. Yaugandharayana
		8. Swapna Vasavadatta
		9. Charudatta
		10. Duta Gatotkach
		11. Karnabhara
		12. Urubanga
		13. Panchatantra
3. Sudraka	Drama	Mrichch Katika
4. Vishnusharma	Story	Panchatantra
5. Harishena	Panegyric (*Prasasti*)	On Samudragupta
6. Vasula	"	On Yesovarman
7. Ravisanthi	"	On Maukhari King
8. Vatsabhatti	"	On Kumaragupta and on Banduvarman
9. Kubje	"	Talgunda
10. Saba	Poetry	Several Poems

Smritis

The *Smritis* of Yajnavalkya, Narada, Katyayana and Brihaspati were written during this period. It is pointed out that the *Smriti* of Yajnavalkya is the most systematic and evenly balanced work on the subject. Some minister of the Gupta kings probably wrote the *Nitisara* of Kamandaka. The *Hitopadesha* or the Book of Wise Counsels was probably written during the Gupta period. Iswarakrishna wrote his famous *Sankhyakarika* a commentary on the *Sankhya* system of philosophy. Vatsyayana wrote *Nyaya-bhashya* on the *Nyaya* system of philosophy. Prasastapada wrote *Padarthadharma*

Samgraha on the *Vaiseshika* system of philosophy. Vyasabbashya has written on *Yoga* philosophy. Philosophers like Baudhayan. Upavarsha and Bhartruprapanch flourished during the Gupta period. Dandin wrote *Kavyadarsa* and *Dasyakumarcharita* during the Gupta period. Asanga, the Buddhist writer, wrote *Yogacharabhumisastra* and *Mahayan Samparigraha*. Vasubandhu wrote many books on *Mahayana* and *Hinayana Buddhist* philosophies. Dinnaga wrote *Pramana Samuchchaya*. Parmartha wrote a biography of Vasubandhu. Chandragomin, a Buddhist scholar, wrote a grammar book called *Chandra Vyakarana*.

Science

Aryabhatta, Varahamihira and Brahmagupta were "the foremost astronomers and mathematicians of the world". Aryabhatta wrote *Surya Siddhanta*. In that book, he explained the true causes of solar and lunar eclipses. Aryabhatta was the first Indian astronomer, who declared the rotation of the earth on its axis. He explained the variations in planetary motions. The *Brihat Samhita* of Varahamihira deals with astronomy, botany, natural history and physical geography. Varahamihira also wrote *Pancha Siddantika, Brihatjataka* and *Laghujataka*. Brahmagupta was a great astronomer and mathematician of his age. He anticipated Newton by declaring that "all things fall to the earth by a law of nature; for it is the nature of the earth to attract and keep things". The *Navanitakam* was written during the Gupta period. This book contains recipes, formulae and prescriptions. Palakapaya wrote *Hastyayurveda* on veterinary science.[7]

Sculpture, Architecture, Painting and Terracota made marvellous achievements in Gupta Age not excelled so far. Some of the most beautiful monuments existing in India today are the heritage of Gupta Arts. Mathura, Banaras and Patna were centres of artistic activity in the Gupta period. Many temples – Vishnu temple at Tigawa (Jubbalpore), Parvathi temple at Ajaigarh, Siva temple at Bhumara and several other surviving temples and the Ajanta Caves are standing monuments of architecture under the Guptas. Stupas (Obelisk), buildings, chapels, monasteries, pillars, coins and terracotta in the Gupta age show the astonishing talents and conceptions of beauty of the artisans of India in that classical age.

Side by side with arts, architecture, literature and amusements, the age of the imperial Guptas was a period of economic affluence and prosperity. There was all round development of agriculture, industry, trade, public works, cities, administration, justice and peace. Another notable achievement of the Guptas was the revival of Hinduism to such heights never achieved before. Mahayanism brought Buddhism nearer to Hinduism. When Sanskrit replaced 'Pali', the common age-old language of the Buddhists, the gap between Buddhism and Hinduism was almost bridged.

The Gupta dynasty lasted for three centuries after Vikramaditya. But the rulers who succeeded Vikramaditya were on the defensive and the Empire shrank and became smaller and smaller. New invaders from Central Asia were attacking India. It is the white Huns, as they were called, who ravaged the law. Their barbarous behaviour and cruelty at last roused the people and a united attack under the leadership of Yashovarman took place. The Hun power was broken and their chief Mahiragula was made a prisoner. But, Baladitya, the descendant of the Guptas, in accordance with the country's custom, treated him with generosity and allowed him to leave India. Mahiragula responded to this magnanimity by returning later and making a treacherous attack on his benefactor.

The decline of the Guptas started after the death of Skanda Gupta. The successors of Skanda Gupta ruled some territories of the vast Empire till the 11th and 12th centruries, not as sovereigns but as vassals of the Huns or Harshas or some other monarchs. A glorious age in Indian history and a renaissance in art, literature and science virtually ended in the seventh century itself leaving to posterity the symbols of a legacy spanning nearly four centuries.

Harsha Vardhan (606-647 AD)

After the end of the Gupta Age, several parts of the Empire declared independence and grew into petty States and no wonder there was struggle for supremacy among them. Four States, Kanauj, Kashmir, Magadha and Rashtrakutas were mainly involved in the struggle. Prabhakar Vardhan was the first ruler who can rightly be called the founder of the hegemony of the Pushpabhuti dynasty. He defeated the Huns, the Kings of Sindhu, the Gujaras, the Gandharas, the Latas and Malavas. On the death of Rajya Vardhan, Harsha at the age of 16 became the King of Thaneswar in 606 AD.

Harshavardhan consolidated the Empire that covered the entire North India and the South India up to the Vindhyas. Arts, Literature, Science, Handicrafts etc. prospered during the Harsha period. The Kumbhamela festival in Prayag (Allahabad) was started during his tenure. The Chinese traveller Hiuen Tsang refers to Harsha period as the period of peace and tranquility in the nation.

Harsha died in 647 AD. The political unity of North India achieved by Harsha was broken after his death. Arjuna usurped the throne of Kanauj. Three kings – Sucandravarman, Bhogavarman and Manorathavarman – ruled Kanauj from 648-688 after the defeat of Arjuna. Several other parts of North India became independent. The Empire of Harshavardhan is the last among the Hindu Empires in North India beginning from Chandragupta Maurya.

Even during the period of Harsha, several strong Hindu dynasties, the Chalukyas, the Pallavas, the Cholas, the Cheras, the Pandyas and the Rashtrakutas ruled South India.

Arab Conquests

The political unity of Northern India achieved under Harsha's was broken after the death of Harsha Vardhan in 647 AD. A large number of sovereign States came into existence. The absence of a centralised government led to a series of struggles among these States to acquire supremacy. Four States, Kanauj, Kashmir, Magadha and Rashtrakutas were the main contestants. At one point of time, the Pratiharas of Kanauj became supreme. Later, the Palas of Bengal replaced them. Rashtrakutas held sway in Western India and South of Deccan. When the Palas disappeared from the scene, the country was divided among the Chalukyas of Anhilwada, Chandellas of Jejakabhukti (the ancient name of Bundelkhand), Kachchapaghapas of Gwalior, Chedis of Dahala, Paramaras of Malava, Guhilas of Rajaputana and Chahamanas of Kadhambhari. The dynasties of South India were not keeping aloof from the struggles in North India. Whenever strong-willed conquerors came to power in South India, they, after consolidating their authority in the South, extended their aggrandisement plans to North India. Dhruva and Govinda III of the Rashtrakutas tried their luck successfully in North India. The rise of Rajputs and other dynasties also posed problems. In short, peace was frequently and continually disturbed in India for five to six centuries after the Harsha period. The turmoil and destruction caused by incessant wars among the dynasties and the expansionist agenda kindled by jealousy, revenge and disunity were a clarion call to foreigners to fish in the troubled waters. Later history of India proved beyond doubt that the West Asian neighbours – the Arabs – made maximum use of this situation according to their whims and fancies.

The rise of Islam is one of the marvels of world history. It was in 622 AD that Mohammed, the prophet of Islam was driven away from his native city. Within a century, his successors and followers were able to set up an Empire, which extended from the Atlantic to the Indus and from the Caspian Sea to the Nile. After the death of the Prophet, Caliphates came into existence. Both civil and religious powers were vested in the Caliphs. The Islamic army of the Arab countries conquered North Africa in 647 AD and converted the people there to Islam. In the first half of the eighth century, the Moors (the North African Muslims) conquered the Iberian Peninsula and threatened many European countries. The Eastern Caliphate at Mecca was transferred to Baghdad. The success of the policy of first conquering the country and then forcibly converting the people to Islam emboldened them to conquer India and convert the Hindus.

The then prevailing situation in India provided them with a favourable atmosphere to accomplish the aim. The successive invasions of India by the Muslims may be viewed in this perspective. The first aim was spread of religion and the second aim was acquisition of wealth. In actual operation, the wealth they acquired far exceeded their expectations. Consequently the second aim acquired precedence over the first.

Under the directions of the Caliph, six futile attempts were made between 636 AD and 664 AD to conquer Sind. Another attempt in AD 711 by one Ubaidullah also failed. In AD 712 a youngster named Mohammed Bin Quasim captured and plundered Sind and Multan, but he was later killed under the orders of the Caliph. Mahmud Ghazni made sixteen conquests in between AD 997 and AD 1030 and succeeded in all of them except one in Kashmir. But, he never thought of establishing an Empire in India. After each expedition, he returned after forcibly converting thousands to Islam, murdering lakhs of people, destroying hundreds of Hindu temples and acquiring immeasurable booty in the form of gold, jewels, diamonds, elephants, horses and whatever he liked. Timurlang, a Tartar by birth and a sadist maniac, in 1398, inflicted more misery than had ever been inflicted by any conqueror. He massacred 50000 men in cold blood on one day, the 12th December 1398 and occupied for 15 days and laid waste the three towns of Siri, Old Delhi and Jahan Panah. After Timur's return, thousands of women and children died of famine, the after-effect of Timur's atrocities.

In 1739, Nadir Shah, the ruler of Iran, conquered and plundered India. The Peacock throne of Shah Jahan, the Kohinoor diamond and many other valuables were robbed. The military of Nadir Shah committed a series of inhuman atrocities and massacred a large number of people. After the death of Nadir Shah in 1747, Ahmad Shah Abdali became the leader of Afghans. He led seven expeditions against India from 1748 to 1767 to establish Afghan supremacy in India. He took advantage of the weakness of the Mughul Empire. In 1748, he invaded Punjab, but the Mughul army defeated him. In 1749, he again attacked Punjab. Muin Khan, the Governor of Punjab agreed to pay Rs. 14,000 as annual tribute to Abdali. As the promised tribute was not paid, he again invaded Punjab and Delhi in 1751. In 1756, he attacked Delhi and stayed there for a month repeating the carnage and arson unleashed by Nadir Shah earlier. On the way back, Ahmad Shah Abdali crushed the Jats and destroyed the sacred towns of Mathura, Brindaban and Gokul. There, he left no atrocity unperpetrated. The outbreak of cholera halted the Afghan march. In 1761, Abdali again came and defeated the Marathas in the third battle of Panipat. The sixth expedition in 1764 against the Sikhs was not completed, as Abdali had to return. The seventh expedition in 1767 against the Sikhs was not successful. However, he retained Peshawar and the areas west of Attock. This lawlessness and confusion benefited only the foreigners. Exploiting the situation of rivalry and infighting between the local chieftains and petty monarchs, the Portuguese, the Dutch, the French and the English captured many areas in India and brought them under their domination.

The above listed plunderers never aimed at gaining political power. Their aims were: (i) conversion of Hindus to Islam, (ii) acquisition of as much wealth as possible, (iii) extermination of Hinduism by destruction of temples and murdering those who resisted conversion, and (iv) molestation of the Hindu womenfolk.

Muslim Empire in India

The first real founder of the Muslim Empire in India was Muhammad Ghori, who ascended the throne in 1175. The entire North India, Bengal, Deccan, Sind, Multan, Anhilwara, Punjab, a portion of Bihar and several other small States came under his sway. He ruled the vast areas through Governors and military commanders. After Ghori, an array of Muslim rulers belonging to six dynasties, as listed below, ruled India:

(i)	The Slave Dynasty	1206 – 1290	
(ii)	The Khalji Dynasty	1290 – 1320	
(iii)	The Tugluq Dynasty (Quaranah Turks)	1320 – 1414	(Timurlang's invasion was during the Tuglaq period)
(iv)	The Sayyid Dynasty	1414 – 1451	
(v)	The Lodhi Dynasty	1451 – 1526	
(vi)	The Mughul Dynasty	1526 – 1707	

The death of Aurangzeb in 1707 witnessed the virtual collapse of the Mughul Empire, though Aurangzeb's son Bahadur Shah and his grandson Muhammed Shah ascended the throne to preside over a shattered Empire. Barring few rulers like Jalal-ud-din Firoz Khalji, Mohammed-bin-Tugluq, Akbar the Great etc., all the Muslim rulers were harshly intolerant towards the Hindus. They kept the Hindus out of any position of authority in government and in the army. Coercive conversions to Islam were common. Those who objected were subjected to inhuman torture, often culminating in death.

The Marathas were badly in need of a leader to uphold Maratha honour and dignity. They found a leader in Shivaji, who can accomplish the hopes and aspirations of the people. Shivaji meticulously planned and executed many guerilla style 'hit and run' attacks against the Mughuls. But, he died in 1680 AD. His son and successor Sambaji (Shambuji?) was tortured and killed under the orders of Emperor Aurangzeb. The resistance on the part of the Marathas later collapsed when the British East India Company defeated them in 1818.

There was widespread disgust among the Hindus against the tyranny and oppression practised by the Muslim rulers. Consequently, frequent clashes between the Hindus and Muslims and social upheavals were common in different parts of the nation.

FOOTNOTES

1. Mahajan V.D., *Ancient India*, p. 10.
2. *Ibid.*, pp. 11-12.
3. Sachidanandan, V.A., *Toynbee Anthology*, pp. VII-X.
4. Jawaharlal Nehru, *The Discovery of India*, p. 59.
5. *Ibid.*, p. 75.
6. *Ibid.*, p. 92.
7. Mahajan V.D., *Ancient India*, pp. 538-41.

Modern India

2

British East India Company

In the first half of the eighth century, the Moors (the North African Mohammedans) seized the Iberian Peninsula and settled there till the eleventh century. After a series of wars, the Christians expelled the Moors and restored their land. It was Portugal, which was in the vanguard in the struggle for the restoration. In AD 1095, Portugal became an independent nation and continued as a superpower in Europe for the next 150 years. Spain, although a superpower, did not take any active part in the restoration as they were engaged in some internal problems. Hence, Portugal unilaterally took the initiative to achieve the three aims of: dismantling the influence and superiority of the Muslims in Africa, thereby preventing their adventurous expeditions to Europe, establishing trade relations with the East, especially South Asia by demolishing the monopoly of trade enjoyed by the Arabs for centuries and the spread of Christianity in the newly discovered lands.

The Pope drew an imaginary line on the globe from the North Pole to the South Pole and entrusted the Western and Eastern parts of the line with Spain and Portugal respectively. Some ecclesiastical powers were also delegated to the Kings of Spain and Portugal to achieve the evangelisation of the newly acquired territories.

In 1497, Vasco de Gama, an adventurous navigator of Portugal, set out to the East, via the Southern tip of Africa (which they named as 'Nathal' – the Cape of Good Hope) and reached Kozhikode in Kerala on the Western coast of India on 20th May 1498. The monarchs in India greeted them and extended help for trade in their respective kingdoms. Gama reached back Lisbon on 14th September 1499 for a tumultuous welcome. The articles brought by Gama – silk, spices, jewels, sandalwood, opium etc. – sold in the European market fetched sixty times the total amount invested for the expedition.[1]

The grand success of Vasco de Gama shocked other European nations. Holland, France and England, the other naval powers in Europe set up companies for trade with India. The Dutch defeated Portugal at Cochin, confining them to Goa, Daman and Diu. It is the British East India Company that changed the course and direction of Indian history. Robert Clive, who joined the East India Company as a clerk and later a soldier in the army, was instrumental in laying the foundation of the British Empire in India. Clive defeated the French army under Dupleix in a long battle extending seven years and captured Arcot in South India confining the French to three small pockets in India, Pondicherry, Mahe and Karaikkal, thus eliminating them from the race for supremacy in India.

In the battle of Plassey in 1757, Clive defeated Siraj-ud-Dowla, the Nawab of Bengal more by treason and treachery than by fighting. Other Nawabs like Mir Kasim were also defeated. Thus, Bengal and Bihar lay at the feet of the East India Company. Only three contestants for supremacy remained in the arena, the Maratha Confederacy, Mysore under Hyder Ali and the British East India Company.

Warren Hastings succeeded Clive as Governor General. He unleashed a series of conquests to improve the finances of the East India Company. Not only the kings but also the common people were squeezed for money. Resultantly, agriculture and industries were weakened. The nation was impoverished. Acute famine has become a frequent feature in India. Even democratic-minded Englishmen protested against the miserable situation in India. Later, Warren Hastings was recalled and impeached by the British Parliament for his omissions and commissions.

Cornwallis succeeded Hastings as Governor General. He was not in favour of the aggressive policies of conquests by the Company. But, later he was compelled to fight against Mysore. Hyder Ali, an uneducated, shrewd, intelligent and ambitious warrior deposed the King and enthroned himself as ruler of Mysore. Not prepared to remain a vassal of the British, Hyder Ali allied with the Nizam of Hyderabad and the Marathas who were also opposed to British domination. But, Cornwallis by the treaty of Salbai in 1782 wooed the Marathas and Nizam and thereby isolated Mysore. Hyder Ali's son Tippu succeeded in Mysore as Sultan. Cornwallis, with the help of Nizam and Marathas, fought against Tippu. After fierce battle for two years, a compromise was arrived at whereby Tippu Sultan was forced to give over a portion of his territory to the East India Company.

In 1798, Lord Wellesley became the Governor General. At that time, Britain was facing the threat of Napoleon in Europe. Ranjit Singh of Punjab and Pazhassi Raja in Kerala were hostile to the British. Lord Wellesley convinced the British parliament of the possibility of an alliance of all these forces against the British and obtained permission to declare war against Tippu Sultan. Tippu was at that time engaged in battles against neighbouring kingdoms to enhance the strength and morale of his forces. In the fourth Mysore war in 1799, Tippu Sultan was defeated and killed. Some portions of Tippu's kingdom were given to the Nizam and Marathas. The legal heir of the expelled ruling dynasty of Mysore was recalled and enthroned as King of Mysore. The company retained some territories. The threat of Mysore was thus eliminated.

The kingdom of Oudh was brought under British sovereignty in 1817 on grounds of maladministration. Ranjit Singh of Punjab died in 1839. After two wars, British dominion was extended to Punjab in 1850. Bengal, Bihar, Marathas, the Punjab, Oudh, Jhansi, Sambalpur, Nagpur, Mysore and many other petty States came under British domination. Thus, the British East India Company became the unchallenged masters of India.

The Great Revolt of 1857-58

A great deal of false and perverted history has been written about this revolt and its suppression. The mutiny started in Meerut by the soldiers was in fact the first planned war of independence. But, the premature outburst upset the plans of the leaders.[2]

After Wellesley, Hastings, Emerst, William Bentick, Auckland and Ellenborough became Governor-Generals. During the period of Ellenborough, Charles Napier conquered Sind. Lower Burma became the territory of the company. While the East India Company was becoming the sovereign of almost the entire India, the people in India were starving. There had been nearly twenty terrific famines in India in between 1770 and 1857. Indian industries were collapsing. Artistic and architectural talents of the Indians gradually faded. Despair and revenge engulfed the people. Discontentment became widespread. The grievances of the soldiers remained a cry in the wilderness.

In this situation, the soldiers in Meerut disobeyed the orders of the British Commanders. This spread to other parts of India like wildfire assuming the character of a popular rebellion. Bahadur Shah, the last Mughul ruler was a leader of the revolt that started in March 1857. By May 1857 it turned into a mutiny. The revolutionists captured Delhi and declared Bahadur Shah, the Emperor of India. Rani Laxmi Bai of Jhansi (a girl of twenty), Tantia Tope, Nana Saheb, Maulavi Ahmed Shah of Faisabad and several others took up the cause of the mutineers. The East India Company resorted to all measures at its command to suppress the revolt. Laxmi Bai who personally led the rebellion in the field was shot dead. Tantia Tope was executed. Bahadur Shah was exiled. It took nearly two years to suppress the revolt.

The British Parliament read the writing on the wall and took over the administration of India from the East India Company, overruling the protests of the Company. Viceroys were appointed in place of the Governor-Generals. Queen Elizabeth of Britain declared that (i) the government shall practise no discrimination between British and Indian nationals. Appointments to the civil services shall be governed by merit alone, not by caste or religion, (ii) The Government shall not interfere in the religious faith of the Indians and no one would be asked to do anything against one's religious faith, and (iii) the right of the ruling dynasties for adoption in the absence of legal heirs would be restored. The government never kept up these promises in the declaration aimed at removing the doubts and anxieties of the Indians.

The Indian National Congress

The second half of the 19th century was marked by a strong wave of reforms in India in the fields of religion and social life. Raja Ram Mohan Roy paved the way for this renaissance to remove the evils and abuses in the religion and society. He founded the Brahma Samaj in 1829 advocating worship of one great God (monotheism) without images or rituals. The Prarthana Samaj in Maharashtra established in 1849 by Keshab Chandra Sen was also Brahma Samaj under another label. Arya Samaj by Swamy Dayanand Saraswati advocated "Go back to the Vedas". The other teachings of Arya Samaj were similar to that of the Brahma Samaj. Another great religious and social movement was the Ramakrishna Mission. Swamy Vivekananda (1863-1902), the most famous disciple of Sri Ramakrishna, spread the message of the mission all over India and abroad. This mission for social and religious reforms had its inspiration from the ancient culture of India. The theosophical society of Mrs. Annie Besant advocated that only the revival and reintroduction of the ancient ideals and institutions of India could solve the problems of India. These movements stressing the religious and social life of the Indian community created a national awakening that resulted in a tremendous upsurge of nationalism.[3]

In 1884, a meeting of the educated class in India in Bombay under the presidentship of W.C. Banerjee gave shape to a political organisation named 'the Indian National Congress' to reverse the trend of degradation through a reawakening. An enlightened Englishman named Allan Octavian Hume, who took the initiative for convening the meeting, was made the first president of the Indian National Congress. The Congress was at the initial stage an expanded form of the earlier organisations – The British Indian Association of 1851 and the Indian Association of 1857 – with wider representation of the people for channelising the collective voice of India for social and economic reforms. It started work by declaring loyalty to the British rule. But the wind for change in the political sphere was blowing everywhere in the country. In the Congress itself, two groups emerged, the extremists and the moderates. Lokamanya Gangadhar Tilak, Aravind Ghosh, Bipin Chandra Pal, Lala Lajpat Rai and several others were in the extremist group. The Indian National Congress, for the first time, brought India with its varied races and religions to a single platform for a common and united effort.

In 1905, Viceroy Lord Curzon introduced a reform for the partition of Bengal. The new province of 'Eastern Bengal and Assam' was formed by the amalgamation of Assam and the Surma Valley with fifteen districts of the Bengal province. (This was annulled later in 1912.) Both the Muslims and Hindus of Bengal opposed the partition and agitated over the issue. Even moderates came into the forefront of the agitation. Curzon's reform poured oil into the fire. The word 'self-rule', 'freedom' etc were echoed in all platforms. The organisation for social and economic reforms was gradually acquiring a political dimension.

India was completely woken up by the partition of Bengal. In 1907, the moderates and extremists in Congress chose separate paths. Tilak, the leader of the extremists, was sentenced for six years imprisonment for his declaration "freedom is my birth-right". In 1916, Tilak came out of the prison and the moderates and extremists joined together. Tilak, in association with Mrs. Annie Besant, organised the 'Home Rule Movement'. With the passing away of Tilak in 1920, the first phase of the struggle for Indian independence ended.

The second phase of the struggle till independence was under the leadership of Mahatma Gandhi. The First World War began in 1914. The British sovereign sent a message to the people of India at the beginning of the war that the war of England would be an opportunity for India. The Indian leaders interpreted it to mean that self-rule would be granted after the war. Accordingly, expecting self-rule, Congress leaders decided to help Britain in the war. With the support of the Muslim League, the Congress even prepared a draft of the outline of self-rule. In 1917, Mr. Edwin Montague, Secretary of State for India announced in the House of Commons "the policy of His Majesty's Government with which the Government of India are in complete accord is that of the increasing association of the Indians in every branch of the administration and the gradual development of self-governing institutions with a view to the progressive realisation of responsible government in India as an integral part of the British Empire."[4] In 1918, the report of the Montague-Chelmsford Committee was published, followed by the Government of India Act 1919. Accordingly, the Central Legislature was thoroughly remodelled and made bicameral. But, the entire powers of administration were vested in British hands. The hopes of the Indians were dashed.

In 1919, massive protest rallys were held in the streets of Amritsar. Dr. Satyapal and Dr. Saifudeen Kitchlu were arrested. Gandhiji, who came to India from South Africa to lead the agitation, was also arrested. People who assembled at Jalianwalabag in Amritsar to express their protests were mercilessly shot down by the army under the command of General Dyer by installing the machine gun at the sole entrance of the stadium, closing all avenues for escape. In this monstrous attack, 379 people died and 1133 were injured. Punjab Governor Michael Dyer and General Dyer together unleashed a reign of terror by declaring martial law in Punjab. 108 people were executed under the martial law.

The Khilafat Movement

When the First World War began in 1914, the Khaliff in Turkey, the head of religion as well as the nation, supported Germany. The Muslims in India supported Britain on the assurance that no retaliatory measures affecting the religious sentiments of the Muslims would be initiated. But, contrary to this assurance, the Turkey Sultan was deprived of his powers to control Muslim sacred places. This stirred up an uprising demanding the restoration of the rights and powers of the Khaliff. The Muslims and Hindus, with the blessings of Gandhiji, jointly began a non-co-operation movement known as the Khilafat Movement. Maulana Mohammed Ali and Shoukat Ali, generally known as Ali brothers, were arrested for leading the agitation. An armed rebellion by the Muslims of Malabar (*the Eranadan revolt*) was a part of the Khilafat movement (some historians are of the view that it was a peasants' revolt nothing to do with the Khilafat). As some Hindus favoured the government, the rebellion turned against the Hindus in some areas. The Government suppressed the rebellion through harsh methods of torture. Gandhiji was arrested for supporting the peasants in Bardoli.

At this stage, a question arose in the Congress as to whether the membership in the legislatures granted by the British need be accepted. Motilal Nehru and C.R. Das who favoured acceptance launched the Swaraj party and contested the elections under the banner of the new party. Motilal Nehru and C.R. Das were elected to the Central legislature and Bengal legislature respectively. The members elected Vithal Bhai Patel, the brother of Sardar Patel as chairman of the Central legislature. He put the government in the docks in the Central legislature on several occasions.

The Simon Commission

In the late twenties, the British Government appointed the Simon Commission to study and report on the situation in India. The Indian National Congress in 1928 decided to boycott the Commission. In reply to this, the Government unleashed a series of repressive measures. Lala Lajpat Rai, a victim of torture, died after one month. This ignited the wrath of the people. On the first anniversary of the incident, Bhagat Singh and his associates murdered the police officer, who tortured Rai. The murderers were later executed, but to the people, they became revered martyrs.

The Indian National Congress in 1929 assembled at Lahore under the presidentship of Jawaharlal Nehru adopted a resolution demanding full freedom. On December 31st midnight, he hoisted the tricolour of the Congress and declared that the people of India would not accept anything less than full freedom for India. It was also decided that 26th January should be celebrated every year as Indian Independence Day.

The subsequent history of India is marked by a series of vigorous and intensified struggles. In 1930 March, Gandhiji along with 79 members of the Congress marched from Sabarmati to Dandi, a distance of 241 miles by foot in 24 days, to disobey the "Salt Law regulations". "Throughout the long journey, Gandhiji received homage and ovation which any Emperor could envy. The villagers flocked from all sides, sprinkled the roads, strewed leaves on them and as the pilgrims passed, sank on their knees."[5]

Similar agitations were held throughout the country. Gandhiji and Nehru were arrested. Later, the struggle was temporarily withdrawn in view of the understanding between Gandhiji and Irwin (the Viceroy).

Gandhiji attended the Round Table Conference at London representing the Indian National Congress. He returned disappointed, as the British Government was adamant on promoting the Muslim interests. In 1932, Gandhiji again exhorted the people for non-violent struggles. The Government responded by arresting Gandhiji and killing many Indians. The struggle was withdrawn in 1934 April. The British Government passed the Government of India Act in 1935 granting self-rule, subject to restrictions. Accordingly, fresh elections to the legislatures were held and the Congress won majority in most of the legislatures and formed ministries. But the ministries resigned in 1939, protesting against the unilateral decision of the British Government to drag India into the Second World War without consultation with India. In fact, India never wanted to hinder the war efforts of Britain. The Indians were against Fascism and Nazism. Britain rejected the demand of the Congress for assurance on freedom for India after the war. British Prime Minister Winston Churchill categorically stated that so long as he was the Prime Minister, the British Empire would not be dismantled.

Gandhiji, on finding the extremists distancing themselves from his policies, preferred to keep away from the Congress and took up creative social work such as uplift of Harijans (Dalits), Khadi etc. At this stage, the direction of the war changed. Hitler's army was advancing in Europe. They marched towards Russia. Japanese planes bombarded Pearl Harbour. Britain's downfall seemed imminent. In the fast developing turn of events, Britain found the support and co-operation of India vital. The British Government deputed Sir Staffords Cripps to India to discuss with Indian leaders and ensure support for the war. Maulana Abul Kalam Azad was then the president of the Indian National Congress. Cripps held discussions with Gandhiji, Azad and other leaders. They presented before the Commission the Indian stand that an assurance by the British Government on the grant of independence to India after the war alone could alter the situation and ensure Indian support for the war-efforts of Britain. As the British Government was not in a mood to accept this position, the Cripps mission failed.

Quit India Movement

In the Congress session at Bombay on 8th August 1942, the Quit India resolution presented by Jawaharlal was unanimously adopted. Nehru told the British Government that it was the last chance.

The Government retorted by arresting Gandhiji, Sardar Patel and other leaders before the dawn of 9th August. There ensued a series of struggles, both violent and non-violent, throughout India. Jaya Prakash Narayan, Aruna Asaf Ali and other leaders absconded and led the struggle. Gandhiji and his wife Kasturba were held prisoners in the Aga Khan Palace, Pune. Kasturba died in the prison. Non-resident Indians also joined the struggle. Subhash Chandra Bose who was under house arrest in Calcutta escaped in disguise and went out of the country. Through Germany, he reached Japan after 91 days journey in a submarine. Ras Behari Ghosh, General Mohan Singh and several others, by then, organised the Indian National Army. Bose, on their request, took up the leadership of the Indian National Army and established a Government-in-exile. A women's wing under Dr. Lakshmi Swaminathan named 'Rani of Jhansi Regiment' was also organised. The Indian National Army hoisted the Indian flag on 14th April 1944 at Manipur. But the British army defeated the Indian National Army in the Arakkan forests. Bose flew back to Japan along with

Col. Habibur Rehman. It is widely believed that they lost their lives in that journey by plane crash. The leaders of the Indian National Army were tried and sentenced to death, but released later, honouring world public opinion.

Britain won the world war. At this stage, a few members of the Royal Indian Navy raised the banner of revolt. Some Air Force personnel followed suit. Britain realised that the loyalty of Indians in any position was no longer reliable. The new Labour Party Government in Britain was convinced that Britain would no longer be in a position to continue their domination in India. Prime Minister Atlee deputed a cabinet committee to India to sort out the issues relating to the transfer of power. In the discussions at Shimla, the Indian National Congress conceded to the bi-nation demand of Mohammed-Ali-Jinnah. It was, therefore, decided to partition India to form a separate nation for Muslims – Pakistan. The Cabinet Committee left India on 29th June 1946.

To work out the modalities of partition and transfer of powers, an interim government was set up under Jawaharlal Nehru in 1946. Later came the declaration of the British Government granting independence to both India and Pakistan with effect from 15th August 1947. Lord Mountbatten, the then Viceroy was appointed Governor General of India to facilitate smooth transfer of power. The central legislature presided over by Dr. Rajendra Prasad functioned as constituent Assembly. The National flag of India was hoisted at the Red Fort in Delhi. Nehru's midnight speech at the flag-hoisting ceremony was an epoch-making one. India and Pakistan became independent nations on 15th August 1947, partition being the price paid for independence.

Independence and its Problems

The interim government had to face gigantic problems – communal riots, massacres, partition, rehabilitation of refugees and the demand of Travancore and Hyderabad for independent Statehood. On 5th July 1947, Sardar Vallabhai Patel took charge of the Indian States Department. The demand of Travancore died out consequent on the resignation of the Diwan Sir C.P. Ramaswamy Iyer. Hyderabad was annexed to the Indian union by a police action by the Indian army. In 1949, Travancore and Cochin were amalgamated to form the Travancore-Cochin State, which later became a part of the State of Kerala founded in 1956.

The ruler of Kashmir expressed willingness to accede to the Indian Union. This position was not acceptable to Pakistan. They conquered Kashmir. India complained to the United Nations. The United Nations interfered, arranged a cease-fire and marked a line of control under which one-third of Kashmir on the other side of the line known as Azad Kashmir remained under Pakistan and two-thirds of Kashmir remained in the Indian Union. This bone of contention between India and Pakistan remains unsolved even today. On 21st June 1948, C. Rajagopalachari became the first Indian Governor General of India. Mohammed-Ali-Jinnah became the first Governor General of Pakistan.

The Constitution of India, promulgated by the Constituent Assembly on 26th Nov. 1949 came into effect on 26th January 1950. India declared itself a Sovereign Democratic Republic and a Union of States without severing its relations with the British Commonwealth. This position was approved by the British Parliament by the India (Consequential Provision) Act of 1949.

India – A Sovereign, Socialist, Secular and Democratic Republic

The Constituent Assembly was an assemblage of men of best talents, erudition and vision, who represented not only divergent shades of opinion but also different classes, castes, religions, localities and political views in India. Dr. B.R. Ambedkar is known as the architect of the Indian Constitution. He, a Dalit (outside the four castes in Hinduism) by birth, was a man of outstanding intellect, wisdom and far-sightedness. He examined almost all the available constitutions in the world, drafted one suitable to the Indian context, convincingly answered all doubts and queries of the members of the Constituent Assembly and got it approved. It took three years to finalise the process.

A specially noteworthy aspect in this context is that while article-wise discussion on the Constitution was going on in full swing inside the assembly, two prominent communities – Hindus and Muslims – were warring outside, competing to surpass each other in the number of massacres on the opposite side. After the partition, the Hindu population in India was 83%. Resultantly, they enjoyed a predominant majority in the Constituent Assembly. Had they so wished, the Assembly could have given shape to a Constitution proclaiming India as a theocratic Hindu nation – *A Hindurashtra*. An assembly gathered in the backdrop of bloodbath and tension was sober and prudent enough to prefer a secular and democratic republic based on universal adult suffrage and equality before law, upholding the age-old traditions and culture of India.

An analysis of the Constitution of India leads us to the conclusion that it is an elaborate and comprehensive document prepared after taking into account the history, culture, traditions and diversities of India. When many countries which acquired independence along with India or afterwards have slipped into autocracy, India survived not only in maintaining its democratic set up and institutions but also with more vigour and strength. After 1951, there had been more than ninety amendments to the Indian Constitution. It shows that the democracy in India is vibrant and sensitive to the needs of the times. The only drawback we notice is the slow progress in the economic front for which the reasons are many. Exploding growth of population, existence of innumerable political parties, corruption at all levels, communal hatred and rivalry among religious factions, growing awareness of rights among the oppressed castes and classes, the Kashmir issue, widening disparity in income due to distortions in the distribution of wealth, unemployment, illiteracy, undeveloped villages etc. retard the progress of development.

The Indian Constitution came into effect on 26th January 1950. The first General Elections under the Constitution took place in 1951. The Indian National Congress became the majority party in Parliament and Jawaharlal Nehru became the first constitutionally elected Prime Minister of India.

"On 20th October 1962, when the Indian Republic was in her early teens, China, with the connivance of Pakistan, declared war against India, as a part of their territorial expansion programme. In September 1965, when India was in the thick of a war against Pakistan, China issued an ultimatum against India, after concentrating their forces in the Himalayan borders. China is still in occupation of thousands of sq K.Ms. of Indian territory. In 1966, a treaty was signed between India and Pakistan known as the 'Tashkent Declaration' accomplished under the initiative of the Soviet Union, but the price paid for it was the life of Mr. Lal Bahadur Shastri, the Prime Minister of India.

On 26th March 1971, the Pakistan government arrested Sheikh Mujibur Rehman and declared war against India on December 3rd, 1971. The Simla Agreement was signed by India and Pakistan in July 1972.

This war was unique on many counts: (i) two hundred thousand cases of rapes, (ii) ten million fled for lives, (iii) the fourth perfidious aggression against India after partition, (iv) a war fought against the forces of darkness, and (v) after all a glorious victory for India forever.

Names of Presidents of the Republic of India	Names of Prime Ministers of the Republic of India
1. Dr. Rajendra Prasad (26th Jan. 1950-13th May 1962)	1. Jawaharlal Nehru (Aug. 15, 1947 to May 27, 1964)
2. Dr. S. Radhakrishnan (13-5-1962 to 13-5-1967)	2. Gulzari Lal Nanda (A) (May 27, 1964 to June 9, 1964)
3. Dr. Zakir Husain (13-5-1967 to 3-5-1969)	3. Lal Bahadur Shastri (June 9, 1964 to Jan. 11, 1966)
4. V.V. Giri (3-5-1969 to 20-7-1969 and 24-8-1969 to 24-8-1974)	

5. Fakhruddin Ali Ahmed (24-8-1974 to 11-2-1977)
6. Neelam Sanjiva Reddy (25-7-1977 to 25-7-1982)
7. Giani Zail Singh (25-7-1982 to 25-7-1987)
8. R. Venkataraman (25-7-1987 to 25-7-1992)
9. Dr. Shankar Dayal Sharma (25-7-1992 to 25-7-1997)
10. Dr. K.R. Narayanan (25-7-1997 to 25-7-2002)
11. Dr. A.P.J. Abdul Kalam (25-7-2002 to 25-7-2007)
12. Pratibha Patil (25-7-2007)

4. Smt. Indira Gandhi (Jan. 24, 1966 to Mar. 24, 1977 & Jan. 14, 1980 to Oct. 31, 1984)
5. Morarji Desai (March 24, 1977 to July 28, 1977)
6. Charan Singh (July 28, 1979 to January 14, 1980)
7. Rajiv Gandhi (October 31, 1984 to December 2, 1989)
8. V.P. Singh (December 2, 1989 to November 10, 1990)
9. Chandrashekhar (November 10, 1990 to June 21, 1991)
10. P.V. Narasimha Rao (June 21, 1991 to May 10, 1996)
11. A.B. Vajpayee (May 16, 1996 to June 1, 1996)
12. H.D. Deve Gowda (June 1, 1996 to April 21, 1997)
13. I.K. Gujral (April 21, 1997 to November 28, 1997)
14. A.B. Vajpayee (March 19, 1998 to May 13, 2004)
15. Dr. Manmohan Singh (May 22, 2004)

FOOTNOTES

1. John Pallathu (Fr.), *Christian Church in the Portugal Age* (Mal.), p. 55.
2. Jawarharlal Nehru, *The Discovery of India*, p. 324.
3. Majumdar, R.C., *An Advanced History of India*, pp. 867-77.
4. *Ibid.*, p. 903.
5. *Ibid.*, p. 974.

Contributions of India to Science of Experiments

3

India is a country of abundant wealth and resources ever since the days of yore, not only natural wealth of minerals, rivers, mountains, seas, forests and the rich cultural and spiritual heritage but also the wealth of human resources and intellectual acumen. Many in the present generation immersed in the theses and practices of modern science and technology fail to realize and appreciate that some of the advances and achievements hailed and trumpeted today by non-Indians were discovered and developed years ago by the ancient Indians. Many the world over would have heard about India in terms of its philosophy, literature, arts, architecture, sculpture and so on, but only a few are aware that India was, once upon a time, the fountainhead of many important foundational approaches to modern scientific developments. Many Western philosophers have often commented that it is difficult to distinguish Indian philosophy from science and religion. The world cannot be blamed for this lack of knowledge and appreciation. It is the fault of Indians, of course, for various reasons. The seeds of many scientific ideas are embedded in India's ancient Sanskrit literature. Even the *Vedas*, considered as religious literature, are repositories of many scientific truths. They are lying latent for several millennia for want of serious efforts to winnow and separate the grains from the chaff and to research, sow and nurture those seeds and seedlings.

Here, an attempt is made to peep into the contributions of India to the world. The main areas of contribution are Science, Religion, World Unity and World Peace. Science covers various branches like Linguistics, Mathematics, Geometry, Astronomy, Chemistry, Physics, Metallurgy, Medicine, Civil Engineering,

Textiles, Architecture, Sculpture, Arts, Agriculture and Philosophy. Actually, what India possesses but not contributed are likely to be more than those contributed so far, as Indians are not yet aware of their possessions. Many scholars have claimed that all modern scientific knowledge existed in ancient India. Some other scholars feel that there were only spirituality and philosophy in India. Whatever be the claims and counter-claims, the fact remains that India never attempted an unbiased approach with true rational vision and scientific temperament to bring to limelight our treasures of knowledge and develop them in a way beneficial to us and to the world.

Science

Sanskrit texts are the prime sources of knowledge of ancient India. To bring out the scientific concepts in them, one has to go deep into the original texts and their commentaries. The results of archaeological observations can provide practical knowledge to supplement theoretical knowledge. Many scientific concepts handed down to the subsequent generations in the course of their applications would provide us with practical knowledge. Metal and alloy samples collected from archaeological excavations can bring to light the metallurgical skills of ancient Indians, e.g. Qutb Minar in Delhi. The information available in the texts could be very often less than that from the available samples. Similarly, systematic approach and application of the *Ayurvedic* and *Sidha* branches of applied sciences can test medicinal concepts. The skills of ancient Indians in civil engineering are visible at Taxila, Harappa, Mohenjodaro, Lothal, Cave temples and the like. The levels of excellence and capabilities of the forefathers of Indians can be ascertained only by a microscopic scrutiny of ancient literatures within the parameters of modern science.

Ancient India's contributions on various branches of science, so far available, are listed below:

(a) Linguistics

Panini's Sanskrit grammar named *Panineeyam* is the highest peak of achievement in linguistics. This is still the most complete book on Sanskrit language and more scientific than any other description yet produced in any language. It contains 4000 Sutras divided into eight chapters. Many Western scholars are of the view that Panini lived in the seventh century BC or at least in the fifth century BC. Buddha's name is not included in the book and, therefore, the presumption is that Panini lived before Buddha. Panini is economical in words and uses symbols as far as possible to indicate the phenomena of languages.[1]

Examples have been taken from almost all the languages of those days. The entire language is shown analysed into its constituent meaningful elements, namely, roots, suffixes and inflections in various ways in which those may be combined. Another notable feature is the use of a symbol for zero in the description to show that there is no suffix in the form of a certain word. This invention of zero to take care of empty places in a system seems to have been due to the linguists; mathematicians used it for *Sunya* (nothingness) only later. Their idea got into philosophy in a modified form, combining with the conception that things are not what they appear to be, but are empty like places in a system and nothing in themselves, (e.g. Nagarjuna). Patanjali has written a commentary on *Panineeyam* that is in no way inferior to Panini's original work and hence known as *Mahabhashyam* (The Great Commentary). This comprehensive work of Panini is not merely a book on grammar but a *Bhashasastra* meaning "Science of Language or Linguistics". There is a legend on the origin of zero. In early Indian literature, if a letter or word were a mistake, the author would round up that letter or word indicating a mistake as a direction to ignore and proceed. This circle later became the symbol of *sunya* (zero).

(b) Mathematics

The layman's knowledge of Indian Mathematics is confined to two Indian contributions: Zero and Pythagoras theorem. Many claim that these two are great achievements. But, the reality is that we have failed to submit proof of even these two. In ancient Indian Sanskrit books, hundreds of scientific informations on mathematics are available. But the crucial requirement is to search important texts. Mathematics including astronomy is the forehead of the *Vedanga Sutras*, compared to the jewel on the brood of a cobra and the sikha on the head of a peacock.

Contributions on Mathematics are enumerated below:

Numbers, square and square root, cube and cube root, use of fractions, discovery and use of zero, infinity, positive and negative numbers, number places, average, ratio and proportions, permutations and combinations, percentage, interest calculations, share and profit sharing in partnerships, loans and interest in banking, rules of charging interest, bodies in motion, progression, determination of unknown numbers, positive and negative numbers, number places, method of presentation of mathematical data, *Aryabhateeya-bhootha sankhya-Katapayadi* number systems, etc.

Mathematical Theorems: Newton Sterling Interpolation, Newton gauss backward interpolations, Newton's power series, Taylor series, Lhuiler formula, Gregory Leibinitz series, Leibinitz power series, De Moivre's approximation to value, modified Leibinitz series, Tycho Brahe reductions, infinite GP, convergent series of Newton, Theorems of Nilakanta, Madhavacharya and Puthumana Somayajee.[2]

(c) Geometry

Geometry is the *Sulbasutras* of Bhoudhayana, Apastamba, Katyayana, etc. Triangles and Quadrilaterals, area of trapezium, cyclic quadrilaterals, diameter, circumference and area of circles, angular dimensions, arc of circles and spheres, arcs and chords of circles, angular relations with arcs and chords in circles, values of sine of angles, relations among sine, cosine and tangent of angles, volume of geometrical figures, volume of cones and partial cones, volume of spheres, etc. Most of these theories come under trigonometry in modern science.

Many authors give explanations on place values of numbers. Aryabhatta says after mentioning one, ten, hundred upto a million 'from one place to the next place, it is the multiple of ten'. In *Vyasabashya*, place values are illustrated as follows: "A woman may be called mother (by her children), daughter (by her father), daughter-in-law (by her mother-in-law), even though she is the same woman. Similarly, even if the digit is the same, depending upon its place in the number, its value varies. In the unit place, the digit has the same value, in the tenth place, ten times the value and in the hundredth place, hundred times the value is given." Adi Sankara (700 AD) in his Vedanta Sutra Bhashya has given similar explanations for writing numbers giving decimal place values.

(d) Astronomy

The Western Scientists feel that Vedic astronomy was primarily concerned with problems and the calendar and with the positions of the constellations, especially the 28 Nakshatras or lunar mansions. Following this, the movements of planets seem to have come into prominence, (e.g.: the 12-year cycle of Jupiter). A Buddhist monk correctly predicted a total solar eclipse of 249 BC. A Buddhist text of the 4th century mentioned about the appearance of a comet.[3] The astronomical investigation of cyclic time of planets as a natural extension of the research on calendar pointed to cyclic periods of millions of years required to contain the calculated complete movements of the planets.[4]

The Indian literature on Astronomy covers definition of celestial and terrestrial circles. Sanskrit glossary and their modern astronomical equivalents, methods for determining astronomical parameters, day diameter and colatitude, day radius and earth sine, division of Zodiac, determination of Sun's prime vertical, determination of earth sine, R sine of moon's meridian and zenith distance, determination of oblique ascensions, winter-summer solstice, celestial sphere, longitude and latitude, determination of ascensional difference, rising of planets, position of planets, precision of equinoxes, visibility of planets, visibility corrections, parallax on visibility, longitude and latitude, apogees of planets, revolution of apogee, revolution of planets, inclination of planet's orbit of revolution, various motions of planets, true planets and mean planets, rate of angular motion of planets, corrections for the calculation of the motions, retrograde motion, studies on tracing Planetary motion etc. are given.[5]

Descriptions of Earth: Cover above the earth, rotation of earth, days and rotation, suspension of earth in space, gravity of earth, four quadrants of earth, north and south poles, meridian equivalent to Greenwich lines of latitude, calculation of latitudes of places, *Sankvarga* (an astronomical observation), calculation of the distance of places from meridian using latitude and longitude, correction for longitude, terrestrial longitude, mean longitude calculations, calculation of time and its relation with longitude, linear measurement – yojna and longitude, meridian and time, time correction from meridian, calculation of distance from prime meridian, sunrise in relation to meridian, celestial latitude and longitude, more parameters related to latitude and longitude.

Description of the Sun and the Moon: The diameter of the sun and the moon, the sun's projection on rising and setting lines, the parallax on the sun and the moon, delineation of the sun and the moon, rising and setting of the moon, visibility corrections of the moon, full moon and new moon, calculation of the illuminated portion of the moon, eclipses, probability of lunar eclipses, true angular diameter of sun, moon and shadow, comparison of the positions of the sun and the moon during lunar and solar eclipses, graphical representation of eclipses, eclipse and parallax, stars, comets etc. Bhaskara gives near accurate values for the sizes of the Earth and the moon and the distance between them. But his figures for the sun (3000000 meters) remain much too small.

In this age of high power telescopes, space vehicles and other technological advancement, we can distinguish between right and wrong in the available data and proceed further for more accurate and advanced discoveries. Now, for whatever is correct in the data available, the credit goes to those who discovered hundreds of years later. This state of affairs should not be allowed to continue for long.

(e) Metallurgy (Chemistry)

Ancient chemistry is reflected in various books, though we have no ancient works on chemistry itself. Metallurgy is the science of practical application of chemistry on metals. Kautilya in his *Arthasastra* has given very detailed illustrations on metallurgy – extraction of metals and qualitative and quantitative analysis for the purpose of detecting malpractices. The list of chemicals known to him in that distant past (fourth century BC) seems most impressive for his times, compared to the histories of chemistry in the Western countries. The existing medical treatises on chemistry have not yet been properly evaluated; they seem to be more centred on the study of mercury.[6]

Ancient knowledge of Metals and Alloys in Indian literature is related to metals, mines, ores, description of metallic ores, impurities in ores, furnaces and kilns, qualities of pure metals, use of flux to remove impurities, corrosion of metals etc. Alloys and pure metals available in those days are referred to as bronze, brass, bell metal, *panchaloha* (alloy of five metals), copper, iron, silver, mercury, lead, zinc, tin and gold. In ancient days and even in modern times, idols of gods for worship were carved in *panchaloha.*

(f) Physics

Physics seems to have been cultivated partly by philosophers as part of their studies on the nature of reality – the elements of which the universe consisted, atomic theories, the study of light, heat, sound etc. – and partly in its application in technology like hydrostatics for irrigation works, military engines, mechanical toys etc. It is also used in studies on theory of music. *The Vaiseshika School* of philosophy was particularly concerned with the problems of physics.[7]

(g) Medicines

According to Hindu belief, Brahma, the God of creation is the originator of the Indian system of medicines. He transmitted this knowledge to *Prajapati* (21 *Prajapatis* were created by Brahma to assist him in creation) and through Prajapati, the subsequent generations bequeathed this faculty of medical science. Later, two systems emerged in this indigenous science; *Ayurveda* and *Siddha.*

(i) Ayurveda

Ayurveda is a supplementary Veda (Upaveda); often described as the fifth Veda.

Ayurveda (lit: knowledge of longevity) is an indigenous medical system based on herbs and plants with a subsystem of physiotherapy associated with massaging along with internal and external application of medicines. Sage Caraka (100 AD) elaborately developed the Ayurveda system in his book *Caraka Samhita* with detailed stipulations on diagnosis, preparations of medicines and their application. In the history of philosophy, this book is remarkable because it contains a section on logic as a branch of knowledge requiring to be cultivated by Doctors both for purposes of making inferences in diagnosis and also for the study of professional ethics.

Later, Sisrutha in his book *Sisrutha samhitha* developed a system of surgery in Ayurveda, thereby making it a comprehensive and scientific system. But, due to the opposition from Buddhists, surgery received a setback. After the advent of the allopathic system with surgery as an integral component, Ayurvedic surgery sank into oblivion.

(ii) Siddha System

Siddha (lit: miraculous): In this system developed by Sage Agasthya, all medicines are prepared in powder-form enabling easy handling and oral consumption, without losing the efficacy of medication. Both Ayurveda and Siddha simultaneously exist in India as sister-systems from ancient period till date.

Dhanwanthari, a man believed to have emerged from ocean, was an expert in anti-venom treatment. Through Dhanwanthari, anti-venom treatment has become a prominent part of Ayurveda. Later, Vagbhata, a Sanskrit scholar of 12th century AD published two books on Ayurveda named *Ashtangasamgraha* and *Ashtangahridaya*. These books later happened to be a comprehensive treatise (like modern encyclopaedia) on Ayurveda. It enhanced the popularity of the Indian system of medicine.

Gradually, the popularity of Ayurveda waned due to the advent of three new systems, (i) *Unani*, an Indian system with Greek base, (ii) Allopathy (the English system of medicine), (iii) Homoeopathy (German system based on the constitution of each body).

Advancement in science and biotechnology put Allopathy in the forefront in accuracy of diagnosis, surgery, speedy recovery etc. The ancient systems prevalent in India failed to cope with the advanced and updated allopathic system. Though the Indian system had the advantages of absence of counter-effects of medicines and rooting out the disease through the treatment of the cause of disease, modern man, who require immediate relief due to the importance of time factor in life, is gradually drifting away from Indian systems due to slowness of recovery, prescription of abstinence during medication etc. It is a pity that no meaningful scientific research and reforms took place in the Indian systems of medicine so far.

(h) Architecture

Viswakarma (the son of Prabhasar and Varastree, the sister of Sage Brihaspati), is the father of Indian architecture and engineering. The *Puranas* (ancient literature) claim that Viswakarma was the architect of an aeroplane, the assembly hall of *Yama* (the king of death), Viswaroopa with three heads, construction of the city of Lanka etc. Even if these achievements are exaggerated facts or fiction, the successors of Viswakarma were renowned architects as is evidenced by the Indus Valley civilization discovered on excavation at Harappa and Mohenjodaro. Two-storeyed houses made of baked bricks, bathrooms, toilets, water supply, drainage, roads etc. in those ancient cities excelled those found in the earlier civilizations in Egypt and Mesopotamia. The palaces and tombs of ancient kings in India with domed roofing, ancient temples, monuments, Asoka's pillars of inscriptions, Rock cave temples etc. testify the architectural skills of the ancient Indians. Hundreds of similar very old monuments of Indian architecture are visible all over India, even today.[8]

(i) Natya Sastra (The Science of Dance)

Bharata Muni (around 400 BC), a critic and commentator, produced a book named 'Natyasastra' with a view to provide the haphazard arts of Indian dance and music with scientific basis and orderliness. *Natya sastra* is a voluminous book containing thirty-seven chapters prescribing scientific stipulations to be followed in these arts, along with detailed illustrations on poetic merits and demerits and commentaries on figure of speech. This is the first book, which provided the Indian music and dance with classicism, elegance and harmony. Many eminent Indian scholars and critics like Mitragupta, Harsha Vardhan, Sankugen, Ulbatan, Abhinava Gupta and others published commentaries of this book. Among these commentaries, the book titled *'Abhinavabharati'* by Abhinava Gupta alone is now extant.

Natyasastra is a book acclaimed all over the world. *Bharatanatya*, a classical dance form named after Bharata, this lover of arts, is very popular all over India even today.

(j) Textiles

Jawaharlal Nehru says:

> Cotton was used for textiles even at that remote period in India. Marshall compares and contrasts the Indus Valley civilization with those of contemporary Egypt and Mesopotamia: Thus, to mention only a few salient points, the use of cotton for textiles was not extended to the Western world until 2,000 or 3,000 years later.[9]

After the advent of the British rule, India became the supplier of raw cotton to the British Textile Industries and the market for the finished goods of those industries.

(k) Sculpture

In Harappa, we come across sculptures in clay, stone and metals. Human figures and animal figures made of clay are found there in very large numbers. The sacred figurines of clay represented Mother Goddess. The Harappa people developed the art of round stone sculptures. In Mohenjodaro, a figure of a bearded man was seen carved in white limestone. The other specimens of sculpture of this period were of high order from the point of view of arts. Two sandstone statuettes from Harappa, representing a youth with muscular body and another a dancer with one leg entwined round the other, were of high artistic value. Great heights were achieved in the art of metal sculptures also. A famous bronze female figure that dances in a special posture was noticed at Mohenjodaro.

Terracotta figurines of human and animals show vigour, variety and ingenuity. All these confirm that sculpture was a prominent art in India even from the days of the Indus Valley civilization.

FOOTNOTES

1. Warder, A.K., *A Course in Indian Philosophy*, pp. 76-80.
2. Gopalakrishnan, N. (Dr.), *Indian Scientific Heritage*, Ch. V.
3. *Ibid.*, Ch. V, p. 49.
4. Warder, A.K., *A Course in Indian Philosophy*, p. 78.
5. Gopalakrishnan, N. (Dr.), *Indian Scientific Heritage*, pp. 201-345.
6. Warder, A.K., *A Course in Indian Philosophy*, p. 80.
7. *Ibid.*, p. 81.
8. Vettom Mani, *Puranic Encyclopaedia*, p. 59.
9. Jawaharlal Nehru, *The Discovery of India*, pp. 58-59.

Science of Experience 4

Today, man has before him a history of 150 years of modern science observing and analysing everything through experiments with the help of modern scientific tools. At the same time, an Indian has behind him an ancient Indian science developed in the days of yore, when everything was accepted solely through the experience of the mind and the body. The Indian *Rishis* (ascetics), who obtained this knowledge through revelations or intuition, practised, proved through experience, confirmed and inherited them to the subsequent generations. India, in possession of this treasure of ancient knowledge, both scientific and spiritual, introduced them into the Indian life style in the form of customs, rituals, beliefs, traditions, practices etc. As such, the facts available before us can be categorised into two groups, one proved through observation and experiments and the other proved through repeated experiences.

Nowadays, even the staunch proponents of modern science recommend this science of experience proved efficacious through experiments with the aid of modern scientific tools. A few of them are listed below:

Yoga – Physiological, psychological and spiritual exercises.

Pranic healing and Indian *Panchaprana* (five stages of respiration) concept.

Vegetarianism and *Brahma Chaitanya* concept (Atma or soul in every living being).

Breathing exercises (*Prāṇāyāma*).

The relation between meditation (*Dhyāna*) and brain.

Childcare through breast-feeding, touch therapy, oily bath, storytelling etc.

Physiotherapy, Music therapy, Aromatherapy, Fasting therapy, Water therapy etc.

Counselling (*upadesasaras*) – expert advice on problems, psychiatric or financial or other problems.

Naturopathy, herbal medicines and health care.

Biofertilisers, biopesticides and fumigation in agriculture.

Relation between body and mind.

Protection of environmental equilibrium and eco-friendly approach.

Management science.

Control of bodily senses and concentration on objects, preferably God.

Morality, ethics and hygiene in life.

In view of the relations of the science of experience with the integrated physiological and psychological development, eco-friendly approach, sustainable consumption, environmental protection etc, this science of experience deserves to be classified among the most sophisticated class of modern science. Today the world is, knowingly or unknowingly, recognising the pearls of knowledge in the Indian Vedas, Upanishads, Philosophies etc. for the survival of life on this planet. In this chapter, a few items of this ancient knowledge are given to assess where Indian thoughts were positioned in the world scenario.

Yoga

The Vedic philosophy of Yoga is a granary of knowledge with physiological and psychological parameters. This Yoga has eight steps or limbs and hence it is known as *Ashtanga Yoga* (Yoga with eight limbs). They are known as (i) *Yama*, (ii) *Niyama*, (iii) *Aāsana*, (iv) *Prānāyāma*, (v) *Prathyāhāra*, (vi) *Dhārana*, (vii) *Dhyāna*, and (viii) *Samādhi*.

(i) Yama

This has five subdivisions, *Ahimsa, Satya, Asteya, Brahmacharya* and *Aparigraha*.

Ahimsa refers to absence of hostility towards other beings. Literally, the word means 'non-violence' or 'non-injury'.

Satya means 'Truth' or 'essence'. '*Satya*' denotes the attempt or investigation to know the essence of a thing – it is the path to the 'Ultimate Truth'.

Asteya refers to the avoidance of exploitation of others. This provides the best approach to the 'techniques of management and maintenance of human rights'.

Brahmacharya denotes self-control and freedom from sexual desires to enable the acquisition of 'Ultimate knowledge'.

Aparigraha refers to restraint and avoidance of material and physical comforts – the understanding of the aim of life.

These five are the cardinal principles of Hinduism and the moral and ethical code of conduct to be followed not only by the Hindus but also by all men to ensure peace in the society, temporal and spiritual contentment and happiness in life.

(Please see more explanatory notes in chapter 10 of Part Two – Hinduism.)

(ii) Niyama

It has five subdivisions:

Soucha: Physical purity, cleanliness and hygiene. Soucha ensures physical and mental health.

Santhosha: Contentment in life or happiness. 'Psychological, social and economic problems are solved by contentment.

Thapas: Process of activation of the body and sensory and functional organs.

Swadhyayas: Learning to acquire the ultimate knowledge. This is the role of education in modern age.

Easwarapranidhana: Submission to the Ultimate Power. By this, endomorphic production takes place in the brain, which heals pain. Unless one has the trust and faith, even the effects of physiological medication are lessened in the body.

(iii) Aāsana

Aāsana means a variety of physical postures for the muscular and skeleton systems. *Aāsana* are the best remedies for several types of body pains and muscular tensions. It directly ensures stability of mind by reducing stress in life. Dozens of postures are prescribed depending upon the type of physiological and psychological stress experienced by the individual.

(iv) Prānāyāma

Prānāyāma is the controlling of the Prana, the life energy of the body (respiration) also called breathing exercises. It can regulate the supply of oxygen to the body. Lactic acid accumulated in the muscle gets easily decomposed and oxidised. It is the best technique to relieve physiological and psychological stress and for regularisation of blood pressure.

(v) Prathyāhāra

This is said to be the first step in meditation in which the sensory organs are withdrawn from the surroundings to obtain concentration. It has a psychological impact whereby many psychosomatic problems can be avoided.

(vi) Dhārana

It is the second step in perfect meditation. By controlling the mind, the brain activity is regulated. In the process of teaching and learning, the level of *Dhārana* is excellent for understanding the subject.

(vii) Dhyāna

This is actual meditation. Concentration of the mind and reduction in brain activities can activate the brain cells by keeping the free flow of the connection of mind with the object matter (or God) without interruption. Different stages of meditation can be perfectly analysed with modern scientific tools. The common state under which the brain cells function is the ***beta*** stage, during which the brain produces electrical waves of frequency between 13 and 28 cycles per second. In the first stage of meditation, the wave number decreases to 8 to 13 cycles per second. This is known as the ***alpha*** stage. When one goes deep in to the meditation, the frequency of electrical waves is further reduced to 3 to 8 cps which is the ***delta*** stage. In the last stage the frequency goes further down to 0.5 to 3 cps. This is explained as the *Samādhi* stage. These results can be measured using the EEG (Electroencephalogram). Hence, meditation is advised for all classes of people like students, workers, bureaucrats and others who work under stress.

(viii) Samādhi

This is the last stage when body activities are minimized and the brain reaches the highest level of accumulation of energy and the senses are focused on one thought or object. This is the ***theta*** stage. Scientific studies have revealed that at this stage of meditation, epileptic brain waves get modified. When music is used along with other factors, it can directly influence the functioning of the brain. *Dhyāna*, *Dhārana* and *Samādhi*, the last three stages of meditation can directly influence the mind, brain, knowledge, awareness and consciousness.

The observations of Dr. B.R. Ramamurthy Neuro Surgeon on brain and mind are reproduced below:

> Until a few years ago the *vaasanās* as mentioned in the Indian scriptures were pooh poohed by the western scientists.... Today we can explain all this based on genetic conditioning.... We know that genes not only determine shape, size, and colour of the body but also the vasanaas as referred to by Indians.

GENE of the modern science is nothing but the JNAANA of the ancient Indian sciences.

We in India say that the *vaasanā* of an individual is due to the pōōrvakarma (action of the past life). This is likely to be proved by modern science within probably a hundred years.

Modern science has accepted the three states of the mind as the *jagrath* (waking), *swapna* (dream) and *sushupti* (deep sleep) as mentioned in the Indian scriptures.

The effect of *Gayathri Japa* and *Manthra Japa* by knowing the meaning and keeping the faith works better and produce chemical changes in the brain.

The meaning of the mind control in all the ancient rituals by saying *manassamaadhiyathaam, Samaabithamanasasma;* let our mind become calm and let it happen to all of us, has the real physiological meaning and message.

The fourth state of consciousness after jagrath, swapna and sushupthi is now proved to be the *Turya* state as mentioned in Turgopanishad.

The present day neurophysiology stops with attributing the thinking process as the highest level function of the brain. It has been common knowledge to oriental thinkers, particularly Indians. There are many further states of the human mind culminating in the state of "thoughtless awareness" and *Turya* is that ultimate functional state of the brain.

In the *Turya* state the energy of billions of brain cells are conserved. Therefore, it may be possible in that state to become extraordinarily aware...as we say *thrikaala jnaani.*

The self-awareness in the thoughtless state will expand and become universal awareness. This brain will transcend time and space. In such a person the *thrikaala jnaana* exists, i.e. the knowledge of past, present and future.

There are also areas in the brain which is responsible for the sense of I (*aham:* in Sanskrit) and also the feeling creating centre of mind (*manha*: in Sanskrit). This centre is known as the temporal lobes. Hence these awareness and consciousness are the knowledge and hence the *prajnaanam Brahma / aham Brahmasmi/thatvamasi* can be correlated with knowledge, and can be directly connected to the divine power as we Indians did, through awareness and consciousness, which is science.

Since the sense of I is the level of awareness, in the higher place of awareness, I is the *drashta* (seer: one who sees). At that level of awareness the brain is receptive to universal power. Hence the name *manha drashta* given to the Rishis is literally correct.

The brain can tap cosmic power if mind is in the fourth state i.e. in *Turya* state. Just like the radio is tuned to receive a particular wave from the sky, the brain can be tuned to receive the universal power. Hearing and conversing with the universal power is possible at *Turya* state.

The above state is the scientific yoga. It is not the unity of the self with the super self, or linking the brain that is aware but understanding by thought, with universal awareness. It is pure science and not philosophy.[1]

Pranic Healing

This science was well-known in India from time immemorial. Through bio plasma explanation, Choa Kok Sui rediscovered the theory as *Praaana, praana, apaana*, *vyaana, udaana*, *samaana* and *Atma*. But this is almost the same as that of the Indian *Panchaprana* described as *Prana, Apana, Vyana, Udanna* and *Saamana*. In this process, energy absorption to the *Praanamaya kosha* is taking place regularly. When there is an abnormality in *Thejomaya kosha* (aura), it is visible in the Kirlin photography. The aura of Rishies, Buddha, Jaina, Lord Krishna etc. can be seen by the scanning done by the pranic healers. The Yoga books explain that there are eleven chakras in the human body absorbing the Prana energy.

Upadesa Saraas (Modern Counselling)

This has already been accepted by the modern science.

Music Therapy (*Raga Chikitsa*, *Naada Chikitsa* and *Sangeetha Chikitsa*)

Gandharva Veda, an Upaveda of Sama Veda, is the Veda of music. Music therapy, combined with other systems, is suggested as cure for headache, cerebral palsy, neuropsychiatry etc. In the Michigan State University in U.S.A., Music therapy was included in the curriculum, decades ago. St. Luke's Hospital, Ohio, Mayo Clinic in Minnesota etc. have separate music therapy departments.

Vegetarianism

The life force known as *Brahma Chaitanya* is manifested as *Atma* (soul) in all animals. Killing animals and eating their flesh are against the concept of *Dharma*. However, extraction is not against *Dharma*. The parts of plants like leaves, flowers, stems, roots etc. can be used so that the plants can grow again. Milk of animals can be extracted and used, but its flesh cannot be used because it tantamount to killing the being. Scientific merit of vegetarian food is another factor accepted by modern science.

Indian Health Science

The Indian system of medicine, consisting of two branches, the Ayurveda and Siddha systems, has been explained in the previous chapter. In those systems, treatment is focused on the patient and not on the diseases. Today, the modern world is more and more veering around the efficacy of this system insisting on vegetarian food, oil massage, hot water massage, herbal medicines and food prepared with cardamom, clove, pepper, turmeric, neem, coriander, dill etc. Modern technology has very much helped the preparation, preservation and marketing of medicines. Flower therapy, Aromatherapy, hot water therapy, massaging, naturopathy etc. are based on Ayurvedic principles. Spirituality is also being prescribed in this system aimed at regularising the mind and thereby controlling the entire physiological system. Physical and psychological exercises prescribed under the Yoga system are also becoming more and more popular all over the world.

Agriculture

Varahamitra, Saarngadhara and many other scientists have explained the Indian approach to agriculture very systematically. They have recommended biofertilisers in the place of chemical, inorganic, artificial and synthetic fertilizers. Higher level of acceptance of biofertilisers shows an ecofriendly approach. Use of plant products, ash, cowdung etc. as manure reduces the risk of adverse reaction and side-effects on the fertility of the land. The antifeedants, allelo chemicals etc. are more ecofriendly pesticides. Extracts of neem, tobaccos etc. are recommended as ecofriendly biopesticides. Fumigation as germicide, pesticide, insecticide etc. affects the fertility recommended not only in agriculture but also as a powerful weapon for atmospheric and environmental cleanliness both inside and outside the houses. Fumigation with camphor or frankincense or some other medicinal plants is an integral part of all *poojas* (worshipping practices) in India. During periods of epidemics, fumigation is the first aid used by all classes of people as a precautionary germicide. Cowdung water is prescribed to eliminate virus, fungus and bacteria-moulds in plants.

Environment

A holistic approach to earth, air, water, plants, animals etc. is recommended in the *Vedas*. It is advised to keep water holy, sacred, clean, pure, cool and free from all germs by the effect of sunrays. The mother earth concept of Vedas has to be accepted by the world to maintain the ecological equilibrium. Variety of trees, creepers, ponds, tiny forests etc. are to be maintained as bioreserve. These are encouraged to maintain the environmental conditions positively.

Family Relations

Today, the world over, family relations are in the process of break up. The result of this breakdown is the abnormality and degeneration of the upcoming generation. The Indians are taught to consider mother, father, teacher and guest equivalent to 'God'. (*Matha Devo bhava; Pitha Devo bhava; Guru Devo bhava; Athithi Devo bhava.*) In caring the aged parents, Indians are instructed to care the elderly parents as a sacred privilege, responsibility and obligatory duty.

Child Care

Compulsory breast feeding, Touch therapy enabling close contact for the baby with the mother, giving food in the hands of the children, oily bath to the babies, allowing baby to play in the Sun, playing in the sand and soil (though little unhygienic), cooked or semi-cooked or specially processed food to the babies etc. are the methods prescribed for child care. These are supposed to aim at building up self-confidence, immunity from diseases, feeling of security, muscular flexibility, growth of brain, physiological and psychological development, learning of ethical values, sociological information and so on. Modern Science has approved many of these practices.

Food, Customs and Rituals

A variety of customs are associated with preparation and consumption of food. Using variety of vegetables, mixing of medicinal plants in food, sitting on the floor while taking food, prayer preceding food, sitting on wooden plank or mat while consuming food, fasting at fixed intervals, diverse food items – change from rice to wheat, wheat to fruits, fruits to leaves with fibre – avoidance of coffee or tea before brushing teeth are some of the items recommended. Many of these are receiving world attention.[2]

Conclusion

Many concepts developed in ancient India – management concepts given in the *Bhagawad Gita*, Indian civil engineering concepts, the *Brahmanda* concept of the universe, transcendental meditation for employees, sudharsana kriya (a type of meditation), the concept of self-awareness of the power of the universe, mental health and neuro-sciences, definition of health as the physiological, psychological, social, mental and spiritual well-being state of the individual etc. – are being examined al' over the world. Much more precious information on multifarious subjects may be lying dormant in the Indian ancient literature. Earnest efforts to scan and bring them to light are till now lacking.

FOOTNOTES

1. Gopalakrishnan, N. (Dr.), *Ancient Indian Scientific Thoughts*, pp. 7-8.
2. *Ibid.*, p. 22.

Contributions at the Level of Religions

5

India gave birth to four World Religions, Hinduism, Buddhism, Jainism and Sikhism; no mean feat in the history of a nation. Before the advent of Communism in China, N. Korea, Vietnam etc., the Indian religions covered half the population of the world. Among these religions, Sikhism is the latest in origin (16th century). All the other three religions originated before the Christian era. Though adherents of Sikhism are found all over the world, with sizeable number in Canada and England, they are either Indian migrants or descendants of Indian natives. There is nothing outstanding mentionable as their contributions to the world.

Jainism is more or less confined to India even today. History does not show any efforts on the part of the Jains to propagate their religion beyond the borders of India. Through many books published by foreigners on Jainism, the ideologies of Jainism would have reached many corners of the world. But, we are still in the dark as to whether the ideologies of Jainism had any reckoning impact or influence anywhere outside India.

But Buddhism stands wide apart from the above mentioned religions. It enjoyed a pivotal position in India for nearly ten centuries, from the fifth century BC to the fifth century AD; in some areas it even replaced Hinduism. The greatest contribution of India in the realm of religions is Buddhism itself. It was exported to all accessible nations in those days and found dear and easy acceptance in many countries. Consequently, Buddhism stands today as the most prominent religion in the East and South-East Asia. Buddha's conception of religion was purely ethical. Unlike Hinduism, Buddhism never cared for worship or rituals. Resultantly, even in the early centuries of its origin, it found easy acceptability in a large number of countries in Asia like Ceylon (Sri Lanka), Burma (Myanmar), Bhutan, Korea, China, Japan, Java, Sumatra, Borneo, Champa, Siam (Thailand), Central Asia, and several other island nations in the Pacific. Many factors contributed for this phenomenal growth of Buddhism. They are:

- Simplicity of the teachings of Buddha.
- Both the philosophies of Buddha and the language of presentation (*Pali*) were simple, familiar and convincing to the people.
- Excessive ritualism coupled with the exploitation by the priests (Brahmins) made the practice of Hinduism very expensive and unbearable to the common Hindu.
- Buddhism, free from casteism based on birth was a very attractive proposition for all those outside the castes.
- The edifying personality of Buddha was a very influential factor in the spread of Buddhism. Buddha was a rare combination of several factors and characteristics constituting a magnetic personality such as:
    - Pure royal descent with no reproach in birth;
    - Sacrifice of the royal privileges, relatives, money and wealth;
    - Pleasant voice with pleasing delivery and politeness;
    - Handsome and pleasant-looking in complexion, fair in colour, fine in presence and stately to behold;
    - Congenial and conciliatory in approach;
    - Master teacher of teachers with righteousness in exhortations;
    - Accessibility to all.
- The Buddha Sanga, priests and nuns were very enthusiastic in propagating their religion.
- The royal patronage of Asoka, Kanishka and Harsha immensely helped the cause of Buddhism. Emperor Asoka deputed his own son and daughter to Ceylon

(Sri Lanka) to propagate Buddhism with impressive results.

- In those days, Buddhism had no serious rivals in the field and
- Adaptability of Buddhism also contributed in a large measure for the rapid spread of Buddhism.

Two other contributions of Buddhism to the world are *monasticism* and *Ahimsa*. Asceticism (*Sannyasa*) was prevalent in Hinduism from the very early days of its inception as an obligatory stipulation in the last among the four stages of life. But, it never had any collective character or import till the advent of Buddhism. It was confined to individual-based hermitages in the forests free from the mundane world where each hermit lived with his disciples. Monasteries were absent. *Viharas* (monasteries) came into existence as an innovative programme of Buddhism which later spread to other regions of the world. Today, monasticism, which originated in India, is a vital limb of the Catholic Church all over the world.

The doctrine of *Ahimsa* (non-violence) was deeply embedded in Hinduism even from the days of its origin. Buddha lifted up this doctrine to the surface and included it as a compulsory dogma of Buddhism to be complied with by all Buddhist believers. According to Hinduism, *Ahimsa* meant not merely abstaining from physical violence or non-injury to others but a concept emphasising love and respect for all. Buddhism gave a wider connotation to *Ahimsa* and substituted it by the words *maitri* meaning friendship and *Karuna* meaning compassion. Jainism advanced this concept further to the extent of insisting refrain from cultivation of land, walking with a stick, covering one's mouth etc. to avoid harm to even tiny creatures. In Bible, we see Jesus Christ advising Ahimsa "If one strike thee on thy right cheek, turn to him also the other" (*The Bible* – Mt. 5:39).

The contributions of Hinduism stand singularly apart from other religions. Being the oldest religion, the main contributions of Hinduism to the world are in the ideological plane. Theism, origin of life, the word 'Om' – Pranava, Revelation, Incarnation, *Saguna Brahma* (personal God), Asceticism, Ahimsa, Trimurty,

Realization of God etc. are concepts originated and developed in Hinduism. Trimurty in Hinduism is parallel to the Trinity in Christianity. Similarly, infancy of Sri Krishna in Hinduism is parallel to the infancy of Jesus Christ in Christianity, with varying interpretations. Priesthood, first developed in Hinduism, is seen in many other religions today. In faith and worshipping practices also, similarities are noticed in Zoroastrianism and Judaism. A few moral and ethical principles noticed in Confucianism and Zoroastrianism resemble those in Hinduism and Buddhism. It is a fallacy to conclude that later religions copied them from the older religions. Similar parallels and analogous terms may appear in different religions with differing connotations. It is more logical to conclude that older religions would have had some impact or influence on later religions, perhaps with diverse interpretations, implications and practices.

Though Hinduism lags behind almost all other religions in the matter of propagation of faith or conversions, it cannot be fully excluded on this score. From the 2nd century BC to the 12th century AD, many Hindu dynasties like Pallavas, Chalukyas, Satavahanas, Rashtrakutas, Cheras, Cholas, Pandyas etc. ruled over the areas of South India and Deccan. Among them, Cholas and Pandyas became superpowers at one time or other. In that remote past, they were strong naval powers too with trade relations with overseas countries both in the East and the West. They propagated Hindu faith in countries where they had trade relations, converted many to Hinduism and resultantly Hinduism became a prominent religion in Thailand, Cambodia (Kamboja), Vietnam, Burma, Ceylon (Sri Lanka), Champa (Annam) and few island nations in the Pacific. But, they failed to withstand for long due to the onslaught of Buddhism. Hinduism gradually dwindled in size. Now, a good number of Hindu temples and Hindu names of places and people remain there. Due to the vicissitudes of history, majority of the Hindus in these nations embraced Buddhism, leaving aside only a negligible number of Hindus at present.

Whatever the demerits and drawbacks of Hinduism, it is the religion that first taught the world on theism. India is the first country to contribute to the world not only the concept of a 'Supreme God, but also to develop and maintain a spirituality based on theism for many millennia, despite many provocations to the contrary'.

Contributions of India to World Unity and Peace

6

India occupies a key position in the world ever since civilization first began to fan out in different directions from its original birthplace in Mesopotamia (present Iraq). India is an epitome of the present world as some of the main problems confronting human race all over the world are present in India as India's national problems and they are being wrestled with by the people of India and the Indian government. Moreover, in India, there is an attitude towards life, and an approach towards handling human affairs that answer to the needs of the present situation. This has an impact not only in India, but also in the whole world.[1]

India's key position in the world is not only geographical but also in holding the balance in the worldwide competitions between rival ideologies. Today, the parliamentary form of democracy has a hold in Asia only because India has chosen it as their own way of political life. If India were to change this option, the effect would be felt not only in India but also in the hearts of Asia and Africa.

Among human activities, politics are more superficial, while religion cuts deeper. In the religious front, India is not a recipient but a donor. About half the living higher religions of the world are of Indian origin. India has been the site of four Empires; Maurya, Gupta, Mughul and British. In the course of 5000 years, Indian peasantry has become accustomed to being exploited in order to provide an urban ruling minority with the amenities of a civilization in which the peasantry has no share. "They have already learnt to take their hard life as they find it without dreaming of the possibility that they might have it in their power to change their life for the better by their own action. It is only in our own lifetime that the consequent fresh spurt of technological advance has gone to lengths which are making it feasible at last to give a fair share in the amenities of civilization to the whole of mankind."[2] This is the present situation in the world as a whole and in India in particular. Population is a world problem and a major problem for India as well. We have succeeded in reducing the death rate without a proportionate reduction in birth rate. It is a titanic task for India to educate and convince millions of wives and husbands on the imperative necessity to limit the number of children. The Government of India is embarking on this enterprise without it being obstructed by superstition. This example will inspire other nations facing this problem.

Another problem that is faced by India as well as the world is linguistic nationalism. It is worth to note that the emergence of their problem is the part of the price for democracy. Though China is a bigger country, this problem is absent as one language is spoken in the entire China. In the case of India, Hindi, the national language has no affinity at all with the Dravidian languages. India cannot afford to allow local linguistic nationalism to go out of hand.

When a government meets with resistance, however morally legitimate, it is easy for it to fall into maintaining its authority by force. This has been one of the common tragedies of history. Gandhi saved India as well as Britain from that situation by inspiring the people of India to keep the struggle on a spiritual plane, above the level of politics. The *Bhoodan* movement was another one in this direction. Asoka substituted religious propaganda for military aggression as his instrument for unifying the world. In this tornado of annihilating material power, mankind cannot save itself from self-destruction unless we manage to practise non-violence in our relations with our fellowmen. This is an abject lesson of immense value for the rest of the world in our time.

Physically, we are all neighbours, but psychologically we are still strangers to each other. We had never been so conscious of our variety as we are now that we have come to such close quarters. This is why India's conspicuous achievement of variety-in-unity is of worldwide importance. It is the spiritual gift that makes man human. It is still alive in Indian souls. Let us go on giving the world the Indian examples of it. Nothing else can do so much to help mankind to save itself from self-destruction.

World Peace

Indian contribution for world peace is, on all counts, greater than those of most other world nations. India became independent only in August 1947. In the 1300 years preceding Indian independence, foreigners determined the future and destiny of India; Indians had absolutely no role in it. From day one after Independence, India followed a policy of peace, whatever be the contention or whoever be the contestants. Though free India was forced to wage few wars unfortunately imposed on the nation, the policy of India had all along been governed by the principles of peaceful co-existence, mutual recognition of the sovereignty and territorial integrity of nations, non-aggression and non-interference in the internal affairs of other nations and solution of problems, if any, through dialogue. Indian Prime Ministers and national representatives in the UN and other international forums unambiguously declared this policy of India, time and again. Not content with high sounding sermons, India has done whatever within its command to achieve the aim of peace. India always co-operated with the peacekeeping efforts under the auspices of the UN by sending forces, whenever she was called upon by the UN to do so.

Indo-Japanese Relations

In the period between 1900 and 1922, the people of India wanted Japanese support in their national struggle, but the attitude of Japan was pro-British because of the Anglo-Japanese Alliance of 1902. But, later, a change occurred in the attitude of Japan towards India. It was not willing to suppress the activities of the Indian revolutionaries in Japan led by Ras Behari Bose. But, in the Sino-Japanese war (1937-39), India sympathized with China. This deteriorated mutual relations. But, after 1945, the relations have undergone vast improvement.

Both countries have concluded several bilateral agreements on trade. Though these agreements were suspended during the Second World War, they were revived immediately after the war. Gradually, cultural relations between the two countries expanded after the cultural agreement of 1956. Today, the relations are normal and friendly.

Sino-Indian Relations

On 20th October 1962, China invaded India with an army of 25000 men, as a part of their territorial expansion programme. Again, when India was in the thick of a war with Pakistan, China not only supported Pakistan but also issued in September 1965 an ultimatum to India, after concentrating their forces in the Himalayan borders. But even after 1962, India supported China's case for membership in the UN. India also expressed their desire to solve border problems through peaceful negotiations. Even though China is still in occupation of thousands of Sq.K.Ms. of Indian territory annexed by them in 1962, India later revived diplomatic relations with China. The border problem still remains unsettled.

Relations with USSR and USA

Ever since Independence, the ties of friendship between India and Soviet Union were gradually becoming stronger, day after day. In 1953, an important trade agreement was concluded. The succeeding years have been marked by consolidation and enlargement of Indo-Soviet friendship. The crisis and conflict between India and Pakistan from 1962-65 came to an end by the Tashkent Declaration, which was accomplished largely due to the intervention of the Soviet Union. In the cultural and economic spheres, the collaboration produced many favourable results for both countries. The major projects like Bhilai and Bokaro steel plants in India were accomplished with the technical support and co-operation of the Soviet Union.

Even after polarization of the world into two Power Blocks under the leadership of USA and USSR, India followed a policy of non-alignment. India kept aloof from the defence pacts of NATO and SEATO under the aegis of the USA or the Warsaw pact under the aegis of the Soviet Union. Equidistance from both power blocks was the considered policy of India. Though the strengthening of the Indo-Soviet friendship was an irritant to the USA, India was very cautious and vigilant to maintain the Indo-U.S. relations without being ruptured.

India's Relation with Arab Countries

India's relationship with Egypt and Arab countries had always been friendly. In the Arab-Israel conflict, India consistently supported the Arab cause without viewing Israel as a foe. The West Asian policy of the Indian Government, during and after the Bangladesh War, was harshly criticized by many quarters. The Arabs never supported the cause of Bangladesh. They were sympathetic towards Pakistan. Despite this attitude, the Government of India maintained friendly relations with the Arab States and supported the Arab cause in the 1973 war. Even in the Iraq-U.S. War, India supported the Iraq cause without straining India's relations with the U.S.

Asia and Africa

A significant feature in the history of the modern world is the awakening of the Afro-Asian nations. India sincerely welcomed this movement. The Asian Relations Conference in March-April 1947, the Conference of Colombo powers (Burma, Ceylon, India, Indonesia and Pakistan) in 1954 and the Bandung Conference in Indonesia in 1955 were convened with India as one of the sponsoring powers. The Declaration of the Bandung Conference itself was on 'World Peace and Co-operation'.[3]

Conclusion

India played an important role in the UN without identifying herself with any block or group.

India sent a peacekeeping force to Sri Lanka to protect that country from the revolutionary army of LTTE, at the request of Sri Lanka. Even though Britain was the oppressor of India, just after Independence, India accepted membership in the British Commonwealth to ensure World Peace.

India won all wars against Pakistan, but she never retained any Pakistan territory. To establish peace in the region, India entered into peace agreements with Pakistan. The Tashkent Declaration, Shimla Agreement to enter into dialogue with Pakistan, the Lahore Declaration etc. are examples. Even now, India has taken the initiative to ensure durable peace in the region.

An organisation called 'South Asian Association for Regional Co-operation (SAARC)' was formed under India's initiative to ensure co-operation and development among all the seven member-nations in South Asia. India played a pivotal role in the Non-Alignment movement and the meeting of Afro-Asian nations.

It not only revived diplomatic relations with China but also still strive to strengthen the ties with that country by mutual visits and trade agreements. India welcomed the formation of the European Union. Many other instances of efforts of India to ensure peace in the world can be cited. India may perhaps be the only nation in the world, which has no rancour or revenge against any other nation. Only a nation with a spiritual basis like India can show that restraint and commitment for world peace, at times, even sacrificing her own interests.

FOOTNOTES

1. Arnold, J. Toynbee, *Lectures in India on India's Contribution to World Unity – A. Toynbee Anthology*, pp. 41-51.
2. Sachidanandan, V., *A. Toynbee Anthology*, pp. 43-44.
3. Majumdar, R.C., *An Advanced History of India*, pp. 1006-29.

PART TWO

HINDUISM

MAJOR WORLD RELIGIONS - UN STATISTICS

All major religions in the modern world originated and spread in the initial stages in Asia, Judaism and Christianity in Palestine, Mohammedanism or Islam in Arabia, Zorostrianism in Iran, Hinduism, Buddhism, Jainism and Sikhism in India, Confucianism in China and Shintoism in Japan. Crude forms of some primitive religions, their number exceeding ten thousand, existed in Africa and some other countries. Many of them have become almost extinct due to the influence of one or more of the other religions. Taoism almost merged in Buddhism and Confucianism. Manichaenism faced a natural death.

UN Statistics, showing the religions in the world are given in the table with explanatory notes.

Continents: These follow current UN demographic terminology, which now divides the world into the six major areas shown in the table. See United Nations, *World Population Prospects*: The 1996 Revision (New York: UN. 1998), with populations of all continents, regions, and countries covering the period 1950-2025. Note that "Asia" now includes the former Soviet Central Asian States and "Europe" includes all of Russia and extends eastward to Vladivostok, the Sea of Japan and the Bering Strait.

Countries: The last column enumerates sovereign and nonsovereign countries in which each religion or religious grouping has a numerically significant and organized following.

Adherents: As defined and enumerated for each of the world's countries in *World Christian Encyclopaedia* (1982), projected to mid-1999, adjusted for recent data.

Christians: Followers of Jesus Christ affiliated with churches (Church members, including Children: 1,863,791,000) plus persons professing in censuses or polls to be Christians though not so affiliated. Figures for the subgroups of Christians do not add up to the totals in the first line because some Christians adhere to more than one denomination.

Other Christians: This term in the table denotes Catholics (Non Roman) marginal protestants, Crypto Christians, and

Worldwide Adherents of All Religions by Six Continents

	Africa	Asia	Europe	Latin America	North America	Oceania	World
Christians	3512760	3064010	5592120	4237130	2587700	248090	1924181
Affiliated Christians	32656900	300917000	53642000	46831200	21045500	2111800	186379100
Roman Catholics	11727700	108437000	28566800	45410500	70652000	8097000	104423600
Protestants	86720000	49140000	77396000	47288000	69523000	7279000	337346000
Orthodox	34549000	14161000	15777200	543000	6275000	691000	213991000
Anglicans	41503000	717000	26628000	1081000	3259000	5386000	78574000
Other Christians	84081000	153105000	29118000	45421000	82320000	1929000	395974000
Unaffiliated Christians	24707000	5484000	22792000	5401000	48315000	3691000	110390000
Non-Christians	4153020	3327878	1697310	3763200	4843200	520900	4004184
Atheists	411000	121467000	23140000	2717000	1628000	360000	149723000
Baha'is	1649000	3382000	128000	850000	770000	108000	6887000
Buddhists	132000	351043000	1533000	635000	2637000	290000	356270000
Chinese folk religionists	32000	380250000	253000	190000	844000	63000	381632000
Confucianists	0	6219000	11000	0	0	23000	6253000
Ethnic religionists	94934000	127260000	1264000	1266000	434000	263000	225421000
Hindus	2312000	792897000	1401000	761000	1308000	349000	799028000

(*Contd.*)

	Africa	Asia	Europe	Latin America	North America	Oceania	World
Jains	65000	4079000	0	0	7000	0	4151000
Jews	212000	4323000	2534000	1133000	6015000	96000	14313000
Mandeans	0	38000	0	0	0	0	38000
Muslims	31052900	807034000	31219000	1646000	4389000	292000	115510900
New-Religionists	28000	99734000	156000	613000	813000	62000	101406000
Shintoists	0	2715000	0	7000	56000	0	2778000
Sikhs	52000	22015000	238000	0	514000	18000	22837000
Spiritists	3000	0	131000	11894000	149000	7000	12184000
Zoroastrians	1000	2407000	10000	0	76000	1000	2495000
Other religionists	65000	23000	235000	96000	591000	9000	1019000
Non religious	4877000	602992000	10747800	15824000	28201000	3268000	762640000
Total Population	7665780	3634279	7289430	4613450	3072020	300180	5928365

adherents of African, Asian, Black and Latin American indigenous churches.

Atheists: Persons professing atheism, skepticism, disbelief, or irreligion, including antireligious (opposed to all religions).

Buddhists: 56 per cent Mahayana, 38 per cent Theravada (Hinayana), 6 per cent Tantrayana (Lamaism).

Chinese folk religionists: Followers of traditional Chinese religion (local deities, ancestor veneration, Confucian ethics, Taoism, universism, divination and some Buddhist elements).

Confucianists: Non-Chinese followers of Confucius and Confucianism, mostly Koreans in Korea.

Ethnic religionists: Followers of local, tribal, animistic, or shamanistic religions.

Hindus: 70 per cent Vaishnavites, 25 per cent Shaivites, 2 per cent neo-Hindus and reform Hindus.

Jews: Adherents of Judaism. For detailed data on "Core" Jewish population, *see* the annual "World Jewish Populations" article in the American Jewish Committee's American Jewish Year Book.

Muslims: 83 per cent Sunnites, 16 per cent Shiites, 1 per cent other schools. Until 1990 the ethnic Muslims in the former U.S.S.R. who had embraced communism were not included as Muslims in this table. After the collapse of communism in 1990-91, this ethnic Muslims were once again enumerated as Muslims if they had returned to Islamic profession and practice.

New-Religionists: Followers of Asian 20th century New Religions, New Religious movements, radical new crisis religions, and non-Christian syncretistic mass religions, all founded since 1800 and most since 1945.

Other religionists: Including 70 minor world religions and more than 10,000 national or local religions and a large number of spiritist religions. New Age religions, quasi religions, pseudoreligions, parareligions, religious or mystic systems, religious and semireligious brotherhoods of numerous varieties.

Non-religious: Persons professing no religion, nonbelievers, agnostics, freethinkers, dereligionized secularists indifferent to all religions.

Total population: UN medium variant figures for mid-1999, as given in *World Population Prospects* in the 1998 Revision.

(*Courtsey*: Britannica Book of the Year 2000)

Many of these religions have no relevance to the topic we deal with in this book. As such, they are only just introduced for general information while the relevant ones are presented in detail.

Current Statistics

The 1998 Revision of the official United Nations World Population estimates and Projections as finalised (Last modified on 6th Sept. 2002) are given below:

Major Religions of the World Ranked by Number of Adherents

Last modified 6th September 2002.

(Sizes shown are approximate estimates, and are here mainly for the purpose of ordering the groups, not providing a definitive number. This list is sociological/statistical in perspective.)

Christianity: 2 billion

Islam: 1.3 billion

Hinduism: 900 million

Secular/Nonreligious/agnostic/atheist: 8.50 million

Buddhism: 360 million

Chinese traditional religion: 225 million

Primal-indigenous: 150 million

African Traditional & Diasporic: 95 million

Sikhism: 23 million

Juche: 19 million

Spiritism: 14 million

Judais: 14 million

Baha'i: 6 million

Jainism: 4 million

Shinto: 4 million

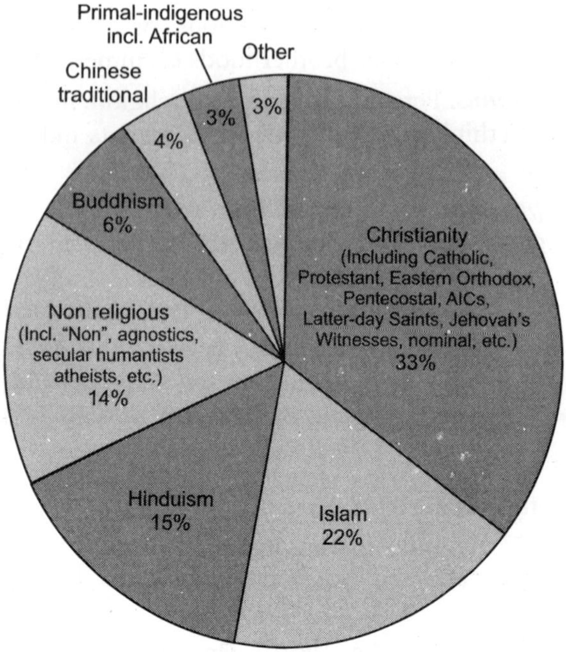

Cai Dai: 3 million

Tenrikyo: 2.4 million

Neo-paganism: 1 million

Unitarian Universalism: 800 thousand

Rastafarianism: 700 thousand

Scientology: 600 thousand

Zeroastrianism: 150 thousand

The adherent counts presented in the list above are estimates of the number of people who have at least a minimal level of self-identification as adherents of the religion. Levels of participation vary within all groups. These numbers tend toward the high end of reasonable worldwide estimates. Valid arguments can be made for different figures, but if the same criteria are used for all groups, the relative order should be the same. Further details and sources are available in the 'Adherents.com' main database.

What is Hinduism? An Introduction

7

Hinduism baffles a definition. The word 'Hinduism' is coined from the word 'Hindu', derived from a root meaning 'to flow' like a stream or river. Here, the reference is to 'Sindhu' flowing through 'Sind', an ancient centre of advanced civilization in India. Today, the term 'Hinduism' is used to denote the system of life of the Hindus or the spiritual part of the Hindu culture. In the ancient period, this part of the Hindu culture that took the form of a religion was called '*Arya Dharma*'. The use of the term 'Hinduism' is only of late origin. This Hindu way of life, which places high value on extreme asceticism, is deeply rooted in a spirituality envisaged in the scriptures and texts known as *Samhitās, Brāhmanas, Aranyakas* and the *Upanishads* together called the *Vedas* and also the *Bhagawad Gita* (the Lord's song), the supposed New Testament of the Hindus. "Hinduism has simply become a convenient and relatively recent way of referring to the complex tradition of faith communities that developed in the earliest centres of civilization in the Indian subcontinent."[1]

When viewed from outside, Hinduism is an extremely confusing and complex system, which does not conform to the generally conceived parameters of religion. The origin and founder of Hinduism are not known. It has no organisational structure or teaching office (*magisterium*) and hence no heresy. In the course of centuries, Hinduism never felt the necessity of a universally applicable creed or a control mechanism to enforce faith and practices. There is no apparatus for propagation of faith or conversion or proselytisation. In the course of its long history spanning four or more millennia, several schools of thought emerged in Hinduism projecting diametrically opposite ideologies. A majority of these schools emphasised theism, whereas few other schools stressed materialism, happiness, naturalism etc., as aims of human life. This naturally led them to sideline the existence of God and soul and resultantly, to refute the theories of life after death and transmigration of souls. A follower is at liberty to worship all the gods or any one of the gods of his choice (*Ishta Devatha*) or to worship none. Gandhiji says, "If I were asked to define the Hindu creed, I should simply say. Search after truth through non-violent means. A man may not believe in God and still call himself a Hindu. Hinduism is a relentless pursuit after truth. Truth is God. Denial of God we have known. Denial of truth we have not known." According to one tradition in Hinduism, the number of deities is 330,000,003. Millions worship *Śiva* (*Parameshwar* – meaning: the supreme God) while other millions worship Vishnu or Ganesh or Rama or Hanuman or Krishna or Kāli or Murugan according to each one's choice. No disciplinary authority is there to watch and initiate correctives.

When viewed from another critical angle, Hinduism is a mass of everything from religion, mysticism, theology and philosophy to myth, idolatry, magic and astrology. The language and pantheon developed in early Aryan culture in the North and North-West India bore similarities to those of classical Greece and Rome. Their deities, personified forces of nature, were arranged in a hierarchical order in which the Lords of the upper regions dominated. This stratification of the society is the nucleus that eventually led to India's caste system. Hinduism's infinite expansiveness and variety seem to be amongst its several aspects of glory. However, these contradictions and divergent views and elements are held together by certain unifying factors – some principles and practices, broadly classified as below:

Quest and search for God

Emphasis on experience as against religion and dogma

Acceptance of Vedas as infallible, being the revealed word of God

Faith in *Karmasamsar* (Transmigration of souls)

Yoga – Jnana Yoga (path of wisdom or knowledge), *Bhakti Yoga* (path of devotion or love), *Karma Yoga* (path of activity or performance) and *Raja Yoga* (path of ethical, physical and psychical exercises) – as means to perfection or *Moksha* (salvation)

Moral discipline through *Śravana* (hearing), *Manana* (thinking or analysing) and *Nididhyāsana* (meditation) according to *Varna* (colour or caste), *Āśrama* (status or station in life) and *Dharma* (duties or obligations or cosmic law).

In its developed form, Hinduism is philosophical pantheism. Its basis is rooted in the faith in the Universal God, omnipresent, omnipotent, omniscient and creator of the universe including man. This formless Universal Spirit, from which all beings issue and into which they all merge, is known by the names *Om* or *Brahman* or *Paramātma*. *Om* is the *Pranava*, the sound of respiration, and the breath of life, life itself, and the vital force. In the Upanishads, this conception is further developed identifying *Prāna* with the concept of 'Soul'. The Chandogyopanishad gives, for the first time, a classification of the *Prāna* (breathings), *Apana*, the exhaling breath, *Yana*, the intermediate breath, the interval between inhaling and exhaling, *Udana,* directing of the stream of air upwards and *Samana,* the inner breath uniting all the other kinds of breath. *Brahman* is defined differently in different texts. According to Brihadaranyakopanishad, "Everything that is, is *Brahman*. The self (*Ātman*) is Brahman." It is the result of the search for the ultimate reality of being. The later Upanishads have given different explanations. The consensus view is that Brahman is the First Cause and that the *Brahman* and *Ātman* (soul) are identical. *Paramātma* is defined as the Supreme Soul from which emanates the *Ātman*, the soul of every creation and to which the *Ātman* ultimately merges. In the early period, the relation between *Brahman* and *Paramātma* was a bone of contention among the Hindu theologians. The ultimate merger of the soul of the creation in the soul of the creator is the realisation of God known as *Mukti* or *Moksha* (liberation or salvation). This realisation cannot be achieved, as a rule, in one life in all cases. Here comes the necessity of rebirths (*Karmasamsar*), the migration of the soul from the body of one creation to another creation, not necessarily human, repeating the cycle till the ultimate realisation or liberation. The consequences of the *karma* (deeds or activity) in the prior life or lives determine the nature and status of the succeeding life (reaping what is sown). The necessity of rebirth ends at the stage at which the realisation is achieved. If anyone does not care to follow the prescribed true paths, he or she may have to undergo the cycle of rebirths. The consequences of wrongdoings are predetermined – here we notice an element of fatalism. No disciplinary enforcement is required. Ascetics are those who strive to release the soul from rebirths at the earliest.

According to another school of thought in Hinduism, whoever perseveres to attain the realisation of the Supreme Soul (known by whatever name – *Ahuramazda* or *Yahweh* or *Allah* or *Christ* or *Brahma*), whatever the methods for attainment, is a Hindu. Any religion that preaches or fosters this realisation is a part of the Hindu religion. Sri Ramakrishna Paramahamsa and his famous disciple Swamy Vivekananda propagated this doctrine envisaged in the scriptures. A quote from the *Bhagavad Gita* by Swamy Vivekananda in his speech at the Inaugural session of the World Parliament of Religions, Chicago on 11th September 1893 is reproduced below.

"Whosoever comes to me, through whatsoever form, I reach him; all men are struggling through paths which in the end lead to me." A Hindu prayer quoted by Swamy Vivekananda reads as follows: "As the different streams having their sources in different places all mingle their water in the sea, so, O Lord! the different paths which men take through different tendencies, various though they appear, crooked or straight, all lead to Thee."[2] According to this doctrine, Hinduism is the mother of all religions and hence does not claim to be the only true religion in this world. It embraces within its fold any religious school or sect, which strives to attain liberation of the soul as aforesaid. Hinduism devises four paths of life for the attainment of liberation. (Please see *Yogas* given on prepage.)

(Further details of these paths are given in the Chapter on Bhagavad Gita.)

Louis Renau says, "Hinduism can be characterised as a system of means appropriate for the attainment of liberation." According to an expanded definition, Hinduism is the spiritual component of a culture originated from the writings of *Rishis* (poets and wise men) and sages and evolved through centuries into a system analogous to that of an eclectic religion (wide range of beliefs or ideas), with individual freedom of choice, for the ultimate liberation of the soul.

An extract of an article published by Shashi Tharoor, a freelance writer, is given below which can provide much insight on Hinduism and an individual Hindu, from a pragmatic point of view.

"Hinduism is thus the name others applied to the indigenous religion of India, what many call *Sanatan Dharma*. It embraces an eclectic range of doctrines and practices, from pantheism to agnosticism, from faith in reincarnation to belief in the caste system. But none of these constitutes an obligatory credo for a Hindu: there are none.

One cannot say, for instance, that a Hindu is someone who prays to Ram, worships at a Shiva temple, believes in caste and in re-incarnation, reads the Vedas, treats the *Bhagavad Gita* as holy writ, heeds the injunctions of the Shankaracharya of Kanchipuram, considers the cow sacred, abjures beef, wears ash on his forehead and washes away his sins in the holy Ganga, because it is possible to do none of these things and still consider oneself a Hindu.

And I am happy to describe myself as a believing Hindu: not just because it is the faith into which I was born, but for a string of other reasons, though faith requires no reason. One is cultural: as a Hindu I belong to a faith that expresses the ancient genius of my own people.

Another is, for lack of a better phrase, its intellectual 'fit': I am more comfortable with the belief structures of Hinduism than I would be with those of the other faiths of which I know. As a Hindu I claim adherence to a religion without an established Church or priestly papacy, a religion whose rituals and customs I am free to reject, a religion that does not oblige me to demonstrate my faith by any visible sign, by subsuming my identity in any collectivity, not even by a specific day or tie or frequency of worship. As a Hindu I subscribe to a creed that is free of the restrictive dogmas of holy writ, that refuses to be shackled to the limitations of a single holy book.

Above all, as a Hindu I belong to the only major religion in the world that does not claim to be the only religion. I find it immensely congenial to be able to face my fellow human beings of other faiths without being burdened by the conviction that I have embarked upon a 'true path' that they have missed. Hinduism asserts that all ways of belief are equally valid, and Hindus readily venerate the saints and the sacred objects of other faiths. Hinduism is a civilization, not a dogma. There is no such thing as a Hindu heresy."[3]

Underneath the confusing outward appearance and apparent contradictions, many of the basic concepts and features of other world religions are seen embedded in Hinduism.

Basic faith: All the classical Upanishads proclaim monotheism in unequivocal terms.

Ekamevadwiteeyam Brahma Meaning: Brahma (God) is one and unrivalled

Many Gods: According to Hinduism, this one and only Brahma has two forms or natures, a static, impersonal and expressionless Brahma referred to as *Nirguṇa Brahma* and a dynamic, personal and expressive Brahma referred to as *Saguna Brahma* who appears in different assumed forms or manifestations. It is the worship of this one and only Brahma in different manifestations that are interpreted as monism or polytheism.

Theology: Badarayana in his monumental work known as *Brahmasūtra*, has provided Hinduism with a comprehensive theology incorporating the theological propositions contained in the *Vedas*, *Upanishads* and the *Bhagavad Gita*.

Law and code of conduct: Manu, Yājnavalkya, Nārada, Brihaspati, Gautama, Vasishta etc. have provided Hinduism, through their *Smritis,* with an authoritative law and code of conduct known as *Dharmasastrās.*

Scripture: In Hinduism, there is a composite scripture known as *Prasthanathrayam* (scriptural trinity) consisting of the *Brahmasūtra*, the *Vedas* and the *Bhagavad Gita.* These form the final authority on scriptural laws.

Goals in human life: Hinduism sets forth four goals in human life:

Dharma	(morality, law, justice, truth etc.)
Artha	(Temporal wealth)
Kama	(Pleasure including sex)
Moksha	(Liberation or Salvation)

Here, a positive and pragmatic approach to family life is envisaged by permitting sex and acquisition of wealth, both with restraint and observance of *Dharma.*

Stages of life: The division of human life into four stages is given below:

Brahmacarya	(Celibacy)
Garhasthya	(family life)
Vanaprastha	(forest life) and
Sanyasa	(asecticism).

These are interlinked with the above goals of life.

While allowing pleasure and wealth in family life, celibacy and asceticism are also stressed with importance. At every stage, *Sanatana Dharma* (eternal order and righteousness) and restraint are insisted on to attain the final goal – *Moksha.*

Incarnation: According to Hinduism, incarnation (Descent of God) is not confined to one only as claimed by Christianity. Hindus generally point out 2 Cor. 5 : 10 in the Bible to refute the contention of 'single incarnation' in Christianity.

'Dharma Samsthapanārthāya Sambhavāmi Yugē Yugē'

(The process of incarnations for establishment of dharma will occur and recur according to necessity, era after era.)

Perfection of religion: Hinduism does not claim perfection. All religions have imperfections as they are handled by imperfect human beings, Hinduism contends.

Exhortations: In order to sustain this world created by God and to enable mankind to live in peace compatible with nature, Hinduism exhorted the world even in ancient times to abide by certain cardinal principles (*Mahāvakyās*) as below:

Lōkā Samastā Sukhino Bhavandu

(Let there be happiness for all living beings in this world.)

Satyameva Jayate

(Truth ever wins.)

Ahimsa Paramōdharma

(Non-violence is the ultimate *dharma* [duty or obligation])

Dharmōsmai Kuladaivatham

(Adhere to Dharma [justice] as God)

Iśa Vāśyam Idam Sarvam

(God lives within everything and beyond all things)

Hinduism is a vast expanse like an ocean. A study of Hinduism in its entirety is practically impossible in one life-span of ordinary human beings. Its scripture, theology, mysticism, philosophy, canons, ethics etc. are contained in thousands of books originated during a long period spanning several millennia. Though some of these books are now extinct, it is happy to note that the basic scripture consisting of the *Vedas* and the *Bhagavad Gita* still exist without any damage. Many of these books, written by different people in different periods covering centuries, were compiled later in book form with or without alterations or modifications. Even in the case of some available books, the names of authors or period of origin have not so far been ascertained. Hence, the preparation of a chronology is not possible. A category-wise classification, though incomplete, is given below to assess the volume and also for some sort of orderliness in introducing them.

1. Vēda Samhitās — 4
2. Branches of Samhitās — 1131

   (According to the *Mahabhāşhya* of Patanjali, *Rig Veda* has 21, *Samavēda* has 1000, *Yajurvēda* has 101 and Atharva Veda has 9 branches)

3. [4]Subsidiary books at the rate of average 13 books for each branch (1131 × 13) 14703

   (Brahmaṇās, Aranyakas, Dharma Sutra, Srauta Sutra, Grihya Sutra, Nirukti, Pratisakya Sūtra etc. containing commentaries and explanations of Samhitās)
4. The Upanishads 108 (or 112?)
5. The Vedangas 6
6. Epics (*Bhagavad Gita* included) 2
7. Saddarshanas (Vedic Philosophies) 6
8. Sramana (Independent) Philosophies 5
9. The Purāṇās (Maha Puranas 18, Subsidiary Puranas 18) 36
10. The Sutras, Sastras and Smritis Number unknown

Besides these, we come across a lot of works in the Christian era produced by eminent scholars and sages in India like Nagarjuna, Vātsyāyana, Manu, Sri Sankara, Ramanuja, Madhavacharya and in modern age by Dayanand Saraswati, Raja Ram Mohan Roy, K.V. Gajendra Gadkar, Dr. S. Radhakrishnan, Aurobindo Ghosh, Sri Ramakrishna, Swamy Vivekananda, Swamy Sharvananda, Balagangadhar Tilak, Tagore, Gandhiji and so on. The list is endless. After the coming of English people in India, we see remarkable enthusiasm among Europeans to study Sanskrit, history, *vedas*, religion, philosophy etc. of India. They conducted deep and wide research in the respective fields and published many valuable books. Max Mueller, Paul Deussen, Bloomfield, Winternitz, Schopenhauer, Aldous Huxley, Theos Bernard and others come under this category. They disagreed with many findings of the Indian authors and put up alternate as well as new propositions.

As the readers can very well understand, in such a situation, a comprehensive treatise on Hinduism is out of the question. Here, the attempt is to introduce Hinduism to the readers, highlighting some salient features.

FOOTNOTES

1. John Renaurd, *Responses to 101 Questions on Hinduism*, p. 20.
2. Ramakrishna Math and Ramakrishna Mission Howrah, West Bengal, *Swamy Vivekananda's Address at World Parliament of Religions*, Chicago, pp. 26-27.
3. Shashi Tharoor, *The Express Magazine – 'The Indian Express,'* 8th February, 1998, p. 5.
4. Sukumar Azhikode (Dr.), *Tatvamasi* (Mal.), p. 37.

A Spiritual Awakening

8

Many centuries after the Indus Valley civilization in Harappa and Mohenjodaro, another civilization developed in the Indo-Gangetic areas. The identity of the originators of the earlier Indus Valley civilization still remains unsure. But, the Aryans who migrated to India from West Asia evolved the later civilization. The time-lag between these two civilizations is even now unknown. Some Indologists put the period of the Indus civilization as third millennium BC and that of the later one as the latter half of the second millennium BC. But there is no unanimity among the historians in this respect. We have reliable evidence to show that these two civilizations stood apart on several aspects. While the Harappa civilization was city-based, the Aryan civilization was fully village-based. In the former, the goddesses and the male gods enjoyed equal status while in the latter; the male gods like Indra, Mitra, Varuṇa etc. enjoyed superiority. Among the Aryan tribes, images played no part (aniconic). The areas occupied by the Aryan tribes such as Bharatas, Yadus, Turvasas etc. are described in the Vedic literature by mentioning some rivers in the area – Kubha (Kabul), Suvastu (Swat), the Krumu (Kurram), the Gomati (Gumal), the Sindhu (Indus), the Sushoma (Sohan), the Vitasta (Jhelum), the Asikni (Chenab), the Parushni (Ravi), the Vipas (Bias), the Sutudri (Sutlej), the Saraswati, the Drishtavadi, the Jamuna, the Ganga and the Sarayu. These details show that the Aryans occupied vast areas stretching from Eastern Afghanistan to the upper valleys of the Ganges. A major part of this area was known in those days as *Saptasindhu*.

Social and Economic Life

The basis of the social and political organisation of the Rig Vedic tribes is the patriarchal family. The members of a family lived in the same house built with wood or reed. A fireplace (*agnisala*), a sitting room and apartments for ladies were arranged in the house. The leader of the family was known as *Grihapati* (the head of the house). There was no classification of people on the basis of occupation. Intermarriages were no taboo. The units above the family were *Grama* (village), *Vis* (group of villages) and the *Jana (*probably modern districts*)*. The form of government was monarchical. In the *Atharva Veda*, there is reference regarding election of *Rajan* (the King). The kings believed that approval of the people was a prerequisite for sovereignty. The King was considered a destroyer of rivals. His foremost duty was the protection of the people and the tribal territory. In the Vedic literature, there is mention of *Sabha* (the Council of the Elders), that took important decisions on matters concerning the *Rashtra* (State) and the administration of justice. There is a *Purohita* (Priest) to advise the King. *Senani*, the leader of the army was an important official. The King was the Lord of the people, but he was expected to govern with the consent of the people.

In regard to the position of women, there was hardly any improvement. Daughters were regarded as a source of misery. Women could not go to the tribal council or assembly (Sabha), neither could they take an inheritance. Married women of the upper classes often had to suffer the presence of rival wives. The life of the queen was miserable. While the *Mahishi* or chief queen, and the *vávâta* or the favourite queens were loved and honoured, others like the *Parivrikti (concubines)* were admittedly neglected. But they continued to have their share in religious rites. The education which some of them received was of a high order and it enabled them to take a prominent part in philosophical disputations at royal courts. The rules of marriage underwent a change towards greater rigidity and there were instances of child marriages.[1]

After the emergence of the caste system, the members of the three higher castes, the *Brahmins*, the *Kshatrias* and the

Vaisyas, were to undergo rigorous discipline of the *Āsrāmas* (station or status of the four stages of life), the *Brahmacharin,* the Vedic student vowed to chastity, the *Grihasthya,* the married householder, the *Vanaprastha,* the forest hermit practising continence and the *Sannyasin,* an ascetic who renounced the world. The nucleus of this system of *Āsrāmas* is already there in the Vedic hymns. At every stage, rigorous practice of self-restraint is insisted on.

Agriculture was the principal occupation of the village folk. The individuals or families owned arable lands and homesteads. But, the grazing grounds *(Khilya)* were common properties. Cultivated lands were known as *Urvara* or *Kshetra.* Ploughing and canal irrigation were prevalent. The usual crops, rice, wheat, barley etc. were harvested with sickle. Rearing of cattle or other domestic animals was equal to or more important than agriculture. Though a pastoral community, they were not indifferent to trade and industry. Commerce was handled by a separate section of people known as *Pani,* probably non-Aryans. Barter was prevalent. The main articles of trade were clothes, skin and coverlets. Coinage was absent. Standard units of exchange were cows and gold necklets (*nishka*). Marine navigation was prevalent in the Rig Vedic period. The word *Samudra* (sea) appears in some literature. Some interpret the word *Samudra* as the lower course of the River Sindhu. But, evidence shows that the early Aryans had intercourse with distant lands beyond the seas. On the industrial front, wood workers (carpenters) made chariots, wagons, houses, boats and finer artistic utensils. The metal workers were engaged in making weapons, implements and ornaments while the tanners made water-casks, bow strings, slings and hand guards in leather. Both men and women were engaged in weaving. Women showed skills in sewing and matmaking from grass or reeds. The potter (*Kulala)* made crafts for the benefit of the people.

Arts, Science and Religion

The art of poetry was in full bloom as is evidenced by the Samhitas. Architecture made some advances in the Rig Vedic

India. The beginning of sculptures is noticed. The medical science succeeded in identifying a few diseases. Along with drugs and herbs, spells and charms were also resorted to in the healing process. Astronomy progressed considerably.

The early Vedic religion had been identified as one of Henotheism or Kathano theism – belief in gods, each god in turn standing out as the highest. Worship of Nature was prevalent. Abstract deities like *Vidhatri* the ordainer, *Viswakarma,* the all-creating, *Prajapati,* the lord of creatures etc. appeared in the later stages. For forgiveness of sins, the people turned to *Varuna*, the Lord of waters. In later age, Vishnu occupied this position. The worship of Varuna, consciousness of sin and trust in divine forgiveness practised by the Aryans happened to be the roots of the later doctrine of *Bhakti.* A salient characteristic of Vedic mythology is the predominance of the male element. Goddesses like *Prithvi, Aditi, Sarasvati, Usha* etc. enjoyed only a subordinate position, contrary to the pre-historic culture of the Indus Valley. A tendency towards monotheism or monism is also noticed among the early Aryans.[2]

Development of a Spiritual Culture

The ancient period of development of the spiritual culture of the peoples of India is known as the 'Vedic Age'. The word 'Veda' has its roots in the word *Vid* (to know) via – the Latin word *Videre* (to see) related to 'wisdom' and 'vision'. The 'Vedas' are the first records on the ancient Indians, their history, religion, philosophy, ethics, culture, aesthetics and many other subjects. According to tradition, the Vedic literature with a historico-philosophical characteristic is classified into four groups:

The *Samhitās*

The *Brahmanās*

The *Āranyakās*, and

The *Upanishads*.

This division is in tune with the historical order of development of the Vedic literature. As regards ancient

Upanishads, this classification was, more or less, in consonance with facts. But many modern thinkers do not include the *Upanishads* as part of the *Vedas* as a series of *Upanishads* which have no relation whatsoever with the Vedas have come up in later periods. Many of them contain independent rational thinking with conclusions diametrically opposed to the spirit and contents of the *Vedas*. Several books titled 'Upanishad' orginated upto the end of the British rule in India (1947 AD) dealing with subjects unconnected with the *Vedas*: *Akbaropanishad* and *Allopanishad* are examples.

For a precise understanding of the structure of the Vedas, one of the cardinal aspects to be noted is that no single group of the Vedic literature is an integral whole. The *Samhitas* (collections) are four in number, the *Rig Veda*, the *Sama Veda*, the *Yajur Veda* and the *Atharva Veda*. The first three known as *Trai* only were originally treated among the *Samhitas*. The Atharva Veda is a later addition. Each *Veda* has its own Brahmanas. The Aranyakas and the *Upanishads* directly adjoin either the *Samhita* or the *Brahmana*. It follows that the 'Samhita' ultimately determines the whole structure or combination of Vedas. Prof. Max Mueller compared the *Vedas* to a tree; the term used by him is 'Veda-tree' (*Kalpatharu* – a tree in heaven). Paul Daussen used the term 'the Tree of the Veda' and compared Bhāgavathā (epic) to the fruit of the tree. Dr. Sukumar Azhicode, the author of the book *Tatvamasi* advanced further by comparing Upanishad to the flower of the tree in full blossom. But, the simile remains incomplete, maimed or mutilated. No one can deny that the Samhitas are the roots of the *Vedas*. Why can't we make the tree whole and perfect with *Brahmanas* as its trunk and Aranyakas as leaves which give the green colour to the forest (*Aranya*).

The Hindus consider the Vedas as revealed scripture and assigned them the titles *Apaurushēya* (not made by man) and *Nitya* (eternal). It is contended that the *Rishīs* who wrote down under inspiration from God handed over them down to the subsequent generations through oral tradition. It is noted that in some cases, illiterate women and people of low castes were authors.[3] The purity of the Vedas was maintained all along, as people who learnt them by heart through hearing transmitted them to another without understanding its meaning. There was no scope for distortion. Thus the Vedas remained unadulterated and free from distortion and, therefore its sacredness was never affected. Being originally learnt by hearing, it came to be known as *Śruti* (hearing). Later, the Rishis (poets and wise men) compiled them as texts in different periods and different places. In the early days, the *Gurus* (teachers) taught their disciples the Samhitas orally with emphasis on phonetics, grammar, meaning etc.

According to Jaimini, the author of *Pōōrvamīmāmsa,* the Vedas are treated as having two divisions, the *Dharmakānda* and the *Brahmakānda. Dharmakānda* consists of laudatory verses for adoration and meditation. The Brahmakānda is aimed at self-sanctification and the experience of bliss through self-realisation.

The age of the Vedas remains a mystery even after four or more thousands of years after its origin. Jacobi puts the period of origin as between 4500 and 2500 BC. But most of the Indian and foreign researchers disagree. There are Indians who assign a long past extending up to 8000 BC. Most non-Indian researchers assign a period between 1500 and 500 BC. Whatever be the age, the value and sacredness of the Vedas remain undiminished or unaltered. Even if viewed in a secular angle, the Vedas provide us with profound awareness on multifarious subjects – ancient history and civilization of India, politics, geography, metaphysics, sociology, philosophy, magic, Indian culture, poetic licence in Indian literature and so on.

The above mentioned premises influenced the Hindu mind to believe that the Vedas, the basis and scripture of their faith are sacred, infallible, eternal, ancient and divine word of God revealed to man in the fullness of time.

We have already seen that *Samhitas* are classified into four texts with separate titles. Before dealing with each one of them, an extract from *The Discovery of India* by Jawaharlal Nehru is given below. Here we see two distinct approaches to the Vedas, a rational approach by Jawaharlal Nehru and a literary and philosophical approach by Rabindranath Tagore. I hope this will enable the readers to have an objective assessment of the differing shades of opinion.

"Many Hindus look upon the Vedas as revealed scripture. This seems to me to be peculiarly unfortunate, for thus we miss their real significance – the unfolding of the human mind in the earliest stages of thought. And what a wonderful mind it was! The Vedas (from the root *vid*, to know) were simply meant to be a collection of the existing knowledge of the day; they are a jumble of many things; hymns, prayers, ritual for sacrifice, magic, and magnificent nature poetry. There is no idolatry in them; no temples for the gods. The vitality and affirmation of life pervading them are extraordinary. The early Vedic Aryans were so full of the zest for life that they paid little attention to the soul. In a vague way they believed in some kind of existence after death."[4]

–Jawaharlal Nehru

The Vedic hymns have been described by Rabindranath Tagore as 'a poetic testament of a people's collective reaction to the wonder and awe of existence'.

"A people of vigorous and unsophisticated imagination awakened at the very dawn of civilization to a sense of the inexhaustible mystery that is implicit in life. It was a simple faith of theirs that attributed divinity to every element and force of nature, but it was a brave and joyous one, in which the sense of mystery only gave enchantment to life, without weighing it down with bafflement – the faith of a race unburdened with intellectual brooding on the conflicting diversity of the objective universe, though now and again illumined by intuitive experience as: 'Truth is one: (though) the wise call it by various names.'"

–Rabindranath Tagore

FOOTNOTES

1. Majumdar, R.C., *An Advanced History of India*, p. 43.
2. *Ibid.*, pp. 24-38.
3. Mahajan, V.D., *Ancient India*, p. 105.
4. Jawaharlal Nehru, *The Discovery of India*, pp. 67-68.

The Vedas

9

Origin of Vedas

The Vedas are eternal divine knowledge originally transmitted by the Origin (God) through the four Seers; *Agni* (fire), *Vayu* (air), *Ravi* (sun) and *Angira* (*Rig*, *Sama*, *Yajur* and *Atharva* respectively). Vedas are not literature created by the seers. Some Western scholars have commented that they are prattlings of children, rubbish and utterances of shepherds.

(a) The Rig Veda Samhita

The Rig Veda is probably the earliest book humanity possessed and the largest among the Vedas. 'Rig' literally means 'hymn' or 'laudatory verse' or *ode*. Other samhitas have only lesser significance than the Rig Veda Samhita. If any of the texts of the Vedas is addressed in the singular as 'Veda' that is Rig Veda alone. It contains 1028 hymns with more than 10500 verses (*Sūktās* good words), equal in size to the Greek *Iliad* and the *Odyssey* together. It is divided into ten *mandalas* (books or chapters). The literal meaning of *Mandala* is 'circle' or 'cycle'. Mandalas two to nine contain the oldest hymns; one and ten are later additions. Mandala 10 contains the *Purushasūkta* (principles of universal man – personified cosmic Law). The laudatory verses are mostly addressed to gods personifying the phenomena or forces of nature regarded as divinities. The Indo-Aryan tribes who crossed over to India in several groups in several periods emerged as a cohesive community by the 10th and 11th centuries BC. The Vedic scholars are of the view that the hymns of this community took shape as the Rig Veda in that period.

Ancient Indians believed that sacrifices accompanied by chanting of appropriate hymns had magic effects in propitiating the gods. Well-being and happiness of people were believed as dependent on sacrifices. The hymns or acts of sacrifices for specific occasions or seasons were generally distributed among the tribes. Nature itself had cult elements ascribed to each phenomenon, e.g. *Indra* (the king of the gods) thought of thunder as the throwing of his mace. The questions as to what was the first sacrifice and who offered it are answered in the hymn to the *Purusa* (X: 90) the personification of the cosmic principle. The gods are supposed to have extracted from the *Purusa,* as it was, the cosmic worlds, the animal world and men. The myth of the origin of the *Varnās* (colours) – each Varna originating from the limbs of *Brahman* (God), the *Brahmins* from the mouth, *Kshatrias* from the arms, *Vaisyas* from stomach, and the *Sudras* from the feet – are projected in Verses 11 and 12 of the hymn. This ascribes a divine origin for the caste system.

The legendary collectors and compilers of the hymns of the Vedas were known as *Rishis* (poets and wise men). They were not historical persons. The aim of the compilers of the Rig Veda Samhita was the preservation of the hymns from oblivion and distortion and not liturgical as is evidenced by the inclusion of several hymns with no bearing on religious subjects or services. The Rig Vedic hymns depict the inquisitiveness of the ancient Indians to know the mysteries behind their own 'existence' or 'being'. Here we notice the emergence of the sparks of philosophical and metaphysical thinking. In the midst of myths and legends, they ask questions to themselves:

> "Why does the Sun not fall, although it is not supported by anything or fixed to anything?"
> "Where is the Sun by night?"
> "Where go the Stars by day?"
> "Whence comes the wind and whither goes it?"
> "Why does it raise no dust on celestial road?"
> "What was that tree, and what was that forest out of which they (the gods) made the earth and the sky?"
> (Hymn X 37)

The hymns refer to the existence of 'matter' from which came or out of which was made the world. But, their conception of this 'matter' is not known. No clear answer is given. The prime substances were believed to be air or water or fire etc. (Hymns X 72, 88 & 121)

The English translation of the hymn (X-129) known as the 'cosmogonic hymn' is given below in full for the academic interest of the readers. This hymn named 'song of creation' is the one to which Max Meuller gave the title 'To the Unknown God'.[1]

"Then even nothingness was not, nor existence.
There was no air, nor the heaven beyond it.
What covered it? Where was it? In whose keeping?
Was there then cosmic water, in depths unfathomed?

Then there was neither death nor immortality,
Nor was there then the torch of night and day.
The One breathed windlessly and self-sustaining.
There was that One then, and there was no other.

At first was only darkness wrapped in darkness.
All there was only unlimited water.
The one who came to be enclosed in nothing,
Arose at last, born of the power of heat (tapas).

In the beginning, desire descended on it –
That was the primal seed, born of the mind.
The sages who have scorched their hearts with wisdom.
Know that which is kin to which is not.

And they have stretched their cord across the word,
And know what was above and what below.
Seminal powers made fertile mighty forces.
Below was strength, and over it was impulse.

But, after all, who knows, and who can say,
Whence it all came, and how creation happened?
The gods themselves were later than creation,
So who knows truly whence it has arisen?

Whence all creation had its origin,
He, whether he fashioned it or whether he did not,

He, who surveys it all from highest heaven,
He knows – or may be even he does not know."[2]

The facts discernible in the hymn are:

It is a magnificent piece of Nature poetry.

The unfolding of the human mind and the unsophisticated imagination of the people in the earliest stages of civilization.

The wonder and awe of existence from which emanated an inquisitiveness to clear their doubts or the quest to find the truth behind the phenomena or forces of nature – a metaphysical research.

"The gods themselves were later than creation." One (*Ēkam*) above the gods created the gods, the personification of the forces of nature.

What is this One (*Ēkam*)? It is answered as follows:

The *One* existed always, it was not born of anything – the *FIRST CAUSE.*

The *One* is the eternally existing of which everything is born – the *CREATOR.*

The *One* that which is and that which is not, top and bottom, night and day, death and immortality – the *ALMIGHTY* or *OMNIPOTENT.*

The *One* which surveys it all from heaven (above all creations) – the *HIGHEST.*

The *One* that breathed by itself without breath – the *SUPREME SOUL.*

The *One* that without an external impetus or impact – the *FIRST MOVER.*

From the above observations, it may be seen that the Vedic Aryans found the answers to their questions (though doubting and non-assertive – "may be even he does not know") on the existence of the One (*Ēkam*), the First Cause, Creator of the Universe, the Almighty, the Highest, the Supreme Soul and the First Mover and therefore the Transcending Consciousness or the Highest Absolute. We can feel the flavour of monotheism here. The manner of presentation of this hymn is religious and idealist. Prof. Max Mueller, Aurobindo Ghose, S. Das Gupta, Dr. Radhakrishnan and many others share this view.

But, materialists like Jawaharlal Nehru and Marxian thinkers view the hymn as a fundamentally realistic work with strong elements of spontaneous materialism and dialectics. They argue that no grounds at all are there for ascribing concepts like 'absolute', 'transcending consciousness' etc. They quote *Enuma Ellis*, the Babylonian hymn of creation and Homer and Hesiod, the representatives of the pre-scientific thinking in Greece to substantiate their arguments. Their standpoints are:

"The original mass of matter contained a contradiction between two irreconcilable hostile forces, the forces of 'order' and 'chaos'. Because of this contradiction, all that it was divided into earthly and celestial phenomena. These phenomena, interacting between themselves, in their turn fell into opposites, the animate and the inanimate, the divine and the non-divine etc. The formation of the world order in this hymn is presented in a mythical and concrete shape rather than abstractly or philosophically."[3]

The *Rig Veda Samhita* also gives an insight into the political, social, economic and religious life of the Indians in the Rig Vedic Age. Sacrifices under this Veda are to be performed by *Gotri* priests only.

(b) The Sama Veda Samhita

The *Sama Veda*, the second among the *Samhitas*, is the Book of *Chants* (Songs). It is a collection of melodies composed mostly for the verses of the *Rig Veda*. It really contains no independent information. 1474 out of the 1549 verses in the *Sama Veda* are already there in the *Rig Veda*. The remaining 75 verses can be traced in the other Vedic literature. These hymns are meant to be sung for the Soma sacrifice by a special class of priests known as *Udgatris*. *Sama Veda Samhita* has nine (or eight?) Brahmanas, the main ones being *Thandya Maha Brahmana* and *Chandogya Brahmana*.

(c) The Yajur Veda Samhita

Yajur means prose. This *Samhita* is the book of sacrifices. There are two main texts in the Yajurveda, the Black *Yajur Veda* and the White *Yajur Veda*. The reference to Black and

White does not represent the colour but the quality. Black refers to impurity and the white refers to purity, purified by removing the elements of Brahmanas. *Black Yajur Veda*, also known as the *Krishna Yajur Veda*, is the oldest one preserved in the *Taittiriya*, *Maitrayani* and *Kathaka* recensions. *White Yajur Veda* also known as the *Sukla Yajur Veda* is of later origin and preserved by the *Vajasanei* recensions. It has commentaries in prose with purity of language for the incantations. *Sathapatha* (hundred paths) *Brahmana*, the most important and famous among the Brahmanas, adjoins the *Sukhla Yajur Veda*. *Advaryu* priests perform the rituals under this *Samhita*.

(d) The Atharva Veda Samhita

Earlier, the three Samhitas mentioned above known as *Trai* were considered as Vedas. *Atharva Veda Samhita*, the book of magic formulae had a stigma as it contained collections of songs, spells and incantations for the healing of diseases, exorcism of evil spirits etc. At the same time, it contained many beautiful songs celebrating the power and omniscience of God and the beneficence of Mother Earth. Here is an example:

> "May earth pour out her milk for us, a mother unto me, her son O'prithvi,
>
> Auspicious be thy woodlands, auspicious be thy hills and snow-clad mountains."

As such, it was later included among the Vedas as the fourth *Samhita*. It is divided into twenty parts containing 75 hymns. From a historical and scientific point of view, it resembles the *Rig Veda* with hymns praising the gods. The magic in this book is believed to have come through the influence of Pre-Aryan people.

Gopatha is the *Brahmana* of the *Atharva Veda Samhita*, but it was not popular as the other *Brahmanas*.

(e) The Brahmanas

The *Brahmanas* are the commentaries of *Samhitas*, each being connected with one of the *Samhitas*. These books emerged during the transition from the Vedic social order to the brahminical social order – the period when the caste system was in the process of taking roots in the community. The *Brahmins* produced the *Brahmanas* for the *Brahmins* (the priests). They are manuals explaining the meanings of various sacrifices and the methods or procedure for the performance of each sacrifice. As such, *Brahmanas* are the liturgies, one branch of the Vedic tradition. According to Jaimini, the *Veda Samhitas* contain only the invocations, the rest are contained in the *Brahmanas*. A.L. Basham concluded that the Brahmanas are the appendices to the *Samhitas*. Sacrifices arising from each *Samhita* are to be performed by separate class of designated priests. The Brahmanas helped the fantastic growth of ritualism that directly and indirectly exalted the status and importance of the priestly class—the *Brahmins*. There was a saying that 'sacrifices are to please the gods and to benefit the *Brahmins* – sacrifices for heavenly gods and ritual fees for earthly ones'.

The connection between the *Samhitas*, *Brahmanas* and the priests are illustrated below:

Samhita	Brahmanas	Priest
I. Rig Veda	1. Aitareya	Hotri
	2. Kaushitaki	
II. Sama Veda	1. Thandyamahabrahmana	
	2. Jaiminiopanishad	
	3. Arsheya	
	4. Devathadhyaya	Udgatri
	5. Vamśa	
	6. Sahitopanishad	
	7. Sama Vidhana	
	8. Shadvimsa[4]	
	9. Panchavimṣa	
III. Yajur Veda		
1. Krishna Yajur	Adhvaryu Brahmana	Advaryu
2. Shukla Yajur	Sathapatha Brahmana	
IV. Atharva Veda	Gopatha	Brahmin

Note: *Aiterayaranyka* and *Aitereyopanishad* are the continuation or extension of the *Aitereya Brahmana*. But, *Kaushitikibrahmana* has no such extension. However, there is an *Aranyaka* named *Kaushitikaranyaka*, which is not related to the *Brahmana*. Two other texts named

Kaushitikopanishad and *Kaushitikibrahmanopanishad* are considered as part of the *Aranyaka* and not of the Brahmana. In both these Brahmanas of the *Rig Veda Samhita*, the rituals described are those of the soma sacrifice. The splendour and vitality of the *Aitareya Brahmana* that attract the people are two folk stories incorporated therein. These stories relate to the escape of two persons from death due to divine grace, one a *Brahmin* boy named Sunashefan and the other the son of a slave woman named Kavashan. The details of rituals in this *Brahmana* are arranged in such a way as to depict the superiority of the *Kshatrias* and to establish that the *Sudra*, being a servant, is essentially the master's property who can be severely punished or even killed at the master's choice (AB: 7:29).

In the *Vamsa Brahmana*, the ethnic details of the Rishis are given. The *Chandogya Brahmana* later became the *Chandogyopanishad*.

The *Sathapatha Brahmana* authored by Yajnavalkya is the most exhaustive, important and interesting among the *Brahmanas* in terms of history and philosophy. Many philosophical questions about 'man' are raised in this *Brahmana*. What is man? What does man consist of? What is his essence? Which of the senses brings man the most genuine information about the surrounding world? Perhaps, neither the one nor the other, but the thought. The subjects relating to the links between the thoughts and the world, human thought and emotion, *Atman* (Soul) as the essence of man, thought as the primary source etc. are discussed in the *Sathapatha Brahmana*. It also deals with the progress of culture from Kuru Panchala to Videha.

One of the sub chapters in the Krishna Yajurveda is treated as its Brahmana. As a Rishi named Tittiri wrote it, it is known as *Taittiriya Brahmana*.

Gopatha Brahmana did not get much recognition due to the stigma attached to the Atharva Veda. This Brahmana has two divisions, the second division is called the Uttara Brahmana. Many stories in the *Itareya*, *Kaushitiki* and the *Sathapatha Brahmanas* are seen in the *Gopatha Brahmana*.

The *Brahmanas* are in prose. Some *Brahmanas* contain a lot of information about non-Aryans. The methods by which the non-Aryans are to be admitted in the Aryan fold are also given. The impression that the *Brahmanas* being commentary literature have no philosophical values is wrong. The *Brahmanas* provide a connecting link between the *Samhitas* and the *Upanishads*. Some important categories of Indian philosophies actually emanated from the *Brahmanas*. Max Mueller complained about the monotony in reading the *Brahmanas*. He states that "greater portion of them is twaddle, and what is worse, theological twaddle". But according to Dr. Winternitz, "the *Brahmanas* may be unpalatable from the point of view of reading, but they are indispensable to the understanding of the whole of the later religious and philosophical literature of the Indians and highly interesting for the general science of religion".[5]

(f) The Aranyakas

'Aranya' means 'forests'. *Aranyaka* means forest books. They are generally described as the concluding portions of the *Brahmanas*. In the ancient days, *Brahmanas* and *Aranyakas* were not distinctly separated. It seems that there were no definite rules in this respect. There are *Brahmanas* with no *Aranyakas* (e.g.: *Sama Veda* and *Atharva Veda*) and independent *Aranyakas* not related to the *Brahmanas* (e.g.: Itarēyaranyaka). According to the Vedic civilization, men in the upper castes had to undergo four stages or stations in life (*Aśramās*). Those who pass through the last two phases of the *Aśramās* (*Vanaprastha* and *Sannyas)* lived in the forests. The *Aranyakas* are supposed to have been written either by these forest dwelling hermits or addressed to those hermits in the forests. The period of origin of *Aranyakas* is not known. Many facts and stories in the *Brahmanas* are seen included in the *Aranyakas* as well. While the *Brahmanas* are mainly concerned with rituals, the *Aranyakas* deal with mysticism and philosophy. The *Aranyakas* resemble the *Brahmanas* in language, style and contents; but they are concerned more with the allegorical significance of rites and the mystic meanings of the texts in the *Samhitas*. Dr. Sukumar Azhikode is of the view that the *Aranyakas* are the rays of light, piercing through the darkness caused by the smoke from the rituals of the *Brahmanas*, to uncover the Vedic vision or Truth. *Aranyaka* is comparatively a small valley in between two mountains, the *Brahmanas* and the *Upanishads*. Therefore, the images of both these mountains are visible in this valley.[6] Many later fruitbearing *Upanishad* trees germinated and grew from the seeds embedded in this valley.

Itarēyaranyaka has five parts, all titled 'Aranyaka'. Part one deals with the rituals of the Soma sacrifice. In part two, scattered images of the Upanishad are seen. Part three is more Upanishadic in character and therefore it is often labelled as *Upanishad.* Parts four and five contain details relating to continence, abstinence, vow of penance etc. of lesser philosophical importance and laudatory. As we have seen, this *Aranyaka* is independent of the *Brahmanas*. The ideas in this *Aranyaka* are developed in the *Upanishad* with the same name.

The Kaushitikaranyaka is also *Rig Vedic*. Parts one to four of this *Aranyaka* form the Kaushitikopanishad. The main difference between the Aitharēyaranyaka and the Kaushitikaranyaka is in respect of their Vedic branch: the former is centred on the 'Whole man' while the latter refers to the 'Brahmin tribe'. This *Aranyaka* is not a continuation or extension of the *Brahmana*.

The Tittiriyananyaka is the Aranyaka of the *Krishna Yajur Veda*. The name of this Aranyaka is not derived from the *Tittiri* bird; but one assigned by the Rishi. The name of the author of this Aranyaka is not mentioned anywhere. It is likely to have been authored by a Rishi named *Tithira* who was the disciple of Yaska Pengi, one of the disciples of Vaiśambayana. This Aranyaka is included in one of the subchapters of the *Sathapatha Brahmana*.

As we have seen, *Sathapatha Brahmana* is the most important among the *Brahmanas*. Its *Aranyaka* and *Upanishad* also stand great and extensive among the respective categories. Here all the three, *Brahmana*, *Aranyaka* and *Upanishad* are linked. We would be dealing with this *Upanishad* later. Brihadaranyaka is the Aranyaka of the *Sathapatha Brahmana* of the *Sukla Yajur Veda*. It is presumed that Yajnavalkya Vajasenaei, the author of *Sathapatha* is the author of both the *Aranyaka* and *Upanishad* known as *Brihadaranyaka* and the

Brihadaranyakopanishad. This *Aranyaka* is found in parts 14 and 17 of the *Sathapatha*. The last chapters of these *Aranyakas* form the *Brithadaranyakopanishad*.

Sama Veda and *Atharva Veda* have no *Aranyakas*. But the early parts of the *Brihadaranyakopanishad* have the nature and character of *Aranyaka*. *Jaiminopanishad* is in fact an *Aranyaka*. Similarly, Gopatha Brahmana of the Atharvaveda has no Aranyaka. *Mundakopanishad* is directly linked with the *Samhita*. *Prasnopanishad*, the continuation of the Mundokapanishad, is situated in the place of the *Brahmana*. Mandukyopanishad also reflects the same character. Gopatha states that Aranyakas have mystical meanings. Here, we notice the gradual drifting of theology from the *Aranyakas* towards the *Upanishads* in this period.[7]

FOOTNOTES

1. The Vedic hymns have no names. From the contents, the Scholars assign some name. E.g.: 'Song of Creation', 'Song of Nasadiya' etc. (Nasad means 'there was not').
2. Brodov, V., *Indian Philosophy in Modern Times*, pp. 45-46.
3. *Ibid*., p. 49.
4. *Shadvimsa* and *Panchavimsa* were parts of *Tandya Maha Brahmana* but later compiled as *Albuthabrahmana*.
5. Mahajan, V.D., *Ancient India*, p. 107.
6. Sukumar Azhicode (Dr.), *Tatvamasi* (Mal.), p. 53.
7. *Ibid*., pp. 53-56.

The Vedangas, Upavedas, Sutras, Sastras, Smritis and Puranas

10

The *Upavedas*, *Vedangas* and *Sutras* are subsidiary Vedic literature.

A. The Vedangas and Sutras

The *Vedangas* are 'members' or 'limbs' of the *Vedas*. They are treated as less authoritative than *Sruti* (Hearing) and therefore styled as *Smriti* (memory or tradition) handed down by the ancient sages to whom the *Vedas* were revealed. These are intended to help the proper reading and understanding of the Vedic literature. The *Vedangas* originated in Vedic Schools (*Charanas*) in condensed prose for memorisation by students and therefore later classified as *Sutras* (guide or clue). Some of them were later versified.

The *Vedangas* are six in number, namely: (i) *Siksha* (Phonetics), (ii) *Kalpa* (rituals), (iii) *Nirukta* (etymology), (iv) *Chandas* (metrics), (v) *Vyakarna* (grammar), and (vi) *Jyotisha* (astrology).

The *Siksha* manuals deal with correct pronunciation and accent. The Siksha School has produced a connected text of the *Rig Veda* as well as the *Pada-Patha* (word-text) which is a grammatical analysis of the text of the *Vedas*. The most prominent composition on Siksha is *Pratisakya Sutras* containing rules regulating the compilation of *Samhitas* (collections).

Kalpa, the treatises on Kalpa are contained in the *Sutras* like *Srautha Sutra, Grihya Sutra, Dharma Sutra, Suluva Sutra* etc. *Srautha Sutras* deal with a large number of ceremonies performed by priests. The *Grihya Sutra* deals with domestic sacrifices and rites to be performed by householders. They also deal with the domestic lives of the people, marriages, *yajnas* to be conducted by them, namely *Brahma Yajna*, *Prithi Yajna*, *Deva Yajna*, *Bhuta Yajna* and *Athithi Yajna*; the obligatory duties of Brahmins, Kshatrias and Vaisyas. *Dharma Sutras* refer to customary law and practices. Gautama, Baudhayana, Apastamba and Vasishta wrote these *Sutras* presumed as originated between 7th and 2nd centuries BC. *Suluva Sutras* deal with the measurement of structures and fire altars for sacrifices. They also contain treatises on Indian geometry. There are supplementary manuals for *Kalpa* known as *Pratisishtas* or addenda.

Nirukta – The book on etymology written by Yaska is supposed to be the authority on *Nirukta*.

Chandas dealing with metrics are contained in the *Dharma Sutras*. Pingalacharaya had written a comprehensive and authoritative book on chandas titled 'Chandasutra'.

Vyakarna (grammar) the earliest book on grammar known as *Ashtadyayi* was written by Panini somewhere between 500-300 BC. Many scholars put the period as 700 to 500 BC. This book gives a lot of information on many regions in India like Kalinga, Sind, Taxila, Kutch and the Swat Valley. He also refers to 22 *Janapadas* (states). The literatures referred to by him include *Rig Veda*, *Sama Veda*, *Yajur Veda*, *Brahmanas*, *Chandas* (metrics), *Kalpasutras*, *Vyakyana* (explanations), *Gatha* (a poem in Manjari metre), *Katha* (historical romance) and *Mahabharata*. *Paniniyam* (the book of Panini) is considered to be the most scientific and comprehensive book on grammar in the world. It contains eight chapters with four divisions each. Panini referred to almost all the literatures produced till his period for examples. There is a legend that Panini performed penance and Siva appeared before him dancing in tune with the sound produced by Siva's big drum. Fourteen different sounds were produced on beating that drum. Panini accepted those fourteen sounds as fourteen *sutras* and incorporated in his book with the title *Maheswarasutras*. 'Paniniyam' is not actually a book on grammar only but a *Bhashasastra* (science of linguistics). But, we do not know much about his early life. Ramabhadra Dikshitar stated that Panini was the son of a sage named 'Pani'. Whatever be the truth in this respect, Panini's work still remains the authority on Sanskrit grammar though many other books on the subject emerged in later years.[1]

Jyotisha – A metrical work on Jyotisha Vedanga alone is now extant.

B. Upavedas

Upavedas are subsidiary *Vedas*. The prominent among the *Upavedas* are: (i) *Ayurveda*, (ii) *Dhanurveda*, (iii) *Gandharvaveda* and (iv) *Shilpaveda*.

Ayurveda means knowledge of longevity. It is the science of long life imparted by Sage Dhanwanthari to Susrutha. Treatments of all diseases are prescribed in this *Sastra* (Science). Diseases are classified into four groups: bodily diseases, mental diseases, uninvited diseases and inherent diseases. Fever and leprosy are examples of bodily diseases; anger, rage etc. are mental diseases, wounds, squash etc. are uninvited diseases and hunger and greying etc. come under inherent diseases. Dhanwanthari was an expert in anti-venom treatment. He divided Ayurveda into eight divisions. Sage Charaka later published his 'Charakasamhita, which is an advanced study on Ayurvedic treatment.

Dhanurveda is the science of ancient warfare. *Brahmins* were the teachers and *Kshatrias* and *Vaisyas* were the students in the Dhanurveda schools. Considering the growing importance of warfare, many comprehensive books have been published on this subject later. Dhanurveda is divided into four parts, usually named *Chathushpadom* (Four legs). These four legs are (i) chariots (a two-wheeler vehicle pulled by horses), (ii) elephants, (iii) horses (cavalry) and (iv) *Kalal* (infantry). This Veda contains descriptions on various fighting postures of soldiers and weaponry. Different types of weapons and the manner of usage of those weapons are also described meticulously. The application of different varieties of warfare and weapons are listed as: (1) *Astra* (bow and arrow-archery), (2) *Khadga* (Sword), (3) *Pasa* (rope), (4) *Sastra* dealing with application of weapons such as (*chakra*) wheel, *Shulam* (pike, spear, trident etc.), *Parasu* (axe), *Gada* (club, mace), *Kripanam* (dagger), *Kshepini* (sling) etc.[2]

Gandharva Veda – *Gandharva* means celestial musician. This *Veda* deals with music and arts, both classical and folk.

Shilpa Veda – *Shilpa Veda* is a part of *Artha Veda*, an *Upaveda*. It deals with architecture. Viswakarmav is the god and father of architecture.

C. Dharma Sastras

The *Dharma Sastras* give us a lot of information on the social, religious, economic and political life of the people in India in the distant past. There are many Sastras, but those considered important are four, written by Manu, Narada, Vishnu and Yajnavalkya labelled *Smriti* (memory or remembrance). All the *Smritis* are in verse except that of Vishnu.

(i) Manu Smriti

It is the most important and authoritative law of the Hindus. The old sayings of Manu were later compiled as *Manusmriti* or *Manava Sastra* (Science of Human Behaviour). The Englishmen who ruled India regarded *Manu Smriti* as the basic laws of the Hindus. Scholars are of the view that this book was written somewhere around 500 BC. It has twelve chapters dealing with subjects detailed below:

- Origin of this book and creation of universe
- Senses and methods to control the senses
- Duties of *grihasthas* and women
- Duties of *Brahmin*
- Food and cleanliness
- *Vanaprasthans* and *Sanyasins*
- King, ministers and justice
- Law, litigation, debt and adultery
- Husband or wife and properties
- Mixed castes and their duties
- Rituals, sacrifices and social evils
- *Karmasamsar* – rebirth

Manu has taken into consideration the *Dharmasastras* of Atri, Gautama, Saunaka and Vasishta for compilation of his book. The jurisdiction of the *Manava Dharma Sastra* was confined geographically to the areas north of the Vindhyas. The Aryans divided these areas into four regions, viz.: *Brahmavarta, Brahmarishidesh, Madhyadesha* and *Aryavarta*. *Brahmavarta* was the territory between the Saraswati and Drishadvati. The *Brahmarishidesh* comprised Kurushetra, Panchala, Matsya and Shursena. *Madhyadesha* was the territory between Himalayas and the Vindhyas and *Saraswati* and *Prayaga*. *Aryavarta* was described as the areas between the two mountains and the two oceans in the West and the East. References to the tribes such as *Shakas, Kiratas, Dravidas, Yavanas, Kambojas, Pahlavas* and *Chinas* are also seen.

Manu Smriti observed that in the absence of any paramount sovereign, States were to be called *rashtras*. The King was known as Raja and the subjects were known as *Praja*. A *Rashtra* was divided into deshas, Janapadas or Vaisyas. There were officers in charge of ten or multiples of ten, even up to one thousand, villages. The King was never an autocrat. Considerable freedom of self-government was given to the people. The King was not a lawmaker. He enforced the laws. *Manu Smriti* divided the Aryan community into two, the *Dvijatis* and the *Ekajatis*. The Brahmins, Kshatrias and Vaisyas formed the *Dvijatis* and the Sudras formed the *Ekajatis*. The Sudras were expected to serve the *Dvijatis* and remove dirt, filth and carcasses. They were not allowed to study *Vedas* or to recite *mantras* except for marriages.

Manu was against freedom for women. He says:

Pitha rakshathi Kaumare
Bhartha rakshathi Youvane
Rakshanthi Sthavire Putra
Na stree Swathanthryamarhati

Meaning: Before marriage, a girl was required to be under the control of her father or brother, after marriage under the husband and on the death of the husband, under her sons. She was not entitled to own any property except her *Stridhana* (the wealth of the woman granted by her father).

Education of children starts after *Upanayana* (wearing of thread) performed at the age of eight or eleven or twelve. The students were expected to live with their teacher for studying *Vedas, Brahmanas, Aranyakas, Upanishads, Vedangas, Darsana, Sastras, Dharma Sastras* etc.

Agriculture was the mainstay of the people. They also engaged themselves in many occupations. They were artisans, mechanics, weavers, potters, tailors, washermen, distillers, blacksmiths and so on. The government fixed prices. Stringent laws were there to punish the law-breakers. Adulteration, false weights and measures etc. were strictly dealt with and punished. Trade flourished both within the country and outside the country. Malpractices in trade invited rigorous punishments. The Government collected taxes and tolls. The officers looked after the collection of taxes. Money was given on credit and interest was allowed to be charged @ 15% per annum. Higher interest rates were allowed for unsecured loans. The gold coin was known as *Swarna* and one gold coin was equivalent to eighty *Krishnalas*. The silver currency consisted of *Krishnalas, Masha, Dharna* and *Shatamana*. The copper coins were known as *Karshapanas* (Pana in common parleys). The smallest coin was 1/8th of a Pana.

The metals known during the period of Manu were gold, silver, copper, bronze, lead, iron, tin and pewter. Precious stones were mined under the control of government. Remarriage was not allowed for women. Manu mentions seven types of slaves. Manu allowed *Brahmins* to marry a *Sudra* girl. He completely disallowed documentary evidences in courts.

(ii) Narada Smriti

Narada wrote his *Smriti* after the *Manu Smriti*. The arrangement of the book and many verses in the book are the same as those in the *Manusmriti*. Manu was against *Niyoga* and remarriage of women. But, Narada did not impose such restrictions. He refers to fifteen kinds of slaves as against seven mentioned by Manu. He also preferred regulated gambling to increase government revenue. The coins mentioned by Narada are Dinaras, Panas and Karshapanas. He laid down rules for apprenticeship and prescribed punishments for dropout students. Partnership in business was legally permitted along with sharing of profit or loss proportionate to the investment. A reference is seen made advocating formation of corporations of the Kula, Sreni, Gana, Puga, Vrata etc. with law-making authority and obligating the King to enforce those laws.

(iii) Vishnu Smriti

This *Smriti* in prose was written after the *Smriti* of Yajnavalkya and therefore many things in the *Yajnavalkya Smriti* are copied in it. According to Vishnu, Aryavarta included the whole of India and not confined to the north of Vindhyas. He refers to the practice of *Sati*. References to Kapalika and Sudra ascetics are noticed. The people are not allowed to talk to *Mlechas* (untouchables) and *Antyajas* (other communities). Gifts to people by King are to be recorded on copper plates with the affixture of the seal of the King.

(iv) Yajnavalkya Smriti

This *Smriti* is more systematic than that of Manu. Many points not discussed by Manu are seen included, but in an abridged form. While Manu referred to only two ordeals, Yajnavalkya prescribed five different ordeals. While Manu permitted marriage of *Sudra* girl by *Brahmins*, Yajnavalkya condemned it. Yajnavalkya favoured gambling under the auspices of the Government for boosting revenue as against Manu opposing it. A lot of anatomical and medical matters are seen discussed in this Smriti. Yajnavalkya discusses the non-acceptance of documentary evidences in courts, at length. He also proposed monasteries for *Brahmins*. He refers to *Vedangas* and fourteen other *vidyas* (knowledge). He clearly defined the rights of widows. Corporations with autonomy proposed by Narada are favoured for *Brahmins* only. The authority of *Dharmasastras* is binding in cases of conflicts with *Arthasastra*, according to Yajnavalkya.[3]

D. The Puranas

Puranas are books on sacred subjects, ancient history, tales, mythological treatises and legends. *Amarakosa*, the Sanskrit dictionary compiled by the great classic scholar Amarasimha prescribed five characteristics for a *Purana*, *Sarga* and *Pratisarga* (cosmogony), *Vamsa* (chronology), *Manvamtharam* (cosmology) and *Vamsanucharitham* (genealogy).

Sargascha Pratisargascha
Vamso Manvamtharānica
Vamsānucaritham Chāpi
Purānam Panja Lekshanam

Sarga and *Pratisarga* deal with creation or origin of the universe, *Vamsa* pertains to fixing of dates of historical events, *Manvamtharam* literally means the period of reign of Manus – the period of origin and development of the universe (cosmos) and *Vamsanucharitham* refers to critical analysis of astrological prophecies and presumptions. Many books classified as *Puranas* do not conform to all the above prescriptions. It is widely believed that *Puranas* existed even in pre-historic days, shedding light on many ancient historical facts and data, often mixed with myth, fiction and exaggerations.

At present, 36 texts of Puranas are available, 18 main *Puranas* and 18 *Upapuranas* (subsidiary *Puranas*). The 18 main *Puranas* in poetry containing more than two hundred thousand *Slokas* (Stanzas) are classified into three groups based on the deity to whom they were linked; Vishnu or Brahmav or Siva.

The details of the classification are given below:

Eighteen main Puranas

Vishnu Section	Brahmav Section	Siva Section
Vishnupurana	Brahmapurana	Vayupurana
Bhagavathapurana	Brahmandapurana	Lingapurana
Naradiyapurana	Brahmavaivarthapurana	Skandapurana
Garudapurana	Markandeyapurana	Agnipurana
Padmapurana	Bhavishyapurana	Matsyapurana
Varahapurana	Vamanapurana	Koormapurana

Eighteen Upapuranas (No classification)

(1) Sanalkumaram, (2) Naarasimham, (3) Naradeeyam, (4) Sivam, (5) Durvasas, (6) Kaapilam, (7) Manavam, (8) Usanas,

(9) Varunam, (10) Kalikam, (11) Sambham, (12) Sauram, (13) Adityam, (14) Maheswaram, (15) Devibhagavathom, (16) Vaasishtam, (17) Vishnudharmotharam, (18) Neelamarapurana.

The last two Upapuranas are related to Kashmir, the first on the Vaishnava sect in Kashmir and the second refers to Neelan, the Naga King of Kashmir. In the *Vishnupurana*, treated as one among the ancient puranas, references relating to the Gupta rule in India are seen. The Gupta age from 320-476 AD was a period of massive revival in art and literature, the climax being reached during the reign of Vikramaditya (Chandragupta II), the third ruler in the Gupta dynasty. As such, the origin of *puranas* remains obscure.

The main puranas are introduced below:

(a) Vishnu Section

(i) Vishnupurana

Vishnupurana is one among the ancient puranas, which conforms to all five attributes of a purana. Sage Parasara compiled this book, according to his own admission, on the basis of materials collected by Sage Vyasa and his disciples. The narration in this Purana is in the form of instructions by Sage Parasara to his disciple Maithreyan. The main theme dealt with in this text is the ten *Poornavataras* (full incarnations of Vishnu – God's descent to Earth).

Matsya: Koorma Varahacha / Narasimhacha Vāmanah:
Ramo Rāmacha Rāmacha / Kriśhna: Kalkir Janardanah:

Here, the five *Poornavataras* are specified with their meanings:

Matsya = Fish

Koorma = Tortoise

Varaha = Pig

Narasimha = *Nara* means man and *Simha* means lion – semi-man and semi-beast

Vamana = a dwarf (a palaeolithic man)

The first four *avataras* were in different subhuman forms. The next five were in human form. Three Ramas appear consecutively. The first is *Parasurama*, the holder of axe. *Parasu* means axe, the weapon of this Rama granted by Lord Siva to his disciple Bhargava Rama (earlier name later changed as Parasurama). The second is Sri Rama, the main character in the epic Ramayana, who is considered as *Maryada Purushothama* (gentleman) and a proficient archer whose weapon was bow and arrow. The third Rama is *Balabhadrarama,* the elder brother of Sri Krishna (some later writers have substituted Sri Buddha for Balabhadrarama). He wields the plough and hence known as ploughman, the cultivator. The ninth avatara is *Sri Krishna* the *Uthamapurushothama* (the full-fledged man or superman), the main character in the epic *Mahabharata*. Sri Krishna's weapon was the *Sudharsana* wheel (a replica of modern missile). The tenth avatara is *Kalki* – it is not sure whether this *avatara* has yet descended or not. *Kaliyuga* (the age of Kalki) is believed to have begun from 3102 BC when Krishna ascended to heaven.

Herein we note the evolution from the primitive man to the modern man or superman. The tenth avatara is awaited. The chronology of the *avataras* depicts an evolutionary character either reminiscent of or analogous to the theory of evolution expounded by Charles Darwin in his book 'The Origin of Species'.

Life originates in water. The 'Fish', the aquatic, is the first *avatar.* The process of evolution begins from the fish.

From fish, the aquatic	to	tortoise, the amphibian.
From the amphibian	to	pig, the land animal
From the land animal	to	Narasimha, the semi-human
From the semi-human	to	Vamana, the palaeolithic man
From the palaeolithic man	to	Parasurama, the neolithic man
From the neolithic man	to	Srirama, the full-fledged man
From the full man	to	Balarama, the ploughman
From the plough man	to	Sri Krishna, the modern man
From the modern man	to	Kalki, the form not known

The Hindu scholars are of the view that the fast degeneration of moral values in the modern age is symptomatic of the *Kaliyuga* (the era of Kalki) and the imminent arrival of *Kalkiavatar* (the incarnation of Vishnu manifested as Kalki).

(ii) Bhagawatha Purana

Bhagawathapurana is the most popular among the *puranas*, the most cherished book of the devotees of Vishnu and the only text translated into all Indian languages. It is divided into twelve *Skandas* (parts). Even though all the incarnations of Vishnu are dealt with in the *Bhagawatha*, the most attractive part is the *Dasamaskantha* (tenth part) dealing with the *Krishnavatara* (the incarnation of Vishnu as Krishna). In this *Purana*, Kapila and Buddha are projected as incarnations.

(iii) Naradiya Purana

The narration is in the form of Narada speaking to sage Sanalkumaran, the disciple of Brahmav. The necessity of observance of *Dharma* in all circumstances is the essence of this Purana.

(iv) Garuda Purana (Garuda – The Eagle is the king of the birds)

The narration in this Purana is in the form of an advice to Garuda by Vishnu. Many subjects like astronomy, Health care, grammar, diamonds etc. are dealt with in this Purana. In the latter half, the state of the human soul after death is described. The Hindus in North India recite the extracts of this Purana during ceremonies for cremation of dead bodies. The origin of Garuda is also seen incorporated in this book.

(v) Padma Purana

This *Purana* is divided into six parts (*Khandas*); *Srishti Khanda* (creation), *Bhoomi Khanda* (Earth), *Swarga Khanda* (heaven) *Padala Khanda* (goddess Durga) and *Uttara Khanda* and *Kriyayoga Saram* (the last). Descriptions on lotus (*padma*), importance of each month, a reproduction of the drama 'Shakuntala' by Kalidasa etc. are the contents. This Purana is seen written after the period of Kalidasa, who lived in the 4th and 5th centuries AD, the period of reign of Vikramaditya of the Gupta dynasty.

(vi) Varaha Purana

Varaha (pig) is one of the incarnations of Vishnu. This *Purana* is in the form of a narration by Varaha itself. The descriptions of many pilgrim centres, incantations, prayer of *Bhoomidevi* (goddess earth) to Vishnu etc. are the contents.

(b) Brahmav Section

(i) Brahma Purana

This Purana is also known as 'Adipurana'. The narration is in the form of instructions issued by Brahmav to Daksha. It contains detailed descriptions of Utkal areas (present Orissa) the Surya temple at Konark near Puri constructed in 1241, an alliance between Siva and Sun etc. The reference to Surya temple proves that this Purana was written somewhere around 13th or 14th century AD.

(ii) Brahmanda Purana

The narration in this Purana is in the form of an advice by Brahmav. It is stated that in the beginning there was a golden egg and that the universe originated from that egg. References relating to *Ramayana* (epic), Radha and Krishna, *Parasurama* (another incarnation of Vishnu) etc. are seen incorporated.

(iii) Brahmavyvartha Purana

The narration is in the form of an advice to Narada by Suvarnimanu. It is divided into four *khandas* (divisions): *Brahmakhanda, Prakrithikhanda, Ganeshakhanda* and *Krishnajanmakhanda*. The story of one Rathandara is seen explained in it.

(iv) Markandeya Purana

This is one of the ancient puranas. Many stories relating to Surya (Sun), *Indra* (the king of gods) and *Agni* (Fire) are described in it. A separate division glorifying goddess *Durga* is also seen incorporated.

(v) Bhavishya Purana

This Purana is in the form of a conversation between *Surya* (Sun) and *Manu* (one of the early kings of the universe created by Brahmav). The contents of this Purana are few prophecies, worship of Fire, Sun, *Nagas* (snakes) etc. The list of the holy places in India and a note on the rights and privileges of pilgrims are seen attached to the main text as appendices.

(vi) Vamana Purana

The narration in this Purana is similar to that in the *Varahapurana*. The incarnations of Vishnu from Vamana onwards are described here. The wedding of Siva and Parvati is prominently explained in detail.

(c) Siva Section

(i) Vayu Purana

In this Purana we see a discourse by the god of air (*Jathavedas*). Banabhatta who lived in the 7th century AD is referred to in this Purana. Some references relating to the reign of Gupta rulers are also seen, which show that this Purana was written somewhere after the 7th century AD. Plenty of verses glorifying Siva are seen included.

(ii) Linga Purana

The topics discussed in this Purana are the instructions on *Dharma* by *Linga* (the genital organ of the male) symbolising the assumed form of Siva. Instances of 28 transfigurations assumed by Siva are also described.

(iii) Skanda Purana

The topic discussed is the murder of *Tharakasura* by Skanda also called Subramanyan, the son of Siva, narrated by Skanda himself. It undeniably resembles the drama 'Kumarasambhava' by Kalidasa.

(iv) Agni Purana

The narration in this Purana is in the form of instructions of *Mathariswar* (the god of Fire) to sage Vasishta. It contains a lot of references relating to *Sivalinga* (Siva manifested as *Linga*) and goddess Durga. The stories of Sri Rama and Sri Krishna are also seen described. Topics like rhetorical poetry, drama, astronomy, sculpture and many other arts are dealt with in this Purana.

(v) Matsya Purana

The tale of *Matsyavathara* (Vishnu's incarnation as Fish), Jainism, Buddhism, *Natyasastra* (the science of dance), dynasty details of Andhra kings and many other irrelevant subjects are dealt with in this Purana.

(vi) Koorma Purana

The narration of the story of Indradyumna by *Koorma* (tortoise, the incarnation of Vishnu) while visiting the hell is the topic dealt with in this Purana. References to seven islands (*Saptadweepa)* and seven oceans (*Saptasamudra)* in the *Prithvi* (earth) are described here. A part of *Jambudweepa* situated in the centre of these islands is the present India. It is believed that this Purana had four *Samhitas* (collections) but one called *Brahmasamhita* alone is now available. The other parts are presumably extinct.[4]

FOOTNOTES

1. Mahajan, V.D., *Ancient India*, pp. 143-46.
2. Vettom, Mani, *Puranic Encyclopaedia*, pp. 617-18.
3. Mahajan, V.D., *Ancient India*, pp. 157-61.
4. Vettom, Mani, *Puranic Encyclopaedia*, pp. 772-75.

The Upanishads

11

What is Upanishad?

The Upanishad is, properly speaking, the philosophical part of the Vedas. They are not books or philosophical treatises in the proper sense of the word, but collections of texts compiled by different persons, often anonymous, at different times and on different subjects. The Upanishads contain "Secret or esoteric doctrines" and deep speculations of a philosophical character that revolve around two conceptions – *Brahman* and *Atman* – the Absolute and the individual self. Although there are quite a few materialist ideas and rational approaches in some modern Upanishads, the idealist view of the nature of the *Brahman* and *Atman* emerges as the main theme of the ancient Upanishads.

Literally, the word 'Upanishad' is a three-syllable word, Upa-ni-sad. 'Upa' means near or close by, 'ni' means below or down and 'sad' with different meanings such as destroy, go, direction, sitting and ending (*Avasadana*). When combined together, we get the meaning 'sitting below close by'. Here we get the clear picture of a pupil sitting at the feet of a preceptor or teacher on an elevated seat. But Sankaracharya, an eminent Indian philosopher and commentator of the Upanishads, gives a deep and logical interpretation. Out of the different meanings of the syllable 'sad', Sankaracharya selected the meaning 'destroy' and presents a different connotation "The acquisition of that knowledge which destroys ignorance is Upanishad." He who distinguishes this knowledge is liberated from the clutches of death or mortality (Katam 1:3, 15). On applying the meaning 'direction', the interpretation becomes "The practice of that knowledge which facilitates the realisation of Brahman is Upanishad." Whoever knows this, knows everything and becomes everything (Prasna 4:10). When the meaning 'ending' (instead of 'sitting') is ascribed to the syllable 'sad', the definition becomes "That knowledge which ends the miseries in life is Upanishad." From these expositions, the final conclusion arrived at is "The knowledge or learning (Vidya) to attain the ultimate realisation of Brahman is Upanishad."[1]

Period of Origin

The ancient Upanishads are regarded as pre-Buddhistic. But, some of the treatises titled 'Upanishad' belong to a much later period. The total number of Upanishads is estimated at 108 (some have estimated 112).

Scholarly opinion is that most of the ancient Upanishads were written before Buddha, in between 1000 BC and 500 BC. The main pre-Buddhist Upanishads, Chandogya, Brihadaranyaka, Taittiriya, Itareya, Kaushitaki, Kenam, Easom and Mandukyam are supposed to have been written in the 7th and 8th centuries BC, according to Max Mueller and Deussen. Dr. S. Radhakrishnan and Das Gupta endorse this view. Deussen has given a classification as below:

Ancient Upanishads in Prose

Brihadaranyaka, Chandogya, Tittiriya, Itareya, Kaushitaki and Kenam.

(The prose is similar to that in the Brahmanas.)

Ancient Upanishads in Poetry or Verses

Katom, Isam, Svetasvatara and Mundaka

(These are not ancient as the above ones, but ancient.)

Later (Non-Ancient) Upanishads in Prose

Prasna, Maitri (Maitrayani), Mandukya

Other Upanishads not related to the Vedas

The relation between the Upanishads and the Veda Samhitas is as below:

Rig Veda: Itareya and Kaushitaki (ancient)

Nadabindu, Nirvana, Bahrucha (modern)

Krishna Yajur Veda: Katam, Taittiriya (ancient)
Kaivallya, Narayana, Amrithabindu, Yogasikha, Katarudra and Varaha (modern)

Sukla Yajur Veda: Isam, Brihadaranyaka (ancient)
Jabala, Niralamba, Paingala, Muktika (modern)

Sama Veda: Kenam, Chandogya (ancient)
Maitreyi, Maitrayani, Vajrasuchi (modern)

Atharva Veda: Prasna, Mundaka, Mandukya (ancient)
Mahanarayana, Atharvasiras, Nrusimhathapani (modern)

The modern Upanishads are classified into six groups, in consideration of their nature and character: *Vedanta, Yoga, Sannyasa, Vaishnava, Saiva* and *Sakti.*

Vedanta: Vajrasuchi, Muktika, Paigala, Jabala, Niralamba and Sarvasara

Yoga: Varaha, Yogasikha, Yogathathva, Thejobindhu, Amrithabindhu, Kshurika, Sandilya and Hamsa

Sannyasa: Jabala, Aaruneya, Katarudra, Maitreyi, Parabrahma, Paramahamsa and Sannyasa

Vaishnava: Narayana, Nrusimhathapini, Ramathapini and Avyaktha

Saiva: Atharvasiras, Atharvasikha, Rudrahridaya and Kaivalya

Sakti: Tripura, Bahrucha and Soubhagyalakshmi

According to Jawaharlal Nehru, "The dominating characteristic of the Upanishads is the dependence on Truth. Truth wins ever, not falsehood. With Truth is paved the way to the Divine." And the famous invocation is for light and understanding.

Asatho ma Sath Gamaya
Thamaso ma Jyotir Gamaya
Mrithyor ma Amritham Gamaya

(Briha-Up 1:3:28)[2]

Meaning: "Lead me from the unreal to the real
Lead me from darkness to light
Lead me from mortality to immortality"

The fundamental doctrine, which pervades all the genuine Upanishads, can be summed up as below:

"The Universe is the Brahman, but the Brahman is the Atman." In other words, "The Word is God, and God is my soul." The two concepts of Brahman and Atman are united in the philosophy of the Upanishads. Deussen has expressed the fundamental ideal of the Upanishads in the following words:

> "The Brahman, the power which presents itself to us materialised in all existing things, which creates, sustains, preserves, and receives back into itself again all worlds. This eternal, infinite divine power is identical with the Atman with that which, after stripping off everything external we discover in ourselves as our real, most essential being, our individual self, the soul. This doctrine has found expression most pointedly and clearly in the Upanishad dictum, which later became the confession of faith of millions of Indians, in the *Tat Tvam Asi* (so often quoted by Schopenhauer). That art thou, i.e., the universe and the Brahman, that art thou (thyself) or in other words, the world exists only in so far as thou thyself art conscious of it."

Schopenhauer, the great German mystic philosopher comments on the Upanishads: "From every sentence, deep, original and sublime thoughts arise, and the whole is pervaded by a high and holy and earnest spirit. Indian air surrounds us, and original thoughts of kindred spirits. And oh, how thoroughly is the mind here washed clean of all early-engrafted Jewish superstitions, and of all philosophy that cringes before those superstitions! In the whole world there is no study so beneficial and so elevating as that of the Upanishads. It has been the solace of my life – it will be the solace of my death."

Dr. Winternitz, in his generous and liberal words, comments: "In fact the whole of the later philosophy of the Indians is rooted in the Upanishads. Their doctrines formed the foundations of Vedanta Sutras of Badarayana.... The theological-philosophical systems of Sankara and of Ramanuja, whose adherents at the present day are still counted by millions, are built upon this textbook. Moreover, all other philosophical systems and religions which have arisen in the course of the centuries...have sprung forth from the soil of the Upanishad doctrines" (*History of Indian Literature*, p. 265). Again, "The Upanishads do not contain 'superhuman conceptions, but, human, absolutely human attempts to come nearer to the truth – and it is this which makes them so valuable to us. For the historian, however, who pursues the history of human thought the Upanishads have a yet far greater significance. From the mystical doctrines of the Upanishads, one current of thought may be traced to the mysticism of the Persian Sufism, to the mystic-theosophical logos-doctrine of the Neo-Platonics and the Alexandrian Christians down to the teachings of the Christian mystics. Eckhart and Tauler, and finally to the philosophy of the great German mystic of the 19th century, Schopenhauer."

According to Will Durrant: "To our own day the Upanishads have remained to India what the New Testament is to Christendom – a noble creed occasionally practised and generally revered. Even in Europe and America, this wistful theosophy has won millions upon millions of followers, from lonely women and tired men to Schopenhauer and Emerson."

Amaury de Reincourt says: "The Upanishadic era represents the zenith of India's cultural growth. The early enthusiasm and joy of living of the Vedic Aryans, now firmly settled in their new land, was sobered by considerable thoughtfulness and an awareness of the deep sorrow underlying all forms of life. The Indian mind began to crystallize slowly and evolve new forms of expression perhaps better suited to a more mature outlook."[3]

According to the Upanishads, the human intellect cannot understand the reality. We require some other organ of perception and understanding than our senses and reason. "Not by learning is the *Atman* (Soul of the world) attained, not by genius or much knowledge of books. Let a Brahmin renounce learning and become as a child. Let him not seek after many words, for that is mere weariness of tongue. The self-evident Brahman pierced the opening of the senses so that they turned outwards, not inward into himself: Some wise man, however, with his eyes closed and wishing for immortality, saw the self behind."

All the religious books in the world deal with salvation. Upanishad is the only book dealing with freedom – liberation from the chains of the world. Upanishad is Vedanta, the end of knowledge.[4]

The Upanishads traditionally learnt are ten. They are Isavasyam (Isam), Kenam, Katam (Katom), Prasna, Mundaka, Mandukya Thaittariya, Itareya, Chandogya and Brihadaranyaka. These are the world famous *Desopanishads* ('Desam' means ten). The foreign scholars call them 'Classic Upanishads'. Sankaracharya has written commentaries for them all. *Svetasvatara* is also an authoritative Upanishad. But, Sankara has not written a commentary for this Upanishad. Hence, it is not included under the *Desopanishad*. It may also be noted that Sankara's *Advaita* is only a subject, not a school. *Dvaita*, *Traita*, *Visishtadvaita*, *Advaitadvaita* etc. are the other subjects related to the ancient Vedic school. In the following paras, an attempt is made to introduce them to the readers; a superficial introduction, without peeping into its depth.

Isavasyopanishad

Isavasyopanishad, popularly known as *Isa* which adjoins the Sukla Yajur Veda is comparatively a small Upanishad in poetry apparently compiled in late Vedic period. Some of the verses and ideas in this text are seen similar to those in the Brihadaranyakopanishad. The language in the *Isa* is tough and difficult to comprehend. This often leads to varying interpretations.

According to this Upanishad, there are two objects of knowledge leading to two corresponding kinds of knowledge. The first and primary object of cognition is the substance (*Atman - Brahman*). This knowledge of substance is genuine knowledge (*Vidya*). Whoever attains this knowledge of the substance has supreme knowledge. The second object of cognition is the object or phenomena. In this knowledge, the genuine nature of the object is not known. This is inferior knowledge or absence of knowledge (*Avidya*). *Avidya* complements *Vidya*. The consideration of the links between *Vidya* and *Avidya* leads to the essence of epistemological problems. In this division, later philosophers faced the question of difference between speculative philosophical reasoning and concrete scientific knowledge. From these poles, it is recognised that scientific methods are inadequate for the solution of the basic problems of human existence.

It is the opening stanza of this Upanishad, more than the philosophy expounded in it that makes this Upanishad world famous.

The stanza reads:

Isavasyam Idam Sarvam
Et Kincha Jagathyam Jagat
Thena Thyakthēna Bhunjēēthāh:
Ma Grudhah: Kasyaswidhanam!!

Meaning: Everything in this dynamic world is the abode of (covered or concealed by) *Paramatma* (God). Therefore, enjoy with restraint. Be free from covetousness.

Sankaracharya in his commentaries on *Isa* used the word *Aachchadaneeyam* for *Vasyam* meaning 'covered or concealed' by God. He attributed this meaning to proclaim that God (Brahman) alone is real and that the world is illusion or unreal, thereby justifying his theory of 'non-dualism'. Sankara's commentary says *Sarvam Characharam Aachchadaneeyam Swena Paramatmane* (The entire universe is covered or concealed by *Paramatma*). Sri Aravindan, the eminent sage, opposed the views of Sankara. According to Sri Aravindan, the first stanza of the Upanishad is the highest peak, from which flows the entire philosophy revealed in the *Isa*.

The meaning given by him for *Vasyam* is 'residing' or 'dwelling' or 'living', or 'covering' or 'wearing'. He supports the 'non-dualism' of Sankara with another interpretation. According to Aravindan, God resides or dwells in the Universe not like a small man living in a big house, but with His presence in every atom or particle of atom in the universe. Here, there is no distinction between God and the Universe. The union is indivisible.

The universe is the residence of God. He is its Vicar and operator. No one has anything of his own in this world. Everything belongs to God and God alone. Hence one should not only covet another's wealth, but also should enjoy, whatever considered his own, with restraint. *Parasya Svasya va dhanam*. He who desires for another's property is worshipping *Avidya*.

According to Gandhiji, Bhagavad Gita is the child of the Isavasyopanishad. He often quoted the first stanza, his most favourite lines among the entire Hindu scripture. Gandhiji has gone to the extent of declaring that even if all the Hindu scriptures were lost, Hinduism would exist so long as this stanza remains.

Those who achieved all the knowledge in this world other than knowledge of Brahman (*Brahmajnana*) are illiterate. They live in darkness. Their sacrifices and efforts are of no avail. If all activities in day-to-day life are not done with detachment, one will move from darkness to darkness.

The substance of the message of Isavasyopanishad is 'the day-to-day life of man in this universe is the gift of God to be used with prudence and restraint as instruments for *Moksha* (salvation)'. This message was declared in loud voice by ancient India to wake up not only India, but also the whole world.[5]

Kenopanishad

Kenopanishad, also known as *Kena,* 'Keneshita' and *Thalavakara*, is considered to be the last among the ancient Upanishads. It adjoins the Sama Veda Samhita. This Upanishad has four parts, the first two parts in poetry and the last two parts in prose. Researchers are of the view that the last parts were later additions. The entire text is devoted to explain the essence of *Brahman*. Here, *Brahman* is presented as the ultimate cause and purpose of existence of the universe and nature: everything originates from Brahman and ultimately returns to Brahman. There is only one path to Brahman, the path of knowledge. Abstinence, Asceticism, Rituals etc. do not lead to Brahman.

The text begins with the question *Kena*? Meaning 'by whom?' The subsequent portions of the book ponder over the answer to this question. After describing *Brahman* in abstract terms, the *Guru* (the teacher – a Rishi) proceeds to illustrate the subject by narrating a story that the disciples were often interested to hear. The story goes on as follows:

Once upon a time, Brahma defeated the *Asuras* (demons or the wicked people) to save the *Devas* (the gods) from troubles frequently caused by the *Asuras*. The gods boasted over their own abilities in the victory over the *Asuras*. Brahman, on learning about the baseless pride and boasting by the gods, one day appeared before the gods in the form of a *Yaksha* (a ghost). The *Devas* (gods) failed to identify the 'being'. They, therefore, requested *Agni Deva* (*Jathavedas*, the god of fire), who was supposed to identify everything, to go and enquire about the identity of that 'being'. When *Agnideva* chased the 'being', Yaksha posed a question "Who are you?" Agnideva answered "I am *Jathavedas*" (the god of fire). Then *Yaksha* posed the next question "What is your forte?" *Agnideva* replied "I can burn to ashes anything in this *Prithvi* (earth)." Then, Yaksha threw a piece of grass before Agnideva and urged him to burn it. In spite of his best efforts, Agnideva failed in the test and returned disappointed. Then, the gods deputed *Mathaviswav* (the god of air) with the mission to identify the 'being'. The process was repeated. *Mathaviswav* who claimed to have power to lift and move anything on this earth failed to lift a piece of grass and returned. Thereupon, *Indra,* the king of gods took up the mission. On seeing Indra, Yaksha hid itself without speaking anything. At that time, Uma, the beautiful daughter of *Himavan* (the personification of Mount Himalayas), appeared before Indra. Uma explained to Indra that it was *Brahman*, who defeated the Asuras that appeared in the form of Yaksha. Then only the gods realised their folly in claiming that the Asuras were defeated by the Devas' power. They accepted the invincible might of *Brahman*.

Guru (teacher) advised his disciples to practise self-restraint, penance (*tapas*) and selflessness (*Nishkamakarma)* and acquire *Brahmajnana* (knowledge of Brahma), that could make them immortal.

The message conveyed by this Upanishad is that there is a force, which is ear of ear, eye of eye, word of word, mind of mind and life of life. This force is inaccessible to human eyes or ears or words or mind. It is one beyond the known and the unknown, one that words cannot describe but that which manifests the word; one that mind cannot analyse but that which infuses thinking in the mind; one that eyes cannot see but that which provides sight to the eyes; one that ears cannot hear but that which gives the sense of hearing; it is one that is consciousness or power or soul or life. It is that one that is Brahman. Whoever boldly and prudently distinguishes and understands *Brahmathva* (the essence of Brahman) becomes immortal.[6]

Katopanishad

Katopanishad stands second among the Upanishads in fame and reputation, the first being *Isavasyam*. The scholars are not in agreement on the Samhita to which it is linked. The general view is that Katom adjoins the Taittireeya Brahmana (of the Krishna Yajur Veda) of the Katom branch with Sage Katan, the disciple of *Vaisambayana*, as *Guru* (teacher). Many researchers link it with either the Sama Veda or even the Atharva Veda. This text contains three parts, each part with three chapters named *Valli*. Prof. Max Mueller is of the view that this Upanishad originally had only one part with three *Valli* and that the subsequent parts were added later. Dr. Radhakrishnan endorsed this view. Sir Edwin Arnold translated this Upanishad into English with title 'The Secret of Death'. In this book, *Valli* is aptly translated as *Lotus stem*. If *Isavasyam* was the most favourite among the Upanishads for Gandhiji, Katom was the most favourite one for Swamy Vivekananda, who hailed it very often in superlative epithets like 'most poetic', 'most beautiful' etc.

The centre of attraction of this Upanishad is a popular story incorporated therein, with sublime artistic beauty, as a vehicle to convey an eternal truth, the message of the book. Though this tale appears in several other Indian literatures, the manner of presentation here is quite impressive so that the reader can grasp the message even without further explanations.

The main character in this story is a Brahmin boy who set out to have a research on the phenomenon of 'death'. The story goes on as follows:

One day, a Brahmin boy named Nachiketas was watching the performance of '*Sarvasvadanam*' (gifting of all assets to the poor – a religious obligation of a Brahmin) by his father. The boy was very much annoyed by the self-deception of his father in gifting the useless, old and barren cows. According to custom, in the last phase, children are also gifted to the *Rithwicks* (the priests performing sacrifices). The ancient Indian literatures show that there were sixteen types of *Rithwicks*. In his eagerness to know about his own future, Nachiketas put one question to his father. 'To which Rithwick are you intending to gift me?' The father failed to respond. When the boy repeated the question twice, the father hesitatingly answered 'I have decided to give you to *Mrityu* (death or Yama, the king of death). On this reply, the boy was very much upset. He pondered long enough on his future and finally decided to personally meet Yama and obtain clarifications. He went to Yama's residence. When he reached there, Yama was out of station. The purposeful and adamant Nachiketas patiently waited for three days in Yama's house without food. When Yama came on the fourth day, he compassionately asked the boy to seek three favours (boons). The boy obediently demanded three favours as below:

When I reach back home, my father should calmly and pleasantly accept me (The natural aspiration of a son coming back to his father after fleeing).

What is the way to reach that heaven free from agedness and deformities?

Will there remain a soul after the death of human beings?

Yama instantly granted the first and second boons. But, before granting the third boon, Yama wanted to ascertain the bonafides of the questioner. With this end in view, he urged Nachiketas to withdraw the third question on the assurance of granting him all means of pleasures in this life; longevity, power, gold, children, women, elephants, horses, cows etc. But, Nachiketas was not a fickle-minded boy; he had his own determination and purposefulness. Least tempted by the assurances of pleasures, he insisted on a proper answer to his question. Valli 2 to 5 contain the detailed answer.

After being convinced that Nachiketas was prudent enough to distinguish between the eternal and the non-eternal, Yama imparted that secret knowledge. The three points repeatedly elucidated by Yama were:

The real nature of the soul
The methods to attain that soul and
The Moksha or realisation of *Paramatma*, the supreme soul.

Yama started by referring to two distinct aims in human life, *Sreyas* and *Preyas*. Sreyas leads one through the path of eternal happiness while Preyas leads through the path of temporary worldly pleasures. The intelligent and courageous man chooses the path of *Sreyas*. The idiot chooses the path of *Preyas*. These correspond to the paths of *Vidya* (knowledge) and *Avidya* (absence of knowledge) respectively. Those who consider that there is nothing beyond this world or its pleasures can never free themselves from the cycles of the life-wheel. By arguments, we cannot determine as to what happens beyond this life. Here, Yama admits that he himself had not yet reached that stage. He, who through spiritual exercises (meditation, devotion, self control etc.) realises that invisible, hidden and eternal consciousness or force which exists only in the intellect, would be liberated from joy and sorrow. That force is beyond the past and the future, action and inaction and virtue and vices. We can call it *Om* (English syllable a, u, m). No glory to man is superior to the knowledge of the essence or meaning of 'Om'. The soul, which is the subject of 'Om', has neithei birth nor death. Even when the body dies, the soul exists.

Sun, stars, lightning, fire etc. have no light before that force or soul which illuminates everything. It is that force that creates the universe and moves everything. It is that force which enlightens spiritual consciousness. After detailed explanations, Yama advised Nachiketas to try to attain realisation of that force. Katopanishad has succeeded in stimulating the yearning to acquire that knowledge among the readers. The importance and reputation of this Upanishad rest on this quality.[7]

Prasnopanishad

Prasna (meaning 'problem' or 'question') is one among the three Upanishads (Prasna, Mundaka and Mandukya) adjoining the Atharvaveda Samhita. Prasna is in refined prose, supposed to have been written late, probably around 500 to 300 BC. Generally, almost all Upanishads follow the style of raising problems and offering solutions. The speciality noticed in this book is that the composition and contents fully justify the title. It contains six chapters, each chapter dealing with one question and its answer. No deviation from the set scheme is noticed anywhere. The questioners, who are free to put forth any question, are the six disciples of the Guru (teacher), the respondent. The identity of the questioners as revealed in the book are: (1) Sukesan, s/o Bharadwaj, (2) Sathyakama, s/o Shibi, (3) Suryapautra of Garga tribe, (4) Kausalya, s/o Aswala, (5) Bhargava of Vidarbha and (6) Kabadi, s/o Kritya. The teacher is a *Maharishi* (*Maha* means great and *Rishi* means a man of wisdom) named *Pippaladan* (who lives on Pippala-fruits) a polite and liberal-minded gentleman. The order of the questioners given above is seen reversed while asking questions, the last one raising the first question.

Question One by Kabadi:

From where do the living beings originate? (A direct and simple question on the genesis of the Universe)

Answer: The world of life originates from the command arising from the power of God's Will.

The Rishi, by referring to creation of *Prana* and *Rayi* representing *Purusa* and *Prakriti*, the consciousness and flesh respectively, the integration of which results in life, further elaborated this answer. This is further illustrated by comparison with the union of Day and Night and *Uttarayana* and *Dakshinayana* (the periods of Sun's travel to north and south – Tropic of Cancer and Capricon – and return to the equator).

Prana – Consciousness + *Jada* – Body or Flesh = Combination

Prana – Day + *Rayi* – Night = Combination

Prana – Uttarayana + *Rayi* – Dakshinayana = Combination

Qn. Two by Bhargava:

What are the forces sustaining the visible body? Among these forces, which is the important one?

Answer: The forces sustaining the body are sky, air, fire, water, earth, word, mind, Sun etc. But, all these forces are subordinate to *Prana*, the vital force. Prana governs entire movements in the body.

Qn. Three by Kausalya:

From where does this life force originate? How it comes into the body? How does it roam about independently? How does it forsake the body and go away?

Answer: *Prana* emanates from the Soul. It joins the body according to the conception of the mind just as the shadow of a body is joined to that body. The *Prana* puts all forces in the body in their respective positions and controls them. It travels through the different organs of the body, the sense organs, the flesh, the tissues, the muscles and others and controls the different functions of the body like the circulation system, the nervous system, system for expulsion of waste etc.

Qn. Four by Souryayana or Suryapoutra:

What all mental dispositions sleep in man or are awake in man? Who actually experience and enjoy the dreams? To what are they fixed?

Answer: When the Sun sets, all the rays of the Sun shrink and become one in the Sun. Similarly, when the mind sets down in deep sleep, all mental faculties shrink and merge in the mind and become one with the mind. In that situation, Prana and other forces control all the non-optional functions of the mind. In sleep, the Jeevatma (the soul of life) experiences joy and sorrow. All other forces in human body fly for safety to the soul like the birds flying in the evening for shelter and safety to their abode or nest on the tree. One, who knows, where the essence of the omnipresent *Jeevatma* dissolves itself, knows everything and gets through everything.

Qn. Five by Satyakama:

What is the world attained by one who meditates on 'Om' without interruption?

Answer: As 'Om' is the symbol or reflection of Brahman, he who meditates on 'Om' will attain *Brahmapadom* (Salvation). We need not meditate on each of the syllables of 'Om' – a, u, m – or the forces of nature in the universe. Instead, we must meditate on the 'Comprehensive Force' – the Brahman – the 'Om'.

Qn. Six by Sukesan:

Please explain the essence of Soul?

Answer: The Soul, the consciousness or the Supreme Force, which is the source of all the sixteen forces of the body including *Prana,* exists in the interior of the body. Just like the river flowing to the sea merges in the sea losing its separate identity, the forces of the body, proceed to the supreme soul, merge in that soul and become one with it.

Thus, Pippiladan, by his dramatic presentation, leads the inquisitive boys through the external and visible matter in the Universe to that Supreme Force, the *Paramatma*, the source and destination of the human soul.[8]

Mundakopanishad

The word '*Mundaka*', meaning 'to shave' or 'to cleanse' is the title of the last part of the *Atharva Veda Samhita*. This Upanishad is generally meant for the *Mundakas*, who are cleansed or free from dirt, errors and ignorance – the ascetics. But, this Upanishad is addressed to the *Grihasthyas* (family men), the questioner himself being a *Grihasthya* who aspires and prepares himself for the next stage of *Vanaprastha*. It adjoins the Saunaka branch of the *Atharva Veda*, but devoid of the stigma attached to the *Atharva Veda*. This text has three chapters, all titled Mundaka, with two *Khandas* (sections) each. As we have seen, three Upanishads, *Prasna, Mundaka* and *Mandukya* adjoin the *Atharva Veda*. Each one is addressed to those in a particular stage in the hierarchical order of *Asramas*, Prasna to the *Brahmacharins*, Mundaka to the *Grihasthyas* and Mandukya to the *Sannyasins* (ascetics). Out of these three Atharvopanishads, the Mundaka alone is the one referred to in the Brahmasutra. Deussen is of the opinion that Mundaka is older than the 'Prasna' and the 'Mandukya'. He puts the period of origin of this, one among the prominent Upanishads, as around the 7th century BC.

The teaching of this Upanishad is contained in the response of Amgirus, the first among the *Agnidevas* (the gods of fire) to a question raised by a family man named Saunaka.

Question: What is the knowledge required for the cognition (understanding) of all that we come across in this world?

The answer to this question is the topic dealt with in all Upanishads. Amgirus begins his answer with the classification of knowledge into two, *Paravidya* and *Aparavidya;* in other words *Vidya* and *Avidya*. *Paravidya* is transcendental knowledge – the knowledge going beyond the limits of human knowledge, experience and reason leading to the realisation of the Ultimate. *Aparavidya* is Vidya other than Paravidya – often confined to the linguistics, phonetics, sound etc. without going deep into the substance or origin. At the end of Aparavidya, one reaches the stage of detachment, continence, disgust etc., and proceeds to *Paravidya*. Thus Aparavidya complements Paravidya.

In the second Mundaka, the form and character of the Brahman, the subject of *Paravidya* are described. Various imaginations emanate from *Brahman the word* and dissolve in itself just like the sparks arising from the fire. This is above the *Prana* and mind, pure and holy and beyond comprehension by all. It is the inner soul of all creations. Fire, Sun, Moon, Stars etc. are its members. The world is its heart and the earth is its leg. Vedas, gods, humans, birds, senses, time and all emanate from that majestic Force. Rivers, oceans, mountains and grains flow from it.

The third Mundaka explains the relation between *Jeevatma*, the soul of life and *Paramatma*, the supreme soul. Here, Amgirus presents a thought-provoking story, which later inspired many poets in this country. Our attention is drawn to a scene of two birds, close companions, sitting on a tree. While one among the birds is eating a fruit, the other bird is simply gazing at it. Allegorically, the tree is the human body and the fruit is the product of past action (*Karma*). The bird eating the fruit represents the *Jeevatma* experiencing the fruits of Karma and the gazing bird represents the *Paramatma*, the supreme Soul, silently watching everything. If the self-knowledge dormant in the heart and the ultimate knowledge independently roaming everywhere outside are the same, why the contradiction of the Jeevatma alone suffering within the constraints of the *Karma*. Here, there is a contradiction, an inescapable contradiction. This dependence or servitude of the *Jeevatma* can end only with the realisation of the Paramatma. Truth, meditation, knowledge and chastity are the instruments to achieve this realisation.

Sathyamēva Jayathe Nānrtham
Sathyena Panthā Vithātho Dēvayānah:

Meaning: Truth ever wins. Untruth never wins.

(The first two words in the first line of this verse is the inscription at the foot of the National Emblem of the Indian Republic.)

The chivalrous and the bold ones who are free from desires achieve the realisation (*Sarvameva Avisanthi*) and get themselves once for all liberated. This is *Sannyasayoga* (asceticism) – the message of the Mundakyopanishad.[9]

Mandukyopanishad

Mandukyopanishad, deriving its name from its author Mandukya, is the smallest among the Upanishads with only twelve incantations in prose. Researchers are of the view that this Upanishad adjoining the *Atharva Veda* is later in origin than the other two Atharvopanishads; its period is estimated as around 400 BC. The subject dealt with in the limited number of incantations in this Upanishad is incomprehensible to the average reader. Only those who possess appreciable knowledge in various other sciences would be in a position to grasp the ideas envisaged in this text. It is said that an aspirant to

Moksha (Salvation) needs only *Mandukyopanishad*. (*Mandukyamekamevalam Mumukkunam Vimukhthaye*). In order to make the ideas in this Upanishad discernible and decipherable, Gaudapada Acharya, the grand great teacher of Sankaracharya also has written a commentary in which he has commented this book as *Sarva Vedanta Sarishtam* (the ultimate essence of the entire Vedanta). All these comments point to the prominence of this small Upanishad.

A speciality of this Upanishad is that it analysed comprehensively the interior state of man and projected each part with its characteristics, before the world. The Western Science has gone beyond the conscious mind of man only with the detection of the subconscious mind by Sigmund Freud, the Austrian Psychologist who developed the systems of Psychoanalysis and Psychotherapy in the latter half of the 19th century. But Rishi Mandukya has gone deep into the role of the human mind, even 2400 years before the findings of Freud. While Freud and his disciples confined their research on two states of mind, Mandukya found four states in the human mind and examined their inter-relationship and the human soul. From this soul, the Rishi proceeded to 'Om' and therefrom to 'Brahma' and concluded on the great Truth – the tenet *Ayamatma Brahma* (whatever we find is Brahma – the human soul).

Mandukya's four States of Mind

(i) Jagrath

Jagrath is the waken state of the mind, that mind which is prepared consciously to receive experiences from outside the mind. This conscious mind comprehends, through the external senses, the experiences from the surrounding universe. The Rishi symbolically calls it '*Viswanaran*'.

(ii) Swapna

Swapna is the second state of the human mind that is sleeping. It is called *Anthaprajna*. This precise mind works behind the conscious mind. This state of the mind experiences the subjects that are inherent in the mind and those directed or ordered by the mind itself. Rishi symbolically calls it *Thyjasan*.

(iii) Sushupti

Sushupti is the innermost state of the mind free from desires or senses or dreams. The sense of diversities created by the mind in the above mentioned two states are absent in this state. Here, knowledge is spread and everything is one like the experience we feel in darkness (*Ekeebhuta* – all elements in one). At this stage, the Soul goes high, beyond all elements in the universe and enjoys happiness. Rishi calls it '*Anandbhuk*' (consumer of bliss). As this condition being not fixed permanently, the soul enjoys the realisation of *Brahma* only tentatively. But being ravishingly delighted, it comes back to the original position. The spiritual consciousness that comes at this state is the power of God, the origin as well as the destination of everything. Though full realisation does not occur, the Rishi symbolically calls it *prajnan*.

(iv) Thurian

The word 'Thurian' is not a name. The Rishi has not named it. 'Thurian' is supposed to be a derivative of the Sanskrit word 'Chathuriyam' (Chathuriyam minus the syllable 'Cha' meaning 'the fourth' or 'the quadrant'). It is a state of the mind beyond consciousness. Actually, it is spread in all the three states referred to above, which through evolution, becomes one with them. Even though it is said to be the fourth, it is really 'Full Consciousness' – Brahma – Atma, the silent 'Om' (*Amathra*) the Supreme Being.

(Here, some incomprehensibility is there.)

For easy understanding, these different states of the mind are given below in a tabular form.[10]

1. *Jagrath*	– It is the waken state of the mind, conscious, comprehends and experiences. (*Virat*, the Universal Body)	*Viswanaran* (Virat) 'A' (The first syllable of 'Om')
2. *Swapna*	– the dreaming state of the mind. Precise	*Thyjasan* 'U' (The second syllable of 'Om')

3. *Sushupti* –	the sleeping state of the mind. No desire or dream Or senses	*Prajnan* 'M' (The last syllable of 'Om')
4. *Thureeyam* –	the fourth state. No state, No name. Full consciousness (*Brahma*)	*Thureeyan* (A+U+M = 'Om')

When *Jagrath, Swapna* and *Sushupti* are states of mind, *Thureeyam* is not a state of mind and it has no name. It becomes one with the other states. Thus, Universe, Man and Brahma are not separate entities. It is Existence + Knowledge + Bliss (*Sat-chit-ananda*). It is Reality, first with no second – the Infinite – the intrinsic power that manifests itself as *Jagat* (Universe) and *Jiva* (Life) Universe and Man. The Reality alone exists. It is Brahma, the soul. The sentence sublime of Mandukyopanishad is *Ayamatma Brahma* (whatever we find is Brahma-the human soul).[11] It is *Saguna Brahma* (Conditioned Reality) in its kinetic state and *Nirguna Brahma* (Absolute Reality) in its static state. The individual soul dissolves itself in the Absolute. This is emancipation according to the *Advaita* (non-dualism) philosophy. The Upanishad, thus, upholds the *Advaita* theory that God, Universe and Man are intrinsic, indivisible and non-dualistic.

As such, whatever we see or hear or feel or experience is Brahma and Brahma alone. There is nothing other than Brahma. 'Om', 'Paramatma', 'Reality', 'Absolute', 'Consciousness' etc. are synonyms of Absolute Reality. Whether static or dynamic, whatever is seen is Brahma, Human soul is Brahma – *Ayamatma Brahma*. This is the message of *Mandukyopanishad*.

Taittiriyopanishad

The *Yajur Veda Samhita* has two branches with separate texts, known as the Taittiriya branch and the Vajasanei branch. Among them, Taittiriya is the first, but Vajasanei is the prominent one. The *Vishnupurana* and the *Mahabharata* contain descriptions on the genesis of the *Yajurveda*. Vaisambayana, who taught his disciples the *Yajurveda*, one day committed a *Brahmahatya* sin (mortal sin) by accidentally killing his own nephew. He appealed to his disciples to practise penance by observing fast for the absolution of his sin. Yajnavalkya, who was a brilliant and beloved disciple of the teacher, in reply, told the teacher that he himself could do penance and obtain absolution; without the help of other students. This haughty behaviour on the part of Yajnavalkya enraged the Guru, who, in a fit of anger, dismissed Yajnavalkya and asked him to leave the *Gurukula* (school) instantly after forsaking whatever he learnt. Yajnavalkya complied with the direction of the teacher, vomited the *Vidya* (knowledge) he learnt and went away. The other students, assuming the form of *Taittiri* (a bird or a red buffalo) consumed the *Vidya* vomited by Yajnavalkya and completed the text of the Yajur Veda known as the Krishna Yajur or Black Yajur Veda.

Yajnavalkya practised *Tapas* (penance – self-exhaustive asceticism) before the Sun god, by way of penance. The Sun, pleased by the Tapas, appeared before Yajnavalkya in the form of a horse (*Vaji*) and replenished whatever Vidya was lost; on regaining his Vidya, Yajnavalkya prepared another text of the Yajurveda known as the Sukla Yajur Veda (also called white). This branch being originated from *Vaji* is known as the Vajasanei branch and the former one originated from *Taittiri*, is known as the Taittiriya Branch.

Taittiriyopanishad is not a separate book, but chapters 7, 8 and 9 of a comprehensive text containing Taittiriya Brahmana, Taittiriyaranyaka and the Upanishad. This Upanishad, supposed to have originated around 600 BC, has three sections titled *Valli; Siksha Valli, Brahmananda Valli* and *Bhrugu Valli* containing 12, 9 and 10 lessons respectively. *Siksha* is the first among the vedangas dealing with phonetics, pronunciation, accent etc. *'Brahma'* means God and *'Ananda'* means bliss or happiness *Brahmananda* means eternal happiness attained by the realisation of Brahma. *Bhrugu* is the name of a boy, son of Varuna, inquisitive to acquire spiritual knowledge (*Atmajnana*) Valli literally means creeper, precisely the stem of a creeper. Here, it represents a part or section or branch.

Siksha Valli

As we have seen, Siksha deals with phonetics, sound etc. The students are taught the methods of reading and learning.

Reading ought to be audible, attractive, sweet and meaning decipherable from the tone and tenor, pronunciation, sound, measure, pitch etc. Here, the Guru is preparing the disciples to handle serious and mysterious subjects like *Atmajnana* and realisation of Brahma in the succeeding *Vallis*. The first lesson in this Valli begins with prayer to *Mitra, Varuna* and *Indra* (three gods) for removal of obstructions in the study. The necessity of mind-control through truth, asceticism, self-restraint, mortification etc. is being stressed. Efforts are also being made to strengthen the intellect through meditation of 'Om'. Before conclusion, some instructions on morality and ethics are imparted. A life based on Truth, Dharma and Purity during study and teaching of Vedas was emphasised.

Sathyam Vada; Dharmam Chara (Valli 1:11) meaning 'Always speak truth; never deviate from Dharma' were prescribed as watchwords in life. Another instruction given was

> *Mathru Devo Bhava : Pithru Devo Bhava:*
> *Acharya Devo Bhava : Athithi Devo Bhava:*
>
> (Valli : 1:11)
>
> *Meaning*: Worship the mother like a goddess: Serve the father like god: Revere the teacher like god: receive and serve guests like god: The First Valli ends with thanksgiving to the gods. Viewed altogether, Siksha Valli is a preparatory exercise for the students; a moral, ethical and spiritual preparation.

Brahmananda Valli

If the Siksha Valli was one concerning preparation and *Upasana* (worship), the succeeding Brahmananda Valli deals with *Brahmajnana* (knowledge of Brahma). The sum and substance of Brahmananda Valli is *Brahma Vidapnothi Param* (Valli: 2:1). Meaning: 'He who knows Brahma attains the most noble state of bliss.' Then, a definition of Brahma is given. *Sathyam Jnanamanantham Brahma* (Valli: 2:1). Brahma is Truth, knowledge and bliss. There is nothing other than Brahma. This is the foundation of human life. To those who analyse life and think over it, this principle comes to light removing the veil covering it. The areas that the human life passes through and interacts are food, prana, mind, wisdom and happiness. These are all, technically speaking, internal cells of human life. After passing through these cells, the human life reaches a stage, the stage of enjoyment of Brahma. This stage is beyond explanation. Word and mind cannot reach there. The most superior happiness in this world is only a neglible part of this eternal bliss.

Anandom Brahmano Vidwan (Valli: 2:9)

He who knows about this *Brahmananda* (the eternal bliss by realisation of Brahma) has no fears. He is not concerned with the distinction between virtues and vices. He looks at them as Soul and appeases it.

Bhrugu Valli

In the previous Valli, the question 'What is Brahma?' was answered. In this Valli, the methods or paths to realise the Brahma are explained. Bhrugu, a boy inquisitive to learn *Brahmavidya* (knowledge of Brahma) approached his father Varuna seeking *Atmavidya* (spiritual knowledge) Bhrugu puts a question to his father *Adhihi Bhagavo Brahmethi* O! Bhagavan; Please advise on Brahma? Varuna is a proficient teacher. Instead of directly answering the question, he posed a counter question to the boy. He asked Bhrugu to seek whether Brahma could be found among the principles underlying food, eyes, prana, ears, mind, word etc. which are susceptible to the human sense organs and thought. In order to help the boy, Varuna provided him with a clue defining Brahma. That from which all living beings originate, that on which those beings sustain in life and that in which all beings enter and dissolve at the end, that is Brahma. The boy failed to find out a correct answer. Whenever he failed, Varuna directed the boy to meditate and try again. After a series of intermittent meditations he found out the correct answer. 'All elements emerge from bliss, live on bliss and at the end dissolve in bliss. Brahma is that bliss.' Varuna accepted his finding and congratulated him. One who realises the Ultimate in the form of Bliss (*Anandarupa*) need not hate or deny temporal life. One who is created on the foundation of this Bliss would become wealthy and famous in this world as well.

In human life, there are five circles or zones. Whatever zones subsequently come should endeavour to complement the existing ones rather than bypassing them. This is the way to achieve comprehensive bliss. The Taittitiriyopanishad conveys this message.[12]

Aitareyopanishad

Aitareyopanishad adjoining the *Rig Veda* is considered one of the oldest Upanishads, presumed to have been written between 800 and 700 BC. The Rig Veda has two Brahmanas. One among them is Aitareya Brahmana. Though Aranyakas are generally linked with Brahmanas, the *Aitareyaranyaka* is not linked with any Brahmana. This independent Aranyaka has five sections, each titled Aranyaka. Chapters 4 to 7 of the second Aranyaka are treated as the *Aitareyopanishad.* Mahidasa Aitareyan, the son of a low caste woman named Ithara, who later became a Rishi with the blessings of *Bhoomi Devi* (Goddess earth) is supposed to be the author of both Aitareya Brahmana and *Aitareyaranyaka.* A reference in Chandogyopanishad (III: 16:7) shows that Mahidasa lived in Kurupanchala kingdom upto the age of 116.

The main theme dealt with in this Upanishad is *Atmajnana* (self-knowledge). The *Mahavakyam* (cardinal message) of *Rig Veda* is *Pranjnanam Brahman* (consciousness is God). This idea is further developed and explained in this Upanishad. One of the biggest problems confronted by man is the attainment of *Mukti* (Liberation) without bypassing or negating altogether this mundane world in day-to-day life. How can one's attitude towards this bondage in life be transformed into one that is conducive to facilitate liberation or salvation? Aitareyopanishad deals with a smooth solution to this problem. According to this Upanishad, the reason for fear and fear-born difficulties in this world is our own perverted vision – the vision of dualism: *Dwidiyath vya Bhayam Bhavathi.* Man can reach the stage of fearlessness only by overcoming the dualist vision of (i) the diversities known under different names in this universe, and (ii) our own self, which is the real form of eternal truth. Gold is the shining fraction of the ornaments, which tempt human beings under different names in this universe. Similarly, Atma is that which shines all elements like consumer, the object of consumption and the instruments of consumption in this world.

This small Upanishad begins with *Atmasabda* (the sound of 'Om') *Atmava Ithameka Eva Agra Asith*. This universe is the real *Atmaswaroopa* (form of the Soul). The oneness, non-dualism and the fundamentality of *Atma* (soul) are expressed here. This chapter contains several subjects from creation of universe to the philosophical principles leading to Brahma. Man is a fine creation *Purusho Vava Sukrutham*. According to Western science also, man is the crown of creations.

The second chapter begins with a warning to pregnant women to go out. After the exit of women, a description of pregnancy and childbirth is given. Man is engaged in the reproduction and generations till the realisation of the knowledge of soul. Man has three births, the first one within the womb of the mother, the second birth in childhood and the third birth on becoming a father. The story of Vamadeva who achieved realisation in the womb of the mother is cited here. After these explanations the pregnant women who were kept out were called in and the author Rishi proceeded to the third chapter.[13]

The third chapter is the concluding chapter. This begins with a question as to whether the soul we worship is *Parabrahma* or *Aparabrahma*. *Parabrahma* is formless and static. It is called *Nirgunabrahma*. *Aparabrahma* with form is dynamic. It is *Saguna Brahma*. The inactive *Atma,* behind the mind, intellect and senses, is the *Satchitananda*, which is the real form of the Atma. It is this Atma we worship.

All universal and mental faculties and matter are manifestations of *Pranjnana* (consciousness). This consciousness is Brahma. Thus *Pranjnanam Brahman.*[14]

The Upanishad concludes with the declaration that realisation of Brahma results in immortality.

Brihadaranyakopanishad

As we have already seen, Vedas are divided into four groups, the Samhitas, the Brahmanas, the Aranyakas and the Upanishads. Each group is meant for people in a particular stage (*Asrama*) in life. Samhitas are incantations for study in *Gurukulas* (residential open-air schools) by students, under vows of chastity and strict restrictions on conduct and discipline in life, known as *Brahmacharins*. Brahmanas contain liturgy and instructions on sacrifices and rituals to propitiate the gods to be performed by family men known as *Grihasthas*. Aranyakas are meant for worship or adoration or meditation during the life of continence and detachment in forests known as *Vanaprastha* Upanishads are for advanced studies in philosophy, theology etc. in the last stage known as *Sannyasa*.

Brihadaranyakopanishad is, as the title justifiably reveals, *Aranyaka* combined with *Upanishad* and *brihat* (big) not only in volume or size but also in age, rich contents, variety, ideology, language, presentation etc. This Upanishad is bigger in size than all the eight Upanishads (excluding Chandogya) we have dealt with in this chapter. It adjoins the *Sathapatha* Brahmana of the *Vajasanei* branch of the Sukla Yajur Veda with two distinct divisions based on two schools of thought, *Maadhyannina* division with 14 subdivisions and *Kanva* division with 17 subdivisions. In both divisions, the last subdivision is the *Aranyaka*. The period of origin is estimated as near about 800 BC. The chapters are titled '*Brahmana*'. Sankaracharya's commentary is for the Kanva division. This Upanishad contains six chapters divided into 47 Brahmanas. These chapters are classified under three khandas, each Khanda having two chapters. The first Khanda (chapters I and II) is *Madhukhanda,* the second Khanda (chapters III and IV) is *Munikhanda* or *Yajnavalkya Khanda* and the third Khanda (chapters V and VI) is *Khila Khanda*, each with separate characteristics; advice, logical arguments and worship respectively.

Two defects pointed out in this Upanishad by Western philosophers are:

(i) The incomprehensibility due to confusingly complicated language and

(ii) The unbearable mixing up of ritualism in plenty.

Chapter I has six *Brahmanas*. The first and the second *Brahmanas* contain elaborate descriptions of a hypothetical *Aswameda* (a horse sacrifice) projecting *Prajapati* (one among the 21 Prajapatis created by Brahmav, the Creator to assist him in the creation of the universe) as the sacrificial horse and the *Devas* (gods) as the members of the body of the horse. In the meticulous descriptions, we notice the marvellous flight of imagination of the Rishi. The third Brahmana describes the enmity between the *Devas* (gods) and the *Asuras* (wicked men) and the important role of *Prana* (vital life). The invocation prayer "*Asatho ma Sathgamaya*" (Briha: 1:3:28) appears in this Brahmana. (The full stanza is given elsewhere with meaning.)

The fifth Brahmana deals with seven items of *Anna* (food) and its distribution among the Devas, cows and other living beings and the retention of the remaining three (word, mind and prana) by Prajapati, being the basis of the universe. The sixth *Brahmana* exhorts to overcome divisiveness due to name (*Nama*), form (*Rupa*) and action (*Karma*) in the universe and to attain realisation by the worship of Atma. Chapter II also contains six *Brahmanas*. In the first *Brahmana* appears a meeting between one Balaki, a pseudo-scholar and Janaka, a real scholar. On finding that whatever Balaki spoke was *Aparavidya* (knowledge other than Brahma Vidya) Janaka took the initiative to teach Balaki on *Brahma Vidya* (knowledge of Brahman). Here Janaka presents a new definition of Brahma *Sathysya Sathya* (the Truth of all Truth) and pointed out that the universe is *Sathya*, being the expression of the 'Ultimate Truth'. The second Brahmana exhorts to worship *Prana* (the Vital Life) supposing it as a calf. The third Brahmana advises to realise Brahma, the *Sathysya Sathya* having two natures, the *Saguna Brahman* (the active or dynamic Brahma) and *Nirguna Brahman* (inactive or static Brahma). Yajnavalkya, the eternal light of Vedic philosophy, appears in the fourth *Brahmana* in a conversation with his two wives, Mithreyi and Karthiyayani. When Yajnavalkya expressed his intention to opt for an ascetic life after distributing his temporal assets among his wives, Mithreyi, one of the wives, posed a question as to whether those worldly wealth would bring immortality to her. When the answer of Yajnavalkya was in the negative, Mitreyi rejected the offer of wealth and sought to teach her on the ways to attain immortality. Yajnavalkya presented before her an eternal truth *Atmanasthu kamaya sarvam priyam bhavathi*. The basis of all love is 'I', the soul that is the *Paramaprema* (Ultimate Love). Therefore, he advised Mitreyi to try to attain realisation of that soul through 'hearing' (*Sravana*), 'thinking' (*Manana*) and 'meditation' (*Nididhyasana*). The fifth Brahmana confirms that *Jeevatma* (the soul of life) and *Paramatma* (the supreme soul) are one and the same. The sixth Brahmana is only a narration of the genealogy of the teachers and students beginning from Brahmav, the Creator.

Chapters III and IV known as Munikhanda contain the essence of the Upanishad. The spiritual truths enunciated in the preceding chapters are further explained here with logical arguments and confirmed. Yajnavalkya stood as the towering personality in the discussions answering authoritatively all questions with supporting logic.

Chapter III contains nine Brahmanas. The first Brahmana begins with the narration of an episode dealing with King Janaka's performance of a sacrifice involving the distribution of a lot of gifts. The King convened a meeting of the *Bramishtas* (eminent scholars in philosophy) for a philosophical discourse. In the meeting, the King announced that the greatest *Brahmishta* among them would be awarded 1000 cows decorated with gold ornaments. When no *Brahmishta* came forward claiming the gift, Yajnavalkya asked his disciples to lead the cows to his *Ashrama* (Monastery). Several *Brahmishtas* present there questioned the action of Yajnavalkya. In reply, Yajnavalkya politely stated that he longed to have the cows. There ensued a series of questions to test the genuineness of Yajnavalkya's claim. Samples of the questions asked by Janaka are given below for academic interest.

Question: Janaka received advice from the Acharayas to worship 'Word', 'Prana', 'Eyes', 'Mind', 'Heart' and 'Ears' as Brahma. He asked whether the advice is right.

Yajnavalkya replied: "These are only parts of Brahma, worship of parts is insufficient."

Chapter III contains similar other questions and the answers of Yajnavalkya to those extempore questions.

Sakalya asked a mischievous question. How many *Devas* (gods) are there? In reply, Yajnavalkya explained the principles underlying the worship of many gods. He stated that the formless, one and indivisible Nirguna Brahma assumes different names and forms in the state of Saguna Brahma. Hence the worship of many gods – the different forms and names of the sole Brahma. *Ekam Sad Vipra Bahuda Vadandi*. Several other questions and subsidiary questions raised by the *Brahmishtas* were convincingly answered by Yajnavalkya in Chapter III.

Chapter IV has six Brahmanas. In this chapter, we find a long dialogue in the form of a question-answer session on philosophical issues. King Janaka raised many questions and subsidiary questions arising from the answers.

Yajnavalkya convincingly answered them as given below:

Question: What is the light that radiates or illuminates in *Purusa*?

Answer: It is the Sun that illuminates the light in Purusa.

Question: When the Sun sets, what radiates the light?

Answer: When the Sun sets, the moon radiates the light.

Question: When the Sun and Moon are absent, what radiates the light?

Answer: In the absence of Sun and Moon, the 'Fire' radiates the light.

Question: When the Sun, the Moon and the Fire are absent, what radiates the light?

Answer: When the Sun, the Moon and the Fire are absent, the 'Word' radiates the light.

Question: When the Sun, the Moon, the Fire and the Word are absent, what radiates the light?

Answer: When the other lights are absent, the *Atma* (the soul) in the body radiates the light.

Question: What is this *Atma*?

Answer: The Purusa, which radiates light in the senses and intellect, is the *Atma*.

Only the gist of the answers is given above due to constraints of space. In fact, Yajnavalkya explained the premises leading to his conclusions. Janaka conceded all these answers as correct. The series of questions culminated in the movements of Atma and transmigration of souls (*karmasamsar*). To a question as to where the Atma goes when it leaves the body, Yajnavalkya explained the different states of the mind, *Jagrath, Swapna, Sushupti* etc. and finally concluded that the *Atma* (soul) goes from one body to another body just as it travels from 'Swapna' state to 'Jagrath' state. About rebirth, Yajnavalkya explained that rebirth is not required for one who is free from desires. Here, the Atma finds refuge in Brahma *Abhayam vy Brahma*.

The fifth Brahmana is a repetition of the fourth Brahmana of Chapter II. The sixth Brahmana deals with genealogy of the Yajnavalkya Khanda.

Chapters V and VI come under *Khila Khanda*. They are only annexures to the Upanishad. No spiritual matters are discussed there. Different modes of worship, prayer at the time of death etc. are prescribed in Chapter V; Chapter VI has six Brahmanas. The importance of *Prana*, the arguments between Swetaketu and Pravahanan, the King of Kurupanchala, *Sreemanthom* prescribing karma for prosperity in life, *Putramanthom* prescribed for *grihasthas* (family men) for childbirth, worship, genealogy, etc. are the subjects dealt with in this chapter.

A materialist view of this Upanishad by V. Brodov in his book *Indian Philosophy in Modern Times* is given below for academic information.

There are different views of Brahman inherent in the text of this Upanishad. In one of the fragments (I, 6) the concept of Brahman is used to denote the substantial basis of the separate groups of homogeneous phenomena: speech is the Brahman of all the names (for "it upholds the names"); eyesight is the Brahman of all the forms (for "it upholds all the forms"); atman is the Brahman of all works (for "it upholds all works"). Another fragment (II, 3) ascribes to Brahman two principal forms of existence *sat* and *tya*. *Sat* is the material or bodily being; it is motionless, inert, transient and mortal. *Tya* is the immaterial being; it is eternally in motion and immortal.

In the main body of the texts (the teachings of the wise man named Yajnavalkya), Brahman is described as the universal common basis (substance) of all that is. Everything proceeds from Brahman, everything returns to Brahman. Brahman has different properties: it has eyesight, sense of touch, hearing, mind and knowing. However, when it is in a purely Brahmanic state ("one without another"), it does not and cannot manifest any of these properties. As for many properties to manifest itself, it is necessary that "another" should exist, that is, some object relative to which this property may be manifested (IV, 3, 31). Yajnavalkya believes this division of that which is into the "one" and "another" to be only possible in this earthly world.

The Brihadaranyaka Upanishad reflects tendencies both towards objective and subjective idealism and towards materialism. Yajnavalkya's teaching contains objective-idealist elements, whereas the fragment "on the Sources of Names, Forms and Works" (I, 6) shows rudiments of subjective-idealism (the individual *atman* as the source of works). The author of the fragment "Water as the Primary Source" (V, 5) takes a materialist view of the basis of all that is.

Epistemologically, of considerable interest is the fragment "Thought, Speech, Breath" (I, 5, 3). The connection between the senses and reasoning is discussed here. There is no sensation without mind ("a person sees with the mind, hears with the mind").[15]

Brihadaranyakopanishad stands above other Upanishads in leading the human mind involved in *Karma* in this world to the peaks of spiritual knowledge enabling one to attain realisation of the eternal bliss.

Chandogyopanishad

Chandogyopanishad, comprising the last eight chapters of the Chandogya *Brahmana* adjoining the Sama Veda, is one among the ancient Upanishads.

The word 'Chandogya' is derived from 'Chandogan' meaning the singer of Sama songs loudly in a special rhythmic style. Researchers assess the period of origin of this Upanishad as around 800 BC. Badarayana, the author of *Brahmasutra* has included 12 quotations from this Upanishad in the Sutra. Gaudapada referred to this Upanishad 809 times, according to Deussen. Sri Sankara's commentary is the oldest among the various commentaries of this Upanishad. All these underline the glory of this Upanishad in the vast granary of Vedic literature.

Chandogyopanishad stands unique in the family of Upanishads on many counts. It enjoins the rich heritage of the Sama tradition.

Compared to the *Mahavakyas* (cardinal messages) of other Vedas – *Prajnanam Brahma*, *Aham Brahmasmi and Ayamatma Brahma* – this Upanishad has coined the most popular, precise, profound and comprehensive *Mahavakya, Tatvamasi*. The word '*Tatvamasi*' is the composite of three Sanskrit syllables, *Tat, Tvam* and *Asi* meaning 'that', 'thou' and 'is' respectively *Tat* denotes something outside and *Tvam* denotes something inside. The most apt translation is 'That thou art'. This *Mahavakya* has influenced and still influences the cultural, moral and religious ethos of the Indians, ancient and modern. Swamy Vivekananda described *Tatvamasi* as the fulfilment of India's spiritual knowledge. Love and compassion, the foundations of the morality of the Indians are contained in *Tatvamasi*, Swamy added.

This Upanishad deals with nearly 135 topics, some of which stimulated the religious and philosophical growth of India. These multifarious subjects are really informative and at the same time provide the Indians with a lot of insight into the ancient history, culture, civilization, social structure, law, geography, education, originality of Indian thought etc. in that remote past. The real spiritual lessons of this Upanishad appear only in two out of the eight chapters – chapter VI with 16 *khandas* and chapter VII with 26 *khandas*.

The poetry in the *Sama Veda* is musical, sublime and inspirational. Seldom can we find in other Vedic literature such poetic beauty of rhythm, metre, measure, lucidity and admirable melody. It is, therefore, widely believed by the Hindus that listening to the Sama songs with devotion, even without understanding the meaning, is an enriching virtue.

In the *Bhagavad Gita* (Lord's song) Lord Krishna introduced himself as the 'Sama' among the Vedas

Vedānām Sāmavedō'smi
Devānām'smi Vāsavah
Indriānam manas ća'smi
Bhutānām'smi ćētanā! (B.G. X-22)

Meaning: I am the Sama among the Vedas, Vasava among the devas (gods), the mind among the senses and consciousness among living beings.

A certificate from the highest dignitary confirms the uniqueness and glory of the Sama.

Now, let us proceed to the Chapters. In the preceding Brahmana (Chapters I and II) the subject dealt with was the liturgy of the Sama sacrifice. The succeeding upanishadic chapters handle a deep and rather incomprehensible subject *Brahmajnana* and *Atmajnana*. The Rishi was fully conscious of the difficulty in the abrupt transition from a simple subject to a complex and serious theme requiring keen attention and intellectual and mental applications. Therefore, in order to bring about a conducive and receptive mood, chapter I begins with an exhortation to meditate on *Udgeetha*, the loud chanting of '*OM*'

Omithi ethadaksharam Udgeetham Upaseetha
Omithi hyudgayatee Thasyopa Vyakhyanam

Meaning: Meditate on the syllable 'OM' famous as Udgeetham. The recitations of the Vedas are generally begun with the syllable 'Om'. It is its explanation that follows.

Many episodes emphasising the glory in the meditation of 'Om' are given here. The incidents of Devas defeating the Asuras by worshipping 'Om' and Ushasthi becoming rich by emphasising the necessity of adoration of 'Om' have been cited. It is further explained that *Udgeetha* is *Pranava* and *Pranava* is *Udgeetha*. Sama is also explained as *Sa* meaning stars and *Ma* meaning moon, together becoming *Sama* and *Sa* meaning the 'Word' and *ma* meaning 'Prana', together becoming *Sama*. Chapter II elaborates the various methods of worship already mentioned in the Sama Veda. The intermingling references to sacrificial paraphernalia in this Chapter may taste sour in sweetness, at least for few.

Chapter III deals with the worship of Sun, which gives vision and light to the entire world. The prominence of the Sun is presented metaphorically with beauty and imagination. The Sun is divine honey (*Devamadu*), sky is hanging honeycomb, the Rig Veda the flowers, the sunrays the eggs and the verses are the bees. Even in the midst of these imaginations, the author guards against the loss of the basic subject in oblivion. He reminds:

> *Sarvam Kwalidom Brahma,*
> *Thajjalanithi Santha Upaseetha* (3:14:1)
>
> *Meaning*: Everything is born in Brahma, exists in Brahma and dissolves in Brahma. Worship the Brahma in peace, without love or hate.
>
> The Chapter concludes with two statements of facts.
>
> *Purusha vava yajna sthasya* (3:16:1)
> (Man himself is his sacrifice)
>
> *Adityo Brahmetya desa* (3:19:1)
> (The Sun is Brahma)

Chapter IV pinpoints the worship of Brahma in the form of *Vayu* (air) and *Prana* (Life or soul). In order to hail the worship of Brahma, the examples of Rykian, Sathyakama and Upakosala are narrated.

King Janasruthi, on hearing about the fame of Rykian, a Brahmin scholar in *Brahmajnana*, wished to learn from him. The King identified Rykian, an uncouth fellow, waiting beneath a bullock cart to push the cart to ease the burden of the bullocks and scratching the itching scabies on his body. The King learnt from Rykian *Upasanavidya* (knowledge of worshipping Brahma) and gave him in return a lot of wealth and even the King's daughter in marriage.

Sathyakama, the son of a maid named Jabala, approached Guru (teacher) Haridruma for learning. The Guru enquired about his tribe. Not knowing the answer, he asked his mother. Jabala replied that she was ignorant of his fatherhood as she worked in many houses in that period. Sathyakama came back and told Guru what he heard from his mother. Impressed by the honesty of Sathyakama, the Guru admitted him as a disciple.

The story of Upakosala learning from Sathyakama the principles of Upasana (worship) is also narrated here. The Rishi by narrating the above stories emphasised the inevitable qualities of humility, charity and honesty in learned men.

Chapter V concentrates on discourses on consciousness. Many world famous characters in Upanishadic literature, Swetaketu, Pravahana, Aruni, Uddalaka, Aswapathy etc. appear in this Chapter. Scenes of Pravahana (a kshatria) teaching Swetaketu, Aruni teaching householders (Grihasthas), King Aswapathy teaching on Viswanara Vidya (knowledge on Universal man) etc. are seen here. The intention in projecting these characters may be to show that the Kshatrias were also interested to teach or learn *Brahmajnana* and *Atmajnana* in those days.

Now, we pass on to chapters VI and VII, where the core of the topic of the Upanishad is discussed. In Chapter VI, we see Aruni teaching his son Swetaketu on 'Tatvamasi'. Chapter VII is devoted to Narada learning Brahmajnana from Sanalkumaran.

Swetaketu, s/o Aruni returned home after 12 years of schooling from the age of 12 to 24. Aruni noticed in the conduct and behaviour of Swetaketu, pride and arrogance quite unbecoming of a learned man. Therefore, Aruni put before Swetaketu a simple question. What is the knowledge by which that is heard without hearing, that is thought without thinking and that is known without knowing? Swetaketu failed to answer the question. Thereupon, Aruni decided to teach his son on the peak of philosophical thought – 'Tatvamasi'.

The discourse begins with a factual statement. We can know an earthen vessel by knowing the clay by which it is made of. Similarly, we can know a gold ornament by knowing the gold by which it is made of. Here, clay and gold are the essence. The earthen vessel and the ornament are forms or *Nama* (name). The essence is the truth. The form or appearance is the *Nama*. In the beginning, this world with different forms and names was One, unrivalled or without a second. When that essence that was One willed to grow in many forms and names, the variegated universe took shape.

Thadykshatha Bahusyam Prajayeyathi (6:2:3)

Meaning: 'That' imagined becoming many. 'That' wanted to prosper. Those names later multiplied into numerous and again and again multiplied into further numerous.

After a series of explanations on this process of growth, Aruni pointed out that the internal cause behind the multifarious forms is the essence, the precise truth – the one and only Truth (*Eka Satyam*). "That is the Truth, that is the Atma, that is you" said Aruni, pointing his finger to Swetaketu.

Tat Sathyam, Sa atma, Tatvamasi Swetaketo ithi. (6:8:7)

This cardinal message (*mahavakya*) of the Sama Veda and Chandogyopanishad is further emphasised with explanations by pointing out several visible examples in nature, viz:

The honey collected from several flowers by several bees become one with one taste.

All living beings – animals, birds, flies, creepers and creatures are one and the same truth.

If we split up and examine the seed of a tree, there is nothing inside. From that nothingness, a big tree germinates.

Salt put in water disappears. The entire water becomes saline. Salt is not visible but its taste persists in the entire water.

All other knowledge becomes ignorance before this wisdom or knowledge. Chapter VII contains a dialogue between Sanalkumaran and Narada. At first, Narada was asked to explain what he knows so that he may be taught what he knows not. Then, Narada presented a long list of Vedas, Puranas, Sastras, Astrology, Grammar etc. Sanalkumaran retorted that whatever Narada listed were only *nama* (names) and not essence, but knowledge of nama is essential to proceed to the essence. Thereupon, at the request of Narada, Sanalkumaran started the discourse. Here, we find a shrewd and proficient teacher revealing not only the depth of his knowledge but also his teaching skill. The magnificent application of the cause and effect theory is visible here in the form of a ladder, the steps of which are arranged from bottom to top in the order of effect and cause culminating in the First Cause. Sanalkumaran guided Narada to climb the ladder of knowledge, step by step. After climbing each step, Narada asked the teacher whether there is any step (knowledge) beyond that which he climbed. Narada repeated this question at each step and the teacher clarified that the next step is the cause of the effect already climbed. Thus, Narada is led from one step to another till he reached the topmost step.

According to Narada's admission, he is already in the first step – *Nama*. The next higher step is the 'Word' which is superior to '*Nama*' because there is no '*Nama*' without the 'Word'. In this way, Sanalkumaran slowly and carefully led Narada from Name to Word, from Word to Mind, from Mind to Imagination, from Imagination to Intelligence (*Chith*), from Intelligence to Meditation, from Meditation to Knowledge (*Vijnana*), from Knowledge to Strength, from Strength to *Annam* (food), from Annam to *App* (water), from Water to Light (*Thejas*), from Light to Sky, from Sky to Memory, from Memory to Desire and from Desire to Prana, the last step – that is Brahma. But, all these steps from Nama to Desire have limitations. There is one that is limitless and beyond all limitations. It is called '*Bhoomav*'. What is *Bhoomav*? That which has none other to be seen or heard or known is *Bhoomav*. There is nothing beyond that and hence that is

Ultimate. Its basis is our own glory; that spiritual glory is *Atma*. As such, Brahma is *Sat* (existence), *Ekam* (One), *Adwiteeyam* (Unrivalled) and *Bhoomav*. Meditate on that Brahma, realise it and attain immortality. Sanalkumaran concluded with this advice.

Chapter VIII prescribes an *Upasana* (worship) that would facilitate speedy realisation of Brahma already explained in Chapters VI and VII. This *Upasana* is known as *Daharavidya*. In the human body described as *Brahmapuram*, there is a house in the form of a lotus flower. This is called *Hridayapundareekam*. Imagine that Brahma is glowing in the small area inside the sky within the flower and search for that Brahma. There is nothing that is not in this sky. Whatever in the earth and not in the earth are available there. There, one can find the *Atma*. Serve this *Atma* with the vow of chastity. That can gain everything. What exists in the middle of these *Nama*, that is Brahma. It is eternal. It is *Atma*.

Conclusion

A cursory view of the ten classical Upanishads creates a feeling of awe and wonder at the resourceful mind of the ancient Indians: their shrewdness in investigation, meticulous and keen observations and philosophical speculations. Explanation of ideas, with similes and metaphors drawn from nature familiar in daily life, is superb. Though the objective methods of modern science are not employed, there is an element of the scientific method in the rational approach in the Upanishads.

The attributes of Brahman, its relation with Jeevatma and the realisation of the supreme God remain the main theme of all these Upanishads. Brahman is viewed in different angles and fractionally defined as each one sees in that angle. Consequently, a lot of attributes emerged; *Om* is Brahman, *Paramatma* is Brahman, *Jeevatma* is Brahman (*Ayamatma Brahman*), Consciousness is Brahman (*Prajnanam Brahman*), I am Brahman (*Aham Brahmasmi*), You are Brahman (*Tatvamasi*), Truth of Truth is Brahman (*Satyasya Sathya*), Universe is Brahman, whatever is visible or invisible is Brahman, there is nothing that is not Brahman and so on. All these are correct but only partly correct, being the result of a fractional view like the blind seeing the elephant. But the essence of all these definitions are welded together and a comprehensive one-word definition is finally arrived at *'Brahman is Satchitananda'*: *Sat+chit+ananda* meaning existence+intelligence+bliss respectively. God being beyond the comprehension of human beings, a more cogent and marvellous definition seems out of human reach.

Contrary to the general belief that Hinduism is polytheistic, all the ancient Upanishads proclaimed monotheism without an iota of doubt. Yajnavalkya has convincingly explained the reason for worship of many gods in Hinduism. The theological essence in the Upanishads is composed and compiled by Badarayana in the *Brahmasutra* and the philosophical essence is contained in the *Bhagavad Gita*, both forming the main scriptures of Hinduism.

Similarly, these Upanishads uphold the *Advaitha (non-dualism)* theory of Sri Sankara that *Jagat, Jiva* and *Brahman* are not separate entities but one Reality – *Brahman* and *Maya* are inseparable. To our dismay, in the Upanishads we find analytical studies on physiology, anatomy and psychology about which the moderm science is still in the process of research. Respiration, mind, metabolism, pregnancy, childbirth etc. are also subjected to minute scrutiny.

One of the greatest contributions of Upanishads is that they present to mankind unadulterated history of ancient India, not only India's religion but also culture and civilization.

Viewed altogether, *Upanishad* is *Vedanta* (The end of knowledge), as proclaimed by Swamy Vivekananda.

FOOTNOTES

1. Sukumar Azhicode (Dr.), *Tatvamasi*, pp. 26-27.
2. Jawaharlal Nehru, *The Discovery of India*, p. 79.
3. Mahajan, V.D., *Ancient India*, pp. 107-09.
4. Swamy Vivekananda, *Foreword to Mundakopanishad.*
5. Sukumar Azhicode (Dr.), *Tatvamasi* (Mal.), pp. 167-84.
   Source: Isavasyopanishad by Swamy Mridananda, Trichur.
6. *Ibid.*, pp. 189-96.
7. *Ibid.*, pp. 217-24.
8. *Ibid.*

9. *Ibid.*, pp. 225-33.
10. Swamy Mridananda, *Mandukyopanishad*, pp. 43-44.
11. Sukumar Azhicode (Dr.), *Tatvamasi*, pp. 224-43.

    C.G. Jung, the great psychoanalyst in his book *Psyche and Symbol* recommended the study of Christian mysticism and Indian philosophy to learn more about the subject. The author of this book also repeats Jung's recommendation.
12. Swamy Mridananda, *Taittiriyopanishad*.
    Source: Sukumar Azhicode (Dr.), *Tatvamasi*, pp. 244-54.
13. Sukumar Azhicode (Dr.), *Tatvamasi*, pp. 255-63.
14. Swamy Mridananda, *Aitareyopanishad*, Trichur.
15. Brodov, V., *Indian Philosophy in Modern Times*, pp. 63-65.

The Itihasas (Epics)

12

What is Itihasa?

Itihasa means ancient history, legend, story and mythological classic (*Puravrutham*). The *Ramayana* dealing with *Sreeramavatara* (Vishnu's incarnation as Sreerama) in the *Tretayuga* by Sage Valmiki and the *Mahabharata* dealing with *Krishnavatara* (Vishnu's incarnation as Sreekrishna) in the *Dwaparayuga* by Sage Veda Vyasa are the two epics of ancient India. The epics took shape in the course of hundreds of years, but composed and compiled later, presumably with alterations. For example, *Sargams* 1 and 3 in *Balakhanda* in the *Ramayana* have two versions. *Uttarakhanda* is a later addition, as this *Khanda* was not existing in the early translations. *Gangavatharanam* was also absent in the original version. Similarly, the original of the *Mahabharata* titled 'Jaya' by Vyasa had only 8800 stanzas. *Vaisambayana*, the disciple of Vyasa, by his additions, made it a book containing 24000 stanzas and changed its title from *Jaya* to *Bharatasamhita*. Later, Acharya Sutan made it a book of one hundred thousand stanzas with the present title *Mahabharata*.[1]

Three distinct styles of narration in the book confirm the later additions. Though they originated in the remote antiquity, these epics all along exerted pervasive influence on the Indians, both the intelligentsia and the village-folk alike, as a living force in life. They deal with multifarious subjects like the early life of the Indo-Aryans, their conquests and expansion, civil wars, internal squabbles etc. These epics, in various degrees, catered to the cultural growth of India, more than any other ancient Indian literature. In these epics, facts and fiction are interwoven together in tales and episodes with heroic conceptions, teaching strict adherence to truth and pledged-word and faithfulness unto death irrespective of consequences, thereby fostering the ideals of courage, charity, good works, sacrifice for others etc. The centre of attraction of these epics is the heroic, daring, chivalrous, justice-conscious and adventurous main characters, around which the epics are built. The divinity of the characters contributed an added attraction.

Some preliminary information on the background of the epics is a prerequisite for a better understanding.

Ancient Measurement of Time

The ancient Indian literature provides us with a table of measurement of time in ancient India; as below:

> The time to pierce a tender tree-leaf with a needle or with any instrument with pointed edge like a needle is called *Alpakalam* (literal meaning – short time).

30 Alpakalam	=	1 Thrudi
30 Thrudi	=	1 Kala
30 Kala	=	1 Kashta
30 Kashta	=	1 Nimisham (Jnodi or Mathra)
4 Nimisha	=	1 Ganitham
10 Ganitham	=	1 Neduvirpu (Panting)
6 Neduveerpu	=	1 Vinazhika
6 Vinazhika	=	1 Khatika
60 Khatika	=	1 Ahorathram (24 hours or full day)
15 Ahorathram	=	1 Paksha (fortnight)
2 Paksha	=	1 Chandramasa (lunar month)
2 Masa	=	1 Rithu (bimonth)
6 Rithu	=	1 Manushyavarsha (human year)
300 Manushyavarsha	=	1 Devavarsha (divine year)
4800 Devavarsha	=	1 Krethayuga
3600 Devavarsha	=	1 Threthayuga
2400 Devavarsha	=	1 Dwaparayuga
1200 Devavarsha	=	1 Kaliyuga
12000 Devavarsha	=	1 Chathuryuga (four Yugas)
71 Chathuryuga	=	1 Manvantharam (period of one Manu)
14 Manvantharam	=	1 Kalpa (Pralayam)

1 Pralayam[2]	= 1 Daylight of Brahma
7.5 Nazhika	= 1 Yama
4 Yama	= 1 Day (12 hours) night excluded
8 Yama[3]	= 1 Full day (24 hours)

Note

In the Vishnupurana, some minor variations are noticed in the table; wherein 15 nimisha = 1 Kashta, 30 Kashta = 1 Kala, 30 Kala = 1 Muhurtam, 30 Muhurtam = 1 Day of Man.

But, 12000 divine years make one Chaturthyuga according to both Bhagavatapurana and Vishnupurana.[4]

The word *Pralaya* is a combination of two syllables *Pra* and *Laya*. *Pra* means Prakriti – the Creator – Brahamav. *Laya* means dissolution – dissolve in water or fire or some other disaster. Thus, *Pralaya* means the end of the world by dissolving in the Creator. This occurs at *Kalpantha*, the end of one *Kalpa*. The celestial planets like Sun, Moon, stars etc. remain. Trimurthi also disappears. Creation, Preservation and Destruction are the three phases of ceaseless activity going on in nature at the end of each Kalpa.

Trimurthy

'Trimurthy' in Hinduism literally means 'three deities' (triad) known as Vishnu, Brahmav and Siva, three distinct forms assumed by God. As we have seen, one Kalpa is one day for Brahmav. His lifespan is 36000 Brahmav days and equal number of Brahmav nights. The lifespan of Vishnu is double that of Brahmav and two Brahmavs appear and dissolve in the supreme God during the age of one Vishnu. The lifespan of Siva is double that of Vishnu. The process of Creation, Conservation and Destruction is repeated after each *Kalpantha* (the end of each Kalpa).

Among the *Triad*, Vishnu appeared first as a baby lying on a banyan tree-leaf floating in water. A lotus plant germinated from the navel of Vishnu. On the top of that plant appeared Brahmav. Several legends exist regarding the birth of Siva. One legend shows that Siva emerged from the curvature of Brahmav's eyebrow when he was in a fit of rage on hearing that his own mental sons opted for ascetic life instead of helping him in creation. Another legend is that Siva emerged from the forehead of Vishnu when Vishnu was in a fit of anger on seeing two *Asuras* (demons) approaching to kill Brahmav.

According to the division of functions among these deities, Brahmav is the Creator (*Shrushti*), Vishnu is the Preserver (*Stithi*) and Siva is the Consummator (*Samhara*). *Shrushti, Stithi, Samhara* are the triple purpose of cosmos. *Samhara* means destruction, but it need not be taken in its literal sense. The function of Siva is to facilitate the beginning of a new cycle of creation at *Kalpantha*, just like a teacher effacing the earlier writings on a blackboard to facilitate writings on a fresh lesson. Being the preserver, Vishnu occasionally descends to earth assuming some form that suits his mission. God Vishnu's descent to earth manifested in a form of his choice for establishing *Dharma* (justice) is known as *Avatara* (incarnation).

In the beginning, Brahma had five heads. Later, Siva, who interfered as a mediator in a dispute between Brahmav and Vishnu, pinched and removed one head. Thereafter, Brahmav had only four heads. Maharishis named Marichi, Angirus, Athri, Pulasthya, Pulakan, Krathu, Dhathavu and Vidhathavu, Rudran, Swayambhumanu, Kamadeva (the god of sex), demons named Gokilan and Madhukan, Maharishi Bhrugu, Jambavan the Vanara, Sanakas etc. were children originated from the mind or body of Brahmav. His weapon is *Brahmastra*.

Vishnu means one who is spread anywhere and everywhere as inner guide. His abode is Ocean and his bed is a venemous snake named Ananthan (the king of snakes, also called *Vasuki*). Vishnu's weapon is *Sudharsana chakra,* a wheel that can follow and destroy any enemy, analogous to the modern missile.

The ornaments of Vishnu are (i) *Sreevalsam* a sign on his chest, (ii) *Panchajanyam*, a white conch, (iii) *Kaumodaki*, a club or mace, (iv) *Kausthubhom*, a jewel, (v) *Nandakom*, a sword, and (vi) *Sharngom*, a bow known as *Vishnuchapom.*

Siva, being originated from rage either of Brahmav or of Vishnu, is instinctively, the ferocious among the three. He is often referred to as *Samhararudran* (climax of ferocity and destruction). He has three eyes, the third eye on his forehead can produce fire. His weapon is trident (*Thrisul*). The matted hair (*Jata*) on his head is the abode of River Ganga and the moon. His necklace is a snake. His robes are of animal skin and his vehicle is *Nandi*, a white bull. Siva resides in *Kailas*, a peak in the Himalayas.

All these deities have spouses; Saraswathi, the goddess of *Vidya* (Knowledge) for Brahmav, Lakshmi, the goddess of prosperity for Vishnu and Parvathi, the goddess of *Shakti* (strength, valour and power) for Siva.

Parvathi, who appeared in the Universe in different forms and names for different purposes, is known under different names. Kali, Gauri, Uma, Karthiyani, Durga, Rudrani, Girija, Chamundi, Sharvani, Bhavani, Dakshayani etc. are Parvathi's synonyms.

Each of these deities are addressed differently by the people, Brahmav as *Brahmadeva*, Vishnu as *Bhagawan* and Siva as *Maheswara* or *Parameswara* (*Deva, Bhagawan, Iswara* – all mean God). In the Puranas, we see few instances of all these three deities transfiguring into one *Viswaroopa* (transfigured cosmic form) proclaiming to the world that they are one and the same godhead in three different forms with equal potentiality. One such instance is when Brahmav and Siva met Vishnu to discuss the churning of the Sea of Milk (*Palazhy*) for *Amruth* (the medicine for health and immortality).

Episodes or Substories

The main themes in the epics are seen complemented and supplemented by a series of episodes. These episodes culminated in fights and victory of good over evil, sanity over insanity, truth over untruth and justice over injustice representing virtue and vice. Mothers and other old members in the households all over the world usually narrate stories or legends wrapped in fancies to pacify children or to dissuade them from mischiefs. Stories in Arabian Nights, *Panchatantra,* Alice in Wonderland etc. are commonly used in households in this respect. But, Indian mothers and elderly womenfolk, particularly Hindus, generally prefer fascinating legends in the epics. One of many such stories in Indian mythology included by F.W. Bain in his storybook on 'creation of woman' quoted by Jawaharlal Nehru in *The Discovery of India* is reproduced below for its thought-provoking imaginative skill of the ancient Indian authors.

"In the beginning, when Twashtri (the Divine artificer) came to the creation of woman he found that he had exhausted his materials in the making of man and that no solid elements were left. In this dilemma, after profound meditation, he did as follows: he took the rotundity of moon, and the curves of creepers, and the clinging of tendrils, and the trembling of grass, and the slenderness of the reed, and the bloom of flowers, and the lightness of leaves, and the tapering of the elephant's trunk, and the glances of deer, and the clustering of rows of bees, and the joyous gaiety of sunbeams, and the weeping of clouds, and the fickleness of the winds, and the timidity of hare, and the vanity of the peacock, and the softness of the parrot's bosom, and the hardness of adamant, and the sweetness of honey, and the cruelty of the tiger, and the warm glow of fire, and the coldness of snow, and the chattering of jays, and the cooing of the *kokila*, and the hypocrisy of the crane, and the fidelity of the *chakravaka*; and, compounding all these together, he made woman and gave her to man."

All these episodes convey a message, either spiritual or moral or ethical to the readers. This practice inculcates the children with the qualities of courage, justice, heroism, service-mindedness etc.

Himsa and Ahimsa (Violence and Non-violence)

In both these epics, we find a lot of armed struggles and fierce fighting ending in the elimination of the enemy. The *Mahabharata* story culminates in the ferocious battle at Kurukshetra. In the battlefield, Arjuna, the well-equipped and chivalrous warrior found himself unequal to the challenges. A mood of despondency prevailed upon him. He wished to refrain from fighting against Bhishma and Drona, persons worthy of veneration by him. It was Lord Krishna who prompted and invigorated Arjuna to fight the enemies to the finish.

How can this exhortation for violence and murder by none other than Lord Krishna reconcile or become compatible with the proclaimed ideal of *Ahimsa paramodharma* (non-violence is supreme dharma) in Hinduism. This is a point agitating the minds of many. Two clarifications on this aspect are extracted below:

The *Bhagavad Gita* exhorts:

"Do the job that is incumbent on you, as a religious act. All attempts to avoid destruction are futile. Waver not as vegetating renegade. A weakling has no place here or hereafter. In the great cosmic plan of action play your part as a hero? Wake up to the reality of this world. Fight the battle of life. Fear nothing. Do not falter in your duty. At the same time, be not a slave to duty either. Perform your duty for its own sake. It is by working in freedom that you rise to the realm of worklessness. To a knowing one, duty such as warfare is as sacred as worship in a sanctuary. This being the message of the Gita it has to be accepted as a gospel of carnage as much as a gospel of preservation of social solidarity. In this world of mutual destruction, practise the science of destruction as religiously as the science of mutual help. He alone is able to save the world that has learnt to slay the wicked in a spirit of worship. In unmistakable terms the Gita exhorts man to sanctify slaughter into a holy act. For this reason the Gita may be proudly proclaimed as the gospel of carnage. Virtue consists in wiping out the wicked."[5]

Jawaharlal Nehru says:

"Yet *dharma* itself is relative and depends on the times and the conditions prevailing apart from some basic principles, such as adherence to truth, non-violence etc. These principles endure and do not change, but otherwise *dharma,* that amalgam of duties and responsibilities, changes with the changing age. The emphasis on non-violence, here and elsewhere, is interesting, for no obvious contradiction appears to be noticed between this and fighting for a righteous cause. The whole epic centres round a Great War. Evidently the conception of *Ahimsa* (non-voilence) had a great deal to do with the motive, the absence of the violent mental approach, self-discipline and control of anger and hatred, rather than the physical abstention from violent action when this became necessary and inevitable."[6]

Avatara (Incarnations of Vishnu)

'*Avatara*' means incarnation and descent to earth by God for some specific mission, commonly known as 'establishment of Dharma'.

Bhagavad Gita says:

Parithranaya Sadhunam, Vinasayacha Dushkritam
Dharma Samsthaparartbaya, Sambhavami Yuge Yuge

Meaning: The process of the protection of the virtuous, elimination of wickedness and the establishment of justice (Dharma) shall go on occurring and recurring age after age.

The word *Dharma* in Hinduism has a wide range of meanings: justice, duty, obligations, action, charity, alms, virtue, law, ethics, morality, righteousness, benevolence, munificence, peace etc.

Vishnu, being the Preserver of the universe, had to descend to the universe at frequent intervals assuming a form of his choice to maintain the eternal law of orderliness and righteousness. The *avataras* of Vishnu are of three types, *Poorna* (full), *Avesa* (momentary inspirations) and *Amsa* (fractional).

The *Dasavataras*, as we have already said, are *Poornavataras* with full potentiality. *Avesavataras* are momentary to meet extraordinary circumstances. *Amsavataras* are fractional; Manus, Devas, Maharishis, sons of Manu etc. are Amsavataras.

There is a legend behind the avataras of Vishnu. One day, the *Devas* (gods) under the leadership of Vishnu went to meet Kavyamatha, the mother of Sage Shukra, the Guru of the Asuras. On seeing the guests, Kavyamatha, by her magical power, numbed and stiffened the Devas. This incident provoked Vishnu to apply his *Sudharsana wheel* killing Kavyamatha. On learning about the death of his mother, Sage Shukra condemned (cursed) Vishnu to descend occasionally to earth as avataras.

Now, let us proceed to *The Ramayana*, the first epic.

The Ramayana

The Ramayana is the first book in poetry in the world. Its original author is Sage Valmiki, a contemporary of Sri Rama, the seventh full incarnation of Vishnu. When Valmiki was bathing in the Sarayu River, he saw a forest-dweller shooting down with his arrow, one among a couple of lovemaking birds. On witnessing this heinous incident, the intense fury and wrath of Valmiki found expression in an outburst as follows:

Mā Nishāda Pratistām twamagamah:
Sāśwathee Samāh:
Yel Krounćhamidhunādeka mavadēē:
Kāmamōhitam.

Meaning: "Oh! Wicked forest-dweller, you have committed a grievous crime by killing one among that couple of birds engaged in lovemaking. You will wander homeless all along your long years."

Brahmav, who heard this voice, instantly appeared before Valmiki and urged him to compose the story of Sri Ramavatara on the lines of the rhythm and metre of that *sloka* (stanza). In pursuance to the instructions of Brahmav, Valmiki composed the Itihasa named *Ramayana* containing seven *khandas* (parts) subdivided into five hundred chapters with 24000 *slokas* (stanzas). This original text known as the Valmiki Ramayana has undergone, in later years, many alterations at the hands of translators and commentators. Three versions, known as the Bombay version popular in North and South India, the Bengal version popular in Bengal and nearby areas and the Kashmir version popular in North West India, came into being. Besides, some other versions titled 'Vasishta Ramayana' also called 'Jnanavasishtam', 'Vasishtothara Ramayana', 'Sita Vijayam', 'Albutha Ramayana', 'Kamba Ramayana', 'Thulasidasa Ramayana' and so on appeared later. It is interesting to note that one among these versions projected Sita as the killer of Ravana, contrary to the common belief that Ravana died at the hands of Rama. In fact, Sri Ramavatara was necessitated to end the misdeeds of Ravana and to thereby to fulfill the promise of Vishnu to *Bhoomi Devi* (the goddess earth), who approached Vishnu complaining against the misdeeds of Ravana.

A synopsis of the main story is as follows:

Ikshvaku, the grandson of Surya (Sun) and son of Vivaswat Manu founded the Surya dynasty. Nemi, son of Ajan, a famous King in the genealogical line of Surya kings, reigned over Kosala kingdom with capital at Ayodhya. King Nemi was assigned the title *Dasaratha* for his ability to wage war simultaneously at ten battlefronts through the swift movement of his chariot. Dasaratha had three wives: *Kausalya* of Kosala, *Kaikei* of Kekei kingdom and *Sumitra* of Kasi. He had one daughter in Kausalya named Santha who was adopted by a childless neighbouring King named Lomapadan. After the birth of Santha, no children were born to Dasaratha in anyone of his three wives. He, therefore, successfully performed *Putrakameshtiyaga*, a customary sacrifice for the birth of sons. Consequently, Kausalya gave birth to one son named Rama, Kaikei gave birth to one son named Bharata and Sumitra gave birth to two sons named Lakshmana and Shatrugna. All the four sons grew up under the care and patronage of Sage Vasishta, the family *guru* (teacher).

Meanwhile, condemned Jaya and Vijaya had their second rebirths as Ravana and Kumbhakarna. By penance, Ravana pleased the gods, acquired immense physical powers through boons, conquered heaven, earth and hell and reigned supreme over all the three worlds with capital at Lanka. By the time the boys reached the stage of adolescence, Vasishta imparted to the boys the required education. According to traditional conceptions, Lakshmana was the fraction of Anantha, the serpent king also called Vasuki and Bharata and Shatrugna were the fractions of the four ornaments of Vishnu; conch, wheel, club and lotus (*Shanku/Chakra/Gadha/Pankaja*).

One day, Sage Viswamitra approached King Dasaratha complaining that the Asuras were obstructing his sacrifice and requested the King to depute Rama, who alone could destroy the Asuras, to the sacrificial venue for protection. Dasaratha, out of fear of the Sage's curse, directed Rama to accompany Viswamitra. Accordingly, Rama and Lakshmana with their weapons, went to the forests along with Viswamitra, killed the ferocious woman demon 'Thadaka' and 'Subhahu', the leader of the Asuras. Another Asura leader Marichan fled to the ocean for safety. The sacrifice was performed peacefully. Viswamitra, pleased by the success of his sacrifice, taught Rama and Lakshmana a few divine techniques in archery. En route their return journey to Ayodhya, Rama and Lakshmana attended the *Swayamvara* of Sita, the daughter of King Janaka and goddess earth. (*Swayamvara* is a custom among the royal families allowing a princess to choose her spouse from among a gathering of kings and princes who display their valour.) Sri Rama, by breaking a bow called *Thrayyambaka,* became entitled to marry Sita. Dasaratha, his sons Bharata and Shatrugna, and the royal entourage went to Janaka's palace, attended the marriage of all the four sons including Rama (Lakshmana, Bharata and Shatrugna married the three daughters of King Janaka's brother) and returned to Ayodhya with all the four sons and daughters-in-law in a ceremonial royal procession. On the way, Parasurama, the preceding Avatar of Vishnu blocked the procession, but on identifying Sri Rama, retraced after surrendering his Vishnu faculties of divinity to Sri Rama.

After reaching Ayodhya, Dasaratha after due consultations with Sage Vasishta, decided the coronation of Sri Rama as his successor. On hearing about the scheme of Dasaratha, Kaikei, at the instigation of her maid Manthara, approached Dasaratha and reminded him of the two favours promised after the Devasura battle. When the battle was in full swing, Kaikei noticed the *Chavi* (key) of the axis of the chariot wheel loosened. She pressed the loose key with her fingers till the end of the battle, thereby averting danger to Dasaratha and his army. Pleased by this instantaneous heroic action of Kaikei, Dasaratha permitted her to seek two favours. Then, Kaikei schematically postponed the issue. She found the occasion of deciding the coronation of successor opportune to raise the issue of the promised favours. Accordingly, she sought for two favours: (i) coronation of Bharata as King, and (ii) deputation of Rama for *Vanavasa* (forest life) for fourteen years. Dasaratha told Kaikei that Bharata could be crowned, but why Rama need go to the forests for such a long period? She remained adamant on her demand. At that time, Bharata was out of station in Kekei kingdom. Dasaratha was very much pained on the separation of Rama. But, Rama consoled both Dasaratha and Kausalya, his mother and set out for forest life along with Sita and Lakshmana. Extremely grieved over Rama's separation, Dasaratha breathed his last when none of his sons was present in Ayodhya. Thereby a curse by an old monk in Dasaratha's young days became a reality.

En route, Rama and party paid obeisance to sages Valmiki and Bharadwaj, obtained their blessings, proceeded to Chitrakoot and halted there. Bharata, on return from Kekei, learnt about the happenings in Ayodhya, went to Chitrakoot and persuaded Rama to return to Ayodhya to take over kingship. Rama pacified Bharata by explaining that return to Ayodhya would tantamount to breach of trust. Bharata returned to Ayodhya with the footwears of Rama for being symbolically revered as King, after pledging that he would commit suicide if Rama failed to return before the day of completion of fourteen years. Thereafter, Rama proceeded to the thick forests, killed the Asura named Viradan, paid obeisance to sages Agustin, Sarbangan and Sudeeshnan and halted at Panchavady on the banks of River Godavari.

At Panchavady, Soorpanaka, the sister of Ravana, infatuated with handsome Rama and Lakshmana, attempted to subjugate them. Lakshmana deformed Soorpanaka by cutting her nose and nipples and chased her away. Thereupon, her brothers with an army of 14000 soldiers attacked Rama and Lakshmana. Rama, within one and a half-hours, annihilated the entire army. Ravana, on hearing about the beauty of Sita, consulted Marichan on the *modus operandi* to attain Sita. Marichan, on instructions from Ravana, proceeded to Panchavady disguised in the form of a fancy deer. Sita, enticed by the beautiful deer, expressed her desire to have that charming and beautiful being. Thereupon, Rama chased the deer to catch hold of it. When Rama failed to return within the normally expected time, Lakshmana, on the insistence of Sita, went in search of Rama. In the absence of both Rama and Lakshmana, Ravana, disguised as a monk, took Sita in an aeroplane to his royal palace in Lanka. On their way to Lanka, Jatayu, a bird devotee of Rama obstructed the flight. Ravana by his sword *Chandrahasa* cut down the wings of Jatayu and proceeded. The bird fell down on the earth. Sita granted Jatayu a boon to remain alive till meeting Rama. Rama, on identifying the deer as Marichan (Asura) killed Marichan and returned to the hermitage. There he found Sita missing. Thereupon, Rama and Lakshmana set out in search of Sita. En route, they learnt from Jatayu that the plane flew southwards. Therefore, they proceeded southwards, reached the banks of River Pamba, blessed Sabari and arrived in the *Vanara* (monkey) kingdom of Kishkinta. There, Rama met Hanuman and entered into an alliance with Sugreevan, the brother of Bali, the King of Kishkinta. In compliance with the terms of the agreement, Rama treacherously killed Bali and enthroned Sugreeva as King of Kishkinta in lieu of the help promised by Sugreeva to detect Sita and to participate in the battle to rescue her. Hanuman went to Lanka, found Sita sitting in a pensive mood in Asokavana (a park adjacent to Ravana's palace), burnt Lanka and returned to Kishkinta to convey the success of his mission to his beloved master Rama. Thereafter, Rama and Lakshmana accompanied by Vanara leaders Hanuman, Jambavan, Angadan, Vividan etc. crossed the sea through a temporary *Sethu* (bridge) built by the Vanaras. They defeated the Lankan army, killed Ravana, Kumbhakarna, the brother of Ravana, Indrajit, the son of Ravana and other leaders, enthroned Vibheeshana, the younger brother of Ravana as King, rescued Sita and came back to the mainland. On the last day of completion of fourteen years' forest life, Rama along with Sita, Lakshmana and a vast entourage arrived at Ayodhya for a tumultuous welcome and took over the reigns of the kingdom. In that period, Sita became pregnant.

According to the moral conceptions of Rama, the King ought to be beyond suspicion of his conduct. One washerman remarked that "Rama's action in accepting Sita, who lived in the apartments of Ravana as wife, was quite unbecoming of a just King" reached the ears of King Rama. To free himself from any shade of doubt on his integrity, Rama secretly decided to divorce Sita. Lakshmana was entrusted with the task of taking Sita to the forests and abandoning her without giving any hint to her. Lakshmana, with abundant grief, fulfilled the mission by leaving Sita near the hermitage of Valmiki. Valmiki identified Sita, accepted her as a daughter and provided her with all facilities for residing in the hermitage. Later, she gave birth to twin sons named Lava and Kusa. The children grew up under the care and protection of the Sage. He imparted to the children a great deal of education including *Dhanurveda* (art of warfare).

In those days, King Rama performed an Aswameda (horse sacrifice). Aswamedayaga is a sacrifice performed by autocratic rulers for atonement of their sins. A horse, with a poster of victory (*Jayapatra*) on its cranium, was let loose to walk freely anywhere and return to Ayodhya. All areas trodden by the horse shall remain the territories of the sacrifice-performer King. The proclamation of the sacrifice itself would be a challenge to all people including other kings. One hundred *Kshatriya* boys followed the horse to confront anyone obstructing its freedom. If anyone tied down the horse, the King would fight and defeat the offender. Any king who successfully performed an Aswameda sacrifice is considered invincible. One, who performs successfully one hundred horse sacrifices, is eligible to become *Indra,* the king of the *devas* (gods).

The *Yagaswom* (sacrificial horse) let loose in Rama's sacrifice, found wandering in the precincts of the hermitage, was fastened by Lava and Kusa. No amount of persuasion to free the horse by even Lakshmana and Hanuman succeeded. At last, they resorted to the use of force. That also ended in vain. The boys relented and released the horse only when their mother told them that the horse belonged to their father Rama. When the boys expressed their desire to personally see Rama, Hanuman physically carried them to the palace. There, at the sacrificial venue, Lava and Kusa recited the entire Ramayana. Thereupon, Rama enquired about the whereabouts of the boys and Hanuman revealed their identity. Rama with intense joy, caressed and hugged the children, repented for his action, summoned Sita to the palace and expressed grief and apologised. He asked Sita to prove her chastity before the world by an ordeal by fire (*Agnipareeksha*). It was a customary practice in those days for women to enter into the fire and return unscathed to prove their innocence and chastity. On hearing the demand of Rama, Sita wept aloud seeking the help of her mother *Bhoomi Devi* (goddess earth). Instantly, there appeared a cleavage on the surface of the earth and Sita disappeared in that cleavage.

According to Ramayana, Rama lived in this earth for 11000 years. At the fag end of his life, Rama abandoned his beloved brother Lakshmana and led a solitary life bearing and suffering alone all the miseries of his life. He divided the country among his sons and nephews, went to Sarayu River, ended his life by *Jalasamadhi* (self-determined attainment of perfection by immersion in water) and merged in Vishnu. All living beings including men, animals and birds that ended their life in water along with Rama attained Moksha (salvation). The epic Ramayana thus ended.[7]

Sri Rama is the only King till his period, who practised monogamy throughout his life and endured so much of pain, agony and miseries on account of the separation of wife. His manifestation as man taught the world that pain and sorrow were integral parts of human life on earth. All along in life, Rama was sober and gentlemanly in conduct, pensive in mood, melancholy in appearance, less talkative, wise, patient, trustworthy and a model philosopher king ever conscious of responsibilities – on all accounts a *Maryadapurushothama* (a gentleman).

Critics generally point out two blackmarks in Rama's life. (i) Murder of Bali by shooting the arrow from a concealed position, and (ii) divorce of Sita for no fault of hers.

Spiritual Contents of the Ramayana

Hinduism claims the Ramayana as a religious book conveying a spiritual message to mankind. But, to a superficial reader, it may appear a fascinating thriller, a novel packed with fiction, legend, flight of imagination, adventure, fight between good and evil, victory, defeat etc. This exciting tale in the Ramayana is only an attractive veil concealing the precious jewels of spiritual lessons embedded beneath the veil. All the characters and incidents referred to in this epic represent or symbolise certain ideas and conceptions or mindsets and realities. Few clues, that may enable the readers to decipher the symbolism and pick up the pearls scattered beneath the veil, are given below:

Dasaratha, a King in the Surya dynasty had three wives and four sons (*Desam* = Ten, *Ratha* = Chariot). Ten represents ten senses, five bodily senses known as *Karmendrias* and five senses of knowledge known as *Jnanendrias*. Body is chariot and *Atma* (soul) is the traveller in the body.

Rama, the eldest son of Dasaratha and the seventh incarnation of Vishnu, around whom the entire epic is built up, is *Viswanaran* (universal man) representing *Jagrath* (awaken state of the mind) which can consciously comprehend and experience the surrounding universe. Rama is the *Sadhaka* (one who accomplishes) in the entire plot in the epic.

Lakshmana – The son of Dasaratha in wife Sumitra and brother and companion of Rama is *Thyjasan* – the dreaming state (*Swapna*) of the precise mind working behind the conscious mind, *Anthaprajna*.

Bharata – The son of Dasaratha in wife Kaikei is *Prajnan* – State of deep sleep (*Sushupti*) of the mind, free from desires or senses or dreams. Here, everything appears as one – *Ekeebhuta* – as in darkness.

Shatrugna – The youngest son of Dasaratha in wife Sumitra is *Thurian*. It spreads in all other states of the mind. It has no name. Free to travel in all other states of the mind and return to the original state.

Sita – Wife of Rama and daughter of King Janaka and *Bhoomidevi* (the goddess of Earth). Represents *Brahmavidya*, the transcendental knowledge that touches and transforms life.

Kausalya – *Sanchita Karma* (Those karmas that bear fruit only in distant future births). Begins in desire, but corresponding

Karma (action) is absent. She represents *Ichha Sakti* (will power).

Kaikei – Prarabda Karma: (lit: Domestic worries). Those karmas that yield fruit in the present birth. Desire plus action *Karmasakti* (power of action).

Sumitra – Agamika Karma: Those karmas that yield fruit in the near future births. Action arising from Prarabda Karma represents *Jnana Sakti* (power of knowledge).

Dasaratha's four sons represent *Jeeva Bhava* (state of life or positive disposition in life) and three wives represent *Karma Bhava* (state of action).

Manthara – Thought behind desire and action.

Vanaras – Represent ficklemindedness in life.

Sugreeva – God-fearing, prudent and dedicated.

Hanuman – Represents Brahmacarya in the pursuit of *Brahmavidya*. Brahmacarya (continence or chastity) is the prerequisite for Brahmavidya.

Vibheeshana – *Rajasa* state (state of kingship or royalty).

Sabari – Primitive devotion (*Gauna bhakti*) – metaphorical expression.

Thadaka – Personification of lust, passion and sex emerging from the wild forests in the mind.

Soorpanaka – Personified lust – a hindrance for spiritual progress.

Bali – Wickedness, arrogance and imprudence in the interior concealed by the seven exterior elements of illusion (*Maya*).

Subahu – represents pleasure.

Mareechan – Desire and sorrow.

Kumbhakarna – State of *Thamas* (darkness).

Ravana – Kingship interlinked with the perceptions of bodily senses and intellect supported by ten heads and twenty hands becoming concrete visible form of darkness (Thamas) symbolising pride, arrogance and lust.

Ayodhya – Place of no war.

Thrayyambaka – The bow symbolising *Pranavopasana* (worship of Pranava).

Pranavo Dhanu: Saravyotma Brahma Thath Lekshyamuchithe.

Rama, the *Viswanaran* is the *Sadhaka*. He studied 32000 stanzas in *Jnanavasishtam* at the feet of his preceptor Sage Vasishta. In his contact with Sage Viswamitra, he proceeded from 'Effect' to 'Cause'. Sage Agustin taught him *Brahmatatva* and presented to him the bow of *Jnana* and the 'sword' of detachment. The association with these ascetics strengthened Rama's commitment and dedication to *Brahmavidya*, the divine knowledge.

In his pursuit to attain the transcendental knowledge, hindrances appear in the form of Thadaka, Subhahu and Marichan representing '*Kama*' (lust), 'Pleasure' and 'Sorrow' respectively. By the elimination of Thadaka the demon, Rama relieved himself from the temptation of lust and sex. Annihilation of Subhahu is symbolic of forsaking the urge for seeking pleasures. Marichan representing sorrow ran away. Thus, Rama overcame the human frailties of lust, pleasure and sorrow in his pursuit to attain *Brahmavidya*.

Rama, keeping his Prana in the appropriate position (*Pranayoga*), attained Sita, the symbol of Brahmavidya by breaking *Thrayyambaka* bow, the symbol of *Pranava*. But, this Brahmavidya (Sita) was subsequently lost when Jadayu's wings were cut down, but regained. When new wings germinated for Sampathi, Sita was rescued.

When the coronation of Rama was interrupted, Kaikei, the symbol of Prarabda karma, in association with Manthara pushed him to the mundane world, the scheming instigator. Life, on reaching the world, engages in several activities, confrontations, pilgrimages, studies, peregrination etc. Rama representing life also indulged in such activites. In this journey, chariot and Sumanthra, the charioteer, the symbols of the pomp and glory of royalty, disappeared.

After reaching Chitrakoot, *Prajnan* and *Thurian* represented by Bharata and Shatrugna appeared before Rama. But, Rama sent them back to Ayodhya for being erected at their high pedestals there.

At the time of cancellation of Rama's coronation and at the dying moments of Dasaratha, Bharata the Prajnan and Shatrugna the Thurain were absent. They were at 'Kekeyam', the place of Kaikei symbolising *Prarabda Karma*, which has become extremely powerful on account of the company of Manthara.

The arrival of Soorpanaka, the personification of lust (*Kama*) happened to be a cause for the germination of desire in the mind of the *Jnani* (the man of wisdom). Cutting her nose and nipples to exterminate the cause for desire deformed her. The chasing of Marichan who appeared in the form of deer was another aberration in the worldly life of Rama. On identifying as a demon in disguise, Marichan was eliminated. Both these incidents were to free Rama from worldly desires, a common feature in worldly life.

The wickedness, arrogance, pride and imprudence of Bali were hidden by the illusion of seven exterior elements. The destruction of the real inner evil was possible only by piercing the exterior illusion. The necklace of Sugreeva helped to identify Bali. An arrow of Jeevatma was shot from a concealed position to pierce the outer illusion and destroy the concealed inner evil.

Rama was *Maryada Purushothama* and Plato's 'philosopher King'. He was very particular to uphold the saying 'Caesar's wife should be above suspicion.' Hence he asked Sita to prove her chastity through an ordeal of fire. But, she disappeared.

Similar symbolisms are visible throughout the text. The readers are advised to study the symbolic narrative style of this book, read it again and again to uncover the spiritual message contained in the Ramayana. It will be an enriching and productive experience.[8]

FOOTNOTES

1. Vettom Mani, *Puranic Encyclopaedia*, pp. 894-98 & 1062-65.
2. *Bhagavatha Purana*, Skanda 3.
3. *Devi Bhagavatha*, Skanda 9.
4. *Vishnu Purana*, 1:3.
5. Swamy Chidbhavananda, *Introduction to the Bhaghavad Gita*, pp. 21-23.
6. Jawaharlal Nehru, *The Discovery of India*, pp. 96-97.
7. Nair, P.S. (Dr.), *Sree Mahabhagavatha*, pp. 188-97.
8. Tunchat Ezhuthachan, *Adhyatma Ramayana.*

The Mahabharata

13

The Mahabharata is an *Ithihasa* (epic). The word 'Mahabharata' is a combination of two words. 'Maha' meaning 'great' and 'Bharata' meaning 'related to Bharata', the first Emperor of Bharat. The title is fully justifiable, as this epic is great both in volume and contents. The commentators of this text often claimed that no subject under the sky is left untouched (leave exaggerations), in this voluminous collection. The topic dealt with in this epic, divided into 18 parts known as *Parva* and subdivided into chapters, is, generally speaking, the rivalry and fight between two factions among the genealogical descendants of Emperor Bharata. But basically it is the description of Sri Krishnavatara at the fag end of the Dwaparayuga. The ancient Indian literatures claim that the Bharata-war was in 3138 BC and Krishna's death was in 3102 BC, 36 years after the war. Vyasa, the author of the original text of the present Mahabharata titled 'Jaya' took three years to compile it. The present Mahabharata is the collection of 18 books named *Parva* divided into 2109 chapters consisting of one hundred thousand *slokas* (stanzas) and an annexure named *Harivamsa* describing the genealogy and life of Sri Krishna.

According to Sri Mahabhagavata, *Saka Varsha* (the Indian calendar) commenced in 550 BC. Based on astronomical calculations, Yudhishthira, the eldest among the Pandavas lived 2566 years prior to the commencement of Saka Varsha; that is 3116 BC. Sri Krishna and Yudishthira were contemporaries, Krishna being one and a half years junior to Yudishthira in age. Based on this data, the Indian scholars calculate the period of life of Sri Krishna as 3208 to 3102 BC.[1]

But, Western scholars do not agree with this conclusion. Based on references in the Mahabharata on Yavanas (Greeks), who came to India in the 4th century BC, on Buddhism that originated in 6th or 5th century BC and similar other references, the Westerners estimate the origin of the Mahabharata as around 300 BC.[2] In the Yajur Veda, there is a reference that two royal dynasties – Kuru and Panchala – joined together some time after a war between them. Brahmav was not prominent in the Vedic Age. Prominence is seen assigned to Brahmav in the Mahabharata. Again, the prominence of Brahmav is seen in the Buddhist period. Megasthenes pointed out the prevalence of popularity for Vaishnavism in India. All these facts lead us to logically conclude that the original text of Vyasa came out in the Vedic period around 10th century BC, the second stage of alteration by Vaisambayan in around 6th century and the third stage by Acharya Sutan in its present form was started in the 3rd century BC. The crowning attraction of this Ithihasa is that the celestial song known as 'Bhagavad Gita', the condensed philosophy of the entire Mahabharata, form part of this Ithihasa.

An introduction of each *Parva* in abridged form is given below.

Adi Parva (*Adi* means beginning or first)

Dhritarashtra and Pandu were brothers and princes in the Chandra dynasty (lit: Chandra means 'moon'). They grew up under the care and protection of their paternal uncle Bhishmar (earlier name 'Devavrathan'). A legend says that Dritharashtrar and Pandu were the sons of Vyasa, the author of Mahabharata. Dhritarashtra was blind by birth. He had hundred sons known as Kauravas, in his wife Gandhari. Pandu had two wives, Kunti and Madri. He had five sons known as Pandavas, three in Kunti and two in Madri. All the incidents narrated in the Epic revolve around the rivalry between Kauravas and Pandavas culminating in a bloody war resulting in the victory of Pandavas and extermination of Kauravas.

Many legends on Bhishmar, Santhanu (the father of Bhishmar), Pandu, Dhritarashtra and several others are described in this Parva.

Sabha Parva (*Sabha* means assembly)

The Kauravas and Pandavas used to assemble in the palace at Hastinapuri, their capital, to engage themselves in studies and pastime; gambling being the common pastime in those days. Yudhishthira, the eldest among the Pandavas was defeated in gambling by the Kauravas through deceit and crookedness by Sakuni, the maternal uncle of the Kauravas. The Pandavas lost everything. They had no means left to afford the stake. It has become imperative for the Pandavas to undergo any punishment imposed by the Kauravas. The unkindest cut of all happened when Kauravas demanded the Pandavas to undergo life in the forests for twelve years and thereafter life incognito for one year. Resultantly, Pandavas along with their wife Panjali set out to the forests.

Vana Parva (*Vana* means forests)

This extensive Parva describes the forest life of the Pandavas in *Kamyakavana* (the name of a forest). Many substories like *Nalacharitha* and *Kiratarjuneeyam* appear in this Parva. *Nalacharitha* is the story of Nala, the king of Nishada falling in love with Damayanti, the princess of Vidarba, their marriage, later separation and reunion. Kiratarjuneeyam is the story of Arjuna performing a long and enduring penance in the Himalayas, Siva appearing before Arjuna and the gifting of *Pasupathastra* (a divine arrow for shooting with Siva's bow named *Pinakom*) to Arjuna. During their life in Kamyakavana, the Pandavas earned the goodwill of many important personalities like Narada, Markandaya, Vidurar and others.

Virada Parva (Virada is a King who sheltered the Pandavas while living incognito)

This Parva deals with the life of Pandavas while living incognito in Virada's capital and the miracles happening there.

Udyoga Parva (*Udyoga* means supplementary efforts – mobilisation of forces for war)

Pandavas returned to Hastinapuri after completing their obligatory estrangement for thirteen years and demanded their due share. The Kauravas were not in a mood to part with even an inch of land, save half of the country for which the Pandavas were morally and legally entitled to. Even the mediation of Sri Krishna failed to bring about an amicable settlement. He pleaded with the Kauravas to be fair to the heirs apparent to the throne and even reminded them of the deadly consequences of a ruthless war, if it should ensue. Covetousness blinded them to see fairness. Resultantly, both parties engaged themselves in preparatory efforts for an armed encounter for final solution of the issue.

Bhishma Parva (Bhishma is the paternal uncle of both groups)

Armed combatants of rival groups arrayed face to face in the battlefield at Kurukshetra. Bhishma was the chief Marshal of the Kauravas. Krishna, the charioteer took Arjuna all around the battlefield to have a glimpse of the strength and capabilities on both sides. On finding Bhishma, his paternal uncle and Drona, his Preceptor on the opposite side, Arjuna, who was very enthusiastic till entering the battlefield, became perplexed. He was between the horns of a dilemma. Here comes the discourse of Sri Krishna known as 'Bhagavad Gita', contained in Chapters 25 to 42 of Bhishma parva. Sri Krishna convinced Arjuna on the necessity of the war and brought him back to the war-mood. He shot down Bhishma. The Parva ends with the fall of Bhishma.

Drona Parva (Drona was the teacher of both groups)

After the fall of Bhishma, Drona, a Brahmin by caste and Preceptor by profession, took over the position of the chief of the Kaurava forces. He fell down at the hands of Drishtidyumna, a classmate of Drona, son of King Drupada and brother of Panjali, wife of the Pandavas.

Karna Parva (Karna is the son of Kunti)

Karna was ignorant of his motherhood. Due to the vicissitudes of history, he happened to be on the side of the Kauravas. On the death of Drona, Karna took up the command of the Kauravas. Karna died at the hands of Arjuna.

Shalya Parva (Shalya was the King of Madra)

Shalya was the brother of Madri, the second wife of Pandu. Though the uncle of Pandavas, Shalyar sided with the Kauravas and took over the command of the Kaurava army on the death of Karna. He waged war against Yudishthira and Bhima. Udishtira defeated him. But he continued the battle with Bhima and died at the hands of Bhima. Thus, all the prominent archers among the Kauravas disappeared from the warfront. Thereafter, the battle of clubs or mace continued. Duryodhana, the eldest among the Kauravas also fell down in his battle against Bhima.

Souptika Parva (*Souptika* literally means in deep sleep)

In the night when the soldiers were in deep sleep, Duryodhana, along with his three archers entered the Pandava camp and done away with all the Pandava soldiers. The five Pandavas alone survived. (Duryodhana's death at the hands of Bhima, referred to in the previous Parva, happened after this incident.)

Stree Parva (*Stree* means women)

This Parva describes the lamentation and blabberings of Gandhari, the mother of Kauravas and other women-folk in the palace.

Shantiparva (*Shanti* means peace)

The war ended. Finally, peace marked the dawn of a new history in the Chandra dynasty. Yudhishthira, the eldest among the Pandavas became King of Hastinapuri. Bhishma was lying in the battlefield on *Sarasayya* (bed of arrows) built by Arjuna. Bhishma already had a boon that he would die only at the time of his own choice. Immediately after coronation,

Yudhishthira went to the battlefield to meet Bhishmar, the grand paternal uncle. There, Bhishma held a long discourse on subjects like duties of a King (*Rajdharma*), emergency measures in calamitous situations, obligatory conduct and behaviour for realisation of *Moksha* and so on to relieve Yudhishthira from the agony and pains due to the loss of kith and kin and guilty conscience.

Anushasana Parva (*Anushasana* means instructions)

In this Parva also, Bhishma continued his discourse on some new subjects like freedom, virtues of Fast or Lent etc. and elucidated them with examples. After concluding the instructions, Bhishma breathed his last.

Aswamedika Parva (*Aswamedika* means 'relating to a horse sacrifice')

This Parva contains the details of an Aswameda sacrifice performed by Yudhishthira.

Asramavasika Parva (*Asramavasika* means residing in a hermitage or monastery)

Dhritarashtra, Gandhari, Kunti and others proceeded to the forests, built a hermitage in the forests and stayed there. After two years, they died in a wildfire in the forests.

Mausala Parva (*Mausala* means a drunken brawl)

This Parva deals with the death of the *Yadavas* (members of Krishna's dynasty) by quarelling among themselves and murdering each other in a drunken brawl, the ascension of Sri Krishna and Balarama to heaven and the sinking of Dwaraka (the place of residence of Sri Krishna) in the ocean.

Mahaprasthanika Parva (*Mahaprasthana* means the great march or journey)

Yudhishtira entrusted the reins of government with his successors and marched (the great journey) towards *Mahameru* (a golden covered peak in the Himalayas supposed to be the abode of Siva) along with his four brothers and Panjali. References are seen that Parikshit, the grandson of Arjuna and son of Abhimanyu succeeded Yudhishitira and ruled for sixty years from 3102 BC to 3042 BC and his son Janamejan succeeded him in 3042 BC.

Swargarohana Parva (*Swargarohana* means ascension to heaven)

This Parva contains details of the Pandavas and their relatives, their death and ascension to heaven.

General

In this epic, we find three styles of narration testifying the handiwork of three distinct authors. Most of the verses are composed in a metric system generally known in Sanskrit as *Anushtippu*, which prescribes a fixed number of letters in a line. Prose is also rarely used in four parvas, on three occasions each in Adiparva and Anushasanaparva and seven each in Vanaparva and Shantiparva – altogether twenty. The poetic style is graceful, imaginative, simple and lucid.

The pivotal role in the Bharata war was that of Sri Krishna who came to the world not only to annihilate the wicked but also to establish Dharma. Krishna said:

Yada Yada hi Dharmasya
Glanir Bhavathi Bharata ।
Abhyuthanam Adharmasya
Thada'tmanam srjamyaham ॥

Meaning: Wherever and whenever there is decay of Dharma and rise of Adharma, I will embody myself, O! Bharata.

In the Mahabharata, we see Krishna personally appearing in the dispute thrice, first as mediator, second under the pretext of sleep and the third as charioteer of Arjuna in the war at Kurukshetra. On the first occasion, Krishna as mediator advised the Kauravas to give the devil his due. They did not pay heed to his advice and the mediation failed. War became inevitable. Krishna triumphed in skillfully creating an occasion for a war to settle the issue once for all.

When conciliation failed, both sides started vigorous mobilisation of forces. The omniscient Krishna knew that both would seek his help. Thereupon, Krishna pretended a sleep on his bed. Arjuna came first. He reverentially stood beside the Lord's feet without occupying the lone chair behind Lord's head. Then came Duryodhana, the eldest among the Kauravas. With his characteristic headweight and arrogance, Duryodhana occupied the vacant chair. When Krishna woke up, his eyes naturally fell on Arjuna. In the conversation that ensued, Krishna promised to help the Pandavas. The presence of Duryodhana was then made known to Sri Krishna. Duryodhana sought help and instantly it was also promised. Sri Krishna put himself unarmed on one side and the men and materials on the other side and allowed them to choose one among the two. Arjuna's choice fell on Sri Krishna. Duryodhana got what he wished – men and materials. Both were satisfied. The result of the war was a foregone conclusion.

As promised, Krishna appeared as the unarmed charioteer of Arjuna at Kurukshetra.

Jawaharlal Nehru in his book 'The Discovery of India' made the following observations on the *Mahabharata*:

"The *Mahabharata* is a rich storehouse in which we can discover all manners of precious things. It is full of a varied, abundant and bubbling life, something far removed from that other aspect of Indian thought which emphasised asceticism and negation. It is not merely a book of moral precepts though there is plenty of ethics and morality in it. The teaching of the *Mahabharata* has been summed up in the phrase 'Thou shalt not do to others what is disagreeable to thyself'. There is an emphasis on social welfare and this is noteworthy, for the tendency of the Indian mind is supposed to be in favour of individual perfection rather than social welfare. It says 'Whatever is not conducive to social welfare or what you are likely to be ashamed of, never do.'

Again: "Truth, self-control, asceticism, generosity, non-violence, constancy in virtue – these are the means of success, not caste or family. Virtue is better than immorality and life. True joy entails suffering. There is a dig at the seeker after wealth. The silkworm dies of its wealth."[3]

The spiritual message of the Ithihasa is dealt with separately (see Chapter 14 on the Bhagavad Gita).

FOOTNOTES

1. Nair, P.S. (Dr.), *Introduction to Mahabhagavatha*, p. VII.
2. Vettom Mani, *Puranic Encyclopaedia*, p. 898.
3. Jawaharlal Nehru, *The Discovery of India*, p. 97.

The Bhagavad Gita

14

Introduction

The 'Bhagavad Gita' literally meaning 'Lord's Song' is not a separate text, but part of the Epic Mahabharata, precisely speaking, eighteen chapters numbered from Chapter 25 to 42 of the Bhishma Parva. The context of origin of this song has already been explained in the previous chapter. The glory and uniqueness of the *Bhagavad Gita* is that it is a discourse between Sri Krishna and Arjuna, the God manifested as man and the man proper with human traits of virtue and vice, the preceptor and the disciple, the Guide (charioteer) and the traveller, the Lord of the senses and the victim of the illusion of senses and two bosom friends and brothers-in-law. The background of the dialogue is the settings of the battlefield at Kurukshetra. The *Bhagavad Gita* is relatively a small poem of seven hundred verses, "the most beautiful, perhaps the only true philosophical song existing in any known tongue".[1]

The condensed philosophy of the Mahabharata is Bhagavad Gita and conversely the expanded version of the Gita is Mahabharata. Gita is the message of poise to the poiseless humanity. It is *Sruti* and *Smriti* blended.

Author

When the discourse was in progress in a chariot, no one else was present in audible distance. If so, who authored this book? It is a normal and reasonable question deserving an answer.

King Dhritarashtra, the father of the Kauravas, was naturally inquisitive to know the progress of action in the battlefront. Being blind, he was unable to personally witness the scene. He, therefore, summoned Sage Vyasa to explain to him the course of events at Kurukshetra. To comply with the wishes of the King, Vyasa endowed Sanjaya, the trustworthiest minister of Dhritarashtra, with the divine faculties of vision and hearing and entrusted him with the task of conveying live to the King the progress in the battlefront. In the Mahabharata, we find several instances of Sanjaya arguing for justice and righteousness in the dispute between the Kauravas and the Pandavas. On one occasion, Sanjaya opposed the decision to send Pandavas for forest life and on another occasion he warned the Kauravas on the consequences of denying to Pandavas their legitimate due. It is this justice-conscious Sanjaya who authored the Bhagavad Gita.

The opening stanza of the Bhagavad Gita is a query posed by King Dhritarashtra to Sanjaya to explain the course of action in the battlefield as follows:

Dhritarashtra Uvaca
Dharmakshetre Kurukshetre Samaveta Yuyutsavah ।
Mamakah Pandava cai va kim akurvata Sanjaya ॥

(B.G. 1:1)

Meaning: Dhritarashtra said:

"Gathered together at Kurukshetra, the field of religious activities, what O' Sanjaya did my war-inclined sons and those of Pandu do?"[2]

At the end of the dialogue, Sanjaya expressed his satisfaction and joy in completing with dutiful devotion the work he was entrusted with by Vyasa. The English translations of Sanjaya's statements are as below:

'Thus have I heard this wonderful dialogue between Vasudeva and the high-souled Partha, causing my hair to stand on end.' (B.G. 18:74)

'Through the grace of Vyasa have I heard the supreme and the most profound Yoga direct from Krishna, the Lord of Yoga Himself declaring it.' (B.G. 18:75)

'O! King, as I recall again and again this wonderful and holy dialogue between Kesava and Arjuna, I rejoice again and again.' (B.G. 18:76)

'And as often I recall that most wondrous form of Hari, great is my astonishment, O! King and I rejoice again and again.' (B.G. 18:77)

'Wherever is Krishna, the Lord of Yoga, wherever is Partha, the wielder of bow, there are prosperity, victory, expansion and sound policy; such is my conviction.' (B.G. 18:78)

The delight that Sanjaya enjoys shows the sublimity of this scripture. These statements of Sanjaya also testify the veracity and authenticity of the book.

Why was Arjuna Chosen?

A pertinent question often raised by the commentators is as to why Arjuna was chosen from among the Pandavas for the discourse. Yudhishthira, the eldest among the Pandavas was already a *yogi* (one who practises yoga), who required no further enlightenment. Bhima, the everthirsty for war never overcame the animal impetuosity dominant in him. It was irrational to expect him to practise Yoga and translate it into action. Arjuna, in between the above two in calibre, had already grown beyond the animal propensities. He represented the normal man in whom normal traits of virtue and vice are intermingled. Arjuna alone had the proper mindset to study and prudently put to practice what he learned. This sermon was for the Arjuna-type people. Hence, the choice fell on Arjuna.

Why Battlefield was Chosen for Sermon?

Another relevant point normally agitating the minds of the readers is the incompatibility in the selection of the battlefield as the venue for a sermon on Vedanta. It seems that Krishna wished to dispel the common notion that silence and serenity were essentially concomitant with Vedantism. According to him, Vedanta is a science that energises man to unfold the best in him. Krishna wanted to teach Arjuna that nothing on earth is achieved without a fight. Earthly life is in itself an endless battle. To equip one to wage the battle of life, the development of a healthy attitude towards one's earthly career is a prerequisite. The exciting settings in a battlefield were found most conducive for the development of the requisite mindset in Arjuna. Hence, Krishna chose the battlefield as the most appropriate venue and the chariot as the pulpit for his sermon on slaughter. It was really a deliberate act.

Influence and Popularity of *Gita*

The influence and popularity of this small book of Pre-Buddhist origin never waned eversince its composition. It maintains in tact its popular appeal even today not only in India but also abroad. The reasons are many. The *Bhagavad Gita* is one among the three, perhaps the most prominent, constituents of the Scriptural Trinity (*Prasthanathrayam*) of Hinduism. If the Upanishads are the cows, *Gita* is the cow's milk.

The *Bhagavad Gita* reveals the path to perfection, the goal of life that everyone has to attain at one stage or other in life. It is the universality of this truth, which enjoys universal acceptance, exalts *Gita* to the status of a Scripture Universal.

The *Bhagavad Gita* is the manual of *Sanatana Dharma* (eternal order and righteousness). The spiritual laws applicable to life are called *Sanatana Dharma*. Yoga is the means to achieve this acme of human aspirations. It is the directory of social fabric and social growth.

It is a poem of crisis, political crisis or social crisis and more so in the spiritual crisis of man. When doubts and conflicts, duties and obligations etc. torture human mind, people turn all the more to *Gita* for light and guidance.

The *Gita* is the basic text on *Yoga*. Perhaps, Patanjali, the author of the book *Yoga Sutras* derived inspiration for his book from the Gita. Several definitions of Yoga like 'Yoga is dexterity of work', 'Even-mindedness is Yoga', 'Disentanglement from contact-born misery is yoga' etc. appear here.

The entire *Gita* is devoted to *Vedanta,* the culmination of knowledge that leads the aspirant from the knowledge perceptible to the senses and intellect to transcendental knowledge and therefrom to absolute knowledge. Hinduism asserts that no religion or theology in the world contained a spiritual law that is not found in the *Vedanta*.

The *Bhagavad Gita* is treated as the fifth Veda as well as an Upanishad – the *Gitopanishad*. The essence of all Upanishads is contained in the *Gita*. Almost all the main philosophical and theological ideologies in Hinduism – Yoga, Definition of Brahma, Vedanta, Tatvamasi, Vidya and Avidya, Preyas and Sreyas, Dualism and Non-dualism, Saguna Brahma and Nirguna Brahma, Spiritual and Temporal, Sraddha and Three Gunas etc. are elucidated with logical reasoning in the *Gita*.

The arrangement and presentation of the various philosophical principles explained and linked together in a coherent chain in the *Gita* are superb, seldom found in other philosophical texts.

Above all, the language of the *Gita* is simple and easy. A faithful translation into a known language is all that is required to bring it within the comprehensibility of ordinary mortals. Devoted and repeated readings, chapter by chapter, are sure to bring to the surface, like the cream in the milk, the sublime ideas embedded therein that can enrich even ordinary students.

What else is required to make a book popular and dear to the people of all ages, classes and nationalities alike, all over the world? The fact that *Gita* is the book, next to the *Bible*, translated into the largest number of world languages confirms its influence and popularity.

Contents

The *Bhagavad Gita* forms part of the *Mahabharata*. When compiled as a separate book, chapters 25 to 42 of the Bhishma Parva were renumbered as chapters 1 to 18 of the *Gita*. These eighteen chapters are unofficially grouped into three groups of six chapters each, conventionally known as *Trisaktam* (three sixes), depending upon the ideas developed in them. Chapters one to six form the first *saktam*, chapters seven to twelve form the second *saktam* and chapters thirteen to eighteen form the third *saktam*. Three separate philosophical principles, – *Yoga*, *Brahma* and *Tatvamasi* are, to our dismay, simultaneously developed in these *Saktams*. *Karma Yoga*, *Bhakti Yoga* and *Jnana Yoga* are also discussed in Saktam one, two and three respectively.

While expounding the definition of Brahma, the three syllables representing the three attributes of Brahma are developed in each Saktam. The syllables *Sat* (existence), *Ananda* (bliss) and *Chit* (knowledge or intelligence) are expounded in Saktam one, two and three respectively so that all the three Saktams together develop the full definition of Brahma – *Sat* + *Chit* + *Ananda* meaning existence, knowledge and bliss – *Satchitananda*.

In a similar fashion, *Tatvamasi* (Thou that art) the *mahavakya* (sentence sublime) of the Chandogyopanishad is developed in these *Saktams*. The constituent syllables *Tat* (Thou), *Tvam* (that) and *Asi* (art) are developed in Saktams one, two and three respectively together forming *Tat* + *Tvam* + *Asi (Thou* + *That* + *Art)*. It is generally used poetically as 'Thou Art that'. Here, 'Thou' represents *Jeevatma* (the human soul) (Please see Sama Veda and Chandogyopanishad). The table appended is likely to elucidate the subject.

The first chapter of the *Gita* contains only the descriptions of the settings in the battlefield. Sri Krishna is seen speaking only from the second chapter onwards. In stanzas two and three of Chapter II, Krishna unfolds his sole purpose of invigorating the faint-hearted Arjuna to wage the inevitable battle of life. Its translation in English is as follows: "At this crisis, wherefrom has this dejection come upon you, O Arjuna, depriving you of your manliness, debarring you from heaven and debasing your earthly career? Son of Pritha, yield not to cowardice. It ill becomes you. Scorcher of foes, cast off this base faint-heartedness and wake up." (B.G. 2: 2 & 3).[3]

The last chapter (Ch. 18) concludes with the statements of Sanjaya, the author expressing his joy and satisfaction in having completed the work he was entrusted with by Sage Vyasa. Three separate chapters are seen assigned for *Karma Yoga* (Ch. III), *Bhakti Yoga* (Ch. XII) and *Jnana Yoga* (Ch. VII).

Many of the main philosophical themes developed in the *Gita* have already been explained in the Desopanishad, which we have already dealt with. Those items are explained below in the form of a chart.

Saktam I

Chap. No.	Name of Chapter	Yoga	Satchitananada	Tatvamasi
I	*Arjuna Vishada Yoga* (The Despondency of Arjuna)			
II	*Samkhya Yoga* (The Yoga of knowledge)			
III	*Karma Yoga* (The Yoga of Action)			
IV	*Jnana Karma Sanyasa Yoga* (The yoga of renunciation of action in knowledge)	*Karmayoga*	*Sat* (Existence)	*Tat* (Thou)
V	*Sanyasa Yoga* (Karma Sanyasa Yoga)			
VI	*Dhyana Yoga* (The Yoga of Meditation)			

Saktam II

Chap. No.	Name of Chapter	Yoga	Satchitananada	Tatvamasi
VII	*Jnana Vijnana Yoga* (The Yoga of Knowledge and Realisation)			
VIII	*Akshara Brahma Yoga* (The Yoga of the Imperishable Brahman)			
IX	*Rajavidhya Raja Guhya Yoga* (The Yoga of Sovereign Science and Sovereign Secret)	*Bhaktiyoga*	*Anandam* (Bliss)	*Tvam* (That)
X	*Vibhuti Yoga* (The Yoga of Divine Manifestations)			
XI	*Viswarupa Darsana Yoga* (The Yoga of the Vision of the Cosmic Form)			
XII	*Bhakti Yoga* (The Yoga of Devotion)			

Saktam III

Chap. No.	Name of Chapter	Yoga	Satchitananada	Tatvamasi
XIII	***Kshetra Kshetrajna Vibhaga Yoga*** (The Yoga of the Discrimination of the Kshetra and the Kshetrajna)			
XIV	***Gunatraya Vibhaga Yoga*** (The Yoga of the Division of the Three Gunas)			
XV	***Purushothama Yoga*** (The Yoga of the Supreme Self)			
XVI	***Daivasura Sampad Vibhaga Yoga*** (The Yoga of the Division between the Divine and the Demoniacal)	*Jnanayoga*	*Chit* (Knowledge)	*Asi* (Art)
XVII	***Sradhatraya Vibhaga Yoga*** (The Yoga of the Threefold Sraddha)			
XVIII	***Moksha Sanyasa Yoga*** (The Yoga of Liberation by Renunciation)			

Yoga

The word *yoga* literally means 'path', 'way', 'method', 'system', 'devotion', 'mind-control through meditation' etc. In the religious context, the word represents the Hindu system of ascetic practice, methods of physical exercises and a school of Hindu philosophy. According to *Agnipurana* (Ch. 373), yoga is the union of the *Jeevatma* (soul of living beings) and the *Paramatma* (Supreme Soul). Knowledge (Enlightenment) illuminates Brahma and therefore, single-minded concentration on Brahma is *Yoga*.[4]

Yoga is a science with two aspects, theoretical and practical. In fact, Yoga is action based in the human body. We may doubt as to how a physical action can help the vision of *Parabrahma* (Supreme God). The sages observe that matter and soul are inseparably related. They are the two faces of 'Existence'. Even atom, the essence of the material world is composed of particles (*Mathra*) known as Neutron, Electron and Proton. *Thanmathra* means the *mathra* of Brahma. According to modern science, the fusion or friction of these *mathras* can produce energy. As such, we cannot outright rule out the possibility advanced by the sages.

Yoga has two branches, *Hatayoga* and *Rajayoga*. They are mutually interdependent and, therefore, both are to be learnt simultaneously. *Hatayoga* is the positioning of the body in a predetermined posture bringing the soul in a particular position. This enables beatific vision and realisation of *Mukti* (Liberation).

Rajayoga is the development of contemplative and meditative techniques associated with physical exercises. This yoga has eight branches known as *Ashtangayoga* (eight members of yoga). They are:

Yamom	(Prohibition or Abstention)
Niyamom	(Tied or bound to something; observation)
Asanam	(Posture)
Pranayama	(Order of respiration or regularity of breath)
Pratyahara	(Free from the world or senses or withdrawal of the senses)
Dharana	(Concentration of the mind on the tip of the nose, navel etc.)
Dhyana	(Meditation or fixed attention)
Samadhi	(The union of mind and soul or concentration)

Patanjali in his book *Yoga Sastras* has given prescriptions in compliance with the practice of each of these eight limbs. Jawaharlal Nehru said, "The yoga system of Patanjali is essentially a method for the discipline of the body and the mind leading upto psychic and spiritual training."[5]

The word '*Yoga*' appears throughout the discourse in the *Bhagavad Gita* and each chapter is also titled *yoga*. The beginning chapter is '*Arjuna Vishada Yoga* (the despondency of Arjuna) and the concluding chapter is *Moksha Sanyasa Yoga* (yoga of liberation and renunciation). The final goal of yoga is

Moksha (salvation). The exercise begins with karma yoga and culminates in the liberation of the soul, confirming that *Moksha* is the end and yoga is the means to achieve that end. The eighteen yogas in the *Gita* are combined and reduced to four categories: *Karma Yoga, Bhakti Yoga, Jnana Yoga* and *Raja Yoga*. These four are compared to the bud, the tender fruit, the unripe fruit and the fully ripe fruit. These yogas need not be mutually exclusive. Some people practise all or combination of several ones.

Karma Yoga (the path of action)

There are countless spiritual paths suited to every level of personal ability and option. This list is expanded accordingly. Karma Yoga originated with the Vedic ritual concerned with the control of the powers of nature. The priests emphasise a direct connection between the ceremony and the order of the Cosmos. Even after the upanishadic thinkers expressed doubts on such efficacy and magical effects, the path of *Karma* (action) remained a spiritual option. In the *Gita*, Krishna revealed to Arjuna that action performed purely out of a sense of duty or dharma, with no selfish motive, leads to spiritual fulfilment. The distinction between obligatory work like *Nityakarma* (eating, bathing, sleeping – daily routine) and *Kamyakarma* (other works, advantages of *Yajna*) are also explained by Krishna in the discourse. The conclusion is 'by doing one's duty without attachment, man can verily obtain the Supreme'. It is *Karma Yoga*. Therefore, try to transform all action into Karma Yoga. Karma Yoga is Karma Sanyasa Yoga that evolves as Jnana Yoga. Karma Yoga and Jnana Yoga are complementary.

Jnana Yoga (Path of knowledge)

Whatever is comprehended with the aid of the senses, mind and intellect is *Jnana* or *knowledge*. The path of knowledge leads to transcendental knowledge and finally to unity with the Ultimate Reality.

The increasingly sophisticated reflections of the Aranyakas and Upanishads offered the way of knowledge as another path to attain *Mukti*. It is knowledge that leads to intuitive and unitive knowledge. The physical exercises called *Hata Yoga* are often associated with the path of knowledge. This path is not accessible to many as it involves disciplined contemplation.

The man seeking knowledge is designated as *Jijnasu* and he who is imbued with wisdom is termed as *Jnani*. The *Jnani* cognises Brahma as the real entity and the very essence in himself. He is, therefore, attached to the supreme reality in himself. That reality gives the *Jnani* his true sense of individuality and thereby the Jnani excels. This is not available to all seekers. The rare who seek shall unmistakably obtain it. Those who obtain it are expected to share it with others.

Bhakti Yoga (Path of devotion or love)

The word 'Bhakti' literally means 'piety' or 'devotion' or 'love'. In our context, it means devotion to Brahma with or without form. Though the goal is the same, the worship of God without form (*Nirguna Brahma*) is difficult for people soaked in body-consciousness. As man thinks of himself as with form, he cannot help thinking of his God as without form. Therefore, the worship of God with form (*Saguna Brahma*) is considered easy and accessible for ordinary man. One who adores Nirguna Brahma has to be free from body feeling right from the beginning. The spiritually advanced soul alone can rise to that level. Hence, the practical option available to ordinary men is the worship of God with form-Saguna Brahma. Krishna said to Arjuna "For those who worship Me, renouncing all actions in Me, regarding Me as the Supreme Soul, meditating Me with single-minded Yoga, whose thought is set on Me, I become the deliverer from the ocean of the mortal *Samsara* (world)."[6]

For those who cannot fix the mind steadily on God, Krishna advised some alternatives. The first alternative prescribed is *Abhyasa Yoga*, which is weaning away the mind ceaselessly from the world.

For those who cannot submit the mind to the *Abhyasa Yoga*, the alternative suggested is performance of actions for God's sake for attaining perfection.

For those who are not able to comply even with the second alternative, a third alternative suggested is to abandon the fruits of all actions with the Self, subdued (B.G. 12:9, 10 and 11). The final advice given by Krishna in his own words is: "Better indeed is knowledge than (formal) *Abhyasa*; better than knowledge is meditation; better than meditation is renunciation of the fruit of action; peace immediately follows renunciation." (B.G. 12:12)

The various categories of devotees dear to God are enumerated by Krishna in Chapter 12:13 to 20.

He who hates no being.
He who is friendly and compassionate to all.
He who is free from the feeling of "I and mine".
He who is even minded in pain, pleasure and forbearing.
He who is ever content, steady in meditation, self-controlled and possessed of firm conviction with mind and intellect fixed on God.
He by whom the world is not afflicted and whom the world cannot afflict.
He who is free from joy, anger (fear and anxiety).
He who is free from wants.
He who is pure and prompt, unconcerned and untroubled.
He who is selfless in all his undertakings.
He who neither rejoices, nor hates, nor grieves, nor desires.
He who renounces good and evil.
He who is full of devotion.
He who is the same to foe and friend and also in honour and dishonour.
He who is the same in cold and heat, in pleasure and pain and free from attachment.
He for whom censure and praise are equal.
He who is silent, homeless, content with anything, steady-minded and full of devotion.
He who follows these immortal dharma described above, looking upon God as the supreme goal and devoted.[7]
The path of Karma and the path of Bhakti are united with the path of Jnana. (B.G. 12:13 to 20)

Preyas and Sreyas

All human efforts are classified into two categories, the *Preyas* and the *Sreyas*. Sense bound pleasures prone to mutation come under the category of *Preyas*. Generally speaking, ordinary men prefer to seek *Preyas* within the ken of senses and intellect. *Sreyas* refers to transcendental knowledge or experience. Only a few among mankind aspire for *Sreyas*. All virtue, strength, sublimity and self-denial emanate from *Sreyas*. Till the dialogue with Krishna at Kurukshetra, Arjuna was a seeker of Preyas. With love and compassion, Krishna imparted the knowledge of Sreyas to Arjuna and transformed him. Terms *Avidya* and *Vidya* (Isavasyopanishad) and *Aparavidya* and *Paravidya* (Prasnopanishad) are synonymous with *Preyas* and *Sreyas*.

Vedanta

The word 'Vedanta' is a compound of two words, *Veda* meaning knowledge and '*Anta*' meaning 'end'. As such, the literal meaning of 'Vedanta' is 'end of knowledge'. The principles enunciated in the Scriptural Trinity are termed as Vedanta. The teachings of the Vedas relate to the mundane world and hence it is relative to worldly knowledge perceptible to the senses and intellect. The realm of Vedanta transcends this world and therefore, the knowledge acquired through Vedanta is transcendental knowledge that leads to absolute knowledge. Absolute knowledge means knowledge of the Absolute Reality. One who has overcome the limitations of the senses and intellect only can reach that level.

Vedanta is the repository of all spiritual principles in all religions, whatever the nomenclature by which they are known. Earnest researchers on the Ultimate Reality have to go beyond the entanglements caused by schisms, dogmas, creeds, cults etc. Vedanta always holds aloft the torchlight of search above all misguidance and focuses attention on the realisation of Truth and Naked Truth only. Vedanta is the culmination or climax of all knowledge.

Sraddha and Three Qualities (Guna)

In Chapter 7 of the *Gita*, we see Arjuna posing a question to Krishna on the nature of devotion of those who disregard the scriptural obligations, but perform sacrifices with *Sraddha* (faith). In reply, Krishna explains that the *Sraddha* of the embodied is of three kinds or varieties inherent in the nature of each individual; *Sattva, Rajas* or *Tamas*. The *Prakriti* is made up of these three *Gunas* (qualities). These are superimposed on the *Prakriti*. In substance, they are one, while in expression they are three.

As beings evolve in existence, free will comes increasingly into play. The higher the being, the more evident becomes the free will. The destiny of man is shaped by the degree of application of this faculty. This endeavour, the prerogative of man, when directed towards self-emulation is called *Sraddha*. The *Sraddha* of every man is in accordance with his natural position. Man is what his *Sraddha* is. Throwing stone soars up in the sky depending upon the momentum imparted to it. A tree grows up in tune with its inherent vitality. A lotus plant shoots up along with the level of the water in the pond. Similarly, a man rises in his worth and attainments corresponding to the quantum of *Sraddha* he is endowed with. Man is nothing more or less than the *Sraddha* in him. The youth Nachiketas in the Katopanishad, who obtained supreme knowledge from Yama, is projected as the model of *Sraddha*.

Men are classified into three categories – *Sattvika, Rajasika* and *Tamasika* – depending upon the *Gunas* (qualities) derived by or found expression in each according to the measure of *Sraddha* in them. The *sattvikas* are only few in number. The other categories form the majority. Their conduct, worship, food, austerity and gift can distinguish them. This division is known as *Sraddhatraya* (Ch. XVII) or *Gunatraya* (Ch. XIV).

The Sattvikas

They are luminous, stainless and unobstructive. They hold aloft the standards of spirituality, morality and ethics in their conduct and behaviour. They worship the *Paramatma* (the supreme soul). When the light of knowledge beams through all the gateways of the body, then it may be known that *Sattva* is 'predominant' (B.G. 14:11). They take food that augment vitality, energy, vigour, health, joy and cheerfulness. They practise threefold austerity, the austerity of the body, the austerity of speech and austerity of mind. The austerities of the body are purity, uprightness, continence and non-injury; worship of the gods, of the twice born, of teachers and of the wise (*deva, dvija, guru, prajna pujanam*) (B.G. 17:14). The austerities of speech are those that cause no excitement, which are truthful, pleasant and beneficial and also includes sacred recitation. Mental austerities are serenity of mind, gentlemanliness, silence, self-control and purity of disposition. A gift is held Sattvika if it is made to one who can make no return with the feeling that it is one's duty to give, and which is given at the right time and right place and to a worthy person.

The Rajasika

They worship the *Yakshas* and the *Rakshasas*. They ardently worship those deities in whom they find the traits of their own character like wrath, revenge and vandalism. They take foods that are bitter, sour, saline, over-hot, pungent, dry and that are productive of pain, grief and disease. The austerity practised with the object of gaining respect, honour and reverence and with ostentation is said to be *Rajasika*; it is unstable and transitory. The gift, which is given with a view to receive something in return or looking for the fruit or grudgingly, is also accounted as Rajasika.

The Tamasika

They are lazy and ignorant. Their conception of godhood is in tune with their disposition. They worship wild deity that delights in hurting and teasing. They take food which is stale, tasteless, stinking, cooked overnight, refuse and impure. The austerity practised with a foolish obstinacy, with self-torture or for the purpose of destroying another is that of the Tamasika. The gift that is given at a wrong place or time, without respect or with insult is also *Tamasika*.

The chapter concludes with the fertile designation of Brahma *Om-Tat-Sat*. *Om* is known as *Nada Brahmom*. *Tat* represents *It* (Brahma). *Sat* represents reality, goodness and steadfastness in sacrifice, austerity and gift. Whatever is practised without *Sraddha* is *Asat.*

Spiritual and Temporal

The *Bhagavad Gita* does not recognise the distinction between 'spiritual' and 'temporal' or the sacred and the secular. According to the Gita, it is only an artificial distinction. Life pertaining to this world is not different from the spiritual. The continuity and homogeneity in life do not change here or hereafter. Change of body or clothing no more changes the personality. It is the mode of action that makes a person what he is. No action by itself is either spiritual or temporal. In the hands of a spiritual man, all actions become sacred. On the other hand, a man with a temporal outlook can drag down even a sacred act to the temporal plane. The Gita exhorts to metamorphose all actions to sacred ones.

By applying another theory also, there is nothing in the universe other than spiritual. God, the Creator of the universe is Spirit and whatever the Spirit creates is spiritual. It is man handling these spiritual faculties or objects, who transforms them as temporal to serve his temporal purpose.

Dvaita and Advaita Philosophies (Dualism and Non-dualism)

Many Hindu philosophers have developed philosophical propositions on the relation between the Universe (*Jagat*), the souls of living beings (*Jiva*) and God (*Brahma*). The accredited commentators on this subject are usually grouped into upholders of three propositions – *Advaita* (non-dualism), *Visishtadvaita* (qualified non-dualism) and *Dvaita* (dualism). The chief proponents of these theories are Sri Sankara, Ramanuja and Madhava respectively. Sri Sankara stands foremost among them. The core of Sankara's theory is that reality is one without a second. It is existence, knowledge and bliss – the Infinite. It has the intrinsic power to manifest itself as the *Jagat* and the *Jiva.* Therefore, *Jagat* (the universe), the *Jiva* (souls of living beings) and *Brahma* (God) are not really separate entities, according to Sankara. This is known as *Advaita* (Non-dualism) theory.

Ramanuja supports the Advaita theory of Sankara with a qualification. According to him, God alone exists. The Cosmos is his body. The *Jivas* (souls) exist only as innumerable life cells in the Cosmos. As the rays of the Sun are inseparable from the Sun, the individual souls cannot be separated from God or the Cosmos. The attainment of this knowledge that man is only an infinitesimal part of the Infinite, leads to emancipation. This theory of Ramanuja is known as *Visishtadvaita* (qualified non-dualism).

According to Madhava, God rules over the universe and the souls. These souls entangled in the universe, through devotion to God and His mercy, free themselves from the bondage of the world and attain the Kingdom of God. This is *Mukti* (Liberation). As such, Madhava concludes that God, Universe and *Jivas* (individual soul) are separate and everlasting entities. This is known as the *Dvaita* theory of Madhava.

These Acharyas are recognised as the chief proponents of the three systems of philosophy. Sri Krishna is the embodiment of broad-mindedness, deep wisdom and great tolerance. A real student of the Gita and a loyal commentator are expected to be approximate to Him. Evidences in support of all these three systems of philosophies are found in the scriptures. It is this Advaita Vedanta philosophy of Sankara, which represents the dominant philosophic outlook of Hinduism today.[8]

Eternal Truths, Adages and Messages Sublime in Gita

God is love. Pure love generates sweetness in all its excellence.

Love expresses as bliss. Supreme bliss is divinity itself.

God is light. What shines through the human frame is none other than the inextinguishable cosmic light.

God is the character residing in the hearts of all.

God and truth are identical

Blessed are the distressed in heart, they shall be comforted in enlightenment

Quieting the body and mind is meditation

Self-perfection is the goal in life

Mind has to be vanquished for attainment of beatitude

The doer of good never comes to grief.

Do the job incumbent on you as a religious act.

The tree is known by its fruit

Seed dies to give birth to the seedling.

A living being knows that it exists. This act of knowing is cognition. When emotion is purified, cognition gets sharpened.

Fight the battle of life. Fear nothing. Do not falter in your duty. At the same time, be not a slave to duty either.

Efficiency to the core is the criterion of a powerful personality.

It is efficiency that makes character.

Creation, preservation and destruction are the three phases of ceaseless activity going on in nature. These may be termed the triple purpose of cosmos.

He who owns a developed mind owns everything.

Zeros gain value when linked with number one. God is the number one and all the worldly things are zeros. Independent of God, they are mere ciphers. (Sri Ramakrishna)

Gita contains many more such sublime messages. A few selected ones only are given above.

An annexure titled 'The Greatness of the Gita' containing 23 stanzas extracted from the *Varahapurana* enumerating the rewards and benefits for those who are devoted to the constant practice or chanting or teaching or listening of Gita is appended to the Gita text. It is stipulated that reading of the Gita by the devotees should begin and conclude with prayer.

FOOTNOTES

1. Jawaharlal Nehru, *The Discovery of India*, p. 98.
2. Swamy Chidbhavananda, *The Bhagavad Gita*, p. 75.
3. *Ibid.*, p. 27.
4. Vettom Mani, *Puranic Encyclopaedia*, p. 1032.
5. Jawaharlal Nehru, *The Discovery of India*, pp. 176-77.
6. *The Bhagavad Gita*, Ch. 12:6-12.
7. *Ibid.*, Ch. 12:13-20.
8. Swamy Chidbhavananda, *The Bhagavad Gita*, the English translation of the stanzas and words in the *Gita* are copied from this book.

Philosophies in Hinduism 15

It is difficult to define 'philosophy'. The characterestic scope of philosophy consists in an enquiry into the credentials of what purports to be knowledge. The Western philosophy originated and developed as dogmatic. The Indian philosophy in ancient times is hardly distinguishable from science and religion. On account of its close relationship with science, a study of the history of science in India is a useful tool in the study of Indian philosophy and its influence on philosophical methods. All human knowledge in ancient days was bound up with myth and rituals. Though Indian philosophy grew independent in later periods, especially during the upanishadic periods, even now it is, at times, difficult to distinguish Indian philosophy from science and religion.

The beginning of the Indian systems of philosophy takes us back to the pre-Buddhist era. In this chapter, the ambit of our enquiry is confined to three schools of philosophy developed in India and their impact on Hinduism. They are:

- *Saddarsanas* (Six visions) – or Vedic philosophies.
- *Sramana* Philosophies (*Sramana* means *Strivers* preferably of truth).
- Modern Philosophies in Hinduism.

Now, we shall deal with each group cited above.

Saddarsanas (Six visions or Philosophies)

These six philosophies, inspired by the Vedas, originated before the Christian era. Each one represents an independent approach with separate arguments. But, they were not isolated from each other. They all are treated as parts of the Vedic literature, given in the form of *Sutras* or aphorisms which are short, definite and free from doubt. The ideas of *Vidya* and *Avidya, Maya, Purusha* and *Jiva* are common to all systems. They all believe in the process of Creation, Preservation and Dissolution of the world. All these systems except *Poorvamimamsa* aim at *Moksha* (release of the soul from rebirth) and propose *Chitasudhi* (purity of mind) and *Nishkamakarma* (selfless acitivity) as the path to attain *Moksha*. These six systems are:

(1) *Nyaya*,

(2) *Vaisesika*,

(3) *Samkhya*,

(4) *Yoga*,

(5) *Poorvamimamsa*, and

(6) *Uttaramimamsa* or *Vedanta*.

1. The Nyaya Darsana (Logic)

This Darsana, written by Gautam Rishi, considers 'Logic' as the basis of all studies. It is the science of all sciences or the science of all reasoning, similar in many ways to Aristotle's *syllogisms*, though there are fundamental differences between the two. The principles underlying logic has been accepted by all other systems as a mental discipline. The *Nyaya Darsana* discusses the problem of doubt and ascribes it to the lapse of memory or irregularities or aberration in recognition or perception. Error is the apprehension of an object other than what it actually is. Truth reveals itself to those who have experience. The soul is real and its attributes are desires, aversions, volitions etc. Consciousness cannot exist apart from the soul, as the brilliance of the flame cannot live apart from it.[1] The Nyaya Darsana believes in God who is full of knowledge and bliss. The theory of rebirth is accepted and the people are asked to release themselves from its bondage.

This system was taught in Indian schools and universities. Though modern education has discarded it, wherever Sanskrit is taught, it is a part of the curriculum. It is an essential mental training for the educated, especially as a preparation for the study of philosophy. It had an important place in the Indian system of education similar to Aristotle's logic in the West. Jawaharlal Nehru comments as follows:

"The method was, of course, very different from the modern scientific method of objective investigation. Nevertheless, it was critical and scientific in its own way, and, instead of relying in faith, tried to examine the objects of knowledge critically and to proceed step by step by methods of logical proof. There was some faith behind it, certain presumptions, which were not capable of logical treatment. Having accepted some hypotheses, the system was built upon those foundations. It was presumed that there is a rhythm and unity in life and nature. There was belief in a personal God, in individual souls, and an atomic universe. The individual was neither the soul alone nor the body, but the product or their union. Reality was supposed to be a complex of souls and nature."[2]

"*The Nyaya Sutra*, as we now have it, seems to have been compiled or revised at the end of the 2nd century AD or even later as it contains a defence against the criticisms of the *Madhyamika School*. The Sutra may also be composite, a combination of two previously existing books, one on the means of knowledge (*Pramana*) and the other on the debate. These were produced by a school or schools of the *Vaisesika*."[3]

Later, the Nyaya school, amalgamating with the Vaisesika, reworked its doctrine as basically an epistemological enquiry and became the *New Nyaya* (*Navya Nyaya*) started by Udayana at the end of the 11th century marking a new beginning in Nyaya philosophy and remained standard texts of the school throughout its history. Udayana through his work *Nyayakusumanjali* attempted to make the philosophical problems a basis for establishing the existence of God. He also aimed at knowledge concerning heaven and release from transmigration.

2. The Vaisesika Darsana

The origin of the Vaisesika School is obscure. Sage Kanada's 'Vaisesika Sutra' is the only ancient book now available on the subject. Vaisesika philosophy has no affinity to any earlier system of philosophy. Asvagosha, the Buddhist poet, who was interested in all systems of philosophy, is silent about this Darsana. The absence of evidence is not a strong argument as regards the works of ancient days.

Kanada does not make any reference to God. His 'Sutra' is not a complete philosophy of the universe. It emphasises the separateness of the individual selves and objects and develops the 'atomic theory' of the universe. The principle of *Dharma*, the moral law, is said to govern the universe and the whole system revolves around this concept. In this Sutra, *Dharma* means 'quality' or 'good quality' that brings about exaltation (*abhyudaya*) meaning 'supreme good' which is release from transmigration.

The Vaisesika philosophy is concerned with *Padarth* (substance or material) which is divided into six categories:

Dravya (substance), *Guna* (quality), *Karma* (activity), *Samanya* (generality), *Visesha* (particularity) and *Samavaya* (inference). Again, the *Dravyas* are classified into nine categories: earth, water, air, light, akasa (essence), time, space, mind and soul. Atoms are the ultimate constituents of concrete things. Atoms cannot be destroyed. What all happened is that atom takes a different shape. Qualities are of seventeen types. *Karma* (activities) is transient and comes to an end at one stage or other. In the actual construction of that system, the sutra applies the methodology of agreements and differences and the parts of the theory of induction.

The Vaisesika doctrine was elaborated long before the second century AD and the school specialised in this study was later recognised under the name *Nyaya*. The other extant Vaisesika works are of much later origin. The most noteworthy among these sources is the medical work of Caraka (100 AD). He refers much more qualities than the standard twentyfour. He is supposed to have identified fortyone qualities. Kanada does not make any direct reference to God.

3. The Samkhya Darsana

The literal meaning of the word *samkhya* is number, sum, knowledge, logic, rationalism, thought etc. The fundamental principle of the Samkhya Darsana is *Dvaita* meaning dualism of *Prakriti* and *Purusa*. Kapila developed this theory in the

7th century BC out of the early pre-Buddhist currents of thought. This philosophy builds its structure on two primary causes, *Prakriti* (an overactive and changing nature or energy) and *Purusa* (the spirit which does not change).

The Samkhya represents a relatively free development of speculation among the Brahmins, independent of the Vedic revelations and in some respects unlike the thought of Uddalaka. In this system, there is neither a personal God, nor an impersonal one; neither monotheism nor monism. There is an infinite number of *Purusas* or souls or something in the nature of consciousness. According to Richard Garbe, 'In Kapila's doctrine, for the first time in the history of the world, the complete independence and freedom of the human mind and its full confidence in its own powers were exhibited.'[4]

Under the influence of Purusa, which itself is inactive, Prakriti evolves and leads the world. This *Prakriti* is developed by three kinds of *Gunas* (qualities): the *Sattvaguna*, *Rajoguna* and *Tamoguna*. Among them, Sattva is the source of goodness and happiness; *Rajas* is the source of activity and pain and *Tamas* is the source of ignorance, sloth and apathy. The world is not regarded as real in the sense that it does not exist forever. The *Jivas* are chained by the bondage of rebirth. The only thing that is eternal is *Prakriti*. *Prakriti* and *Purusa* are independent; they do not depend upon God.

Causality is accepted, but it is said that the effect really exists in the cause. Cause and effect are the developed and undeveloped states of one and the same thing. From the practical point of view, cause and effect are different, but there is identity between them. "From the unmanifested *Prakriti* or energy, through the influence of *Purusa* or consciousness and the principle of causality, nature with its immense complexity and variety of elements, has developed and is ever changing and developing." Between the lowest and the highest in the universe, there is continuity and unity. The whole conception is metaphysical and the arguments based on certain hypotheses are long, intricate and reasoned.[5]

Speculations in the direction of the *Samkhya* can be found in the early Upanishad, particularly in the

Brihadaranyakopanishad. As presented by the *Kathopanishad*, the whole system looks more like a variant on the speculation of Sandilya or Yajnavalkya than the independent *Samkhya* and of course it is assimilated to the doctrine of *Brahman* as Ultimate Reality.

Udayana in his book *Atmatattvaviveka* produced a famous defence of the doctrine of the eternal soul against the Buddhist critiques. In association with the Nyaya philosophy, he attempted to prove the existence of God and produced the *Navya Nyaya* philosophy, a combination of *Nyaya* and *Samkhya* philosophies.

4. The Yoga Darsana

Detailed notes on the 'Yoga' are given in the previous chapter.

The essence of the Yoga philosophy is that by concentration of mind, a person can be liberated from the chain of rebirths by the practice of Yoga. The greatest contribution of Patanjali is not the *Yoga Darsana*, but the classic commentary (*Mahavashya*) of Panini's grammar. Prof. Stchersatsky of Leningrad is of the opinion that "the ideal scientific work for India is the grammar of Panini with the Mahabashya of Patanjali".

An observation on this aspect by Jawaharlal Nehru is reproduced below for academic interest.

"Yoga is a word well-known now in Europe and America, though little understood, and it is associated with quaint practices, more especially with sitting Buddha-like and gazing on one's navel or the tip of one's nose. Some people learning odd tricks of the body presume to become authorities on the subject in the West, and impress and exploit the credulous and the seekers after the sensational. The system is much more than these devices and is based on the psychological conception that, by proper training of the mind, certain higher levels of consciousness can be reached. It is meant to be a method for finding out things for oneself rather than a preconceived metaphysical theory of reality or of the universe. It is thus experimental and the most suitable conditions for carrying out the experiment are pointed out. As such a method it can be adopted and used by any system of philosophy, whatever its theoretical approach may be. Thus the adherents of the atheistic Samkhya philosophy may use this method. Buddhism developed its own forms of Yoga training, partly similar, partly different. The theoretical parts of Patanjali's Yoga system are therefore of relatively small importance; it is the method that counts. Belief in God is no integral part of the system, but it is suggested that such belief in a personal God, and devotion to him, helps in concentrating the mind and thus serves a practical purpose."[6]

5. Poorvamimamsa Darsana

'Mimamsa' means investigation of the proper interpretation of the Vedic texts. Jaimini is the author of the *Poorvamimamsa Darsana*. It is mainly concerned with rituals, tending towards polytheism. The authority of the Vedas is accepted. According to this Darsana, the Self is different from the body, senses and understanding. The plurality of souls is recognised. There are two kinds of activities, the *Nityakarma* (the daily routine functions like bathing, sleeping etc.) and the *Kamyakarma* (action for specific objects). Offerings are to be made for a number of deities. Here, there is no relevance for a benevolent and active God. This Darsana is more concerned with mechanical ethics. Life based on Dharma is insisted. It is concerned only with *Karmakand* or the performance of sacrifices.[7] This Darsana and its rules have influenced modern popular Hinduism and Hindu Law.

In the polytheistic Hinduism, there is a vast number of *devas* (gods) who are supposed to be of a lower order of creation than man. Both Hindus and Buddhists believe that human birth is the highest stage that the Beings have reached on the path to self-realisation. Even the *devas* (gods) can achieve this freedom and realisation only through human birth. Buddhists say that only man can attain the supreme consummation of Buddhahood. In practical polytheism, this concept stands far from truth.[8]

The Poorvamimamsa is strictly Vedic (sometimes called *Vaidika*) and admits no authority other than the Vedic texts, eliminating even speculation, contrary to the spirit of the Vedic texts themselves. The problem of interpretation of the Vedic text leads to much interest in philosophical study and the *mimamsa* itself becomes a kind of discipline, intermediate between linguistics and logic. Thus, the problem of interpretation of the Vedic texts led to much philosophical studies. Where the direct statements of the Vedas were found not to cover necessary points, rules were framed extending them by implication, context, injunctions etc. This study known as Mimamsa in fact overlapped both linguistics and logic, especially the former.

6. Uttaramimamsa Darsana or Vedanta

Badarayana is the author of this system of philosophy. He wrote 555 *Sutras* divided into four chapters. The first chapter deals with Brahman and his relation with the world and individual souls. The second chapter deals with objections. The third deals with the ways and means of attaining *Brahma Vidya* (the knowledge that transforms life). The fourth chapter deals with the fruits of *Brahma Vidya* and the future of the soul after death. The Vedanta system that rose out of the Upanishads developed and took shapes and forms, but it was based on a monistic philosophy of the universe. The *Purusa* and *Prakrit* of the Samkhya system are not considered independent substances but as modification of a single Reality – the Absolute.

On the foundation of the early Vedanta, Sri Sankara developed a system called the *Advaita Vedanta* (Non-dualist Vedanta). It is based on pure monism, the only Ultimate Reality in the metaphysical sense being the Absolute Soul – the *Atman*. That is the subject; all else are objective. How that Absolute Soul pervades everything and yet retains its 'wholeness'? The Upanishads described this Atman as below:

> "Whole is that; whole (too) is this; from whole, whole cometh; take whole from whole, (yet) whole remains."[9]

> (For further information, please refer to the notes on 'Vedanta' in the previous chapter.)

Conclusion

In all these philosophies, we find independent and rational thought. Whether the existence of God is accepted or not, these thoughts have influenced the Hindu faith and law in a small or large measure. The uniformity in acceptance of many Vedic concepts testifies the inspiration from the *Vedas*. This prompted many modern thinkers to express apprehensions as to whether all these contemporaneous theories were parts of a larger plan. Anyhow, many ideas and thoughts developed in these *Darsanas* were fruitfully used by Hinduism to check or counter Buddhist and Jainist ideologies.

Sramana Philosophies

The development of philosophy outlined so far known to us is only from the *Vedas* preserved as Brahminical Canon. But, after the sixth century BC, several philosophies, independent of the *Vedas*, grew up. Several factors contributed for this development.

The Pourava Empire in North India, which protected the Aryan-speaking India for seven centuries from the 13th century BC onwards, shattered in the sixth century BC.

The traditional values sown and nurtured by the Brahmin priests were replaced by economic progress, consequent on the opening up of the Ganges Valley and the expansion of the manufacturing industries and trade.

A money economy generated by new source of wealth paved the way for the emergence of an affluent class.

The burden of Hindu ritualism imposed by the *Brahmin* priests on the common people became unbearable and incurred the wrath and resentment of the masses.

The Brahmins, the highest in the ladder of castes, who were expected to be spiritual guides, were gradually degenerating into a wretched class of vices. The *Kshatrias*, the second in the caste hierarchy, ventured to come to the open and lead the people against this tyranny, oppression and exploitation.

In the backdrop of these situations, new philosophies challenging the old ones found easy acceptance. Those philosophers who repudiated the basis of the old value system were known as *Sramanas* (meaning 'Strivers' – presumably of truth). They rejected the Vedic tradition and the rituals prescribed by the Brahmins. Most of them were generally empiricists, appealing to experience as source of knowledge. The origin of the *Sramana* movement is not known. From among the work of many individuals and groups, five major systems of philosophy grew up somewhere around 500 BC or few years later and dominated the Indian philosophy for several centuries thereafter. They are known as *Lokayata, Ajivaka, Ajnana, Buddhism* and *Jainism.*

1. Lokayata

The word *Lokayata* is derived from the word *Loka*, implying a kind of natural philosophy, which can be interpreted as *Naturalism*. According to another traditional interpretation, *Lokayata* means 'widespread in the world' which sounds to mean a 'popular philosophy'. The early Buddhist literature mentions a *Sramana* named Ajita Kesakambalin, a contemporary of Buddha, expounding a theory named 'annihilationism' (*Ucchedavada*). We find numerous references in ancient times about the existence of a book *Lokayata Sutra*, usually ascribed to one Brihaspati. This Brihaspati is saluted as teacher in Kautilya's *Arthasastra*, which claims to follow the Lokayata philosophy. Another *Kambalasvatara* has expounded a theory of five winds in the human body. From these references, the inference drawn is that Brihaspati is the exponent of the Lokayata philosophy, the other names mentioned above are likely to be synonyms. In modern terms, this philosophy can be designated as 'materialism'.

The main teachings in this Sutra can be summed up as below:

There are no such things as sacrifice, meritorious giving, results of good and bad actions etc. There is no other world as heaven or future life, any mother or father in a religious sense.

Man is a compound of four elements (bhuta), viz., earth, water, heat and air. On death, these elements amalgamate with the respective elements in the world; Earth amalgamates with earth, water with water, heat with heat, air with air and faculties pass on into the space.

Aryadeva, the Buddhist Philosopher, in his book *Satasastra* has projected the view that happiness is happiness by its 'own-being' just as salt is salt by its 'own-being'. Moreover, happiness can impart happiness to other realities just as salt can make other realities salt, 'own-being' (*Svabhava*) is a concept of the Lokayata School that is often referred to as *Svabhavavada*. As such, happiness (*Sukha*) should be the only aim of man (*Sarvadarsanasamgraha*).

It is meaningless to say that happiness cannot be aimed at because it is mixed with unhappiness. One should enjoy the happiness while avoiding the unhappiness just as one should avoid the bones while eating fish or by removing straw from the grain. Happiness should not be abandoned for fear of unhappiness.

In the union of the elements, there forms the body, senses, the faculties and perception (*Samjna*). From these come consciousness (*caitanya* – thinking). Consciousness (*vijnana*) is like the intoxicating power that comes from the ferment (as in liquor). Consciousness arises through the 'own-being' of the qualities and effects of the body itself from the mingling of the five winds.

The conclusion arrived at is – one should be happy as long as one lives, no one is beyond the range of death, and if one is extinguished by the ashes of cremation, how can there be any coming back?

We are free to pursue pleasure or happiness and should spontaneously do so in accordance with our 'own-being'.[10]

2. The Ajivaka

The name *Ajivaka* appears as derived from the term *Ajiva* meaning 'Way of Life' – in the sense of the special way of life of the *Sramanas* – that of being wanderers not stationed in the ordinary society. A school named *Ajivakas* was formed probably in 489 BC by the *Sramanas* in the city of Sravasti. Three prominent leaders who contributed one characteristic doctrine each were Gosala, Purana and Kakuda. Here, we find the versions of doctrines of each one of them.

Gosala Doctrine

This doctrine is called 'purity of transmigration'. There is no cause or condition whereby beings are defiled. In the same way, they are purified (eventually escaping from transmigration) through no cause or condition. Men do not accomplish anything at all, either by themselves or through the efforts of others. There is no such thing as strength or energy. Due to the combination of Destiny (niyathi) the experience of happiness and unhappiness change them in nature. Gosala specifies innumerable forms of life that every soul has to experience in the course of transmigration with no power to influence destiny. It agrees with the Buddhist sources in stating that the total time a soul takes to complete its transmigration is 84,00,000 *mahakalpas*. It goes further in giving a calculation that this time is equivalent to thirty million million million years multiplied by the number of grains of sand in the bed of river Ganges. No mathematician is able to calculate the grains of sand. The main point of the doctrine is that everything is predetermined by 'Destiny' and nothing men attempt to do can have slightest influence on what happens, their imagined actions are illusory. The object of the Ajivaka philosophy was, presumably, to reconcile oneself to Destiny and accept everything with equanimity, if one is prepared to endure its blows and shocks in anticipation. Thus, the process of the universe is endless. Man can only adjust to that.

Purana Doctrine

Consistent with the teaching of Gosala, Purana argues that all supposed actions of men, popularly regarded as good or bad are not really good or bad at all. The means they produce are of no effects, are not moral causes, are not really actions at all.

Kakuda Doctrine

Kakuda contributed a theory of elements or substances (*Kaya*). There are seven among them, earth, water, heat, air, happiness, unhappiness and soul (*Jiva*). They are uncreated, uncuttable, sterile, immovable and rigid. They do not change or do not affect one another. Resultantly, such supposed actions, as injuring or hearing or being conscious of anything or causing other persons to do such action, do not exist. This is evidently an atomic theory.

Therefore, the Ajivakas maintained that everything 'is', 'is not' and 'both' is and is not. Everything 'is living', 'is not living' and 'both living and not living'. A further method is that things can be considered in three ways as schemes (*nayas*), as substances (*dravya*) or as modification or transformation (*Paryaya*). On this basis, the Ajivakas were in the habit of taking up a non-committal or critical position in relation to any proposition, reminding us of the famous remark '*Hapeya*' (it may be).

3. *Ajnanavada*

For the term *Ajnanavada*, the term 'Agnosticism' is used by Silanka for one of the ancient schools of Indian philosophy and is so named in one of the early Jaina texts, the *Sūyagada*. The Jainas seem to have regarded these Agnostics as simple wandering ascetics who dismissed knowledge as useless. The Buddhist *Digha Nikaya* ascribes to a *Sramana* by name Sanjay in following the view that it is 'equivocation'. "If you were to ask me 'Is there another world?' – Then, if I thought there was another world, I would explain it thus. There is another world. But I do not do so. I do not say it is true. I do not say it is otherwise. I do not say it is not so. I do not say it is not not so." This is a method of evading to answer the question. Those who take up this position are called 'perpetual equivocators'.

"From this scanty record we may perhaps conclude that the agnostics held that no conclusions about any of the speculative questions raised by the philosophers were possible, that it is best to avoid discussing them, especially as argument tends to produce bad tempers and loss of peace of mind (which all were presumed to be seeking) and possibly that it is best to cultivate friendship. There scepticism is shared to some degree by all the *Sramana* schools, and is an important element in the development of a critical philosophy, though of course they carried it to an extreme degree according to their opponents."[11]

(Two other Sramana philosophies are Buddhism and Jainism. They are dealt with in separate chapters, elsewhere in this book.)

Conclusion

All the Sramana philosophies are materialistic. God is sidelined in all of them. The Lokayata upholds the theory of happiness – happiness as the sole goal of life. The Ajivakas present a theory of 'destiny' exhorting man to reconcile with destiny with equanimity. The theory of Ajnanavada evades direct answer to all questions. They are 'perpetual equivocators'. Buddhists sideline the existence of God. The founder of Jainism was formerly a member of Gosala's Ajivaka School. All these Sramana philosophies seem to have emerged to challenge the Vedic philosophies by questioning the existence of Brahma.

Modern Philosophies in Hinduism

The middle of the 19th century was a turning point in the history of India. The British colonialists completed the conquest of India by the crushing of the uprising in 1857-59. As a result of the devastating impact of the British industry in India, the foundation of the Indian social structure – Indian handicrafts, peasant family industries and the village commune – disintegrated. India became an appendage of Great Britain, a source of agricultural products and raw materials and the market for the finished goods of British capital. In other words, the old order was ruined and a new one was not built.

The railway network facilitated the transport of the industrial products of the colonialists even to the remote corners of the country. To add fuel to the fire, branches of British industries were established to exploit the resources like coal, cotton and other minerals. The situation of the Indian workers was not much better; they had to work 14 to 15 hours a day under very hard conditions and starvation wages. The ideology of the Indian national liberation movement contained features characteristic of the ideology of the bourgeoisie in the colonial and semicolonial countries. Simultaneously, ideological struggle for liberation from Christianity spread throughout India. This struggle essentially went on at three fronts. Swamy Dayanand Saraswati of Gujarat was the most brilliant representative of this struggle, who took up the tasks of reforming and reviving the Hindu religion and opposing

Christianity. He founded the *Arya Samaj* in Mumbai. Similar reformist organisations were set up elsewhere. The Hindu Tract Society in Madras, the Hindu Free Thought Union etc. are examples. The second trend of the struggle was the mystic trend of spiritism and theosophy. The Theosophical Society of India established in New York shifted its headquarters to India. The third direction was linked with the Brahma Samaj, a religious reformist movement. The Brahma Samajists were never prepared to yield their ideological positions to anyone. But the defeat of India in the struggle against the British Colonialists forced the reformists to assimilate Christian ideas in Hinduism. The results of this assimiliation will be clear in the views of Sri Ramakrishna, Vivekananda and Aurobindo Ghose, which we shall take up in brief in the succeeding pages.

1. Dayanand Saraswati

Dayanand Mulshankar (1824-83), who acquired the title '*Saraswati*' became widely known as the founder of the reform movement named *Arya Samaj*, founded in 1875. He criticised the 'Vedantists' idealist monism suggesting the idea of the existence of three independent substances; God (*Brahman*), the Soul (*Atman*) and Matter (*Prakriti*). Dayanand in his book *Satyartha Prakash* (Light of Truth) expressed his proposition that *Brahman* alone is worthy of cognition, for everything in the universe is born, lives and disintegrates owing to *Brahman*. Thus, God, the soul and *prakriti* are co-related within the universe as 'three causes', the efficient, the auxiliary and the material. God is the highest form of being, the 'supreme spirit' dominating all and needing no matter for its existence.

Dayanand says that all the laws of the material world function under the power of God; any action which we observe in the surrounding world is intended for the benefit of souls and fulfilment of their desires; matter creating the conditions for the souls, without depriving them of freedom. He distinguished three elements in the process of cognition: cognition through the senses (*Indriya*), cognition through the reason (*manas*) and cognition through the soul (*atman*) or the ego. In Dayanand's view, reason is a sixth sense that, in conjunction with the *indriyas*, provides man only with perception. The sense organs are not the gates through which all impressions may pass. Knowledge arising from sense perception is called deduction (*anumana*). For example, the conclusion that there is fire on a mountain cannot be made until smoke is seen.

Dayanand distinguishes three kinds of deduction; progressive deduction, regressive deduction and attendant deduction. Progressive deduction is deduction of effect from cause. E.g.: a cloud is coming this way, consequently it will rain. Regressive deduction is deduction of cause from effect. E.g.: Streams have started running into the valley, consequently, it has rained up there in the mountains. Attendant deduction has no cause and effect relations with phenomena, but certain attendant circumstances are there. It is the law of causality in the final analysis. For instance, no one can move from one place to another without travelling the distance between them.

According to Dayanand, perception affords man the knowledge of attributes, that is of concrete things and their properties, but not of substance. Dayanand refers to knowledge obtained by the soul as *Pratyaksha*, or intuition. Intuition is recognised only on three conditions. The first condition is that the intuition must have for its object substance or attributes or terms expressing them. The second condition is constancy or immutability. Knowledge, which disappears is called variable and cannot be included as intuitive knowledge. The knowledge, which carries conviction or confidence alone can be considered intuitive.

The characteristic of his socio-political views is his adherence to the idea of rebuilding Indian society on bourgeois principles in which all men would be equal in the face of God and headed by a just and impartial monarch. The obstacles in the way of formation of an ideal society, according to him, are foreign ideology, encroachment of other faiths, especially Christianity and Islam, as well as the economic dominance of the foreigners.

Dayanand preached the worship of a single God and condemned polytheism. He opposed caste restrictions, early marriages, the *purdah* system, conservatism and illiteracy. He advocated abolition of untouchability, emancipation of women and the development of education in Sanskrit and Hindi. He organised a *Shudhi* (purification) movement for returning to the womb of Hinduism. In his works of translations from the Vedas, Dayanand revived the democratic traditions of the Hindu religion, which the Brahmins passed over in silence. He criticised idol worship, inescapable power of fate and man's impotence in the face of fate. He concluded by exhorting his followers to act vigorously and expressed the hope that the forces of nature can be exploited with the aid of science to improve the condition of man's existence.[12]

2. Aurobindo Ghose

Aurobindo Ghose (1873-1950) was a major objective idealist philosopher of Integral Vedanta and leader of National Liberation Movement. There were three principal currents in the Indian philosophical systems of the Vedanta: (1) unrestricted monism (*advaita*), (2) the restricted monism (*visishtadvaita*), and (3) the pluralism or dualism (*dvaita*). In Aurobindo's views, these trends were one-sided, for materialism and idealism, rationalism and mysticism, monism and pluralism appeared in them as opposites in a state of implacable conflicts. In the integral Vedanta, all these opposites are fully reconciled.

He recognised *Brahman* as the primary basis of all that is. According to the previous Vedantists, the essence of *Brahman* is restricted to one of its attributes.

According to the *Upanishads* and the *Bhagavad Gita*, there are three real forms of *Brahman*; the infinite *Brahman* (*the Nirguna Brahman*), the definite *Brahman* (*Saguna Brahman*) and *Brahman* as the absolute consciousness, as soul (*Atman*). In fact, there is only one *Brahman*, the indefinite *Brahman*, that is the substance. *Brahman* cannot be expressed or defined, neither this, nor that, not a third one *ad infinitum* (*neti neti*) but despite the fact that all is Brahman, we cannot fix it to any concrete thing, even through any infinite series: it is this, it is that (*iti iti*) etc. The only properties of *Brahman* are (1) He is, (2) He knows, and (3) He is full of bliss – Sat Chitananda.

According to Ghose, all that exists in space and time are an endless number of qualities, forms and construction out of matter and consciousness. These existences are named the phenominal world of nature. Ghose says that the theory of spiritual evolution is not identical with the scientific theory of evolution of Darwinism, for "if the facts with which science deals are reliable, the generalisation it hazards are shortlived". From this angle, Ghose considered human life and life in general. He believed that our existence was a kind of refraction of divine existence in reverted order. In summing up his philosophical studies, Ghose arrived at the following conclusions:

Everything emerges out of Brahman, everything reverts to Brahman: the cycle is eternal.

Life and death are two phases of a single cycle; what happens is reincarnation of the soul.

Karma, the eternal moral law of the universe, determines the destiny of the human soul as well as the destiny of all nature.

Man's goal is 'life divine' merging with Brahman. The path to life divine lies through cognition of the self.

Aurobindo's philosophy contained another progressive element, namely, his criticism of Indian asceticism for its neglect of the material conditions of life and for 'excessive' mysticism.

Integral Sociology

Aurobindo's sociological views are directly linked with his philosophical vision. According to Ghose, "man is not a social being, but rather an autonomous independent individual being, his material practice and thinking not as a concrete manifestation of social being, but rather as a 'separate existence' based on the development of his life, satisfying his "mental tendencies, emotional and vital needs and physical being according to his own desire governed by his reason".

From this position, Ghose views the entire history of human society as the history of separate individuals and their 'aggregate states'. The men's actual inequality is the result of the imperfections of the 'aggregates' (economic, political and other types). Under the conditions of imperfect 'aggregate states', evils such as oppression, racial discrimination, poverty, lack of rights etc. emerge. The essence of the ideal common law of social development consisted in the free development from within to perfect one's individuality. The law for humanity is to pursue its upward evolution towards Brahman and merging with it. The principal propositions and ideas of integral sociology developed by Ghose had progressive significance in India at that time even though it had its inherent contradiction. His positions, at times, were inconsistent and vacillating.[13]

3. Sri Ramakrishna Paramahamsa

Sri Ramakrishna Paramahamsa was not a philosopher. He was far more than a philosopher. His views, words, deeds and life were philosophical and his solutions to problems were pragmatic. What he expounded to others were none other than his personal experiences, the result of his prolonged and intense spiritual life.

One of the major reformists in India in the 19th century was Gadadhar Chatterjee, later known as Ramakrishna Paramahamsa. Ramakrishna (1834-1886) was born in a poor *Brahmin* family. In his young days, he did not receive any systematic education. He never wrote any book or philosophical treatise. He expressed his views orally with the help of images and parables. He had a striking intellect and sharp insight into the nature of things and phenomena. Sri Ramakrishna was a God-intoxicated soul. He picked up his parables from everyday life of ordinary men and illustrated even deep spiritual laws and philosophical principles with a 'down to earth' approach that compelled even very rigid minds to grasp his ideas with the beauty and grandeur, that were his life.

Ramakrishna believed that all religions ultimately teach one and the same thing, and that the gods of the different religions are the same Being, though referred to under different nomenclature, just as water is known under different names. Sectarian strife between different religions was not only meaningless, but also harmful, according to Ramakrishna.

Assertion that "my religion is the truth and others are false" cannot be true. God has an infinity of aspects. "God is formless and with form and many are His forms, which no one knows". He "can take the form of Krishna, Christ or any other incarnation". Being 'formless', he is 'invisible existence' – intelligence – bliss absolute (*the Satchitananda*). Ramakrishna was a follower of the Vedanta philosophy, not those linked with Sankara or Ramanuja. He extended his objective idealism to the phenomena of social life.

According to the monistic Vedanta (*advaita*), *Paramatman* is the witness of three states of consciousness; the waken state, the dream state and the dreamless sleep. In the views of Ramakrishna, all these are only ideas. The state of sleep is just as real as waken state. He establishes this view with the help of a parable of a monist farmer, who realised that the waken state was as unreal as the dream state and that the one permanent reality was the *Atman*. He accepted *Samadhi* as the fourth state and referred to his experiences of falling in to the *Samadhi* state. He, therefore upheld the existence of *Brahman* the Absolute and *Maya* (illusion), *Jiva* (the individual soul) and the world.

Good and evil, virtue and vice are to be found in this world of relativity, but *Brahma* is unaffected by them. He compares *Brahma* as the light of a lamp. By the same light, one can recite the Holy Scriptures and another can forge a document, while the light remains unaffected. *Brahma* is like the Sun who shines equally upon the virtuous and the wicked. Only the highest form of animation – human animation freed from the concrete relativity of human existence and from being part of the phenomenal world – merges with the highest form of animation – the World Consciousness or *Brahman*.

While distinguishing between *Avidya* and *Vidya*, he asserts "Knowledge of diversity is ignorance. The egotism bred of erudition proceeds from ignorance. That knowledge by which we know that God exists everywhere is true knowledge." "He who has realised *Brahman* becomes silent." "What the Absolute is, no one can tell, He who has attained the Absolute, through *Samadhi* cannot give any information on it." One can only perceive Brahman with one's soul, merging with it and dissolving in it just as salt dissolves in water.

Ramakrishna answers the reason why souls are so bound to the world. It is the sense of 'I' that is the whole cause. When 'I' is dead all troubles cease. This sense of 'I' is like a thick cloud that hides the glory of the eternal Sun. On account of the sense of 'I', soul has forgotten its real 'self' and has become entangled in the meshes of the various limitations of mind and body. From the standpoint of the soul, all men are equal. But, everyone cannot immediately understand that standpoint or still less, make it the rule of one's personal behaviour.

Ramakrishna resolutely objected to fighting evil on the principle of 'eye for eye' and 'tooth for tooth'. Here he speaks like a mystical idealist. To a question 'what attitude should we hold when wicked people come to disturb our peace or do actually offend us? Ramakrishna answered, 'A person living in society should have a little *tamas* (darkness, anger etc.) for purpose of self-protection.' In another context, he said, "There is no harm in 'hissing' at wicked men and your enemies showing that you can protect yourselves, but be careful not to pour your venom into the blood of your enemy. Resist not evil by causing evil in return."

Ramakrishna exhorted his disciples to serve man, seeing God in him. Each individual soul according to his religious mystical views is immortal and potentially divine. Seeing God in man meant viewing his soul as part of the absolute spiritual substance. In the words of Ramakrishna "the non-dualist Vedantins hold that the Self has no attachment to anything. Pleasure, pain, virtue, vice etc. can never affect the Self in any way; but they do affect men who think that their soul is the same as the body."

Ramakrishna's world-view is very complex. On one occasion, he advocated escape from reality while on some other occasion, he exhorted his audience to be closer to the practical interests of men. On one occasion, he advised of giving oneself up entirely to God, while on another, he warns against excessive enthusiasm for religious cults. He criticised spiritualism and theosophy. On theosophists he said that those who seek powers... belong to an inferior class. To substantiate his point, Ramakrishna quoted a parable. One day, a man, who acquired the ability to walk over water after 14 years of rigorous ascetism, told his teacher about his great feat. The teacher replied "what you attained by fourteen years strain is attained by common people who give small coins to a boatman".

The goals and tasks of the religious reformist movement started by Ramakrishna were in broad outline, as below:

"Postulating as an eternal truth the idea that God is one but has many aspects, and that each religion is merely one of the aspects of worshipping one and the same God; proceeding on this monotheistic idea, eliminating the contradictions (establishing harmony) between the various faiths and doctrines of different sects; proving that each individual soul is immortal and potentially divine, and preaching equality of all men on that basis; proving that 'this world' is real, by developing the objective-idealist philosophy of the Vedanta under the new historical conditions; promoting in every way the growth and enrichment of man's life in this world, gradually getting rid of the superstitions, religious strife, sectarian bigotry, theosophy, and other imperfections and errors; resisting the Indian people's external and internal enemies, "hissing" at the enemies but avoiding fighting evil by causing evil in return. Ramakrishna's world-view reflected the passive form of protest of the liberal circles of the Indian public against the oppression of the British colonialists."[14]

4. Swamy Vivekananda (1862-1902)

Swamy Vivekananda (earlier name – Narendra Dutt), one of the rare spiritual luminaries of India and a man of originality and erudition, wrote one of the most exquisite pages in the history of Indian philosophical and social thought. He hailed from a rich and educated family in Bengal, studied philosophical literature at a very early age and enrolled himself as a disciple of Sri Ramakrishna. In his own words, he is "I met Ramakrishna Paramahamsa with whom I lived for a long time and under whom I studied.... All that I am...is owing to my master,

Sri Ramakrishna."[15] John Stuart Mill's *Three Essays on Religion* profoundly influenced him. He studied the works of many prominent Western writers like Descartes, Spinoza, Hegel, Hume, Kant, Schopenhauer, Darwin etc. and evolved his own conclusions that may fit in with the Indian context.

Vivekananda's family was ruined in 1884 and resultantly, he was on the verge of starvation. He knocked at many doors, but rejection was the result everywhere. From experience, he learnt what human sympathy meant. He discovered that the weak, the poor and the abandoned had no space on this earth. After observing the development of social relations in Western democracies, he commented, "They that have money have kept the government of the land under their thumb" to rob the common people.

With the desire to build up a new India, Vivekananda paid considerable attention to philosophical heritage of India as a whole and championed exclusively the philosophies of Vedanta and *Yoga* in Hinduism. On Vedanta, he produced three books: (a) On the Vedanta Philosophy, (b) the Vedanta in all its phases, and (c) the Vedanta Philosophy and Christianity.

These books contain criticism of the traditional Vedantist interpretation of the basic philosophical problems from the *Vedic* period to his own times. According to him, Vedanta is philosophical algebra and at times a synonym of Hinduism.

He says, "Whether we are conscious of it or not, we think the Vedanta, we live in the Vedanta, we breathe the Vedanta and we die in the Vedanta; and every Hindu does that."

After considering the philosophical heritage of Vedanta as a whole, Vivekananda created a "New Vedanta" on the basis of the most valuable and progressive elements in the various Vedanta philosophies. In this endeavour, he admits that the different "Vedantic schools are not contradictory, that they all necessitate each other, and one, as it were, is the stepping stone to the other". Vivekananda divided all Vedantic trends into two large groups; *dvaita* (dualism), and *advaita* (non-dualism). He gave a new interpretation to the term 'dualism' one that is different from the European, recognising the existence of two worlds, the other world (the essence of the world – *Brahman-Atman*) and this world (the world of phenomena, nature and the universe).

Vivekananda believed in the division of all philosophers into materialists and idealists depending on their choice of the primary principle to be devoid of any meaning, for both matter and spirit are phenomena of this world. Matter and spirit are both natures, the former is crude and the latter fine. One party says thought caused by matter while the other party claims that matter is caused by thought. Vivekananda says that both parties are wrong, as both are co-existent and that both matter and thought are products of *Brahman-Atman*. Matter and mind are really forces; at root, they are one. Thus, nature is homogeneous. Differentiation is only in manifestation. To substantiate this statement, Vivekananda puts forth an example. "If I do not eat for ten days, I cannot think. I am very weak and perhaps do not know my own name. Then I eat some bread and in a little while, I begin to think, my power of mind has returned. The bread has become mind. Similarly, the mind lessens its rate of vibrations and manifests its effect in the body and becomes matter."

Brahman is the absolute, eternal, motionless, without qualities, infinite and amorphous. It is at the same time the cause of the universe. In the objects and phenomenon of nature, it becomes relative, transient, moving, finite and having form. The one question that is difficult to explain is the relation between *Brahman* and the universe. Vivekananda asks as to how the Infinite, the Absolute has become the finite. He himself answers the question. This Absolute (1) has become the universe (2) by coming through time, space and causation (3) this is the central idea of the Vedanta. Time, space, causation are like the glass through which the Absolute is seen, and when it is seen on the lower side, it appears as the universe.

All the Vedantists are in agreement on three points: (1) Belief in God, (2) Belief in the Vedas as revelation, and (3) belief in cycles as the mainline of the development of all that is. The doctrine of cycles is as below. All that exist in the universe are the result of the manifestation of the primary matter known as *akasha* (essence). All that exist in the universe are the result of the primary force called *prana*. Acting on the amorphous *akasha*, *prana* projects or constructs the universe (nature). At the beginning of the cycle, *akasha* is immobile and does not manifest. Then, *prana* acts with a growing force, creating forms (plants, animals, men, stars etc.) of higher magnitude and contents. These evolutions attain the climax in millions of years. After attaining the climax, involution or decline starts and the objects and phenomena assume finer forms and finally revert to the original state of *akasha* and *prana*. In addition to *akasha* and *prana*, a cosmic reason called *mahat* also exists. According to Vivekananda, *mahat* is neither created by *akasha* or *prana* nor *vice versa*, but *mahat* is transformed into *akasha* and *prana*. While form is active and creative, matter is passive.

Aristotle believed in four causes for any phenomenon of nature, the material cause, the formal cause, the efficient cause and the final cause. Aristotle illustrated this by an example of the construction of a house. Material cause is the building materials, the formal cause is the plan of building the house, the efficient cause is the architect and his art and the final cause is the finished building. Aristotle's form signifies the action of the divine cause whereas Vivekananda's *prana* and *mahat* are 'astral' or cosmic forces.

According to Vedantists including Vivekananda, man is an organic mixture of the materials of the universe; it is a synthesis of the universe, or a mini-universe. Man contains the physical matter, the vital force of the vegetable kingdom, ability to feel and desire, the intellect and the soul – which makes the true man. The soul constitutes man's essence, it is immortal. Birth and death are to be viewed from this standpoint as changes in matter rather than as changes in ourselves. The cycles of reincarnations through which the soul depart for the other side and return to earthly life, another depart and another return etc. (the process is called *Samsara* in Sanskrit) culminate finally in the so-called release, which means that the individual soul has attained through an enormous number of reincarnations such a degree of purity that during the current departure for the other side, it fully merges with Brahman and becomes identical with *It*.

As distinct from Christian, Vedantists believe that the problem does not lie in the soul reaching the heaven, but in stopping the soul's departures to heaven, that is, stopping the cycle of reincarnations, of deaths and births. The Hindu belief is that the soul is neither mind nor body. The body is always changing, and the mind is subject to even greater changes – it never has the same thoughts for even a few minutes. Vivekananda says, "Behind the body, behind the mind, there must be something, viz.: the soul, which unifies the man. Mind is merely the fine instrument through which the soul – the master – acts on the body. In India we say a man has given up his body while you (Christians) say a man gives up his ghost. The Hindus believe that a man is a soul and has a body while Westerners believe he is a body and possesses a soul. Death overtakes everything that is complex. The soul is a single element, not composed of anything else, and therefore it cannot die. By its very nature, the soul must be immortal."

"The national laws at best are embodied will of a majority of the nation."[16] "Law itself is the operation of cause and effect. Certain things happen according to certain other things that have gone before. Every precedent has its consequence."[17]

There are no causeless phenomena in nature, there can be no freedom in it either. Any will is causally conditioned. "Everything that I do or think or feel, every part of my conduct or behaviour, my every movement – all is caused and therefore not free.... There is no such thing as freedom of the mind, it cannot be."[18] When he is free, nature becomes the slave.

"The awakening of the soul to its bondage and its efforts to stand up and asserts itself – this is called life."[19] The eventual triumph "when all the slavery is blown away, is called salvation, *nirvana*, freedom etc.".

Yoga

Vivekananda dealt with *Yoga* in detail. This subject is dealt with in the previous chapter on *Bhagavad Gita*.

Some salient quotations from Vivekananda's philosophical treatise on *karma yoga* are given below for additional information.

"Although a man has not studied a single system of philosophy, although he does not believe in any God, and never has believed, although he has not prayed even once in his whole life, if the simple power of good actions has brought him to that state where he is ready to give up his life and all else for others, he has arrived at the same point to which the religious man will come through his prayers and the philosophers through their knowledge."[20]

"...what I meant was, that a man must be active, in order to pass through activity to perfect calmness."[21]

Here is the final appeal of Vivekananda to his compatriots.

"Awake, arise, and stop not till the desired end is reached."[22]

"The philosophical and sociological views of Vivekananda can be summed up in the following way. Vivekananda was an adherent of the objective idealist Vedanta philosophy, but he also raised Vedantism to a new and higher level, making some concessions to materialism."[23]

Conclusion

India, in the period between the 18th and 20th century, produced many illustrious and eminent philosophers deserving high recognition on many counts. From among them, selected four of representative characters only have been introduced above. Others have been omitted not wilfully but due to constraints of space.

Dayanand Saraswathi was a dedicated religious activist and reformer, a nationalist to the core, a philosopher of repute and the founder of Arya Samaj.

Aurobindo Ghose was an objective idealist philosopher of 'Integral Vedanta' and a leader of the national liberation movement. He developed an integral sociology linked with his philosophical vision; suitable for his period.

Sri Ramakrishna, a prophet of the modern age, was an ascetic of a high order with direct transcendental experience and a world-view on religion. He championed the cause of non-violence and his approach to problems was with passive shrewdness. His proficiency in presenting high philosophical and theological ideas in simple language with the help of parables picked up from daily life of man, is superb and beyond comparison.

Swamy Vivekananda was a scholar, an extraordinary genius with a gifted tongue, an ambassador of Indian culture and religion and a philosopher, who stood apart from other Indian Philosophers. He blended world philosophy from Aristotle to his times with Indian philosophical heritage and shaped new philosophies of his own, picking up the most valuable and progressive elements in various other philosophies.

Hence, four philosophies of a representative character have only been chosen.

FOOTNOTES

1. Mahajan, V.D., *Ancient India*, p. 115.
2. Jawaharlal Nehru, *The Discovery of India*, p. 175.
3. Warder, A.K., *A Course in Indian Philosophy*, p. 135.
4. Jawaharlal Nehru, *The Discovery of India*, p. 176.
5. *Ibid.*, p. 176.
6. *Ibid.*, p. 177.
7. Mahajan, V.D., *Ancient India*, pp. 113-14.
8. Jawaharlal Nehru, *The Discovery of India*, p. 180.
9. *Ibid.*, p. 181.
10. Warder, A.K., *A Course in Indian Philosophy*, pp. 32-38.
11. *Ibid.*, pp. 43-44.
12. Brodov, V., *Indian Philosophy in Modern Times*, p. 181.
13. *Ibid.*, pp. 310-36.
14. *Ibid.*, pp. 193-208.
15. Swamy Vivekananda, *The Complete Works of Swamy Vivekananda*, Vol. V, p. 150.
16. *Ibid.*, Vol. III, pp. 235-36.
17. *Ibid.*, Vol. V, p. 335.
18. *Ibid.*, Vol. VI, p. 31.
19. *Ibid.*, Vol. VIII, pp. 245-49.
20. *Ibid.*, Vol. I, p. 84.
21. *Ibid.*, Vol. I, pp. 37-38.
22. *Ibid.*, Vol. II, p. 138.
23. Brodov, V., *Indian Philosophy in Modern Times*, p. 290.

Hinduism vs Hindutva

16

Hinduism

Hinduism never claimed that it is the only true religion in the world. It allows its members the widest freedom in matters of faith and worship. Resultantly, we come across in Hinduism a variety of beliefs, practices and philosophies dealing with the nature of God, man and the universe and different methods for God-realization. Hinduism, all along its history, had been tolerant towards other religions. Its policy had always been 'let good thoughts come from all sides'. This freedom, openness and flexibility helped Hinduism to withstand the onslaughts of other religions and maintain its separate identity. Moreover, it had always shown willingness to accept and assimilate some of the positive elements in other religions. In the Hindu scriptures, we do not come across the use of the term "Hindu Dharma" designating an exclusive religious identity.

The concept of Hinduism developing as a separate religion seems to be a later occurrence. In fact, Hinduism, as we see it today is the meeting point of various religious traditions developed in various parts of India in different epochs of its long history just like various rivers (Ganga, Yamuna, and Saraswati) joining together at *Triveni Sangam* to form a mighty river. The Aryan branch in Hinduism is a typical example. The spirit of openness, assimilations, and tolerance contributed to the synthesis of various religious traditions. It is logical to conclude that it is the advent of other religions of foreign origin that prompted Hinduism to assume a separate distinguishing identity as a religion. Hinduism does not acknowledge any single individual or institution as a final and definitive authority in matters of faith and practice. The

Dharma Sansad occasionally convened at *Kumbha mela* tried to assume the role of a final religious authority, but it failed to muster the consent and recognition of the Hindu masses.

The Hindu religion does not have a stereotyped form insisting conformity by all. Each one is free to pick up and choose according to one's preferences. In this respect, we come across two concepts, *Adhikara* (eligibility) and *ista* (personal preference). A man of intellectual and mystical frame of mind may find it easy to enjoy union with God without the need of temples or rituals or symbols of worship, whereas an ordinary person may feel at home with God whom he can love, touch and see in the form of an idol. For him, rituals and symbols of worship help to express his inner feelings and sentiments. Hinduism gives equal respect for both.

Sri Krishna in the *Bhagavad Gita* states that the distinction between spiritual and temporal or sacred and profane is meaningless. The *Isavasyopanishad* begins with the statement *Isavasyam Idom Sarvam* meaning 'the whole universe is the dwelling place of God' (please see notes on *Isavasyopanishad* in Chapter-11). The Lord envelops whatever is there in this moving world. According to the *Brihadaranyakopanishad* "And everything that is, is Brahman." The *Kathopanishad* says that the transcendental one is greater than the greatest (*Mahato mahiyan*) and smaller than the smallest (*anor aniyan*) as it is intimately present in the heart of every being. There is the touch of the divine in every fibre of being, in every flower and in every leaf. All are charged with the grandeur of God.

In the Bible (Ex: 3:5) we find Yahweh telling Moses from the burning bush "Take off your footwear from your feet, for the place on which you are standing is holy ground." Similarly, the sacredness of all things can be found in Hinduism as well, through the respect towards the universe, towards every form of life, the variety of symbols they use, the use of idols (*murti*) etc. The *Svetasvatara Upanishad* (VI: II) affirms that the Supreme Spirit present in a hidden manner in all beings (*sarvabhutesu gudhah*) as their foundation makes itself visible in an image (*visesadhisthana*) for the sake of His devotees.

God is present in everything. Whatever special quality, special excellence, special beauty, strength, height, length, width, depth, etc. possessed by the creation indicates a special presence of God and therefore deserves special reverence and honour. Thus, mighty Himalayas, large rivers like Ganga, gigantic banyan tree, strong lion, etc. manifest the special presence of God. Sri Krishna identifies himself (B.G. X:22) with the best of all categories of creations; Samaveda among the Vedas, mind among the senses, *Sumeru* among the mountains, *peepul* tree among the trees, Vyasa among the sages, etc. Again Krishna says:

> Whatsoever is glorious, good, beautiful and mighty, understand thou that go forth from a fragment of my splendour. (B.G: X: 40-41)

In the *Rig Veda*, the term '*deva*' was used to signify the special presence of God. For example, the Sun god stands for the special presence of the divine power giving life-nourishing light and energy to the whole of creation. Whatever God creates is sacred and divine. If everything is sacred and divine, the most sacred of all God's creations is undoubtedly man, the human being. The *Bible* says (Gen. 1:28) that man is created in the very image and likeness of God. In essence, God and human being are spirit, (*atmah*), pure awareness (*caitanyamatra*). Not only that they are of the same nature, but also there is an intimate relationship between them. The *Paramatma* and the *Jeevatma* are related like the fire and the sparks, the whole and the part or the soul and the body. Sri Sankara named this relationship as *Tadatmya* (becoming one with). The *Mundakopanishad* (III: 1:1-3) presents a story of two birds, representing the divine spirit and the human spirit sitting on a tree. (Please see notes on *Mundakopanishad* in Ch. 11)

"The affirmation of the fundamental divinity of the human being makes it the object of special reverence and respect. All forms of violence towards human beings, therefore, go against the true spirit of Hinduism. Fundamentalism and religious intolerance, leading to atrocities against others in the name of God and religion, are negations of one of the cardinal principles of Hindu religion. More than a temple, mosques and churches, the human being is the living temple of God. To desecrate this temple by thought, word or deed is indeed to commit sacrilege against the one true God known by different names."[1]

Service of the human being is the true service of God. This is illustrated in Hinduism in the concept of *Nara-Narayana*. The human being, especially the poor is the visible manifestation of God Himself. In the *Gita* (B.G. III:20) Sri Krishna tells Arjuna the example of King Janaka who attained perfection through action for the welfare of the world. Swamy Vivekananda advised to integrate the ideal of service to humanity with Indian monasticism that is by and large acosmic. Vivekananda adds that a man with the simple power of good actions for others, even without believing in any God or even without praying once in the whole life, can reach the stage where the religious men and philosophers reach through their knowledge.[2]

The Cardinal Virtues of Hinduism

Hinduism has five cardinal virtues, very dear to Gandhiji and generally acceptable to all; *ahimsa, satya, asteya, brahamacarya*, and *aparigraha*. These are the five subdivisions of *Yama*, the first among the eight steps of yoga.[3]

Ahimsa: The traditional and literal translation of this word is non-violence or non-injury. But it has a connotation wider than its literal meaning, namely love and respect towards all. Hinduism proclaims *ahimsa* as the greatest virtue and highest duty of all human beings (*Ahimsa paramo dharma*). This attitude is expected to flow from the heart, rejecting the options of anger, revenge, hatred and other similar vices. The Buddhist virtues of *maitri* (spirit of friendship) and *karuna* (compassion) are akin to *Ahimsa*.

Satya: Satya means truthfulness in thought, word and deed (*Manasa vacha karmana*). This emanates from love for fellow beings. Intolerance and harshness are opposed to the virtue of *Satya*.

Asatya: It literally means 'non-stealing'. It implies the recognition of the right of others to hold wealth as a means for livelihood. One's property is the outer life of the person. Avoidance of all sorts of exploitation of others for one's self-interests falls within the ambit of this virtue.

Brahmacarya: It literally means continence, meaning conduct which puts one in touch with God, as against the general narrow interpretation as abstience from sex. According to the Upanishad, *Brahmacarin* means one who seeks the liberating knowledge of the Supreme Spirit, one who is loving and compassionate towards other human beings, recognising the presence of God in others.

Aparigraha: This means non-accumulation of material possessions and avoidance of avarice. The principle of trusteeship advanced by Gandhiji is based on *Aparigraha*. One's possessions have to be looked upon as a trust to be utilized for the welfare of others. The *Isavasyopanishad* says *Ma Grudha: kasyaswidhanam* (covet not the wealth of others). Gandhiji stresses that one who accumulates more than what is necessary for oneself is truly a thief.

Secularism

The word 'secularism' literally means a belief that laws, education etc. should be based on facts and Science rather than on religion. This word originally developed in the West to indicate a political concept advocating strict separation of State and religion; in other words, state and religion mutually keeping distance from the other. This concept emerged in the West in the struggle between the Church and the rulers for political supremacy. The rulers won in this struggle. In other words, secularism means separation from political rule. In India, neither *Dharma* exercised absolute power over rulers nor rulers sought absolute power over *Dharma*. This continued during Muslim rule also. The Indian languages translate the word 'Secularism' as *Dharmanirapekshata*. According to genuine Hinduism, religious and moral values ought to play an important role in nation building. Religion is an integral and inalienable part of Indian culture. The impact of religion is found in every aspect of human life. From birth to death, religion surrounds a person through rituals, feasts and other observances. From the Hindu point of view, this factor has to be kept in mind while defining secularism.

Any socio-political system that ignores or discards moral and spiritual values is against the core and spirit of Hinduism. The *Ramarajya* of Gandhiji, a concept built on the solid foundation of moral and religious values, is akin to the 'kingdom of God' proclaimed by Jesus. Sacred and profane are not separate watertight compartments.

In examining the relations between the State and religion, three schools of thought or interpretations have emerged and have come to the forefront.

1. *Theocracy*: It upholds one religion as State religion and grants preferential treatment to that religion. This is diametrically opposed to the concept of secularism.

2. The State keeping equidistant from all religions or the view that the State has nothing to do with religion or religious values.

3. *Sarvadharma Samabhava*: State recognising and treating all religions equally with due respect and honour (*Sadbhava*) with no special treatment for any religion. It ensures a positive and harmonious relation between all religions also.

The Constitution of India has adopted the concept of "Secularism" described in item (3) above as the one that suits the country and as the only one that reconciles with the Hindu faith and the age-old traditions and culture of the nation. The Indian nation has complied with the constitutional stipulations in the past more than fifty years, thereby preserving the integrity of the nation and checking, then and there, fissiparous tendencies, if any, in every isolated nook and cranny.

India is a multi-religious country, with the population crossing the thousand million mark. The religion-wise distribution of % of population is as follows:

Adherents	Population %
Buddhists	0.8
Christians	2.3
Hindus	82.0
Jains	0.4
Muslims	12.1
Sikhs	1.9
Others	0.4

Note: (1) This excludes Assam and Jammu and Kashmir.
(2) Figures of 1991 Census (2001 tentative figures do not show much difference).

Hindutva

In recent years, a fundamentalist minority in Hinduism has advanced a new concept named *Hindutva.* The literal translation of the word *Hindutva* is *Hinduness.* Veer Savarkar, a Hindu leader is said to be the first to have used this word. It is not known whether this word finds a place in any ancient Indian literature or whether it is a newly coined one. The protagonists of Hindutva fail to explain the full implications of this concept. But, we get some hints about their intentions from some of their utterances. Anyhow, the prevailing use of the term 'secularism' has become a tool in the hands of the Hindutva sponsors to brand their opponents as pseudo-secularists who allegedly try to keep God and religion out of the lives of the people. This approach clearly reveals that the present 'secularism' as followed by the nation is not acceptable to them. They find it as appeasement of minorities for political motives. They equate Hindutva with Hinduism and links it with Indian nationalism so that those who do not abide by the concept may be labelled as anti-nationals. From these utterances, there is reason to doubt whether their ultimate aim is to make India a theocratic nation (as successfully practised by India's neighbours) throwing the present secularism to the winds. But, a vast majority of the Hindus, as on today, do not subscribe to the Hindutva ideal. They are happily content with the present Hinduism evolved through millennia and preserved singularly apart from all other world religions.

Historical Background of Hindutva

Hindu fundamentalism of the present day has to be looked upon as the cumulative effect of various historical, socio-political and economic factors. Hindutva ideology is in itself a deviation from the true spirit of Hinduism. Similar aberrations have made their appearance, from time to time, in many world religions including Christianity and Islam. Let us briefly examine these factors.

The political unity of North India achieved under the Harshas was broken after the death of Harsha Vardhan in 647 AD. The absence of a centralised government in India emboldened the Arabs to conquer India and convert the Hindus to Islam. The success of the conquests and conversions in North Africa and the Iberian Peninsula served as a fillip to repeat similar expeditions. The transfer of the Eastern Caliphate from Mecca to Baghdad accelerated the tempo and frequency of the conquests of India. Under the directions of the Caliph, six futile attempts were made in between 636 and 664 AD. Another attempt by one Ubaidulla in 711 AD also failed. In 712, one Mohammed Bin Quasim succeeded in capturing and plundering Sind and Multan. But he was executed under the orders of the Caliph. Thereafter, the Hindushahi kingdom in the North-West India resisted the pressure for the subsequent 200 years. In the beginning of the eleventh century, Mahmud Ghazni made sixteen attempts and succeeded in all of them except one in Kashmir. After each expedition, he returned after forcibly converting thousands to Islam, ravaging the areas, destroying hundreds of temples, murdering thousands of people and acquiring immeasurable booty in the form of gold, jewels, diamonds, elephants, horses and whatever he liked. It is Muhammad Ghori who established the first Muslim Empire in India consisting of North India, Bengal, and Deccan. After Ghori, the Turks established the Turkish rule in India at first through the Slave dynasty followed by the Khalji and the Tuglaq dynasties. After the death of the last Tuglaq in 1394, there was no effective government due to the struggle between the rival claimants for the throne. This provided an opportune occasion for Timur, a Tartar, to plunder India. The number of massacres by Timur is estimated as not less than one hundred thousand. On 12th Dec. 1398 alone, fifty thousand men were murdered in cold blood. He occupied for 15 days and lay waste the three towns of Siri, Old Delhi and Jahan Panah. Even after Timur's return, thousands of women and children died due to famine, the after-effect of Timur's atrocities. Many historians are of the view that Timur had only one motivation; the extermination of the unbelievers. Amassing as much wealth as possible was only a subsidiary motive.

After the return of Timur, the Sayyid dynasty occupied the throne of the Delhi Sultan. They were succeeded by the Lodhi dynasty. Ibrahim Lodhi, the last among the Lodhis was defeated by Babur, a Mangolian by maternal genealogy and a Turk by paternal genealogy and established the Mughul Empire in India. During the Mughul rule, Nadir Shah, the ruler of Iran conquered and plundered India. He robbed the Kohinoor diamond, the peacock throne of Shah Jahan, and many valuables and committed innumerable massacres and atrocities. Ahmad Shah Abdali, the successor of Nadir Shah led seven expeditions and repeated the atrocities and murders of Nadir Shah. With the death of Aurangzeb, the Moghul Empire almost collapsed though his son and grandson ascended the throne as nominal successors.

Thus, for more than ten centuries, India was under Muslim domination. Many rulers (Sultans), except a few like Jalal-ud-din Khalji, Mohammad-Bin-Tuglaq and Akbar, were against religious tolerance. The atrocious and brutal persecution of the Hindus under Mohammad Bin Quasim (712 AD), Mahmud Ghazni (1006-1024), Timur (1398), Humayun of Bhamani kingdom (1458), Nadir Shah (1739) and Ahmed Shah Abdali (1748) remain notorious chapters in Indian history.

Thereafter came the Portuguese rule in Goa and the British rule in India. In Goa, the Portuguese were not behind anyone in the religious persecution of the Hindus. But, it was limited to only a small area. The British never unleashed any notable religious persecution. They were concerned more with trade and wealth, rather than religion.

In the British period, Indian agriculture was ignored, village industries collapsed, the artisans were thrown out of employment, labourers were to work in pitiably miserable conditions and famine became a rampant and recurring feature in India with death toll in thousands each time. They impoverished India by converting the country as supplier of raw materials and provider of market for the finished products of the British Industries. All agitations and challenges to their actions were mercilessly suppressed with an iron hand.

In this historical, socio-political and economic background, no one need be surprised if a section in Hinduism has become fundamentalists with grim determination for revenge. But, the unkindest cut of all happened later by the partition of the Indian nation on communal lines. A nation is a community of people usually sharing a common history, culture, language and living in a particular territory under one government. Hinduism is a religion closely intertwinned with the nation, its geography and natural environment. The partition of the country into Hindu India and Muslim Pakistan wounded the hearts of not only the Hindus, but also the whole Indians irrespective of caste or community. To add fuel to the fire, the partition was accompanied by the outbreak of a series of massacres on both sides. The current crisis in the relations between two nations and two religions must be seen against the backdrop of these historical facts.

Dharma as Science

Meera Nanda, a fellow of the American Council of Learned Societies at Columbia University has revealed the intentions of the Hindutva ideologues, claiming as 'intellectual *Kshatrias*', planning to defend *dharma* as science and for declaring astrology and the entire vedic tradition as 'scientific'.

Excerpts of her Article in the *The Week* magazine are reproduced below, in this context:[4]

"Hindutva is in the process of creating a myth of 'Vedic science' which can co-opt and absorb modern science into Hindu traditions by declaring these traditions to be scientific. Hindutva ideologues argue that just as modern 'Western science' is scientific from a Judeo-Christian perspective, Hindu traditions of astrology, *Yajnas*, *Ayurveda*, *Vastu Shastra*, Hindu ecology, Hindu meterology, etc., are scientific from a Hindu perspective."

"Take for example the argument for scientificity of astrology. It is the neo-Gandhian Ashis Nandy and his followers who have long argued that astrology can't be condemned as a superstition. On the strength of the argument that all 'ethno-science' has no greater claim to objectivity, Nandy has argued that modern science is the myth of the imperialist West, and astrology is the myth of the weak, who are the victims of the West. If that is granted, Nandy argues, the weak should have the right to challenge the 'myth' of science."

"Secular intellectuals and progressive social movements have for too long decried it as a ploy of westernised elites. At a time when modern science needed to establish its cultural authority so that it could set new norms for public discourse and provide a more rational world-view, it remained besieged from all sides. Ever since the scientific temper debate in early 80s, which marked the beginning of the end of the Nehruvian consensus over secularism and modernity, there have been few voices that have actively challenged the many signs of unreason and arbitrary authority in our society."

India's Cultural and Religious Heritage

If the Hindutva adherents succeed in establishing scientific basis of Vedic traditions, *Dharma*, Astrology, *Yajnas*, *Ayurveda*, *Vastu Sastra*, etc., there is absolutely no ground for any Indian to be unhappy. The fear is only on the future of secularism and the relations of Hinduism with the main minority religions in India, Islam and Christianity. Once that relation becomes strained, skeptical or hostile, it is a matter of grave concern for the nation as well as the whole people of India. Fundamentalism and fanaticism, wherever they are found, are in fact a negation of a true religion. When these factors masquerade as religion, it is factually the denial of it. All religions, in principle, stand for promoting unity and harmony rather than division and discord. An indepth analysis reveals that *Hindutva* concept resembles a perverted form of Hinduism diametrically opposed to the grand ideals of *Sanatana Dharma* and *Loka Samasta Sukhino Bhavandu* proclaimed to the world by Hinduism alone. If *Hindutva* is one germinated from the urge for revenge for past actions, it is nothing but 'burning the castle to kill the rat'.

Toynbee says:

"One Indian virtue that has impressed me greatly and touched me deeply is the Indian people's freedom from rancour." He adds, "Non-violent revolution is a characteristic Indian accomplishment." "But, who are still alive are now living the full blast of the Atomic-age. In this hurricane of annihilating material power, mankind will not be able to save itself from self-destruction, unless we all of us manage to practise non-violence in our relations with our fellowmen. We have to practise it in the teeth of provocation, however, wanton and however deliberate the provocation may seem, in our eyes, to be. If India were ever to fail to live up to this Indian ideal which is the finest, and therefore the most exacting legacy in our Indian heritage, it would be a poor look-out for mankind as a whole."[5]

(Please see list of 23 civilizations and further details in Chapter 1 of Part one.)

Conclusion

After the success of the independence struggle, Indians certianly did not brood over the past or nurse grievances. India joined the British Commonwealth and still maintains cordial relations with our oppressors in the international arena without grudge or ill-will or hatred. This is the typical example of *Indianness* that no other nation in the world can claim. This is what our great teachers like Buddha, Mahavira, Asoka, Gandhiji and others taught us. Our endeavour ought to be the resurrection of this heritage.

Let us hope that the essentially liberal and secular core of Hinduism would reassert itself, in the course of time and disown its own fundamentalist and ugly image. The prime need of the hour is a genuine critique of religion in dialogue. Islam, preaching universal brotherhood and Christianity preaching 'love' as the core of its teachings should realise the genuine grievances of the Hindus and should take the initiative for a purposeful and fraternal dialogue with Hinduism without delay to avert a future catastrophe. Let wiser counsel prevail.

FOOTNOTES

1. Joseph Vellaringhatt, S.J., *The Secular Face of Hinduism*, p. 650 of VJTR 9/2001.
2. *Complete Works of Swamy Vivekananda*, Vol. 1, p. 84.
3. Gopalakrishnan, N. (Dr.), *Ancient Indian Scientific Thoughts*, p. 1.
4. Ms. Meera Nanda, Article in *The Week*, 24-06-2001.
5. Sachidanandan, V., *A. Toynbee Anthology*, pp. 48-49.

PART THREE

OTHER RELIGIONS OF INDIAN ORIGIN

Buddhism

17

Introduction

In the Vedic age, several schools of philosophy based on the *Vedas* emerged in Hinduism. From the 13th to the 8th century BC, there was a strong Empire in North India that claimed to unite the Sanskrit-speaking Aryans by protecting the *Vedic* philosophies and rituals. In that period, it was rather unthinkable for any philosopher to do anything outside the *Vedic* tradition, unless and until social changes took place deeply disturbing the *Vedic* framework of *brahminical* society protected by the political system. But, between the 8th and 6th century BC, for reasons unknown, the Empire broke up into a large number of independent States. These States differed widely not only in their governmental system, but also in their degree of adherence to the age-old traditions. The resultant expansion of trade and economic affluence accelerated the shattering of the traditional values. In the changed scenario, several independent philosophers and teachers came to the limelight, in the sixth century BC. These philosophers and teachers, who were exponents of independent thoughts outside the *Vedas*, were generally known as *Sramanas* (Literally meaning 'Strivers', presumably of Truth).

Sramana Philosophies

Many of the *Sramana* philosophers repudiated the monopoly of the *Brahmins* in the hereditary *Vedic* traditions and rituals. The prominent among these philosophies were *Lokayata* (worldliness or naturalism), *Ajivakas* (materialism or happiness emphasizing fate or *Niyati*), *Ajnana* (ignorance), 'Buddhism' and 'Jainism'. They rejected life after death, transmigration of souls (*Karma Samsar*) and advocated happiness as the main goal of life. According to the *Vedic* philosophies, the goals of life in Hinduism or *brahminical* traditions were *Dharma* (obligations, duties, virtue, righteousness etc.), *Artha* (wealth), *Kama* (pleasures of the world including sex) and *Moksha* (eternal bliss or salvation) in the order of priority. The Sramana philosophers changed this order of priority by putting *Kama* and *Artha* above *Dharma* (*Dhamma* in Buddhism). The seeds of *Sramana* philosophies were sown in a ground made fertile by the discontentment and opposition to the vested interests, excessive ritualism and exploitation by the priests in Hinduism.

The influence of Aryans was strong and more widespread in North-West India. North-East India, which remained comparatively free from the influence of *brahminical* traditions, became the breeding ground of many heterodox sects. Religiously, this was a time of doubt, turmoil and experimentation in North-East India and, therefore, new philosophies found easy acceptance.

Buddha

Gautama (563-483 BC) also known as Siddhartha or Sakya Muni, the founder of Buddhism, is considered one among the *Sramana* philosophers. The term 'Buddha' is a title meaning 'the enlightened'. Gautama, a member of a royal Hindu family of Kapilavastu (recently, some scholars are of opinion that Kapilavastu is in Nepal and not in India) after long meditation under a *Bodhi* tree in Gaya in Bihar (India) claimed to have discovered certain truths and became a *Buddha* (meaning – the enlightened). He founded his teachings on the truths that he discovered from his experiences. In his lifetime, the school founded by him was very small compared to the widespread organisation of the *Ajivakas,* another *Sramana* philosophy. But, in the long run, Buddha became the most successful among the *Sramanas*. Though Buddha disagreed with the *Sramana* philosophers on many aspects, he endorsed their views of sidelining the existence of God or Soul. The Buddhist Era begins from the year of death of Buddha (483 BC). Many Japanese scholars put Buddha's life 100 years later, from 448 to 368 BC. The era, which gave birth to Buddha, was one of tremendous mental ferments and philosophic enquiries not only in India but also in many parts of the world. Lao-Tze, Confucius, Zoroaster and Pythagoras were the products of that age.

Whether fact or fiction, many miracles were reported to have "occurred when Gautama was born. The heavens glowed with glorious light, the lame suddenly walked, the blind regained sight, the decrepit were made strong and throughout the world musical instruments stuck up majestic hymns of praise, though untouched by human hands or lips. Even the gods rejoiced and sent cascades of flowers showering down upon the earth. The infant himself quickly revealed that he was no ordinary child."[1]

Buddhism eschews all speculations about God and the Universe. The avowed aim of Buddhism is similar to that of Hinduism – the liberation from the bondage of suffering – but the way prescribed by Buddhism for liberation is more ethical than that of Hinduism. In Buddhism, attention is focused on man's inner attitude through which the process of detachment and disentanglement from the world has to be achieved. A true Buddhist strives for salvation mainly through meditation in which he becomes aware of the nothingness of all changeable things and in deep confidence and full devotedness prepares himself for the Absoluteness – (*Nirvana*) – which means an existence beyond all limitations.

Buddha wrote nothing himself. But some 300 years after his death, his teachings assumed a canonical form being collected in the *Tripitaka* or Triple basket. The early Buddhist texts emphasize 'cessation' as a practical programme to be undertaken by each student personally verifying the truth through one's own experience. There is no question of believing anything on authority, not even the authority of Buddha and he personally disclaimed his own personal authority.

The sacred writings of Buddhism are in three parts: (1) for the laity, (2) for the devotees, and (3) a metaphysical section. Buddhism embraces four sublime Verities:

That suffering exists

That it is caused by desire

That there is a way to end it.

That this way consists in following eight-fold path of:

(a) Right Doctrine,

(b) Right Purpose,

(c) Right Discourse,

(d) Right Behaviour,

(e) Right Purity,

(f) Right Thought,

(g) Right Lowliness, and

(h) Right Rapture.

Hinayana and Mahayana Systems

Buddha used the popular language of the area he lived which was *Prakrit*, a derivative of Sanskrit. From this *Prakrit* developed the *Pali* language of the early Buddhist scriptures. Buddha's dialogues and discourses were recorded in *Pali* long after his death and this formed the basis of Buddhism in Ceylon (Sri Lanka), Burma (Myanmar), etc. where the *Hinayana* (small vehicle) form of Buddhism prevailed. This is also called the *Theravada* School (meaning Elders School).

Hundreds of years after Buddha, there was a revival of Sanskrit in India and the Buddhist scholars in India wrote their philosophical and other works in Sanskrit. These Sanskrit writings of Indian scholars spread to China, Tibet, Central Asia etc. where the *Mahayana* (big vehicle) form prevailed. Today, the *Mahayanas* constitute 56 per cent of the Buddhist population. The *Hinayanas* come to 38 per cent. The rest are *Tantrayanas* (Lamaism).

Buddhism has multiple forms, but the two basic forms are the *Hinayana* and the *Mahayana*. The *Hinayana* form is orthodox in doctrine, strictly non-personal and tends to eliminate man's personality and the reality of the world leading to man's liberation. The *Mahayana* is less rationalistic and considers Buddha as a supernatural being and an object of worship. According to this sect, compassion for all who suffer is a fundamental virtue. In man's striving towards liberation, he is supported by superior beings, the *Bodhisattavas* (those who aspire to become Buddha), who help him not only for liberation but also to become at the final stage an 'enlightened' one, a 'Buddha'.

While the *Hinayana* adhered to the ancient pure doctrine circumscribed in a *Pali canon*, the *Mahayana* spread out in every direction, tolerating and adapting itself to each country's distinctive outlook. Some of the earliest Buddhist thinkers moved away from the agnostic attitude that Buddha had taken up regarding the existence of the soul and rejected it completely. In the *Mahayana*, the means of salvation are available to a larger number of people and hence treated as 'Big Vehicle'. In *Hinayana*, the means of salvation are alleged to be restricted to a smaller number of people and hence it is only a "Small Vehicle". In the growth, development and acceptance of the *Mahayana* system in India, the role of Nagarjuna, who lived during Kanishka's reign about the beginning of the Christian Era, a scholar in Sanskrit and both Hindu and Buddhist philosophies, is worth mentioning. He was instrumental in settling all ideological controversies and establishing the *Mahayana* system on a strong logical foundation in India.

Outside the *Mahayana* and *Hinayana* groups, there is a group known as Lamaism or Tantrayana that constitute roughly 6 per cent of Buddhists.

Buddha's Message

The teachings attributed to Buddha were transmitted orally by his disciples prefaced by the phrase "*evam me sutam*" (thus have I heard). Therefore, it is difficult to say whether his discourses were related as he spoke them. In the early centuries after Buddha's death, the Buddhist Councils made an attempt to establish his true and original teachings and claim their findings as original and genuine. But many scholars are still skeptical.

Buddha was a rebel. But he hardly cut himself off from the ancient faith of the land. Mrs. Rhys David says "Gautama was born and brought up and lived and died as a Hindu. There was not much in the metaphysics and principles of Gautama which cannot be found in one or other of the orthodox systems and a great deal of his morality could be matched from earlier or later Hindu books. Such originality as Gautama possessed lay in the way in which he adapted, enlarged, ennobled and systematised that had already been well-said by others.... The difference between him and other teachers lay chiefly in his deep earnestness and in his broad public spirit of philanthropy."

The essence of Buddha's message was universal benevolence of love for all. It was an ideal of self-righteousness and self-discipline. His own words quoted below will help to have an insight into his message.

"Never in this world hatred ceases by hatred: hatred ceases by love."

"Let a man overcome anger by kindness, evil by good."

"One may overcome a thousand men in battle, but he who conquers himself is the victor."

"Not by birth, but by conduct alone does a man become a low caste or a Brahmin."

"Victory breeds hatred, for the conquered is unhappy."[2]

Buddha preached without any religious sanction or reference to God or another world. To a question regarding the existence of God, he neither affirms nor denies. He says:

> "If the Absolute is meant something out of relation to all known things, its existence cannot be established by any known reasoning, how can we know that anything unrelated to other things exists at all? The whole universe as we know it is a system of relations: we know nothing that is or can be unrelated. So we must limit ourselves to what we can perceive and about which we can have definite knowledge."[3]

The Absolute is often referred to in Buddhist philosophy as *Shunyata* or nothingness (In Sanskrit, *Shunya* means Zero) yet it is something different from our conception of nothingness. "It is on account of *Shunyata* that everything becomes possible, without it nothing in the world is possible" says a Buddhist scholar. Metaphysics developed in Buddhist philosophy, but the method was based on a psychological approach.

The aim of religious practice is to get rid of the delusion of "Ego", thus freeing oneself from the fetters of this mundane world. One who is successful in doing so is said to have overcome the cycle of rebirths and to have achieved enlightenment. This is the final goal – *Nirvana* – not a paradise or a heavenly world.

In later years, there developed in India a movement called *Vajrayana* or *Esoteric Buddhism* that aimed at liberation more speedily. Gnosticism and magical currents pervasive in those days influenced this movement. But, the historians of Christianity attribute the *vice versa* – Buddhism influenced Gnosticism in the West.

Different Philosophies

Four definite schools of philosophy developed in Buddhism, two in the *Hinayana* branch, another two in the *Mahayana* branch. Dr. Radhakrishnan describes the logical movements of Buddhist thoughts as found expression in the four schools. It begins with a dualistic metaphysics looking upon knowledge as a direct awareness of objects. In the next stage, ideas are made, the media raising a screen between mind and objects. These two stages represent the *Hinayana* school. The *Mahayanas* went further, abolished the things behind the images and reduced all experiences to a series of ideas in the mind. The ideas of relativity and subconscious self come in. In the last stage, mind itself is dissolved into mere ideas, leaving us with loose units of ideas and perceptions, about which we cannot say, anything definite. This is the middle way (*Madhyamika* philosophy of Nagarjuna). Thus we finally arrive at airy nothing or something that is so difficult to grasp for our finite minds. The utmost we can say is that it is some kind of consciousness, *Vijyana* as it is called.

Impact of Buddhism on Hinduism

Initially, Buddhism was only a *Kshatria* movement, but with a popular appeal. Buddha may not have thought of himself as the founder of a religion. He probably looked upon himself as a social and religious reformer only. But his dynamic personality and forceful messages attacking many social and religious practices led to conflict with the entrenched priesthood. He never wanted to uproot the existing social order or economic system; he accepted their basic premises and only attacked the evils that had grown under them. His revolutionary approach angered the *Brahmin* classes, who were the beneficiaries of the existing practices and privileges. But, many *Brahmins* joined it. It may perhaps be because the *Brahmins* found that it developed more along metaphysical and philosophical lines.

Buddhism influenced Indian life in a hundred ways as it was a living, dynamic and widespread religion in India for over a thousand years.

Much of the ritualism and ceremonial associated with the *Vedic* religion of the Hindus, especially animal sacrifice disappeared.

Buddhism emphasized the idea of non-violence already present in the *Vedas* and the *Upanishads*.

A new respect for life and kindness to animals emerged. The total effect of Buddha's teachings was one of pessimism towards life. Sexual continence and vegetarianism were encouraged. In Aryanism, the emphasis was on an all-round life, according to which there were four stages (*Ashramas*) in life:

Brahmacarya – sexual continence and discipline.

Garhasthy – The householder participating fully in life's activities including sex (Here, sex is treated as a natural and essential component of life).

Vanaprastha – gradual withdrawal from material world and concentration on public service and self-improvement through prayer, detachment and meditation (formerly, it involved living in forest settlements).

Sannyas – full withdrawal from life's normal works and attachments and leading an ascetic life, the last stage at the fag end of life.

By the coming of Buddhism, huge monasteries grew up everywhere and there was regular flow of people towards these *Viharas*, as they were called. The State of Bihar derived its name from *Vihara* indicating that a large area there was full of *Viharas*.[4]

Another significant effect of Buddhism was in the social structure in India based on the caste system. Buddhism never accepted caste, but approved its base. Importance to births was replaced by importance to character, capacity, occupation etc. The caste system was not altogether eliminated, but its rigidity and sanction were weakened resulting in a change in the perspective of the people.

In the Indo-Aryan social structure, agriculture was a honourable occupation entitling a higher place in the social ladder. By the emphasis on non-violence by Buddhism (more by Jainism) the tilling of the soil involving destruction of animal life was considered a lowly occupation degrading the agriculturist to a lower rank in the social hierarchy.

The worshipping practices, rituals, ceremonials, monastic systems etc. in Buddhism were copied by Hinduism, thereby reducing the distance between the two religions in outward appearance that ultimately led to the vanishing of the gap in between.

Decline of Buddhism in India

Even when Buddhism reached its zenith in India, Hinduism was not exterminated, but remained side by side with Buddhism. After being the prominent religion in India for more than thousand years, Buddhism gradually declined. All the factors that contributed for this decline are not known. Many believe that Buddhism was so tolerant of other faiths that it was simply reabsorbed by a revitalised Hinduism.

Even after the destruction of numerous monasteries by the *Huns* in the 6th century AD, Buddhism revived in the North-East India under the patronage of the Pala kings. The kings protected the great *Mahavihars* (Monasteries) and built up new ones. One among them at *Odantapuri* near Nalanda flourished under the Pala kings and the University of Nalanda became a world centre for the study of *Tantric* (*Vajrayana*) Buddhism. With the decline of Pala dynasty in the 12th century AD, Buddhism in India lost its glory from which it never recovered.

Another important factor contributed for its decline is that Buddhism, being a monastic movement, never paid due heed to the laity. Monasticism lost its esteem and image among the public when monasteries degenerated by becoming wealthy enough to have slaves and hired labourers to care for the monks and lend the lands they owned. When the Muslim invaders sacked the monasteries in the 12th century, the Buddhist laity did not come forward to revive them. Above all, the propaganda onslaught of the Hindu reformers like Sri Sankara contributed in a large measure to accelerate the downfall of Buddhism.

The people of ancient South India followed Dravidian practices, which were not based on any religious philosophy. Their way of life was a mixture of primitive rites and practices. The sharp division between castes and communities were conspicuously absent and the rigours of social exclusiveness were unknown. The exact period of Brahmin migration to South India is not known. Though there was no large-scale migration at any point of time in the BC, all historians agree that stray presence of Brahmins was there even during the BC. Anyhow, Brahminism or *Aryadharma* was not an influential factor in the 3rd century BC when Buddhism spread to South India during the period of Asoka. The social and religious life of the South Indians provided a congenial atmosphere for Buddhism to grow rapidly. Its decline started in the 8th century and finally disappeared in the 12th century, leaving behind its legacies and remnants even today. Historians are unanimous in their view that Buddhism was absorbed by Hinduism in South India as well along with its worshipping centres, forms of worship and impressive ceremonials. Many prominent Hindu temples like the Vadakkumnatha Temple at Trichur, Kurumba Bhagavathi Temple at Kodungalloor, Durga Temple at Paruvassery, the famous pilgrimage centre at Sabarimala, Buddha images at Kunnathoor, Ambalapuzha, Mavelikkara and Karunagapally Taluks in Kerala were originally Buddhist shrines. Some scholars are of the view that the famous deity at Sabarimala (*Sastha*) named *Ayyappa* in the sitting posture is the Hinduised version of Buddha. The prior vow for pilgrimage to Sabarimala involving non-violence, vegetarianism and abstinence of worldly pleasures including sex and the sing-song repetition of *Saranam Ayyappa* by the pilgrims echoing the *Saranam* formula of *Buddha*, *Dharma* and *Sanga* are reminiscent of the Buddhist doctrine of *Ahimsa* (Non-violence). The practice of *Kettukazhcha* or *Kuthirakettu* associated with some temple festivals had its origin in Buddhism. The Buddhist *Vihars* (monasteries) were generally known as *Palli* in the vernacular and the educational institutions attached to the *Vihars* were known as *Ezhuthupalli*. *Ashtangahridaya* written by Vagbhata, a Buddhist scholar and *Amarakosa* written by another Buddhist scholar Amarasinha are very popular in South India even today.

The Kings of Chola, Chera and Pandya dynasties in South India were staunch Hindus who propagated Hinduism in their territories and even abroad. They have played a very important role in the revival of Hinduism. On the whole, the mutual interaction and give and take by Hinduism and Buddhism resulted in the survival of the fittest-Hinduism – one swallowing the other.

Buddhism Outside India

Buddhism spread to other countries in Asia through the efforts of Emperor Asoka in the 3rd century BC and Emperor Kanishka in the 1st and 2nd centuries of AD. By the 11th century, Buddhism in Central Asia faded through the influence of Zoroastrianism, Christianity and Islam. Buddhism took roots in Sri Lanka with the arrival of Asoka's son Mahinda and his companions. In the first millennium of AD, the Theravada tradition (Hinayana) co-existed with Hinduism, *Mahayana* Buddhism and *Tantric* Buddhism in Sri Lanka. The monastic community in Sri Lanka is divided into three denominations: (1) the *Siam Nikaya*, founded in the 18th century, a conservative and wealthy sect which admits only members of the *Goyigama*, the highest Sinhalese caste, (2) the *Amarapura* that admitted lower castes, and (3) the *Ramanya*, a reformed group separated from *Siam Nikaya*.

In Myanmar (Burma) and Thailand, the *Hinayana* form remained the prominent one, though *Mahayana* and *Vajrayana* forms and Hinduism were present. In Kampuchea (Cambodia) and Vietnam, the *Mahayana* and *Vajrayana* Buddhism became prominent along with Hinduism. Though Buddhism entered China in the 3rd century BC, it became popular only during the rule of the Han dynasty. Its golden age is during the T'ang dynasty (618 to 907 AD). Among the various schools, the prominent ones are the Ch'an School (better known in the West as Zen) with emphasis on meditation and the Pure Land School emphasising devotion. The Chinese Buddhists underwent great persecution in 845 AD and severe repressions during the Cultural Revolution (1966-69).

Buddhism was introduced in Korea when it was divided into three kingdoms, Paekche, Koguryo and Silla. It came first from China to the kingdom of Koguryo and therefrom spread to other kingdoms. After World War II, growth of Buddhism was hampered by Communist Rule in North Korea and by the great vitality of Christianity in South Korea.

Buddhism was initially introduced in Japan in the 6th century AD from Korea. It was then regarded as a talisman for the protection of the country. It was accepted by the powerful *Soga* clan and rejected by others, which led to a controversy. During the *Nara* period (710-784 AD) Buddhism became the State Religion of Japan. Under the Tokugawa shogunate (1603 to 1867) Buddhism became an arm of the government. Temples were used for registering the populace for preventing the spread of Christianity regarded as a threat to the feudal government.

Buddhism spread to Tibet in the 7th century and Mongolia accepted the Tibetan tradition. In the beginning of the mid-19th century, Buddhism was introduced in the United States and other Western countries by the large number of immigrants from China and Japan, but more recently from other countries of South-East Asia. It gained a foothold among a significant number of Western intellectuals especially among young people seeking new forms of religious experience and expression. Japanese Scholar D.T. Suzuki and Tibetan Buddhist teachers have succeeded in the 20th century in creating interest in Buddhism among the Westerners. In each of these countries, Buddhism adapted itself to the religious, cultural and philosophical *ethos* of the respective countries, sinking and swimming along with their historical currents. Today the world population of Buddhists according to UN Statistics for 1998 is 356 million, of which 98.5 per cent are in Asia.

Contemporary Revival in India

At the beginning of the 20th century, Buddhism was extinct in India. In the early decades of the 20th century, a number of Buddhist Societies were organised by Indian intellectuals who found in Buddhism an alternative that was part of the Indian heritage. Following the Chinese conquest of Tibet in late 1950, there was an influx of Tibetan Buddhists to India. They established a Buddhist community in North India. The incorporation of Sikkim into the Republic of India in 1975 brought a strong Buddhist community to the Indian nation, following the *Vajrayana* Buddhism of Tibet. Another major component in the resurgence of Buddhism in India is the mass conversion of people from the so-called Scheduled Castes (formerly untouchables) under the leadership of Dr. B.R. Ambedkar. These neo-Buddhists follow the Theravada version of Buddhism.

Thus, after being extinct for seven centuries in India, the land of its origin, Buddhism is showing signs of revival in the modern age, gradually increasing the number of its followers. According to 2001 Census in India, all the groups together, the number of Buddhists in India is 63,87,500. This is likely to go up further in the years to come for several reasons, caste system (not under the law of the land but persisting deep-rootedly in the minds of the people), urge for revenge against exploitation of the outcastes for centuries, newly acquired political strength in a democratic set up and above all educational and economic advancement of the downtrodden communities.

Buddhism and Hinduism

1. It is rightly pointed out that Buddhism was merely a phase of Hinduism.
2. It is also pointed out that Buddhism borrowed a lot from Brahminism.
3. Buddhism puts emphasis on the necessity of removing pain by the elimination of desires. The authors of the *Upanishads* gave similar ideas.
4. It is contended that the monastic system was one of the greatest contributions of Buddhism. But even before the time of Buddha, there did exist a large number of monastic orders.
5. It is rightly pointed out that Buddha himself was a product of the *brahminical* system that prevailed in his own time.
6. The *brahminical* writers also anticipated the Buddhist idea of *Nirvana*.
7. Hinduism believes in God, Matter and Soul and considers God as the creator of the universe. Buddhism believes in Matter and Soul and there is no place for God. The God as creator is simply ignored.
8. Hinduism considers the *Vedas* divine and the *Vedic* rituals as a necessity for salvation. However, Buddhism denies the authority of the *Vedas* and it has absolutely no faith in the efficacy of the sacrifices or the *Yajnas* or *Samskaras*.
9. There is no personal element in Hinduism. However, Buddhism introduces such a personal element in the form of Buddha as the Saviour.
10. Hinduism puts emphasis on the caste system and considers it as the bedrock of the whole social system. However, caste system based on birth does not find any place in Buddhism.

11. Buddhism is a missionary religion. It aims at converting the entire mankind to the doctrines of Buddha. However, such is not the case with Hinduism.[5]

12. According to Hinduism, prayers could please the gods.

Conclusion

Buddha's method was one of psychological analysis, and again it is surprising to find how deep was his insight into this latest of modern sciences. Man's life was considered and examined without any reference to a permanent self, for even if such a self exists, it is beyond our comprehension. The mind was looked upon as part of the body, a composite of mental forces. The individual thus becomes a bundle of mental states, the self is just a stream of ideas. All that we are is the result of what we have thought.[6]

"Buddha had the courage to attack popular religions, superstitions, ceremonials and priestcraft and all the vested interests that clung to them. He condemned also the metaphysical and theological outlook, miracles, revelations and dealings with the supernatural. His appeal was to reason, logic and experience; his emphasis was on ethics and his method was one of psychological analysis, a psychology without a soul. His whole approach comes like the breath of the fresh wind from the mountains after the stale air of metaphysical speculation."

Jawaharlal Nehru – *The Discovery of India*

FOOTNOTES

1. *Reader's Digest*, "Great People of Faith and Wisdom," pp. 61, 178-200.
2. Jawaharlal Nehru, *The Discovery of India*, p. 117.
3. *Ibid.*, p. 117.
4. *Ibid.*, p. 167, para 3.
5. Mahajan, V.D., *Ancient India*, pp. 197-200.
6. Jawaharlal Nehru, *The Discovery of India*, p. 118.

SUGGESTED READINGS

Arnold, Sir E., *The Light of Asia.*

Bapat, P.V. (ed.), *2500 Years of Buddhism*, New Delhi, 1956.

Brown, B., *The Story of Buddha and Buddhism.*

Carus, Paul, *The Gospel of Buddha.*

Coneze, E., *Buddhism, Its Essence and Development.*

Coomarswamy, A., *Buddha and the Gospel of Buddhism.*

Dutt, Nalinaksha, *Early History of the Spread of Buddhism*, 1925.

Dutt, Sukumar, *Buddhist Monks and Monasteries in India*, London, 1962.

Gangulee, N., *The Buddha and His Message*, 1957.

Geiger, W., *The Mahavamsa*, 1908.

Hardy, R.S., *Manual of Buddhism*, 1860.

Humphreys, C., *Buddhism.*

Jennings, J.C., *The Vedantic Buddhism of the Buddha.*

Kashyap, *The Abidhamma Philosophy.*

Keith, A.B., *Buddhist Philosophy in India and Ceylon.*

Law, B.C., *Concepts of Buddhism*, 1966.

——, *Geography of Early Buddhism*, 1932.

——, *Buddhistic Studies*, 1931.

——, *Concepts of Buddhism.*

Malalasekar, G.P. (Ed.), *Encyclopaedia of Buddhism* (Colombo).

Max-Mueller, *Dhammapada*, Oxford, 1898.

Jainism

18

Introduction

Jainism, a religion originated around the 6th century BC in India, is popularly believed to have been instituted by an ascetic named Vardhamana Mahavira, the 24th *Theerthankara* (prophet) among the Jaina teachers. One of the schools in Jainism refutes this claim by pointing out that the real founder of Jainism, according to the secred books, was Rishaba, the father of the famous King Bharata in Indian history. Twenty-three *Theerthankaras* (prophets) succeeded Rishaba and Mahavira was the last and the 24th among them. According to Prof. Jacobi, the founder of Jainism is Parsavanath, the 23rd *Theerthankara*. Buddha and Mahavira, the most successful among the *Sramana* philosophers, were contemporaries and *Kshatrias* by caste. The adherents of this religion are known as 'Jains' or 'Jainas', derived from the word 'Jina', the conqueror of passions.

Swetambaras and Digambaras

Like the Buddhists, there are two classes in Jainism, the ascetic class and the lay people. Some secondary texts extracted from the original ones, supposed to have been codified towards the end of the 4th century BC, are called *Angas*. There are two schools of Jainas, the *Swetambaras* (white gowns) and the *Digambaras* (the air-clad or naked). At the time of meals, which they take in common, the *Digambaras* strip naked. The *Swetambaras* claim to be in possession of the *Angas*. The Digambara school declares that the authentic texts have been totally lost and therefore they rely on the traditions handed down by the teachers of their school and later codified in textbooks written by some of them. They abstain from animal food, drink only filtered water, breathe only through a veil and move on sweeping the ground before them for fear of swallowing or crushing any living being. Some of the beautiful *Jaina* temples are exquisite examples of Indian architecture.

Mahavira was earlier in the *Ajivaka* school, one of the *Sramana* philosophies, advocating materialism or happiness emphasising *Fate* or *Niyati*. But, later he disagreed with the *Ajivaka* doctrine of 'fatalism', which implies ineffectiveness of human action. Therefore, he seceded from the *Ajivaka* school and founded a separate school. (Basham's book on *Ajivakas* mentions about Mahavira's association with *Gosala* and their eventual break.) Though Mahavira rejected the fundamental doctrine of 'fatalism' of the *Ajivakas*, he retained most of the other *Ajivaka* conceptions, an eternal soul in transmigration passing through a vast number of incarnations and eventually attaining release or final peace, a theory of elements and atoms, the dialectics of different schemes etc. The *Acaranga* and the *Sutrakrtanga* appear to be the oldest texts now available. These are supposed to be the authentic copies of the *Angas* codified at the end of the fourth century BC. The former is a book on discipline for *Jaina* ascetics while the latter deals with, to some extent, doctrinal matters. The *Sutrakrtanga* states its theme as the soul and its release. This is a doctrine of 'possible action' (*Kriya*) by which one can release his soul any time, not waiting for a predestined course. This action is more a matter of restraint from the worldly actions tending to continue transmigration than of 'positive action'. The way to release the soul consists of very severe asceticism, having no possessions, exercising complete self-control and avoiding ordinary actions. The most important point made in connection with avoiding actions is the insistence on *Ahimsa* (non-violence). The *Sutrakrtanga* criticises all other *Sramana* schools and *Brahminism*. According to it, the arguments that 'ritual is useless', 'there is no God', 'the universe is eternal or non-eternal' etc. are to be avoided. The most projected characteristic of *Jaina* doctrine is a *modified skepticism*. Everything can be considered as either substance (*dravya*) or modification (*Paryaya*). There are five substances which exist: Matter

(*Pudgala*), Soul (*Jiva*), Space (*Akasa*), Activity (*Dharma*) and Inactivity (*Adharma*). (In the definition of the word *Dharma*, Jainism deviates from the meaning of the word both in Hinduism and Buddhism.) Matter, composed of atoms, indivisible and too small to be sensed, is eternal, while all combinations of atoms, as we sense, are non-eternal. Activity and inactivity or motion and rest, as originally conceived, deserve merit or demerit in relation to soul. On the other hand, the conception of *Dharma* as a natural activity (not a static quality or principle) may be used to illuminate the Buddhist concept of *Dharma* as a natural activity, suggesting that this meant an event, rather than a quality.

Both Buddhism and Jainism emerged as rebel movements against the parent religion – Hinduism – and both are in many ways utterly different from Hinduism. Buddhism, which could not reconcile with casteism, faded away in India after remaining a predominant religion for nearly thousand years. Jainism, which was tolerant to casteism, adapted itself to it, survives and continues in India as an offshoot of Hinduism with 0.4 per cent of the Indian population as its adherents.

Jain Philosophy (*Nav Tattvas*)

Jain philosophy can be described in various ways, but the most acceptable tradition is to describe it in terms of the *Nav Tattvas* (nine fundamentals). They are:

Jiva (soul)
Ajiva (non-living matter)
Punya (results of good deeds)
Pap (results of bad deeds)
Asrava (influx of *karmas*)
Samvar (stoppage of *karmas*)
Bandh (bondage of *karmas*)
Nirjara (eradication of *karmas*)
Moksha (liberation)

Now, let us use a simple analogy to illustrate these *Tattvas*, generally quoted by the Jains. There lived a family in a farmhouse. They were enjoying the fresh cool breeze coming through the open doors and windows. The weather suddenly changed and a terrible dust storm sets in. Realizing it as a bad storm, they got up to close the doors and windows. By the time they could close all the doors and windows, lot of dust entered the house. After closing the doors and the windows they started clearing the dust to make the house clean.

We can interpret this simple illustration in terms of *Nav Tattvas* as follows:

The people represent *Jivas*.

The house represents *Ajiva*.

The enjoyment resulting from the nice cool breeze represents *Punya*.

The discomfort resulting from the sandstorm, which brought dust into the house represents *Pap*.

The influx of dust through the doors and windows of the house represents *Asrava* that is similar to the influx of *Karman* (sin) particles to the soul.

The accumulation of dust in the house represents *Bandh*, which is similar to bondage of *Karman* particles to the soul.

The closing of the doors and windows to stop the dust from coming into the house represents *Samvar*, which is similar to the stoppage of influx of *Karman* particles to the soul.

The cleaning up of accumulated dust from the house, which is similar to shedding accumulated karmic particles from the soul, represents *Nirjara*.

The cleaned house represents *Moksha*, which is similar to the shedding off all *karmic* particles from the soul.

Jiva: All living beings are called *Jivas*. *Jivas* have a consciousness known as the soul, which is also called the *atma* (soul – *chetan*). The soul and body are two different entities. The soul cannot be reproduced. It is described as a sort of energy that is indestructible, invisible, and shapeless. Jainism divides *Jivas* into five categories ranging from one-sensed beings to five-sensed beings. The body is merely a home for the soul. At the time of death, the soul leaves the body to occupy a new one. *Thirthankaras* have said that the soul has an infinite capacity to know and perceive. This capacity of the soul is not experienced in its present state because of accumulated *karmas*.

Ajiva: Anything that does not have a soul is called *Ajiva*. *Ajiva* does not have consciousness. Jainism divides *Ajiva* in five broad categories: *dharmastikay* (medium of motion), *adharmastikay* (medium of rest), *akashastikay* (space), *pudgalastikay* (matter), and *kala* (time).

Punya (virtues): By undertaking wholesome activities, we acquire *Punya* or good *karmas* (deeds). Some such activities are providing food or other items to the needy people, doing charity work, propagating religion, etc. When *Punya* matures, it brings forth comfort and happiness.

Pap: By undertaking bad activities, we incur *pap* or bad *karmas*. Some such activities are: being cruel or violent, showing disrespect to parents or teachers, being angry or greedy, showing arrogance or indulging in deceit etc. When *pap* matures, it brings forth suffering, misery, and unhappiness.

Asrava: The influx of *Karman* particles to the soul is known as *Asrava*. Wrong belief, vowlessness (observing no vows), passions, negligence, and psychophysical activities cause it. Such influx of *Karman* is facilitated by mental or verbal or physical activities.

Samvar: This is the process by which the influx of *Karman* particles is stopped. This is achieved by observing *samiti* (carefulness), *gupti* (control), *yati-dharma* (Monkhood), contemplating on the twelve *bhavanas* (mental reflections), and *parishaha* (suffering).

Bandh: This refers to the actual binding of *Karman* particles to the soul. Bandh occurs when we react to any situation with a sense of attachment or aversion.

Nirjara: The process through which we shed *karman* is called *Nirjara*. *Karman* can be shed either by passivity or active efforts. When we passively wait for karman to mature and to give their results in due time, it is called *Akam*.

Nirjara: On the other side, if we put active efforts for *karman* to mature earlier than supposed to be, it is called

Sakam Nirjara. This can be achieved by performing penance, regretting, asking for forgiveness for the discomfort we might have caused to someone, meditation etc.

Moksha: If we rid ourselves of all *karmas*, we will attain *Moksha* or liberation.

Definition of Religion

The Jain definition of religion is as follows:

"Unlike other living beings, we, human beings, have reasoning mind and capacity to think rationally. We have curiosity. We want to live a peaceful, happy and simple life. Since the beginningless beginning, we, curious human beings have been seeking answers to the questions such as: Who am I? Who am I not? Who made this universe? What is my relationship with the universe? What is my real nature? How can I achieve my own nature? What is my original self? How do I achieve permanent happiness? Right answers to these questions form the religion."

The Jain belief about the universe is distinct from that of other religions.

The Jains believe that God did not create the universe. If God created this universe, who created that God? Who created the creator? If the God has created the universe, he ought to have a desire to create. The desire makes the God imperfect and He cannot be imperfect. If God carries out the task of creation and destruction without any purpose, then it becomes a foolish game. If he had created the universe, then he would have made all *Jivas* (soul) equally happy. But we have 87 per cent people on earth living in poverty and misery and only 13 per cent people have some prosperity. Therefore, God must not be managing the affairs of the universe. As God is omniscient, omnipotent, and devoid of desires and passions, He could not be interested in the matters of the universe. Some claim that all creatures are God's images. If we accept that God created the earth, He manages the earth and He decides who gets what, then countless questions are raised and we do not have rationale answers to these questions. Therefore, it appeals to our commonsense that God did not create the universe.

The Jains use a rosary with 108 beads, each bead representing a unique quality of the Supreme Being. They are:

Arahants (supreme human beings, 12 unique qualities).
Siddhas (pure souls, 8 unique qualities).
Acharyas (master teachers, 36 unique qualities).
Upadhyayas (sages who teach, 25 unique qualities).
Sadhus (all sages, 27 unique qualities).

They are also called *Panch Pameshthi*, *panch* means five and *Pameshthi* means the live supreme beings, the best ones among all living beings. These five souls have given up worldly pleasures. There are a total of 108 unique qualities of these five supreme beings. Therefore, each bead represents one such unique quality.

Regarding necessity of temples, their answer is:

"The worshipping place provides the necessary environment for spiritual upliftment just as the school provides for education. Once one has advanced spiritually, he/she can continue the spiritual activity at any place. But for most of the *samsaris* (householders) we need to depend upon outside source such as temple to make initial progress in the spiritual direction. It is also acceptable that one practises his/her religion from home as long as he/she achieves similar or better results. For most people, the combination of both is recommended."

Worship

Eight types of rituals for *upasana* (worship), each type with different articles, are detailed below:

Jala Puja (water): Water symbolizes life's ocean of birth, death and misery. This *puja* reminds that one should live his life with honesty, truthfulness, love and compassion towards all living beings. This path is supposed to enable one to cross life's ocean and attain liberation (*Moksha*).

Chandan Puja (Sandal wood): *Chandan* symbolizes knowledge (*jnana*). By performing this *Puja*, one should thrive for right knowledge. Jainism believes that the path of knowledge is the main path to attain *Moksha* or liberation.

Pushpa Puja (Flower): The flower symbolizes conduct. Our conduct should be full of love and compassion towards all living beings, like flower provides fragrance and beauty without any discrimination.

Dhup Puja (incense): *Dhup* symbolizes monkhood life. While burning itself, incense provides fragrance to others. Similarly, true monks and nuns spend their entire life selflessly to benefit all living beings. This *Puja* reminds that one should thrive for an ascetic life.

Dipak Puja (light): The flame of *dipak* (light) represents pure consciousness, i.e. a soul without bondage of any *karma* or a liberated soul. By perfoming this *Puja*, one should thrive to follow five great vows: non-violence, truthfulness, non-stealing, chastity, and non-possession. Ultimately these vows will lead to liberation.

Akshat Puja (Rice): Rice is a kind of grain that is nonfertile. One cannot grow rice plants by sowing rice. Symbolically, it means that rice is the last birth. By performing this *Puja*, one should thrive to put all the efforts in life in such a way that life becomes one's last life, and after the end of this life one will not be reborn again.

Naivedya Puja (Sweet food): *Naivedya* symbolizes tasty food. By performing this *Puja*, one should thrive to reduce or eliminate attachment to tasty food. Healthy food is essential for survival, however one should not live for tasty food. Ultimate aim in one's life is to attain a life where no food is essential for survival.

Fal Puja (Fruit): Fruit is a symbol of *Moksha* or liberation. If we live our life without any attachment to wordly affairs, continue to perform our duty without any expectation and reward, be a witness to all the incidents that occur around us, truly follow monkhood life, and have love and compassion to all living beings; we will attain the fruit of liberation. This is the last *Puja* symbolizing the ultimate achievement of our life.

Conclusion

Parsavanath advocated four vows: not to injure life, not to lie, not to steal and not to possess property. Mahavira added the fifth vow of chastity. Even during the life of Mahavira, there were two sections in Jainism, one following Parsavanath and the other following Mahavira. Even the parents of Mahavira followed Parsavanath. The possibility of *Swetambaras* following Parsavanath and the *Digambaras* following Mahavira cannot be ruled out. Mahavira brought out unity among the two sections. But, disunity continued.

Mahavira did not believe in the existence of God. He was against the belief that God created everything and controlled the universe. Performance of sacrifices and recitations of *mantras* (incantations) were a waste of time, according to Mahavira. Right faith, right knowledge and right actions are the essentials of a good life. Death by self-imposed gradual starvation was permissible. Even suicides were recommended. Marriages were forbidden and a life of celibacy was insisted on. The followers were asked to go about naked. The body was to be given every kind of pain to realize the truth. Without 'intuitive knowledge', everyone is bound to commit sin, which will inevitably lead to the cycle of rebirths.

Both the *Swetambaras* and the *Digambaras* accepted *agama-siddhanta*, the sacred book of Jainism. In later days, Sanskrit was accepted as the *lingua franca*. A major part of Jain literature in Sanskrit consists of scholastic and philosophic works defending the faith of Jainism. In Tamil literature, Jain poets were honoured with high esteem. *Jeevaka chintamani* in Tamil is the finest of Tamil poems. Thiruvalluvar, the author of *Thirukkural* is believed to be a Jain. Once upon a time, Jainism was a religion of standing in Tamil Nadu, Andhra, and partially in Karnataka. Many Jaina temples were visible in many parts of North India. A lot of works have been done on Jainism by Prof. Jacobi, Dr. Hornie, Prof. Buhler, Dr. Banarsidas Jain, Mrs. Sinclai Stevenson etc. But today the strength of Jainism is gradually nose-diving.[1]

FOOTNOTE

1. Mahajan, V.D., *Ancient India*, pp. 171-77.
   [*Sources*: 1. Jawaharlal Nehru, *The Discovery of India*, p. 108;
   2. *The Britannica – Internet – Jainism*].

SUGGESTED READINGS

Barodia, U.D., *History and Literature of Jainism*, 1909.

Bloomfield, *The Life and Stories of the Jain Saviour Parsvanath*, 1911.

Buhler, J.G., *On the Indian Sect of the Jains*, 1903.

Guseva, N.R., *Jainism*, Bombay, 1971.

Jacobi, H., *Jain Sutras*, Oxford, 1884-5.

——, *The Metaphysics and Ethics of the Jainas*, 1908.

Jaini, Manak Chand, *Life of Mahavira*, 1908.

Jhaveri, J.L., *First Principles of Jain Philosophy*, 1912.

Lattha, A.B., *An Introduction to Jainism*, 1905.

Mehta, Mohan Lal and Hira Lal Kapadia, *History of Jain Literature*, V & IV.

Shah, C.J., *Jainism in Northern India*, 1932.

Stevenson, (Mrs.) Sinclair, *The Heart of Jainism*, 1915.

——, *Notes on Modern Jainism*, 1910.

Sikhism

19

Introduction

The word 'Sikh' means disciple. According to Sikhism, a Sikh is a person who believes in one God (Monotheism) and the teachings of the ten *Gurus* (Teachers) enshrined in the *Guru Granth Sahib*, the only Holy Scripture of the Sikhs, provided he or she has undergone *Amrit* (Sikh baptism). The founder of Sikhism is Guru Nanak born in 1469 AD in the Village Talwandi near Lahore in Pakistan. He found all religions in his times unacceptable as they enforce meaningless rituals, superstitions and dogmas on the innocent people. Therefore, he founded a new religion free from superstitions, rituals, casteism and exploitation. Guru Nanak and nine *Gurus* who succeeded him led a full spiritual life, simultaneously taking active part in the secular life of the world. Guru Gobind Singh, the tenth and the last *Guru* passed away in 1708 AD. Guru Arjan Dev, the fifth *Guru* compiled in 1604 AD the *Guru Granth Sahib*, the ultimate spiritual authority of Sikhism and built the *Darbar Sahib* popularly known as Golden Temple at Amritsar, the nucleus and highest seat of Sikhism. The temporal authority of religion is vested in the *Khalsa Panth* (the Sikh Commonwealth).

Canons of Faith

(a) Belief in one Supreme God, the Absolute, the Eternal, the Creator, the Cause of Causes, not the God of one nation, but the God of Grace. He created man not to punish him for his sins but for realisation of his true purpose in the Cosmos and to merge in from where he or she issues forth.

> "O my mind, the Lord is ever with thee
> Through the Guru's word enjoy his love
> Knowing thy essence, thou knowest thy Lord."
>
> (*Guru Granth*, p. 441)

(b) Sikhism does not recognise caste, idol worship, rituals and superstitions; gods and goddesses are non-entities.

(c) It claims to be a religion of practical living, rendering service to humanity and engendering tolerance and brotherly love towards all. Retirement from worldly life is not necessary to attain salvation. Anyone who earns an honest living and leads a normal life can attain salvation.

> "He alone O Nanak knoweth the way,
> Who earneth with the sweat of his brow,
> And then shareth it with others."
>
> (*Guru Granth*, p. 1245)

(d) Riches and worldly possessions are not hindrances to a spiritual life.

> "Those who are attuned to the Lord
> By Guru's grace attain the Lord
> In the midst of Maya (wealth)."
>
> (*Guru Granth*, p. 921)

(e) Ideology of pessimism is not acceptable, but advocates optimism and hope. The maxim 'whosoever smite thee on the right cheek, turn to him the other also' does not find any place in the life of the Sikh.

> "When an affair is past every other remedy,
> it is righteous indeed to unsheath the sword."
>
> (Guru Gobind Singh)

Distinctive Identity

Every Sikh is expected to have five distinctive symbols of identity known as *Kesha* (long unshaven hair), *Kangha* (a comb), *Kara* (a steel bracelet), *Kachha* (a pair of shorts or underwear), and a *Kirpan* (a sword). These symbols are to foster a disciplined outlook and a sense of brotherhood. Any Sikh without these symbols is treated as a non-entity.

Code of Conduct

The Sikh has a code of conduct known as *Sikh Rehat Maryada*. This is to enforce a uniform discipline of faith. Intoxicants like alcohol, tobacco and its derivative products, trimming of the hair and eating meat prepared as per Muslim rites (*Hallal*) are forbidden. Adultery is a sin.

Amrit (Baptism)

Baptism is a must for every Sikh irrespective of sex, nationality, race or social status.

Women

Woman receives utmost reverence for her role in family and society. Marriage is not a contract, but a sacrament. Divorce or dowries are not permitted.

> "They are not wife and husband who only sit together
> Rather are they wife and husband who have one spirit in them."
>
> (*Guru Granth*, p. 788)

Widows can remarry. Women can perform all ceremonies including baptism. They need not put on a veil. The only restriction is regarding wearing clothes exposing the body breeding lustful thoughts. Sikhism does not believe in celibacy. Marriage and family life are considered honourable, natural and ideal.

Gurudwara

The Sikh temple is called *Gurudwara*; it has two parts, a hall and a kitchen. The Holy Scripture is installed in the main hall for prayer and worship. Any person is allowed entry in the *Gurudwara*, provided footwear is removed and head is covered. Salient features of the *Gurudwara* are *Sanghat* (congregation) and *Pangat* (community kitchen). Free food is provided for all devotees including visitors, maintaining full equality, at the expense of the community. Hymns, lectures and prayer (*Ardas*) are the items for service and worship.

All *Gurudwaras* are believed to have equal sanctity, but a few of them (five in number) with historical importance are treated as *Takhats* (Seats or throne or authority). They are *Takhat Patna Sahib* in Bihar, *Takhat Damdama Sahib* at Talwandy Sabo in Punjab, *Takhat Keshgarh Sahib* at Anandpur, Punjab, *Takhat Hazoor Sahib* in Maharashtra and *Akal Takhat Sahib* at Amritsar, the supreme one from where *Hukam Namas* (Injunctions) are issued from time to time for the guidance of the community, which has the binding force of Sikh personal law.

On the top of each *Gurudwara*, a yellow flag surrounded by a *Khanda* (double edged sword) is erected which is supposed to be the Logo of Sikhism. There is no priesthood. The person who conducts or leads the services in the *Gurudwara* is called *Granthi.* The hymns are called *Kirtans* (hymns praising the Lord) and the singers are known as *Ragis*.

Festivals and Ceremonies

Sikh festivals are:

(a) the birth and death anniversaries of the Ten *Gurus*,

(b) the Installation Day of the Holy *Granth Sahib*,

(c) the birth of the *Khalsa* (*Baisakhi day* generally 13th April),

(d) the martyrdom of the prominent Sikhs, and

(e) the important events in Sikh history.

The main ceremonies are:

(a) Births, (b) Naming of a child, (c) *Amrit* (Baptism), (d) *Anand Karaj* (Marriage), and (e) Death.

The dead is cremated and the ashes are thrown into some canals or rivers. Erecting monuments over the remains of the dead are forbidden. Recitation from the scripture is a must for all festivals and ceremonies.

Daily Life of a Sikh

A strict daily routine is prescribed for every Sikh. Get up before dawn, bath, meditation and recitation of prescribed compositions for prayer three times a day, morning (*Japji sahib*, *Jaap sahib* and *Ten Swiyyas*), evening (*Rehras*) and Night (*Sohila*). Attendance at *Gurudwara* is also a part of daily routine.

Sikhism claims to be a practical religion, a faith of hope and optimism. They have blended some elements of faith of other religions, which they considered progressive while rejecting some other cardinal principles. Many of the canons they prescribe are more ethical or moral than theological or philosophical. In the early stages of Sikhism, they were subjected to oppressions and suppressions at the hands of the authorities as well as the fanatics in other religions. They had to live in constant threat of a surprise attack from any quarter at any time. This social necessity moulded their soldier-like form and character, uniform, carrying of weapons, distinctive identity and preparedness to defend themselves and their religion. This background prompted them to turn towards theocratic nationhood. They achieved this ideal in the 18th century through Maharaja Ranjit Singh (1780-1839 AD), who established a kingdom of the Sikhs in Punjab. This kingdom lasted for nearly half a century. In 1839, the English under Governor General Dalhousie conquered Punjab and annexed the Sikh Kingdom to the Empire.

Again, in the second half of the 20th century, a few extremist Sikhs attempted to establish an autonomous nation for the Sikhs named *Khalistan*, organised a terrorist group and unleashed a guerilla-model attack killing hundreds of innocent people. When this guerilla warfare reached its zenith threatening the peace and integrity of the Indian nation, the army cordoned off the *Akal Takhat*, flushed out the terrorists and crushed them. The terrorists revenged their defeat by assassinating Mrs. Indira Gandhi, the then Prime Minister of India who ordered the military action. The non-Sikhs avenged the assassination by murdering hundreds of Sikhs outside Punjab. The terrorists who escaped lingered on with stray attacks. But the State Government crushed the menace and re-established peace in Punjab.

At present, the Sikhs constitute 1.8 per cent of the Indian population. But they have earned a name for themselves in almost all walks of life in India such as the armed forces, agriculture, industry, transport, engineering, politics, sports, civil service and so on. They are a set of well-built people, who work hard with missionary zeal in all their engagements. Their enterprising, adventurous and risk-taking nature earned for them in the entire nation a reputation as a heroic and reliable community. Today, Sikhs in India enjoy a position far surpassing their numerical strength in all spheres of the Indian nation: community-wise, they are the most prosperous community and State-wise Punjab leads other States in the production of wealth.

Now, Sikhs have spread to many other nations of the world, especially England, Canada, the United States of America and several other countries in Europe.

Short Notes

(a) Tradition of Devotional Hymns (Shabad Kirtan)

Music has been recognised as a form of meditation and worship in itself in almost all-major religions, because of its potential to constrain the human mind to a mood of concentration. Sikhism is no exception to this practice. Seven out of the ten *Gurus* in Sikhism were great poets and musicians who composed melodious devotional hymns of outstanding merit for recitation in worship. In the course of time, the particular form of devotional music is known as *Shabad Kirtan* (*Shabad* means *Shabda* or voice and *Kirtan* means devotional songs). Guru Gobind Singh has compiled a separate book of hymns known as *Dasham Granth*. The main scripture of Sikhism known as *Guru Granth Sahib* is a combination of the holy precepts in verse form, composed by Muslim Rabbis and Hindu saints of the medieval period. To sum up, Sikh devotional music is a symphony, rich and magnificent, into which, within the last five centuries, diverse musical elements, styles and modes were assimilated with remarkable oneness, harmony and piety.[1]

(b) Harminder Sahib (Golden Temple)

Harminder Sahib, popularly known as the Golden Temple situated in the city of Amritsar (lit: a pool of nectar), the universal headquarters of the Sikh religion, is a two storey marble structure with an imposing dome of pure gold. This temple enshrines the *Guru Granth Sahib* the holy book installed in 1604. The fourth *Guru* of Sikhs, Guru Ram Das (1534-1581) founded Amritsar. The fifth *Guru* of the Sikhs, Guru Arjun Dev (1563-1606) completed the temple in the 16th century. The gilding, marble and glass works were done in the 19th century under the leadership of Maharaja Ranjit Singh. The 6th Sikh *Guru*, Hargobind (1595-1644) established the *Akal Takhat* or immortal throne, the supreme seat of the Sikh religious authority. The building is a blend of Indian and Arabic architecture. It is believed that the temple is situated at the site where Saint Valmiki wrote the epic *Ramayana*. The legend says that Rama and Sita spent a short time at this site. The Harminder Sahib is the symbol of abiding faith and tolerance held in high esteem by every Sikh, who so often dreams of visiting.[2]

(c) Guru Granth Sahib

As we have already seen, *Guru Granth Sahib* is the final authority on the scripture of Sikhism. The hymns in it have a special significance as the sole authentic record of the fundamental doctrines of Sikh faith. It is the central object of worship in all *Gurudwaras*. According to the Sikh philosophy, the "Reality" is one. It is transcendent. God is the creator of the universe and the whole cosmos is under the binding law of God. Soul is the light of God. The *Guru Granth Sahib* is compiled in *Gurumukhi* script that has a lot of words from Persian, Arabic, Sanskrit and Braj. India, being a multi-religious society, real harmony among people will come only through tolerance, social justice and equality. As such, integration of different strands of social fabric is a major concern of the *Guru Granth Sahib*.[3]

The main appeals of the *Granth Sahib* are its secular character, utter simplicity, universal appeal and its relevance to India's social conditions.[4]

To conclude, it will be interesting to reproduce here a stanza in the daily prayer of every Sikh.

O! God, give us light, give us understanding
So that we know what pleaseth Thee
And may all (the whole mankind) prosper by Thy Grace.

To the Sikhs, Guru Nanak is creator of a *New Man* in the *New World* supported by a *New Morality*.

FOOTNOTES

1. Delhi Sikh Gurudwara Management Committee publication, *Tradition of Shabad Kirtan.*
2. *Amritsar* – Internet, p. 1 of 1.
3. Delhi Sikh Gurudwara Management Committee publication, *What is Sikhism*?
4. Delhi Sikh Gurudwara Management Committee publication, *Sri Guru Granth Sahib.*

PART FOUR

CHRISTIANITY IN INDIA

The Pre-Portuguese Period

20

St. Thomas Christians

Christianity is traditionally believed to have spread to India in the first century AD through the evangelization mission of St. Thomas (also called 'Didymus' and 'Judas Thomas'), one of the disciples of Jesus Christ. No conclusive historical evidence in support of this belief is readily forthcoming. Mr. T.K. Velu Pillay, a Hindu historian and editor of *Travancore State Manual* has aptly commented in the Manual of the erstwhile Travancore State "St. Thomas came to India to preach Christianity, not to create historical evidence". Though few historians in the early Church like Origen (185-254), Eusebius (260-340), Hippolytus etc. asserted in unequivocal terms the Indian mission of St. Thomas, some historians like Chaplain James Hough and George Milne Rae do not subscribe to the veracity of this tradition. Several books on St. Thomas mission in India are now available with varying conclusions, a few of them rejecting outright the St. Thomas mission in India. The conclusions arrived at by the historians are categorized and summed up below:

St. Thomas came to India by the land route via. Thakshashila (Taxila), an ancient seat of learning in India, confined his mission in North-Western India, mainly in the kingdom of King Gondophornes and never came to South India.

It is St. Bartholomew who came to India and not St. Thomas. The evangelisation work of St. Bartholomew was in and around the present Bombay (Mumbai). In the sixth century AD, there was a bishop appointed by Persia in *Kalyan*, they point out.

Both St. Thomas and St. Bartholomew visited India; the former worked in South India and the latter in North-West India.

St. Thomas landed at Muzuris near Kodungalloor on the Western coast of India in 52 AD (Kodungalloor, Cranganore, Mahadevarpattanam, Mahadevarpuram, Muzuris, Shingly etc. are synonyms). Maliankara, the word Malankara supposed to be a derivation, an island near Kodungalloor is now extinct. In those days, Kodungalloor, situated at the mouth of Periyar river was an important cosmopolitan port-city and trade centre on the Western coast of India and also the capital of the King of the Chera dynasty (Later, the capital was shifted to Kollam). St. Thomas preached Christianity and established seven Christian congregations at Kodungalloor (Maliankara), Palayur, Kottekkavu (in Parur), Kokkamangalam, Niranam, Kollam and Chayal (also called Nilakkal) – all in Kerala. Therefrom, St. Thomas proceeded to the Eastern coast of South India and established one congregation at Calamina (present Mylapore) near Chennai, which has subsequently become extinct.

St. Thomas never came to India. Christianity spread to India through the immigration of Persian Christians in the subsequent centuries.

Whether fact or fiction, a few historians are of the view that St. Thomas first visited Mylapore and thence came to Malabar and again returned to Mylapore. Some other historians are of the view that St. Thomas visited China and returned to Mylapore after a sojourn in China. He was speared by a lance to death in 72 AD at Calamina (present Mylapore) under the orders of King Mazdai of that area and was buried at the place where the Mylapore Cathedral Church, with the sepulchre of the Apostle at the centre; stands at present.

St. Thomas

St. Thomas, appearing in the Gospels in different contexts, provides us with pointers to assess the depth of faith, temperament and traits of character of the Apostle. A few instances are given below:

"The Jews then took stones to stone him.... They sought therefore to take him and he escaped out of their hands and he went again beyond the Jordan, into that place where John was baptizing first and there he abode" (John X 31: 39-40 – *Bible*).

"And when a messenger came there to call him to Lazarus who was dying and Jesus said to his disciples 'Lazarus is dead ...but let us go to him'. Thomas therefore who is called Didymus said to his fellow-disciples: Let us also go that we may die with him" (John XI 14-16 – *Bible*).

"And Thomas...who is called Didymus was not with them when Jesus came, the other disciples said to him 'We have seen the Lord'. But he said to them 'Except I shall see in his hands the print of the nails, and put my finger into the place of the nails, and put my hands into his side, I will not believe'. And after eight days again his disciples were within and Thomas with them, Jesus cometh, the doors being shut, and stood in the midst and said: 'Peace be with you'. Then he said to Thomas: 'Put in thy finger hither, and see my hands, and bring hither thy hand and put it into my side; and be not faithless, but believing'. Thomas answered and said to him, 'My Lord and my God'. Jesus said to him 'because thou hast seen me, Thomas, thou hast believed: blessed are they that have not seen and have believed'" (John XX 19-29 – *Bible*).[1]

As Thomas has not only seen, but also touched the Resurrected Christ, who can any longer doubt the Resurrection? The curiosity of doubting Thomas confirmed the faith of all Christians. When Jesus resolved to return to Judaea, where the Jews were seeking to kill him, Thomas said "Let us also go, that we may die with him." This shows his quick-tempered courage of conviction and sincerity of purpose. When he addressed Christ "My God", it was the announcement of a new relationship between him and Christ. He was a fearless man prepared to undertake, irrespective of consequences, any sacrifice for preserving his faith and conviction, as is evidenced by his readiness to undertake long and tedious journeys and miseries which eventually led to his martyrdom.

In the early Church records, the division of evangelisation work among the Apostles are recorded as follows: "St. Thomas evangelized the Parthians, St. Andrew the Scythians, St. Bartholomew went up to India and to Southern Arabia, Philip died at Herapolis in Phrygia." According to the Encyclopaedia, "Parthia is an ancient country corresponding to Northern Iran. It was inhabited by a Scythian people of Aryan speech and manners, who, after being tributary successively to Assyria, Media, Persia, Alexander the Great and Syria, set up an independent kingdom in 250 BC, which was Rome's greatest and most continuous rival for the domination of the Near and Middle-East. Ctesiphon was their capital; the Euphrates lay between them and Rome. Ardashir, who founded a Persian Empire about 224 AD, overthrew them."[2]

Some historians are of the view that a few territories of North-West India, especially Western Punjab, were part of the then Parthian Empire. The claim of the St. Thomas Christians in India that the spiritual head of their Church was the ecclesiastical dignitary at Ctesiphon stood vindicated by the fact that St. Thomas first evangelized Parthia and introduced a worshipping system in Chaldean Syriac, the *lingua franca*. St. Thomas thereafter evangelized India and put the Churches in India and Parthia under one liturgy – the East Syrian, which in subsequent centuries, developed into a prominent liturgy in the Church. He also put the Church in India under the guidance and guardianship of the head of the Parthian Church – a natural, logical and purposeful decision. This weighty evidence proves beyond doubt the mission of St. Thomas in Malabar. The logic is simple.

St. Thomas evangelized Parthia. There is no doubt about it at all. Ctesiphon, the city on the bank of the Tigris, was the capital of Parthia. In the early days of the Church and even in modern age, the capital city of a kingdom enjoys preponderance over other cities even in the ecclesiastical sphere. E.g.: the General Council of Constantinople in 381 AD approved a canon which made the bishop of Constantinople (New Rome) the ranking Prelate in the East with primacy next to that of Pope. Ctesiphon thus became the seat of the highest ecclesiastical dignitary of the Parthian Church. When St. Thomas established a Church in India, it was naturally put under the spiritual guidance of the Church dignitary in Ctesiphon. Two reasons would have influenced St. Thomas to arrive at such a decision: (i) Fear of the possibility of the small Christian congregations established by him being swallowed in the longrun, by the powerful Indian religions, and (ii) The anxiety to preserve from oblivion the seeds of the East Syrian liturgy (Chaldean) that he himself has sown in Malabar, especially when Chaldean (East) Syriac was a foreign language for the people of Malabar. Had someone other than St. Thomas evangelized India, the possibility for linking the Indian Church with the Parthian Church would have been far remote. Till the schism in 1653 in the Indian Church, bishops were occasionally sent to India (Malabar) by the Persian Church (Seleucia-Ctesiphon by then became the capital of the Persian Empire) to attend to the spiritual needs of the Malabar Church.*

Prior to the schism in 1653, three Bishops, one Jacob, one Joseph and one Abraham of the Chaldean Syriyan Church were deputed one after another in a row of the Malabar Church to attend to the spiritual needs of the faithful. But, the Portughese detained Mar Jacob and Mar Joseph in custody under some pretext or other. Mar Abraham was a shrewd and experienced person who visited Malabar on an earlier occasion as a Nestorian prelate. He later embraced the catholic church, got himself ordained as a chatholic prelate, escaped from the grips of the Portuguese and reached Angamaly incognito. The faithful in the locality accorded a rousing reception to Mar Abraham and his entourage. He attended a meeting of the synod convened by the Goan Archbishop at Goa on the assurance of protection guaranteed by Pope Gregory XIII. Mar Abraham continued as the Chaldean Syrian Metropolitan of the Angamaly See till his death in 1597 A.D. No Chaldean prelate entered Malabar after 1597 A.D.

---

* Seleucus Nicator, one of the Generals of Alexander the Great, who on the death of Alexander secured the rule of Babylon and Syria, founded the Seleucid dynasty. This dynasty founded many cities named Seleucia. One among them was Seleucia on the Tigris, on the opposite side of Ctesiphon. These twin cities on both sides of River Tigris, situated on the N.E. of Babylon, later became the capital of the Persian Empire, popularly known as Seleucia-Ctesiphon.

The Catholic Directory of India 1998 published by the Catholic Bishops' Conference of India, while describing the history of the Bombay Archdiocese, stated that "it is now seriously held that the India supposedly evangelized by St. Bartholomew, the Apostle in the first century and visited by Pantaneus of Alexandria in the second century may have been the present territory of the Archdiocese".[3] This corroborates with the Church records relating to the assignment of the mission in India to St. Bartholomew. He did not continue for long with the mission in India, perhaps due to the antagonistic attitude of the natives or to take up the mission in Southern Arabia. Inasmuch as no one in the Bombay area put forth any claim of succession of those baptized by St. Bartholomew, it is to be presumed that the congregation, if any, established by the Saint ceased to exist pretty long ago.

The earliest reference to the mission of St. Thomas appears in a book titled 'Acts of Thomas' in Syriac, supposed to be written by one Bardesan of Edessa (154-222 AD). He was a Christian and a historian in the court of the King of Syria, probably Abgar VIII.[4] This book was treated as apocryphal because a king named Gondophornes in India mentioned by the author was found fictitious. But this book was very popular in early Christianity and was recognized by *Encyclopaedia Britannica* as an authoritative document on the early Christian Church in the East. Later, archaeological excavation at Takshashila (Taxila) under the supervision of Sir John Marshall unearthed coins and Takt-i-bahi stone with inscriptions of King Gondophornes. Thus, the grounds for treating 'Acts of Thomas' as apocryphal withered away. These archaeological findings enabled historians to trace the genealogy of Gondophornes and his predecessor kings to the Indo-Parthian dynasty which ruled the North-Western Frontier Province comprising Afghanistan, Sind, Punjab etc. from 95 BC to 50 AD. Sir John Marshall has indicated that St. Thomas visited Gondophornes in 40 AD.[5]

The reference in the 'Acts of Thomas' confirmed by archaeological research has sealed once for all the doubts about the visit of St. Thomas to Taxila. If so, the possibility of

St. Thomas visiting Malabar coast by sea cannot be ruled out for two cogent reasons.

The early targets of the disciples of Christ for evangelisation in those days were the Jews. Knowledge about the presence of a Jewish community in or around Kodungalloor would have motivated St. Thomas to reach Malabar. (In Parthia, he would have learnt from the traders about the migration of the Jews to Malabar.)

Central Asian countries enjoyed the monopoly of the trade between Arabian countries and Malabar. The trade vessels frequently plying between Arabian countries and Malabar would have facilitated travel to Malabar.

Dr. Xavier Koodapuzha quotes a lot of testimonies supporting the Indian mission of St. Thomas in his book *Christianity in India*. How far these non-contemporary records can succeed to correct the sceptics, remains a mute question.[6]

The Martyrology and liturgical calendar of the Roman Catholic Church associated the Church in India with Apostle St. Thomas. According to the Roman Breviary, Apostle Thomas was martyred at Calamina (the present Mylapore). The Byzantine liturgical tradition also refers to the martyrdom of St. Thomas by a lance. The Alexandrian tradition follows the Byzantine calendar. The local tradition confirmed in Malabar gradually penetrated to Egypt, Arabia, Syria, England and Europe. In the 4th century AD, a Syrian merchant named 'Khabin' took the relics of St. Thomas to Edessa in 394 AD (165 AD?). Later, the Portuguese opened the tomb and took away certain particles of the relics to Lisbon and Rome. Mylapore developed gradually into a pilgrim centre of repute attracting many pilgrims from inside and outside India. No one, by pointing out a substitute or parallel tomb for St. Thomas, had ever challenged this heritage of Mylapore, a pride for both Christians and Non-Christians in the area.

The Catholic Church, the oldest organisation in the world, is in possession of the requisite infrastructure, wherewithal and services of experts to investigate and conclude on matters relating to faith. The Church, after due investigations, upheld the mission of St. Thomas in the Malabar coast and, though late, explicitly declared this fact to the world through the mouth of Popes Pius XII and John Paul II.

In 1952, Pope Pius XII declared: "During centuries that India was cut off from the West and despite many trying vicissitudes, the Christian Community formed by the Apostle (Saint Thomas) conserved in tact the legacy he left them, and as soon as the Sea passage at the close of the fifteenth century offered a link with their fellow-Christians of the West, their union with them was spontaneous. This apostolic lineage, beloved sons and daughters, is the proud privilege of many among you who glory in the name of Thomas Christians, and we are happy on this occasion to acknowledge and bear witness to it."[7]

Pope John Paul II in 1980 while greeting Syro Malabar Hierarchy made a special reference to the origin of their church from St. Thomas and the appellation after the Apostle as 'St. Thomas Christians'.[8]

Mr. T.K. Velu Pillai, a Hindu historian and Editor of the *State Manual* of the erstwhile Travancore State in 1940 stated in the *State Manual* as follows:

> "If the desire for trade and the exigencies of political ambition made travelling anything but an abnormal enterprise, the missionary who desired to carry the Word of God to the remotest confines of the earth would find no difficulty in arriving at Malabar Coast from Socotra or Edessa or Antioch. The learned Chaplain (Chaplain James Hough) emphasizes the absence of what he calls 'the faintest vestiges of authentic history' in support of the coming of St. Thomas and finds an easy way to reject the tradition. What is the authentic evidence of the facts of history, which are said to have transpired nearly two thousand years ago? It is not reasonable to hope that the visit of St. Thomas could be proved by certified records in the archives of Government nor is it right to think that the transactions should, if true, be recorded on stone or copper. St. Thomas came to India to preach Christianity,

not to create historical evidence."[9] (Pages 653 & 654 – *Travancore State Manual*)

(*Please note*: This is the editor's (T.K. Velu Pillai) response to the criticism of Chaplain James Hough & George Milne Rae.)

Dr. Rajendra Prasad, the first President of the Republic of India and a scholar of International repute, hailed the St. Thomas tradition of India, which has become a part of the religious heritage of India. His words are reproduced below:

> "Remember, St. Thomas came to India when many of the countries of Europe had not yet become Christian and those Indians who trace their Christianity to him have a longer history and a higher ancestry than that of the Christians of many of the European countries. And it is really a matter of pride to us that it so happened."[10]

President Dr. Sankar Dayal Sharma, another President of the Republic of India and an erudite and colourful scholar, on the solemn occasion of his installation as the President of India specifically referred to the origin of Christianity in India from St. Thomas, one of the twelve Apostles of Jesus Christ. He mentioned it to point out the antiquity and indigenous identity of Christianity in the Indian soil.[11]

A. Sreedhara Menon, a historian of high repute in his book, *A Survey of Kerala History* has emphatically declared the existence of Christianity in Kerala in the first century AD. His words are reproduced below:

"Christianity was introduced in Kerala in the first century AD, i.e. three centuries before it gained official recognition in Europe or became the established religion in Rome. Legend has it that Apostle St. Thomas landed at Maliankara, a place adjoining Muziris, in 52 AD, converted several *Brahmins* and others and founded seven churches on the Malabar coast, i.e. at Maliankara itself, Palayur, Kottekkavu, Kokkamangalam, Kollam, Niranam and Nilakkal. The belief in the St. Thomas tradition is firm and widespread among the Christians of Kerala, though many modern historians have rejected the evidence on which it rests. In the background of the extensive trade relations that existed between Kerala and the Mediterranean countries before the Christian Era, it must be stated that there is nothing intrinsically improbable in the St. Thomas tradition. The traditional accounts preserved by the Jews who came to Cranganore in 68 AD contain a reference to the existence of a Christian community at the place. The statement of Pantaneus, the head of the Alexandrian school who visited Kerala in the 2nd century AD that he found a flourishing Christian community here is also cited as evidence in favour of the Apostolic origin of the Kerala Church."

"Since its introduction in Kerala, the Christian faith, though alien in its origin, came to be accepted as an indigenous faith and it made steady progress. The Ecumenical Council held at Nicaea in 325 AD Johannes who is described as the "Metropolitan of Persia and Great India" attended at the instance of Emperor Constantine, among others. The number of Christians on the Kerala Coast was reinforced in 345 AD by an influx of Syrian immigrants consisting of 400 Christians from 72 families belonging to seven tribes in Baghdad, Nineveh and Jerusalem under the leadership of the merchant Knayi Thoma (Thomas of Cana). Cosmos Indicopleustus, the Byzantine monk who came to the coast early in the 6th century AD, testifies to the existence of a Christian community here. The Christians became gradually prominent in the field of trade and commerce and before long they received several privileges and favours at the hands of the ruling monarchs. During the period of the Second Chera Empire (800-1101 AD) they were a prominent business community in the land. The Terisapalli Copper Plate executed in 849 AD by Ayyan Atikal Thiruvatikal of Venad during the reign of Emperor Sthanu Ravi (844-885 AD) confers to two Christian merchants, Chathan Vadukan and Iravi Chathan, who were members of the Manigramam being conferred certain privileges. The Copper Plate Grant (1225 AD) issued by Vira Raghava Chakravarti, the ruler of Mahodayapuram, confers on the latter, the office of Manigramam, i.e. the headship of the merchants of the place, in addition to several other rights and privileges. The Christians were treated all along on a footing of equality with the Hindus and assigned a very important place in the economic and social life of the State."[12]

Conclusion

In arriving at a conclusion, the following facts have to be considered:

- The relation of the Malabar Church with Seleucia-Ctesiphon, both evangelised by St. Thomas and the East Syrian Liturgy followed by both the Churches.
- Visit of St. Thomas to the kingdom of Gondophornes as recorded in the 'Acts of Thomas' confirmed by archaeological excavations and the possibility of St. Thomas proceeding therefrom to Malabar coast through trade vessels plying between Arab lands and Kodungalloor, to visit the Jewish colony there.
- The erstwhile state of Travancore, a major geographical component of the present Kerala State admitted the fact of St. Thomas mission in the first century AD.
- The declaration of the Catholic Church, after deep investigations and minute scrutiny, on the mission of St. Thomas in the Malabar Coast of India.
- Two eminent Hindu scholars and Presidents of the Republic of India declaring with pride the antiquity and indigenous identity of Christianity in the Indian soil through St. Thomas, the disciple of Jesus Christ.
- The absence of any trace or claim by anyone in the world on the death and burial of St. Thomas.
- The above mentioned premises and certifications crowned by the staunch, unanimous and traditional belief of eight million St. Thomas Christians all over the world conclusively settle the subject once for all.

Malabar is the only place, which has claimed the proud patrimony of St. Thomas. Those who matter have already endorsed the St. Thomas mission. It is a futile exercise to correct and convince the skeptics. Let us close the subject with the words of Wald "Whenever St. Thomas is mentioned, in breviary or liturgy, in poem or history, he is the Apostle and almost invariably associated with India. All patristic writings, whether Greek, Latin or Syrian bear testimony to the connection of the Apostle Thomas with India."[13]

The Growth of the St. Thomas Church in India

The growth and history of the St. Thomas Church in India can be classified into three distinct periods:

- the period from the first to the sixteenth century, otherwise called the Pre-Portuguese period,
- the origin and expansion of the Latin Church in India or the Portuguese period,
- the modern period beginning with the British rule in India or from the advent of Protestantism till date.

The Pre-Portuguese Period

The information available about this period is scanty. But, generally speaking, this was the most prosperous period in the history of the St. Thomas Christians in India. The seeds sown by St. Thomas germinated and grew remarkably into a well-knit and cohesive community with ecclesial solidarity, one faith, one liturgy, equality within the Church, social status, economic prosperity, political influence and the amenities of a privileged class. The rulers in Malabar were conspicuously tolerant towards all religions. The Indian church maintained cordial ecclesiastical relations with Ctesiphon till the fall of the Parthian Empire in 224 AD and thereafter with Seleucia-Ctesiphon, the capital of the Persian Empire. The East Syrian bishops visited intermittently and spiritually stimulated and invigorated the Indian church. Conversely, many members of the Indian clergy visited Seleucia, Edessa, Antioch etc. for higher studies. Travel across the seas was taboo for the Hindus in those days. Hence, Christian laymen were deputed to go abroad for trade. This interaction at various levels between Persia and India not only fostered the strengthening of the spiritual content of the Church but also helped to boost the trade between Malabar and the Arab lands. Being efficient navigators and shrewd traders, Christians almost monopolized the trade. The flourishing trade enhanced the wealth of the country. Resultantly, the Kings were well pleased with the Christians, who gradually became an indispensable faction in the community enjoying the confidence of the monarchs. As an offshoot of this royal patronage and recognition, Christians were held in high esteem and treated on par with the upper classes in the hierarchical social ladder, of course next to the *Brahmins*, who were teachers and priests of the royalty. This upgradation in the status of Christians naturally distanced them from the people in the lower strata of the society with consequential practice of untouchability, thereby risking the primary mission of evangelisation. If at all any evangelisation work was done, it was confined to the upper classes. In short, the Christians became entrenched in some sort of elitism with its inherent practices and customs. This is the background in which A. Sreedhara Menon, a reputed Kerala historian, remarked that the "St. Thomas Christians were Christian in faith and Indian in all other respects".

The noteworthy events during this period were: (a) Visits by foreigners, (b) The Knanaya immigration to Malabar in 345 AD, (c) The arrival of two Prelates named Sapor (Mar Sabariso) and Prodth (Mar Aphrodth) at Kollam, (d) The infiltration of Nestorian bishops, (e) Separate Provincial status for Mar Thoma Christians followed by Metropolitan dignity, (f) Detection of Persian Cross at Mylapore, Kottayam, Kadamattom, Muttuchira etc.

(a) Visits of Foreigners

The first among the foreign visitors was Pantaneus, an Alexandrian philosopher of the stoic sect and a man of great erudition deputed to India in 190 AD by Demitrius, the bishop of Alexandria to settle some disputes in the St. Thomas Church.[14]

The second visitor was Bishop Dudi (David) of Basra in Persia, an eminent Doctor who evangelised many in India.[15]

A palm leaf document of 293 AD shows that few Vellala (a caste) converts in Kaveripooppattinam, fearing persecution by their King, arrived at *Korakkeni* (Kollam) by some sea vessels and settled in Kollam, where there were Christians at that time.

One Theophilos the Indian, deputed to India by Roman Emperor Constantius in 354 AD, is said to have introduced many reforms in the Indian church.[16] Constantius, the son of Constantine, who became Emperor in 350 AD favoured Arianism (a heresy in those days) and tried to crush the Nicenes (those who follow the Nicene Creed). As such, we are not sure of the nature of reforms this delegate introduced in the St. Thomas Church, probably Arian heresy.

In 522-525 AD, an Alexandrian merchant Cosmos Indicopleustus visited India and published a book on his visits titled Universal Christian Topography wherein he referred to the presence of Christians in Ceylon and Malabar. According to him, in the island called Socotra in the Indian Sea, there were a 'multitude of Christians', and in the country called Male (Malabar) where pepper grows, there was a Church at Kalliana and a bishop appointed from Persia.[17]

St. Gregory of Tours (538-593) referred to the removal of the Holy Remains of St. Thomas to Edessa and the existence of a 'monastery Church of striking dimensions at that part of India'.[18]

In AD 852, an Arab traveller named Sulaiman visited Kaulam-mala (Kollam). He had given detailed descriptions about 'Kollam' described as *Chemmala* by the Greek travellers.[19]

Marco Polo visited Malabar in 1292. He highlighted the honesty of the people of Malabar and their justice-minded King. In 1291, Monti Corvino, a Dominican missionary visited India as a representative of Pope Innocent. Under his initiative, few Dominican Friars came to the Western coast of India and settled at Thane near Bombay. All these Friars except one (Jordanus de Severac, a French missionary) were murdered at Thane. Jordanus visited many parts of India (called by him as 'greater India', 'lesser India' etc.) including Kollam in the 1320s, converted many to Christianity, returned and submitted a fascinating report of his travels titled *Mirabilia Descripta* to Pope John XXII (1316-1334), then residing at Avignon in France. A Malayalam translation of the full report *Mirabilia Descripta* is available in the book *Kollam Christians* (Mal) by

Msgr. A.J. Rozario. An English translation is reported to be available in the Dominican Generelate. (This author had no occasion to see it.) The Pope, very much impressed by the dedication of Jordanus, appointed him 'Bishop of India and the East' with Headquarters at Kollam.[20]

But we have no evidence to prove either the arrival of Jordanus at Kollam as Bishop or the establishment of a diocese at Kollam in the 14th century.

An extract of the Catholic Directory of India 1998 (page 946) is reproduced below, "In 1329, Pope John XXII by a Bull in Perpetuam Memoriam of 9-8-1329, constituted as an episcopal See, the first diocese in the Indies, and at the time, the only one in the country, as suffragan to the Archdiocese of Sultany in Persia." By a Bull 'Venerabili Fratri', the same Pope John XXII on August 21st, 1329 appointed the Dominican Friar Jordanus de Severac as Bishop of Kollam. Both these Bulls remained in theory. Nothing practically materialised. Kollam became a diocese only on September 1st, 1886[21] when Pope Leo XIII established the Indian Latin Hierarchy. It leads us to conclude that the diocese instituted by Pope John XXII in 1329 has not materialised for some reason or other, presumably the death of Bishop Jordanus on his way back to Kollam.[22]

Twenty years later, one Marinjoli, Pope's delegate to China, *en route* his return journey, visited Kollam and stayed there for sixteen months. He refers to the gift of one hundred gold coins to him by the Kollam Christians. A reference is also seen about his visit to a Church in the name of St. Mary at Kollam.

(b) The Knanaya Immigration

A landmark event in the history of St. Thomas Christians in India took place in 345 AD by the immigration of 72 families consisting of about 400 Jewish Christians from Mesopotamia to Muziris under the leadership of one 'Thomas of Cana'. Historians have attributed two reasons for this immigration.

Consequent on recognising Christianity as the official religion in the Roman Empire by Emperor Constantine, King Sapor II of Persia (309-375 AD) hated Christianity and unleashed persecution of Christians. Brigadier General Parcy Sykes in his book *History of Persia* gives an account of the nature and harshness of the persecution as follows:

"The first order issued against the Christians was that they should pay double taxes as their contribution to the cost of the war in place of personal services. Mar Shimum, the Catholicos, who was required to collect the money, foolishly refused, on the two-fold grounds that the people were too poor and that the bishop was not a tax-collector. He was arrested with many of his colleagues; and on Good Friday 339 AD, Mar Shimum, five bishops and one hundred priests were executed at Susa, the ancient capital of forgotten Elam. Massacres and the destruction of churches for fully forty years continued the persecution. Monks and nuns, especially, being subject to pitiless persecution, because they conspicuously violated the sane tenets of Zorostrianism."[23]

The general impression among historians is that this severe persecution unleashed in Persia account for the exodus of Christians. The other reason attributed by few historians is a dream of Bishop Mar Joseph of Edessa in which St. Thomas appeared and asked him 'Wilt thou not help India'? The bishop conveyed the message of the dream to his superior Catholicos, who in turn, summoned Thomas of Cana and urged him to proceed to Malabar to save the St. Thomas Church from disintegration. Accordingly, Thomas of Cana organised the expedition to help the Malabar Christians. The participants in this expedition were Jewish Christians, victims of persecution, who willingly assembled together from different areas of the Persian Empire.

When Thomas of Cana and party reached Muziris on the Malabar Coast, the King personally greeted and welcomed them. The King was very much impressed by the latter's remarkable bearing and wealthy following. In the words of P. Thomas, the author of *Christians and Christianity in India*, 'the standing of Cana Thoma with the Perumal (King) was very high'. His vast resources and personal ability won for him many honours from the Perumal. In appreciation, the Perumal allotted to Thomas of Cana a suburb of Muziris called

Mahadevarpattanam (the city of great God) and granted 72 privileges confirmed by the royal charter in three copper plates known as *chepped*s in the local language. These *chepped*s are now extinct in India. The 72 privileges granted by the Perumal are listed in pages 21 and 22 of the book *Knanaya Church in Kerala History* (Mal.) by Dr. Jacob Kollaparambil.

In the land gifted by the Perumal, Thoma built a Church and residential houses for him and his associates on the southern side of Mahadevarpattanam. The native St. Thomas Christians continued in their traditional houses on the northern side of Mahadevarpattanam. To distinguish the identity of the two sects of Christians, the people addressed them in colloquial tongue as *Thekkumbhagar* (Southerners or Southists) and *Vadakkumbhagar* (Northerners or Northists). These terms are in vogue even today.

A few historians have questioned the authenticity of the claims of the immigrants on three scores: (i) Dutch writer Visscher puts the date as 745 AD, Hough gives the date as 780 AD and Paoli assigns the date as 825 AD. Archbishop Menezes dates it as 9th century. Another theory is that Cana Thoma was a Nestorian bishop who came in 900 AD and not a merchant. (ii) As regards the claim of the immigrants that a bishop named Mar Joseph of Edessa accompanied them, some historians point out that there was no bishop named Joseph in Edessa in that period. (iii) In the light of the missing copper plates, some others doubt the details of the privileges granted to Thoma by the King. Whatever be the merits or demerits of these claims and counter-claims, the Knanaya community, claiming to be the descendants of the 72 families, now numbering about two hundred thousand (1,31,000 in the Catholic Church and 68,000 in the Jacobite Church) continues today as a strong arm of the Christian Church in Kerala. Till today, they have followed the faith and doctrines of Christianity, the Syriac liturgy and their Jewish customs and practices to which they were accustomed to, without distortions or deviations. They maintained cordial relations with other Christian churches and non-Christian religionists. They are traditionally healthy and industrious and also shrewd businessmen.

In the early centuries, they stayed at Cranganore. Later, due to several factors like increase in their number, the communal flare up between the Jews and the Muslims in Cranganore and the vicissitudes of history, they first migrated from Cranganore to Kaduthuruthy and therefrom to other parts of Kerala in the medieval period. This community maintained its cohesiveness till the schism in the Malabar church in the 17th century. Consequent on the schism, the Knanites parted company into two factions, a major faction continuing in the Catholic Church and the other group driven to the lap of the Jacobite Church accepting the Antiochean Jacobite Patriarch as their head and the consequential change-over from their age-old Chaldean Syriac liturgy to the Antiochian Syriac liturgy. In 1911, Pope Pius X instituted the Vicariate of Kottayam exclusively for the Sudhists (Knanayites) in the Catholic Church. In 1923, Pope Pius XI raised the Vicariate of Kottayam to a diocese with Mar Alexander Choolaparambil as the bishop. Recently, the Holy See elevated the Kottayam diocese to the dignity of an Archdiocese under Archbishop Most Rev Kuriakose Mar Kunnassery.

After the retirement of His Grace Most Rev. Kuriakose Mar Kunnassery, His Grace Mathew Mar Moolakkatt has been elevated to the dignity of Archbishop of Kottayam Archdiocese.

In 1909, the Jacobite Patriarch Mar Abdullah consecrated a bishop, Mar Severiose Edavazhikal exclusively for the Knanayite faction in the Jacobite Church. In 1932, this Knanayite Jacobite Community became an independent con-fraternity with a separate diocese. (Details on the schism are given separately.)

One serious allegation generally raised against the Kerala Knanaya Community by both Christians and non-Christians alike is the racial discrimination in marriages practised by them. They insist on marriages strictly within their sect, allegedly to maintain purity of blood and race, under the penalty of expulsion of the offenders from the sect. According to the critics, this practice is not only against the fundamentals of Christianity but also against civility and morality. The critics argue that in such a set-up, the congregation becomes sectarian with no scope for individual or collective mission for evangelisation in a religion that teaches that every Christian is automatically a missionary. They also allege that this practice is a religious, social and political evil and an anachronism in a civilised society.

The community's defence for this is as below: The Knanaya community is population-wise negligible in a country like India with a population exceeding one thousand million. They are the descendants of people emigrated from another nation and hence of a different ethnic origin. Unity and emotional solidarity of the sect are essential prerequisites for survival and self-protection of this small community. If restrictions for marriages are relaxed, solidarity is likely to vanish and even the very existence of the sect would be in jeopardy, in not so distant a future. Marriages detrimental to the very existence of the sect are discouraged solely for survival and self-protection and not anything connected with racism or apartheid as alleged or feared by the critics. Both the Catholic and Jacobite Churches allowed separate dioceses after in-depth study and realisation of the gravity of this life-and-death situation. Here there is no question of any discrimination against anyone. In India, almost all sections of people enforce similar restrictions. The *Brahmins* marry *Brahmins*, the *Kshatrias* marry *Kshatrias*, *Sudras* marry *Sudras*, the *Sunni* Muslims marry *Sunnis*, *Shias* marry *Shias*, all denominations of Christians prefer marriages from their own sect. Similar restrictions are prevalent in various sects all over the world in some way or other and offenders are even ostracised in certain sects. Despite restrictions, the number opting to go out of the sect is on the increase year after year. In such a situation, relaxation of restrictions would be self-annihilation; the community argues.

In the present fast changing hi-tech world, with the advancement of science and technology, economic affluence, women's education, women's employment, craze for Westernisation, loosening of the grip of religions, growing internationalism, precedence of pragmatism over idealism, growing consciousness of individual rights and freedom etc., all these restrictions are likely to wither away in the course of time. There seems to be no necessity for any alarm or hue and cry on this score.

(c) Two Prelates in Kollam

In 823 AD, two prelates named Sapor (Mar Sabariso) and Proth (Mar Aphrod) along with a batch of followers arrived at Kollam. The King of Kollam Sthanu Ravi Varma gave them land for the construction of a Church and other privileges of honour inscribed in *Cheppeds* (Copper plates of guarantee). A Mingana, in his book *Early Spread of Christianity in India* said that Syrian bishops and Metropolitans were used to visit Kollam. The *Cheppeds* known as *Therissappalli Cheppeds* are available even today. The King granted two sets of *cheppeds*, three copper plates in the first set and four plates in the second set. Out of them, one of the first set and three of the second set are kept in the Catholicate House, Kottayam. One each of the first and second sets is kept in the Marthoma Church, Tiruvalla. One among the three plates in the first set is missing. Historian A. Sreedhara Menon says:

"The first Venad ruler about whose reign we have any authentic information is Ayyan Atikal Thiruvatikal. He has immortalised himself in the famous Therisappally Copper Plate grant issued by him in 849 AD (The 5th Regnal year of Sthanu Ravi Varma Kulasekhara) in the presence of important officers of the State and the representatives of the Anchuvanam and Manigramam. The inscriptions record that one Maruvan Sabriso also had built a church named Terisapalli and a *Nakaram* (Trading centre) at *Kurakkeni* (Kollam) and the Venad Chief made the gift of a plot of land to the Church and the Nakaram along with several families of labourers and proprietary rights."[24]

After being settled, the descendants of the immigrants spread over to nearby Kundara, Chathannoor and Kayamkulam.

(d) Nestorian Bishops

The traditional belief of the Christian Church is that Christ is God and man. Some extremists in the Antiochean School conceived the distinction between the two natures of Christ, divine and human, as of two persons. Nestorius, a priest of that school, later became the Patriarch of Constantinople

(428-431 AD). The General Council of Ephesus in 431 AD condemned the theory of Nestorius and deposed him. One of the byproducts of the Nestorian theory was that Mary is not the mother of God but only mother of Christ in whom the person of the Word of God united 'Himself – the word of God dwelling in Christ as in a temple'.

The Seleucians who lived outside the Roman Empire were not in touch with these controversies. Many Nestorians fled to Seleucia. Nestorianism in its strict sense does not admit the unity of person in Christ. But the Seleucian Christology, often accused of Nestorianism, does admit the personal unity of Christ. About the primacy of Peter and his succession, they were in full agreement with the teachings of the General Council of Nicaea. In the 16th century, when the patriarchal office fell vacant, the Seleucians elected one John Siud Sulaqua and sent him to Rome for the Sacred Pallium. Cardinal Maffei who presented the new Patriarch for the Pallium commented, "These Nestorians seem to have kept rather the name of the heretic Nestorius than his heresies. For, I see nothing in these men that are here which may have any leaning to that sect."[25]

These comments of Cardinal Maffei are fully relevant in the Indian context. Many Nestorian bishops would have come to Malabar and the Indian Church would have incognito accepted them, believing their claims and robes. In the absence of proper communication facilities, the probability of such things happening cannot be ruled out. In the history of Malabar Christians, there were instances of bishops identified as heretics being driven out from the Church. At one point of time, four bishops of Nestorian persuasion, Mar Thomas, Mar Denha, Mar Jacob and Mar John were found in position in Malankara. But none of them dared to teach Nestorianism, fearing the possibility of unpleasant reaction from the people.

From the very days of inception, the St. Thomas Church believed in the personal unity of Christ. Devotion to Mary as Mother of God was also unshakeably deep-rooted in them. The congregation at Niranam founded by St. Thomas in the name of St. Mary even today remains as St. Mary's Church. Papal delegate Marinjoli is reported to have visited at Kollam a

Church in the name of St. Mary. Hundreds of ancient churches in the name of St. Mary are visible all over Malabar, celebrating the festival of Our Lady every year and addressing St. Mary, 'the mother of God'.

All these evidences establish beyond doubt that though there were infiltrations by Nestorian bishops into Malabar, there had never been the infiltration of Nestorianism in the St. Thomas Church in Malabar. A small Chaldean Church in Trichur in Kerala, earlier labelled as Nestorians, now disowns Nestorianism, though they still address Mary as "Mother of Christ" only.

(e) Status of the Indian Church

As a result of a compromise between Seleucian Patriarch Timothy I (in the 8th century) and the Persian Church, the Indian Church was raised to the status of an ecclesiastical province directly under the Patriarch. Later, Patriarch Sliba Zcha (714-728) raised the Indian Church to the Metropolitan dignity. Patriarch Theodosius (852-855) granted certain concessions to the Malabar Church, subject to mutual communications and offerings (tribute or gift) every sixth year, for the maintenance of the patriarchate. The official title of the Metropolitan of India was 'the Metropolitan and the Gate of all India'. The Vatican Syriac Codex 22 written in Cranganore in 1301 mentions the name of Metropolitan Mar Jacob as 'the Metropolitan Bishop of the See of St. Thomas and the whole Church of the Christians in India'. According to Fr. Campori S.J., 'the Bishopric of Serra was always an Archbishopric and is the most ancient in the whole of India'.[26]

(f) Persian Crosses

Few carved granite crosses believed to be of Persian architecture with inscriptions in Pahlavi language were detected at different places in Malankara. Pahlavi was the language in use in Persia during the rule of the Sassanid dynasty. It is presumed that these Persian crosses were erected in Malankara in the seventh or eighth century. These crosses, representing the strong relationship between the Churches in Persia and Malabar, are still preserved in the Knanaya Jacobite church at Kottayam, the Jacobite Church at Kadamattom and the Syrian Catholic Church at Muttuchira. A similar cross was later unearthed at the St. Thomas Mount, Madras, now known as 'St. Thomas Cross'. The translations of the inscriptions vary among the scholars. B. Vadakkekara observed "These crosses were revered because they were expressions of their Christian faith. Labelling it Manichaen or Nestorian finds justification neither from tradition nor from history. The St. Thomas cross continues to be rightly venerated as it is the most ancient Christian emblem as yet discovered in India."

Manichaens never developed any veneration of the cross. Even though we are still in the dark as to from where or through whom or when these crosses came to India, the St. Thomas Christians venerate them as a rich heritage of the Syrian church and the solid evidence of the Indo-Persian fraternity in the ecclesiastical sphere.

Liturgy, Social Life and Administration

The most remarkable developments in the life of the St. Thomas Christians in the Pre-Portuguese period were in the areas of liturgy, social life and the administrative system in the church. By giving an Indian colour, shape and flavour in these areas, the St. Thomas Christians consciously prevented themselves from being isolated from their fellow-citizens. In the social sphere, they developed a social system of their own by insisting on the Seleucian canons only where obligatory local usages, customs and practices were not prescribed by the Indian Society. Their caste-based life helped them to preserve and keep up the traditions among the Hindus. They pursued only those occupations considered noble by all.

A passage from the notes of Rev. Dr. Placid throwing much light on the life of the St. Thomas Christians is reproduced below:

"The Church architecture in its externals, the musical instruments and the paraphernalia used in churches, the flag staff in front of the Church to hoist flag on during the celebration of feasts, the pilgrimages, the Church processions, the offerings made in churches etc. resembled the corresponding items kept in Hindu temples, but were all christianised.

Eg: In the Church processions the priests carried small crosses in their hands, which the faithful kissed devoutly, while the priest celebrant carried a copy of the *Bible* which, says Vincent Maria, OCD, 'was not taken out for private use, since they thought it improper to take out of the sanctuary the foundation of the faith'. In place of *prasad* given to Hindu devotees in their temples, Christians who made offerings were given a little fried rice or a piece of bread. There is no wedding ring, instead the boy ties the 'thali' to the neck of the girl. The Christian 'thali' was distinguished from the Nambudiri *Brahmin* 'thali' by the cross of 21 beads on its front. The thread to suspend the 'thali' was drawn out from the bridal veil as among the Nambudiri *Brahmins*. The East Syrian ritual was followed for the funerals. But, everything that followed the burial was Hindu, but christianised. The priests presided at the above mentioned feasts (Chatham and pulakuli) and prayed for the deceased together with the faithful."[27]

The St. Thomas Christians had a three-tier system for the administration of the Church as detailed below:

The Palliyogam at the parish level,

The Archdiaconate at the community level, and

The Metropolitan and the Patriarch at the top hierarchical level.

Palliyogam

Palliyogam is the local assembly consisting of the heads of the Christian families and the clergy of the *edavaka* (parish), the modern developed form of the traditional village assembly known as *Manram* in the ancient Dravidian communities. The Palliyogam assembles under the leadership of the local parish clergy known as the *Dessathupattakar* (native priests). All are bound to abide by the decisions of Palliyogam on matters concerned with the parish such as:

Selection of candidates for priesthood.

Christian life of the members of the parish.

Upkeep and maintenance of the temporalities of the parish.

Punishment for public sinners.

Finance and its management.

Reconciliation in cases of conflicts.

Dessathupattakar

One of the members of the parish selected and recommended by the Palliyogam duly ordained by the bishop is the *Dessathupattakar.* His jurisdiction was confined to the parish for which he was ordained. Generally, they were married. As such, each parish was independent.

The Archdeacon

The Archdeacon, responsible for the administration of the whole church, is traditionally a member of the Pakalomattom family, one of the *Brahmin* families believed to have been converted by St. Thomas. General assemblies, consisting of the representatives of all parishes convened to handle issues concerning the whole church or regional issues, were presided over by the Archdeacon who had a decisive role in such meetings. He is the leader of the entire St. Thomas Christian community in India and hence designated as 'Archdeacon of All India'. At one time, there could be only one Archdeacon while there was no limitation regarding the number of bishops. He was the Chief Co-ordinator of various local communities and the Chief Administrator of the entire church. From 1576-1586, Pope Gregory XIII addressed five papal Briefs to the Archdeacon acknowledging the traditional dignity, position and responsibility of his office.[28] A Portuguese document written between 1780 and 1786 speaks of the important position of the Archdeacon "The Archdeacon is the first among the 72 princes of the kingdom known as *Perumpadapu*: the said Archdeacon is, according to custom, the man to crown the king in order that the king may be recognized as king; the coronation consists in this that the Archdeacon puts a gold cross on the neck of the king, and he (the King) must wear this for five days before he is called King of Perumpadapu" (the name of the kingdom). To sum up, the Archdeacon was held in high esteem and he commanded the respect of not only the Christian community, but also the entire people in the kingdom including the King and the royal entourage.

The Bishop

The Bishops were ascetics held in high esteem and social status. They, being foreigners, were concerned only with spiritual obligations and responsibilities. The bishops neither confer sacred orders nor absolve from ecclesiastical censures without the official request from the community, which submits the formal petition to the bishop after assembling in the Church and hearing the candidates to sacred orders. This unique administrative set up of the St. Thomas Christians resembled a civil republic.

On analysis of history of the early fifteen centuries, the St. Thomas Church of Malabar is credited with achievements galore in several areas. But, no student of history can ignore the dismal failure of the Church on two vital counts:

- Practice of untouchability with its inherent vices, and
- Neglect of the primary mission of evangelisation.

Both are opposed to the fundamental basis of Christianity. Had the Church been vigilant in these areas, Christianity would have presented a different picture in India.

In short, the St. Thomas Church was, as Dr. Placid Podipara has aptly commented, 'a community, Christian in religion, Hindu in culture and Oriental in worship'. Thus, when the Indian church was peacefully marching forward, the Portuguese landed in India, marking the beginning of a period of strife, chaos and schisms with far-reaching consequences.

FOOTNOTES

1. George Menachery (Prof.), *The St. Thomas Christian Encyclopaedia of India*, Vol. 2, p. 1.
2. *The Great Encyclopaedia of Universal Knowledge*, p. 803.
3. CBCI, *The Catholic Directory of India*, p. 234.
4. David Daniel, *The Orthodox Church of India*, p. 4.
5. John Marshall (Sir), *A Guide to Taxila* (1960).

6. Xavier Koodapuzha (Dr.), *Christianity in India*, pp. 33-37.
7. *Ibid.*, p. 47.
8. *Ibid.*, p. 47.
9. David Daniel, *The Orthodox Church of India*, p. 3.
10. Xavier Koodapuzha (Dr.), *Christianity in India*, pp. 46-47.
11. *Ibid.*
12. Sreedhara Menon, A., *A Survey of Kerala History*, pp. 97-98.
13. Xavier Koodapuzha (Dr.), *Christianity in India*, p. 46.
14. Eusebius, *Historia Ecclesiastica*, Ch. V, Book V.
15. Cherian, C.V., *A History of Christianity in Kerala*, (1973), p. 72.
16. Joseph, T.K., *The Malabar Christians and their Ancient Documents*, (1929).
17. Kuriakose, M.K., *History of Christianity in India*, Source materials CLS, Serampore.
18. Perumalil, A.C., *The Apostles in India*, p. 71.
19. Rozario, A.J. (Mons), *Kollam Christians* (Mal.), p. 99.
20. *Ibid.*, p. 67.
21. CBCI, *The Catholic Directory of India*, p. 946.
22. Firth, C.B., *The Orthodox Church of India*, p. 23.
23. Percy, Sykes, *History of Persia*, Vol. 1, p. 415.
24. Sreedhara Menon, A., *A Survey of Kerala History*, p. 160.
25. George Menachery (Prof.), *The St. Thomas Christian Encyclopaedia of India*, Vol. 2, p. 30.
26. *Ibid.*, Vol. 2, p. 31.
27. *Ibid.*, Vol. 2, p. 32.
28. Xavier Koodapuzha (Dr.), *Christianity in India*, pp. 71-75.

The Portuguese Period

21

The sixteenth century was a turning point in the history of the St. Thomas Christians in India. Portugal, a comparatively small Christian country in Europe situated in the Iberian Peninsula, between Atlantic Ocean and Spain, planned a voyage of expedition to India in the fifteenth century. The impetus for this planning had many contributory factors.

As a part of the Islamic expansion programme, the North African Muslims (the Moors) occupied Spain and were poised to advance further to North and East Europe, in the eighth century. Although the Christians recovered Spain in the eleventh century, the European nations were apprehensive of the possibility of another similar adventure by the Islamic militia with adequate reinforcements. The failure of the Crusades to achieve the desired ends and the conquest of Constantinople by the Turks in 1453 strengthened their apprehension.

The Arabs monopolised trade of spices with the East and established their dominance in the seas in between India and the West.

The success of the voyages of exploration of Amerigo Vespucci and Christopher Columbus encouraged and triggered Portugal to attempt similar explorations to discover and colonise unknown lands.

In the 15th century, Portugal was a developing nation growing fast into a strong maritime power in Europe. Being born and brought up in a seafaring nation, there was no dearth of efficient and valiant sailors and navigators in Portugal. Their King himself was a reputed navigator.

Above all, the Pope entered into an agreement with the Kings of Portugal and Spain, known as *Padroado*, by which several ecclesiastical rights and privileges were granted to the Kings in order to enable them to evangelise the newly discovered lands. (Please see notes on Padroado in Part Five – Chap. 39)

Portugal made several attempts in the 15th century under the captaincy of Bartholomew Diaz to discover the sea-route to India, but those attempts did not succeed due to inclement weather and fatigue of sailors. Thereupon, the King arranged the construction of three new ships named *Savo Gabriel, Savo Raphael* and *Savo Michael* and bade happy voyage to Vasco de Gama from Lisbon to India in 1497.[1]

Gama, armed with the support and blessings of the King and the Pope, symbolically the sword and the cross, reached Kozhikode on 20th May 1498 after 346 days strenuous journey. The St. Thomas Christians were immensely happy to receive and welcome Gama and his companions, their fellow Christians from the West. In 1500, the Portuguese Viceroy Cabral arrived at Kozhikode with 13 ships and 1500 men. Gama returned to Portugal with his merchandise and came back to India in 1502 with few missionaries to harvest the ripe crops in India. These missionaries belonged to four congregations; the Society of Jesus (known as Jesuits and also called Paulists, the name related to St. Paul's College run by the Jesuits), the Franciscans, the Augustinians and the Dominicans. The relations of the missionaries and the Portuguese authorities with the St. Thomas Christians were calm and cordial in the initial period, but things moved from bad to worse and to the worst later, the initial calm being the calm before the storm.

The Portuguese had a three-fold agenda, religious, commercial and political. The conflicts between local kingdoms in Malabar provided them with ample opportunities to intervene in local squabbles and twist matters to their advantage. The native monarchs competed among themselves to curry the favour of the Portuguese. Lucrative profits in spice trade, high social status, the support of the trained militia of St. Thomas Christians, a naval fleet consisting of several ships with hundreds of armed sailors, arms and ammunition, friendship with local rulers, voluntary service of dedicated missionaries etc. put the Portuguese in a commanding position. They found the time and environment most conducive to straightaway proceed to accomplish their avowed aims of evangelisation, extermination of the Muslims from the trade sector, monopoly of trade and colonisation. The Arab monopoly of trade had already crumbled with the arrival of the Portuguese. Their domination in the seas was also completely shattered by inflicting heavy loss to them; many innocent women and children sailing in the Arab vessels were drowned in the sea. By the defeat of the Arabs, the Portuguese scored two goals at one stroke, the shattering of the Arab domination in the seas and acquisition of the complete monopoly of trade with Malabar.

The capture of Goa from the Adil Shah of Bijapur was also a well-calculated step to achieve two birds at one shot: (i) gaining total control over the Western coast and the seas, and (ii) colonisation of Goa. This provided the Portuguese with a port-city and a base camp for military operations. The territories acquired earlier in Malabar remained well-fortified as support bases for limited operations.

In the realm of evangelisation, they employed all methods at their command to convert non-Christians. In all spheres, they believed in the dictum 'the end justifies the means'. The missionaries, being patronised by the King, were primarily concerned with the continuance of the royal patronage. Mixed marriages with the natives, humanitarian aid, political protection, use of force etc. were prudently and effectively applied to gain conversions. Morality and ethics were all subsidiary matters.[2]

Mass conversions of the Parava community by Francis Xavier was a fillip to establish solid foundation for the Latin missions in Goa, Bassein, Cochin, Travancore, Tuticorin, Mylapore etc. In 1600, there were 28,379 Latin Catholics in the small Salsette peninsula alone. By 1630, there were 1500 Latin Catholics in and around Bombay through the untiring efforts of the Franciscans.

The Portuguese identified with and accustomed to Latin practices and traditions failed to understand the churches of the eastern traditions. According to their conception, absolute conformity with the liturgy and practices of the Roman Church was a prerequisite to claim communion with the Holy See of Rome. In the assessment of the Portuguese and Jesuits, the Church in Malabar was a pagan conglomeration with pagan rituals and practices with the label of Christianity under the leadership of an incalcitrant archdeacon who was held in high esteem not only by his followers, but also by the general public. The question of handling this puzzling situation was a headache for them; being sour, neither could they swallow; being sweet, nor could they spit it out.

After serious thought and careful planning, they set forth their aims: (i) achieve the conversion of non-Christians using all the means, fair or foul, (ii) prevent the arrival of Syrian bishops to India, (iii) to get rid of the archdiaconate, and (iv) latinise the entire Thomas Christians and put them under the control of Latin Bishops, preferably foreigners. Once the goals have been identified and set forth, a multi-pronged strategy was also drawn up and set in motion to achieve the goals. The strategy consisted of: (a) establishment of seminaries on Latin pattern for training and formation of priest, (b) establishment of a new Latin diocese after suppressing the existing Syrian diocese at Angamaly, (c) granting cash subsidies to priests, churches, institutions etc. (money is the most effective weapon to command docility), (d) confinement and deportation of incoming Syrian bishops, (e) handing over the incorrigible elements to the Inquisition for appropriate action, and (f) to deal with the Archdeacon with the help of the local rulers, if necessary, by bribing them, followed by abolition of the post itself.

The Jesuits were put in charge of the execution of the above-mentioned methodology; the missionaries of the other congregations were sidelined for their allegedly favourable disposition towards Thomas Christians. In the succeeding paras, let us see how things moved on.

In 1541, Vincent Lagos started a seminary at Cranganore to train Thomas Christians. As the training imparted was of Latin pattern, those ordained there were not acceptable to the Thomas Christians. Therefore, that endeavour met with a natural death. Pope Paul III created the first Latin diocese under the 'padroado' in Goa in 1534 with its territory extending from Cape of Good Hope to China. In 1577, Goa was raised to an archdiocese with two suffragan dioceses, Malaca and Cochin. Simultaneously, the East Syrian bishops were induced to adopt Latin practices. Mar Jacob accepted some of them. His action invoked the wrath and displeasure of the community and resultantly he had to spend his last years at Cochin with the Portuguese. Mar Joseph who succeeded Mar Jacob in 1556 was detained in a Franciscan monastery. The Superior of the monastery told Mar Joseph that 'those who want to minister the sacraments to the Christians of Malabar without the permission of the Bishop of Goa were thieves who did not enter through the door to the sheep-pen. But, Mar Joseph, on reaching Malabar, had to follow the East Syrian liturgy. He was, therefore, taken into custody and transported to Portugal to be subjected to the Inquisition. On finding him quite orthodox, Portugal sent him back to India. In India, he was arrested again and sent to Portugal and thence to Rome, where he died in 1569. Giusseppe Beltrami, who conducted a thorough study on the mission of Mar Joseph certified his 'death a martyrdom which took place close to the tomb of St. Peter, a sign of his constant fidelity to the Petrine See of Rome'.

Meanwhile, another East Syrian bishop Mar Abraham, who was very cautious against being caught hold of by the Portuguese, skipped them and reached Malabar in 1570. He was welcomed and accepted by the Thomas Christians. Here, it has to be specially noted that Mar Abraham, on an earlier occasion, arrived in Malabar as a Nestorian Metropolitan in 1556 and became a Catholic at Cochin in August 1558. He was deported by the Portuguese in 1559, escaped to Mozambique, joined the Catholic Patriarch Mar Abdiso, went to Rome, was reordained priest and bishop by order of the Pope, returned to India as Metropolitan of Angamaly, was detained in Goa, escaped and reached Malabar in 1570.[3]

The Archbishop of Goa decided to convoke a council at Goa and invited Mar Abraham to attend the council. Mar Abraham, on account of his previous experiences at Goa, declined the invitation and referred the matter to the Pope. Pope Gregory XIII, in reply, assured Mar Abraham of safe return and addressed the King of Portugal and the Archbishop of Goa on the imperative necessity of ensuring protection and safety to Mar Abraham, a fellow catholic bishop. On the assurance of Pope, Abraham attended the Council. In the third session, the council passed ten decrees urging the Thomas Christians to adopt Latin practices. As follow up of the decrees of the council, a Jesuit seminary was started at Vaipicotta for latinisation of the Thomas Christians. The response of Mar Abraham to this endeavour was lukewarm. The strained relations continued till the death of Mar Abraham in 1597.

Thus, in the crucial year 1597, marking the centennial year of the first arrival of Vasco de Gama in India, one chapter in the episode on Indo-Portuguese relations ended. Compared to the action-packed chapter that followed, the preceding century was not a noisy one. Before proceeding to the tumultuous chapter in this episode, it would be interesting for the readers to have a feedback on the issues that actually distanced the St. Thomas Christians from the Portuguese. A detailed description of the contentious issues in the canonical, liturgical and social spheres given by Dr. Jacob Kollaparambil in his book *The St. Thomas Christian Revolution in 1653* is reproduced below:

"But one thing disturbed the missionaries – the difference in rites and customs. Quite a number of practices and customs – canonical, liturgical, and social – of the St. Thomas Christians were different from those of the Portuguese. For example, they had a married clergy. Their liturgy was Oriental, even having an anaphora attributed to Nestorius. They celebrated the Holy Eucharist only rarely, and that with leavened bread and wine made out or raisins soaked in water, breaking the bread into many parts not elevating the chalice even once, giving the Communion in hands and in both the species. They had only general confession, but even that was not obligatory before each Communion. Their baptism was by immersion and with anointing of the chest and head, but with no salt, and the sacrament was delayed sometimes even to old age for lack of proper minister, or allegedly for lack of the required minimum offering of three fanams. They had no confirmation as a rite distinct from that of baptism. Their bishops conferred holy orders on married men and those below canonical age. Their clerics grew a tuft of hair on the top of the head instead of the clerical tonsure. They held as valid child marriages, clandestine marriages, and marriages contracted between parties in forbidden degrees of consanguinity or affinity. They blessed their sick reading scriptural passages and placing written verses from the *Bible* over the sick instead of the 'extreme unction'. They addressed Holy Mary 'Mother of Christ' and not 'Mother of God'. They commenced the liturgical days on the previous evening, and Lent on 'Quinquagesima Sunday', not on Ash Wednesday. They could eat no fish, egg, or milk-products on days of fasting. They had only crosses and no statues in the churches. Their churches were built like temples in architecture and decorations. They charged interest on loans."

"In the missionaries' view, such practices were wrong. They wished that the St. Thomas Christians abandon those 'wrong' practices and conform themselves to the Western Christians in everything. Obviously, the missionaries were under a mistaken concept that whatever was in use in the West by positive laws of the Latin Church was binding on every Christian all over the world, and that for the very salvation of one's soul. They had, however, various schemes to remedy the situation. The most rigid wanted to strike a perfect uniformity, while others, considering the fact that the Western positive laws had never been promulgated among the St. Thomas Christians, thought that some of the practices could be allowed to continue under dispensations granted by the Holy See."

"To achieve their goal, the missionaries tried to coerce the Chaldean bishops into changing some of their traditions, rites, and practices in Malabar, and into accepting some Latin ones instead, but such efforts scored only limited success. Mar Jacob's time saw the beginning of common cemeteries in the Churchyards. Previously, it is asserted, the St. Thomas Christians used to bury their dead in their own premises. So too in church building the Portuguese style began to be adopted. Mar Jacob introduced private confession, translating the formula of absolution from *Rituale Romanum* into Chaldean."[4]

Over and above those mentioned in the foregoing paras, we have already seen the practices of untouchability, neglect of evangelisation mission, Hindu rituals for marriages and processions etc. among the Thomas Christians. Here, one fact deserves to be mentioned. Before becoming Christians, the Thomas Christians were Hindus, a part and parcel of the Hindu culture. They continued to adhere to that ancient culture wherever those practices were not against their Christian faith. In doubtful cases, they christianised those practices and adhered to them. These were *prima facie* inconceivable to a European Christian wont to Latin practices.

"As in the other Oriental Churches, also in Malabar, Baptism and Confirmation were administered together, and their solemn administration, it seems, was reserved to the bishops. A ceremony of naming the child and feeding it with rice for the first child and for the first time usually preceded the rite of Baptism. Communal confession and general absolution was the norm for the sacrament of penance. Public penance was required of public sinners, and such sinners were absolved at the Church door, the priest striking the penitent slightly with a bundle of sticks. In place of the anointing of the sick, the Malabar priests had a special blessing, placing on the sick some scriptural verses written on paper or cadjan."[5]

Even from the early days of Christianity, the Eastern and Oriental churches (Eastern churches mean churchs in the Eastern Roman Empire and Oriental churches are those in the East, outside the Empire) had their own liturgies and practices originated even before shaping of the Latin liturgy in the West. Christianity first spread among the Jews and later among the Gentiles in Palestine and nearby areas like Antioch, Edessa, Parthia, Persia, Babylon, Alexandria etc. St. Peter went to Rome only later in his life, after gaining a foothold for Christianity in the above mentioned areas. (He chaired the Jerusalem Synod of the Apostles in 48 or 49 AD.)

The Eastern schism and the emergence of Orthodox churches occurred only in the 11th century. A section of the Christians in the Eastern Empire did not opt for the Orthodox churches. They continued in communion with Rome, following their ancient traditional liturgies like Byzantine, Antiochean, Alexandrian and Chaldean. Difference in liturgies never created any obstacles for them to continue in communion with Rome. Even now, they continue with both; their liturgies and allegiance to the Holy See of Rome.

In consonance with their characteristic aggressive approach, the Portuguese, on the strength of the Padroado, without caring to verify the validity of the East Syrian (Chaldean) liturgy, insisted on an abrupt and wholesale change-over to the Latin Rite. The St. Thomas Christians, who considered sacred their liturgical tradition, perhaps older than that of the Portuguese, naturally resented. When the Portuguese attempted to compulsorily enforce it, the St. Thomas Christians would have objected or even revolted against it. They (the Portuguese) purposely avoided referring to Rome for clarification or advice on the liturgy issue because they were fully aware that Mar Abraham was consecrated as bishop by Rome with the express sanction of the Pope and posted as the Archbishop of the Angamaly See of the St. Thomas Christians. Moreover, on an earlier occasion, when the question whether Syriac need be taught in the seminary was referred to Rome, the answer was a direction to the missionaries to work harder for the preservation of Syriac, correcting only errors and abuses. The strong defence of Rome was that variety made the Church beautiful. In short, the Portuguese view of the St. Thomas Church was that of a community immune to correctives.

The next irritant in the eyes of the Portuguese was the archdiaconate. The incumbent holding the office in their period was a hard nut to crack. The archdiaconate was an innovative device founded by the Thomas Christians in ancient days to tide over emergent situations in the absence of the Syrian bishop; at times it may take years for a new bishop to come from Seleucia-Ctesiphon. And whenever they came, they had difficulty to interact with the faithful due to the language problem. The Archdeacon held no spiritual authority. It remained the exclusive prerogative of the bishop. The Archdeacon, the symbol of unity of St. Thomas Christians, was responsible for the co-ordination and administration of the temporalities of the whole Church. He would have hesitated to abide by the dictates of the Portuguese bishop or Jesuits. Being an important functionary, he could take decisions only after weighing the merits and demerits of each issue. This enraged the Goan bishop and the Jesuits. According to their assessment, the Archdeacon was a man not amenable to wiser counsel.

This is the background of the confrontation between the Portuguese and the Thomas Christians. The main grievance of the community was the imperious and haughty behaviour of the bishops and the Jesuits. The Thomas Christians were in the lookout of ways and means to get out of the stranglehold of the 'Padroado'. The Portuguese wanted the latinisation of the Thomas Christians, the expulsion of the archdeacon and the abolition of the archdiaconate itself. After the death of Mar Abraham, there was no bishop for the Angamaly See. Dom Menezes, the shrewd Archbishop of Goa (1595-1610) found the situation most opportune to personally interfere in the internal affairs of the Angamaly See. He came to Malabar, camped at Vaipicotta and personally monitored the execution of his plans.

Synod of Diamper (Udyamperoor) and its Aftermath

'Diamper' is the Western version of the place named 'Udayamperoor' situated a few miles south of Cochin. The scheming and charming Archbishop Menezes, on reaching Vaipicotta engaged himself in attending to the preparatory spadework for accomplishing his aims. He first visited the local kings who were eager to win the support of the Portuguese against their rivals. After ensuring the support of the Kings, he arranged a tour to the parishes accompanied by the Archdeacon and his own entourage. In consonance with his inborn instinct for high-handedness, the Archbishop administered sacraments of confirmation and ordination of priests in the parishes he visited. When the Archdeacon sounded about the validity of his actions, the Archbishop silenced him by mentioning the name of a rival candidate to Archdeacon's office. The exasperated

Archdeacon again yielded to subscribe his assent and signature to a list of ten points presented by the Archbishop. The list is reproduced below:

- To condemn Nestorianism and to acknowledge Nestorius, Theodore and Diodore to be in hell fire.
- To confess the Law of Thomas to be the same as the Law of Peter.
- To make a profession of faith according to the formula prescribed by the Archbishop.
- To hand over all books to be corrected or burned.
- To accept the Pope's supremacy.
- To condemn the Patriarch as a heretic and schismatic and to swear not to have relations with him.
- To obey Dom Menezes as his superior by an oath until the arrival of new bishop.
- To swear not to receive any bishop other than the one sent by Rome and approved at Goa.
- To promise to convoke a synod in the place appointed by Dom Menezes to accept everything that would be settled there, and to convoke to it priests and representative laymen and not to go about accompanied by soldiers.
- To travel always in the company of Dom Menezes and in the same conveyance.

Refusal to accept any of these was refusal to accept all.[6]

After taming the Archdeacon, the Archbishop dispatched convocatory letters from Vaipicotta inviting the entire Parish priests and lay representatives to the Synod to be held at Diamper from 20th to 27th June 1599. The Archbishop already had the drafts of the decrees of the Synod prepared beforehand. The participants of the Synod, except a few priests, were incapable of understanding the discourses and decisions. They had only the role of silent spectators. The decrees visualised radical changes in the liturgy, theology, spirituality, administrative system, discipline, tradition etc. of the St. Thomas Christians. Once implemented, the decrees would have transformed the entire Syrian community in India into a full-fledged Latin community in form and contents. Archbishop Menezes accomplished what he desired. He planned ingenuously and executed his plans with precision. All prospective trouble-shooters – the Kings, the Archdeacon, the indigenous priests, and the laity – were either numbed or silenced. The Kings were trapped by promises, the Archdeacon was intimidated and subdued and the priests and laity were convinced of his spiritual authority and made happy by the administration of sacraments, especially the ordination of their kith and kin. He had neither mandate nor jurisdiction to convoke a Synod or to ordain priests in a diocese in the absence of the diocesan bishop, according to canons. The Archbishop was a very knowledgeable person fully aware of the legal and ecclesiastical intricacies and implications of his actions. He single-handedly managed everything without dissent, chaos or confusion. He rectified the errors and supplied the omissions in the minutes or decrees, after the Synod. By any yardstick, what an amazing personality of brilliance and calibre he was? Had he not been transferred from Goa to Braga in Portugal in 1610, what would have been the destiny of the St. Thomas Church in Malabar and Christianity in India as a whole, is left to the readers to guess.

Three letters written on the proceedings of the synod by Bishop Francis Roz to the Jesuit General in Rome and to the Portuguese Assistant Fr. Alvarez in Rome are extracted below:

Letter dated 20th November 1603 to the Jesuit General

"I request Your Paternity, for the love of our Lord, on receiving this information, to use your influence in the court of Rome so that this state ruinous to souls, may be averted; and let the Holy Father be informed of it; let not these Christians say that we have duped them; for, to tell you the entire truth, some of the canons of the above mentioned Synod the Archbishop himself added after the Synod was over; not a single canon was discussed or altered. So much so that there was no form of a Synod and it cannot be said to contain anything more than directive principles; they heard them without understanding what was being said, and I can myself bear ample witness as also the other Fathers who understood the language."

Letter dated 27th December 1603 to the Jesuit General and Fr. Alvarez

"The Archbishop of Goa, I think, intends to send to Rome the Synod he conducted at Diamper when he came here, because he has written to me asking for signatures which I was keeping. It was no Synod since no consultation was made and the Christians were unaware of what was being enacted. If they put their signatures it was due to my importunity. Hence the Synod should on no account be presented to the Holy Father."

Letter dated 1st January 1604 to Fr. Alvarez

"Now I should not like to leave out here a thing of great importance, namely that when the Archbishop of Goa came to visit this Malabar, he conducted a council, to tell you the truth, with little form and order of a council; and he of his own accord, even afterwards, added some things which were never read public. And much of what was read, was done in such a hurry and confusion that the Christians did not understand, not consequently accept it."[7]

The follow up on the decisions of the Synod with far-reaching repercussions, were:

- Appointment of a Latin bishop (Bishop Francis Roz) for Thomas Christians. (Nov. 5th, 1599)
- Suppression of the Metropolitan See of Angamaly, which was a suffragan of Goa. (Dec. 20th, 1599)
- Extension of the Portuguese Padroado over the Thomas Christians. (Aug. 5th, 1600)
- Consequent on wide protests from the St. Thomas Christians, the metropolitian dignity of the Angamaly See was later restored. (Dec. 22nd, 1608)

- After the restoration, Bishop Roz and his successors became archbishops from 1608 onwards, as detailed below:

Francis Roz as bishop	1600 - 1608 and
Do as Archbishop	1608 - 1624
Archbishop Stephen Britto	1624 - 1641
Archbishop Francis Garcia	1641 - 1659

All of them were Jesuits. Bishop Roz convened a synod at Angamaly in 1603. He published a statute known as Rozian Statute whereby the powers of the Archdeacon were curtailed. The Archdeacon conveyed his protests to the Portuguese Assistant Fr. Alvarez. But there was no tangible effect for his protests. Tension was mounting up. Bishop Britto allowed few relaxations in the powers of the Archdeacon. Franciscans, Dominicans and Augustinians were strong supporters of the Archdeacon. They accused the Archbishop of arrogance and authoritarianism.

Archdeacon George died in 1640. This was followed by the death of Archbishop Britto in 1641. Fr. Thomas, nephew of Archdeacon George, succeeded as Archdeacon in 1640 and Archbishop Garcia succeeded Britto in 1641. During Garcia's period, the relations with the St. Thomas Christians became further strained. These Archbishops were not successful due to their ignorance of language, liturgy, customs and administrative systems of the St. Thomas Church. The *padroado* jurisdiction of Portugal was very vast, extending from Gibraltar in the West to East Indies in the East and it was not running smoothly. Protestant countries like Holland, England and Denmark created conflicts and divisions in the missions, posing threats to the Portuguese. Financially, the *Padroado* was not in a position to subsidize the missions. Open conflicts between the Portuguese and the Thomas Christians were not rare. This complex situation in the missions prompted Rome to think of reorganising the missionary activities. In 1627, Pope Gregory XV established the College of Propaganda Fide to impart proper formation and training to the missionary personnel. Rome, in 1633, issued instructions to the Latin religious orders in India to work as a team and not to make any exclusive claims on the mission territory (the Jesuits often claimed the mission in Malabar as theirs).

Archbishop Garcia was a man adamant in his views and aggressive in their implementation. The community had many grievances like Padroado jurisdiction, latinisation, harsh treatment to the Archdeacon, absence of gentlemanly behaviour on the part of the Jesuits and so on. The Archbishop had never been lenient towards their grievances. This attitude of the Archbishop and the Jesuits has alienated the community. Whenever there was any crisis somewhere, the Archbishop approached the local kings to suppress the rebels. The net result of all these actions or inaction was the mounting tension between the community and the ecclesiastical authorities that would naturally erupt like a volcano in the fullness of time. Meanwhile, the archdeacon wrote to the Syrian Patriarchs to depute a bishop to rescue the St. Thomas Christians from the precarious situation in which they were put into.

At this stage, the Thomas Christians received information that a Metropolitan named Ahtallah from Syria landed at Surat in 1652 and thence came to Mylapore and the Jesuits took him into custody. This information fanned the emotions and imaginations of the people. They found a light at the end of the tunnel.

Koonan Kurisu Sathyam (The Slant Cross Oath)

In the beginning of 1652, Archbishop Garcia and his supporters were in a mood of complacency under the impression that the Malabar Church would soon be entering into an era of peace, not known to it in the immediate past and that the Thomas Christians, barring the archdeacon and few of his associates, would remain loyal and obedient to their Prelate. But, those who were closely watching the situation underneath the apparent calm in the surface were apprehensive of some explosion. They cautioned the Archbishop of the danger that is likely to erupt, once the shadow of an 'Armenian' (a Syrian Prelate) appearing in Malabar. Later events justified their apprehensions.

In September 1652, three Seminarians and one layman, returning to Malabar from a pilgrimage to Mylapore, brought some exciting news. Along with it, they carried one (or three?) letter addressed to Archdeacon Thomas from a Syrian Prelate in Mylapore, claiming his identity as Patriarch Ignatius Mar Ahtallah sent by Pope Ignatius to govern the St. Thomas Christians. They told the Archdeacon that the Patriarch was detained at the Jesuit College, Mylapore and that he was a holy person.

The Malabar Christians took Ignatius as a synonym for Innocent and innocently believed that Pope Innocent X had sent Ahtallah. Though Archdeacon and his associates had initial misgivings about the identity of the newcomer, they were tempted to forgo all doubts so long as the so-called Prelate or Patriarch was a Catholic. The news spread far and wide. The St. Thomas Christians all over Malabar became ebullient at the prospects of their dream coming true. On Archdeacon's invitation, priests and lay representatives assembled at Diamper and discussed the ways and means to bring the Patriarch to Malabar. Meanwhile, the Archdeacon publicised the first letter he received. After prolonged discussions, they arrived at a decision to write a letter to Archbishop Garcia seeking his co-operation to bring Mar Ahtallah to Malabar. The Archbishop replied on a small slip of paper, a token of his arrogance and contempt, that "even if the Patriarch is sent by the supreme Pontiff, we cannot grant him to you, for he has not brought the consent of our King". The Thomas Christians, outraged by the conduct of Archbishop Garcia, clamoured for breakaway from Garcia's rule. Two priests pacified the participants and proposed to send a delegation to personally meet the Archbishop and apprise him of the grave consequences of his decision. Unrelenting by the threats, the Archbishop told them that 'if his subjects rebelled, he would know how to tame them and that all the money he might spend for that purpose would be later recouped from them'. In the light of the failure of their moves, the meeting at Diamper concluded with the resolution that all should reassemble at Mattanchery when the ship, with the Patriarch on board, would arrive at Cochin.

Considering the influence of the letters of Mar Ahtallah on the subsequent events and the disagreement among historians on the bonafides of the second and third letters, the full text of the first letter alone is published below:

First Letter

"In the name of the Almighty and Eternal Essence, Patriarch St. Thomas, the Apostle, peace of God, the Father, blessing of our Lord Jesus Christ, and the descent of the Holy Spirit. Behold! I, Ignatius, Patriarch of All-India and China, send to you a letter through the clerics who came here from your place. When you have read the letter diligently send to me two priests and forty men. If, however, you wish to send them from your place, send them cautiously, quickly, and soon, so that seeing your people they would release me without hindrance. Come sons, listen to me and learn from me that I am empowered with all powers by my Lord, Pope Ignatius, who holds all powers. Now then, have no fear, for I have with me many treasures and other riches according to your necessities. Do your best, therefore, to get me to you. Meanwhile, in the name of Mary, the Mother of God, I inform you priests, clerics, and all the elders of the holy flock that I came to the city of Mylapore thinking that many people come here, and that priests would get me to your place of the Indians. In the year 1652 of our Lord, in the month of August, on Monday, I arrived at Mylapore in the monastery of the Jesuits. In the same monastery I stay, and they help me very much; may their reward increase here and there. Peace be with them, with you, and with us now and always, Amen.

This document is written in the year 1652 of our Lord in the holy city of Mylapore.

I, Ignatius, Patriarch of All-India and China."[8]

In the meantime, the Archdeacon's camp was not keeping quiet. He wrote to all civil and ecclesiastical dignitaries in Cochin; the Captain, the City Council, the Commissary of Inquisition, Superiors of Religious Orders etc. seeking their support and blessings. The Thomas Christians, aware of the undermining efforts of the Jesuits, naturally reacted disrespectfully not only to the Jesuits, but also to Archbishop Garcia. Meanwhile, the Archdeacon and other leaders were engaged in closed-door brainstorming exercises to find solutions to their problems; How to ascertain the identity of the so-called Patriarch?, How to rescue him if his claims were genuine?, If rescued, how to accommodate him so long as Archbishop Garcia was in position? Who are the persons to meet Ahtallah? Whether the second and third letters were genuine or forged by cassanar Ittithomman as alleged by people? etc.

The Archbishop's camp was also not idling their time. They were seriously collecting whereabouts and materials to portray the so-called Patriarch as an imposter and chalking out ways and means to prevent the Thomas Christians from meeting Ahtallah, at any cost. At one point of time, on the advice of his well-wishers, Archbishop Garcia was inclined to allow the Archdeacon and his people to meet Ahtallah. But, Fr. Hyacinth de Magistris, the secretary of the Archbishop vehemently opposed any leniency towards the Thomas Christians and dissuaded the Archbishop. In short, both camps were busily preparing for the rehearsal of their respective scenes in the drama to be staged at Mattanchery on the crucial day of arrival of Mar Ahtallah.

As expected, the Metropolitan was taken on board a Portuguese ship at Madras bound for Goa. *En route*, it touched Cochin. The 25,000 strong (leave exaggerations) Thomas Christians marched to the Harbour demanding the immediate release of their Metropolitan. A step by step narration of the events by Fr. Jacob Kollaparambil is copied below:

"Seeing that the Archbishop thus turned a deaf ear to their insistent pleas, the crowd became extremely exasperated. To their mind Dom Garcia's conduct of the whole affair bespoke his defiance of the Holy See and his contempt for his flock. Hence they assembled in the Church of Our Lady of Life at Mattanchery and passed six resolutions by which they declared that they would no longer obey Archbishop Garcia or any other Prelate from the Society of Jesus, nor would ever again admit the Paulists (Jesuits) into Malabar or to their churches, chose Archdeacon Thomas as their ecclesiastical governor and assigned to him four prominent cassanars as councillors, promised to uphold his authority even at the cost of their lives, sanctioned the forfeiture of the high-caste status for non-observance of those resolutions and finally invited all to meet again at Edappally* on the three-day fast of Jonas."

"Then, having a crucifix with lighted candles placed over a buffet in the center of the Church, the Archdeacon and the cassanars** touching a *Bible* at the main altar, they all together confirmed their resolutions with a solemn oath. This so-called Koonan-Cross Oath was made on Friday, January 3, 1653. After the oath Mar Ahtallah's letter was read to the crowd, and explained as though it conferred all the necessary powers on the Archdeacon. Cassanar Chandy Kadavil then made a speech in praise of the Babylonian Church. Further, the assembled issued a manifesto and posted it in public places justifying their declaration of independence from Dom Garcia and the Jesuits on the ground that the latter defied the Pope's orders by deporting the Patriarch whom the Pope had sent to govern the Malabar Church. Having done these things, the crowd dispersed. On orders of the Archdeacon the six resolutions were read in all the Churches of Malabar, and by all of them. Thomas was recognized as their ecclesiastical governor, independent of Archbishop Garcia. Informed of the Koonan-Cross Oath, Archbishop Garcia reportedly said in the presence of several people, "They espoused me to a black spouse, but if she doesn't want me, and repudiates me, frankly I don't care; the devil can take her."

"Evidently, at first Archbishop Garcia and his trusted councillors did not give much importance to the Koonan-Cross oath. They took it for granted that before long the Christians would be back to the Archbishop, as in the past, seeking ordination for their children, relatives, or parishioners."

---

* Edappally = A place north of Cochin where a famous Church in the name of St. George is situated.

** Cassanar = An ordained priest in the Malabar Church is designated 'cassanar' or 'kathanar'.

"That year the *Moonnu Noyambu* (Three-day Lent festivities) at Edappally drew an unusually larger crowd from all over Malabar, for the word was out that a papal brief brought by Mar Ahtallah would be read during the feast. Before closing the festivities, on Wednesday, February 5, at about 3:00 PM, Archdeacon Thomas took a decorated seat on an elevated platform built in front of the Church. A few of the prominent Cassanars were with him on the stage. The rest of the clergy and about eight thousand people crowded around. Then, as directed by the Archdeacon, Cassanar Chandy Kadavil read aloud a letter in Syriac, and explained it in Malayalam. Cassanar George Bengur also joined him in giving the necessary clarifications. The people were told that the Patriarch (Mar Ahtallah) had sent that letter by which he conferred upon Archdeacon Thomas all the powers of jurisdiction needed to govern the Malabar Church, such as to grant matrimonial dispensations including that of consanguinity in the second degree, to inflict or lift ecclesiastical censures, to appoint or remove the vicars, to decide litigations, and to conduct other affairs of the Church. As for the powers of the episcopal order, namely to bless the holy oils, to confer Holy Orders or the sacrament of Confirmation, etc., they announced that the Archdeacon had another letter from the Patriarch with directions to be implemented in case the Patriarch would be impeded by death or other causes from coming to Malabar. Hence, for the powers of episcopal order they would wait for definite news from Goa about the Patriarch's fate. In the meantime, however, as already acknowledged by the Mattanchery Yogam* on the authority of the Patriarch's letter then read, Archdeacon Thomas would function as the governor of the Archdiocese, helped by the four councillors named by the same yogam. On hearing these explanations the crowd at Edappally enthusiastically cheered and acclaimed their new ecclesiastical governor and his councillors. Then, in a collection taken up immediately, the crowd contributed towards the initial expenses of the new administration."

* Yogam = meeting, assembly, conference.

"Instead, accepting the counsel of the Inquisitors and the Patriarch of Ethiopia (Afonso Mendes, S.J.), then living in Goa, the Viceroy summarily decided to send Mar Ahtallah to Portugal. Accordingly, he was put on board the ship 'Nossa Senhora da Grace' which set sail from Goa on January 30, 1653. The Archbishop of Myra was also given passage to Lisbon on board the same ship. To inform the King of Mar Ahtallah's case the Viceroy wrote a letter dated January 28, in which he stated that the 'Syrian Patriarch' was generally held to be a schismatic and that on his account the Christians of Malabar, who were naturally schismatic, had revolted. Referring to the reports that the Jesuits would be sending for further information on Mar Ahtallah's life, the Viceroy recommended the case to the King to be disposed of as it would fit the King's interest."

"Then from Cannanore, the Viceroy sent a reply to the protests and complaints of Archdeacon Thomas and his followers, informing them that Mar Ahtallah had already embarked for Lisbon, and exhorting them to submit themselves to Dom Garcia and to receive the Jesuit missionaries as before. Yet feeling that such exhortation would not pacify the rebels, the Viceroy wrote again to the King on March 4, 1653, giving him more details about the revolution of the St. Thomas Christians and their resolution against accepting Dom Garcia and the Jesuits. He pointed out that for those Christians still inclined to follow their ancient errors, their own will was their law. Since they lived in territories of the Hindu Kings, there was no way to punish them for their disobedience. Besides, their hatred for the Jesuits was so high that in his opinion the best way to solve the problem was to oblige them by appointing a non-Jesuit successor to Dom Garcia, and by sending them missionaries of other religious orders, who would in the meantime reform them and reduce them to obedience. The Viceroy urged the King to come to the rescue of that Christianity by whatever means he deemed fit."

"The Inquisitors and the municipal council of Cochin also sent formal replies to the protests and complaints the St. Thomas Christians had written to them from Mattanchery. Those replies contained excuses for not letting Mar Ahtallah land at Cochin, and a half-hearted exhortation that the Archdeacon and his followers unconditionally submit themselves again to Archbishop Garcia and admit the Jesuit missionaries to the Churches of Malabar. Nobody among the civil and ecclesiastical authorities of Portuguese India, however, seemed concerned enough to intervene and seriously discuss peace and reconciliation. Rather any Portuguese who happened to be in the Sera for whatever business usually avoided communications with the 'rebellious' Christians."

"In these circumstances, after receiving reliable reports about Mar Ahtallah's deportation from Goa, the leaders of the revolt decided to make Archdeacon Thomas a bishop, mainly to prevent anyone from going to Archbishop Garcia for ordination. The understanding was that Thomas would relinquish the government of the Church in favour of the Patriarch if he returned, or in favour of any other bishop who might be sent by the Pope."

"Some of the cassanars, and George Bengur among them, objected to such a procedure, because they had read in one of Mar Abraham's books that no one could be consecrated bishop except on the Pope's orders...and by three episcopal consecrators. But those who claimed to know better argued that the Pope had sent Patriarch Ignatius to India to see that the missions did not suffer from the Holy See's continued refusal to confirm Portugal's nominee to her Padroado Sees. That the Malabar Church had made an Archbishop in place of Dom Garcia, they reasoned, was nothing new, for in the same way the people of Portugal had made a King for themselves, excluding the King of Spain. They justified the unusual procedure by pointing out, from the Floss Sanctorum by Fr. Henriques, S.J., that in the past many bishops, for example St. Augustine, St. Martin, St. Pauline, St. Blasé, St. Nicholas, St. Lazar, and St. Maximin, had been appointed by other bishops, or by Kings, or by the faithful themselves. Further in favour of twelve priests ordaining a bishop on orders of the Patriarch sent by the Pope, they made an argument out of a note in their Syriac sacramentary (translated by the Jesuits from Latin) which stated that simple priests with special faculties granted by the Pope could bless the Holy oils, and confer the sacrament of confirmation. Finally, Cassanar Bengur and others who had objections, except one or two, gave in to the majority opinion."

"Accordingly, the Patriarch's letter, most likely only the pertinent portion of the second letter, was read at the Church of Alangad on May 22, 1653, during the solemn celebration of the Feast of the Ascension. Immediately the priests and people assembled there acclaimed Archdeacon Thomas as their bishop, and twelve priests proceeded with the rite of episcopal ordination according to the old Chaldean Pontifical. The band belonging to the Cochin captaincy played, adding to the solemnities. Reportedly, the King of Alangad also was present at the ceremony, and some pagan rites, such as the throwing of strangled fowls with the performer and the spectators screaming, were part of the festivities."

"After this episcopal ordination, they sent letters to all the Churches of Malabar requiring them to recognize Thomas as their Archbishop. The acceptance was almost total. Only two Southists churches of Kaduthuruthy and Diamper and a very few people elsewhere, at first expressly refused to recognize Thomas as the Archbishop, and that was because they regarded his episcopal ordination by twelve simple priests as invalid. According to several testimonies made later at the informative processes conducted by the Apostolic Commissaries, those who never recognized Thomas Parambil as a validly ordained bishop were an insignificant minority among the Christians of Malabar. They numbered only two hundred laymen and fifteen to twenty priests, as one witness testified. According to another, they were about a thousand laymen and fifteen priests."[9]

As the number of people assembled being large, it was not possible for all to touch together the Cross. So they connected themselves to the slant granite cross outside the Church building by means of ropes tied to it in all directions. The phrase 'Slant Cross Oath' (*Koonan Kurisu Sathyam*) originated from this incident.

In some books, the wording of the oath in the *Koonan Kurisu Sathyam* is as below:

> "To submit no longer to the ecclesiastical authority of Rome and to obey none save their archdeacon Thomas until they get a bishop from the Eastern Church."[10]

This sounds illogical and self-contradictory. Even before the period of the Latin bishops, the St. Thomas Christians were under East Syrian Catholic bishops like Jacob, Joseph, Abraham and others. Pope Gregory XIII has written to the King of Portugal and the Archbishop of Goa certifying Mar Abraham as a Catholic bishop. The King of Portugal sent Mar Joseph back to India after ascertaining the loyalty of Joseph to the Holy See of Rome. The oath itself was the expression of protest against Archbishop Garcia for not accepting Ahtallah, a bishop sent to Malabar by the Supreme Pontiff. After the Slant Cross oath, the Archdeacon himself has written to Bishop Sebastiani to obtain recognition by the Holy See for his episcopate, by rectifying the defects in his consecration. Many more evidences are available. In this situation what is the *locus standi* for an oath against the Holy See?

Mar Thoma I, a few weeks after his consecration, began ordaining clerics and priests to pre-empt the faithful approaching the Archbishop for benefices. The Archbishop, till then optimistic about bringing back the rebels to his obedience, realised the gravity of the situation. But things attained a dimension beyond the reach of his hands. He lost the leverage in the tussle. Many of his well-wishers and impartial leaders blamed the Archbishop and the Jesuits for their tactlessness in allowing the events to drift to such a culmination. The Viceroy suggested to Bishop Garcia to withdraw the Jesuits temporarily and to depute few leaders of other congregations to pacify the Thomas Christians and to pave the way for reconciliation. But the Archbishop's trusted lieutenants, the Jesuits, were not in a mood to give in. They advised him to approach the Hindu Kings, bribe them and bring back the rebels to his obedience. He, therefore, rejected the suggestions of the Viceroy and approached the Kings. It is reported that he gave *fanams* 6000 each to the Kings of Cochin and Kaduthuruthy, *fanams* 3000 to the King of Parur and *fanams* 1500 to the King of Alengad. The Kings gladly accepted the money, but nothing tangible turned out. Even at this stage, the Archbishop was not prepared to budge an inch. The tense situation continued.

On being informed of the troubled situation consequent on the *Koonan Cross Oath*, Rome decided to conduct an enquiry through two Carmelites, Guisseppe Sebastiani O.C.D. and Vincent Hyacinth O.C.D. As Apostolic commissaries, Sebastiani reached Malabar in February 1657 and Hyacinth reached in March 1658. Sebastiani submitted a report to Pope on 7th March 1658. His suggestions were not favourable to the Jesuits. On the basis of the report, the Congregation of Propaganda fide decided to intervene in Malabar by establishing a new ecclesiastical unit known as the 'Vicariate Apostolic of Malabar' and made Sebastiani the first Vicar Apostolic. In 1659, Sebastiani was appointed the Administrator Apostolic of the Archbishopric of Cranganore also.

Archbishop Garcia died on Sept. 3, 1659. Fr. Hyacinth died on Feb. 10, 1661. Bishop Sebastiani reached Malabar on May 14, 1661. Thus, the high-handedness of Bishop Garcia and the Jesuits resulted in the explosion of the pent-up emotions of a people that were reeling under the yoke of the Padroado. As Cardinal Tisserant has aptly commented "Neither negotiations nor threats nor forcible measures used by the Portuguese authorities curbed in anyway the resistance of the Archdeacon's party."[11] Bishop Sebastiani came to Malabar with ample authority even to consecrate Thomas Parambil as bishop. He summoned a meeting of Thomas Christians and explained to them that the purpose of his visit was reconciliation. In the meeting, the Thomas Christians demanded the recognition of Mar Thoma I as bishop, which Bishop Sebastiani rejected outright. Mar Thoma I also demanded that the Holy See should recognise him as bishop, rectifying whatever defects there had been in his episcopal ordination by twelve priests.

In 1663, the Dutch defeated Portugal, occupied Cochin and expelled all foreign missionaries from Malabar. Bishop Sebastiani was under orders from the Dutch to leave Malabar. In his absence, an indigenous bishop was found essential to lead the Thomas Christians. He, therefore, consecrated as Bishop Alexander Parampil (Alexander de Campo), the nephew of the (pseudo) bishop Thomas, on February 1, 1663. After the consecration ceremony, Bishop Sebastiani publicly and solemnly declared the excommunication of Thomas Parambil and his close associate, Cassanar Ittithomman. Bishop Sebastiani pointed out in that meeting that Thomas, unfortunately, failed to come to terms with him, as he showed no inclination to repent and do penance for his misdeeds.

Even after excommunication, Thomas enjoyed the support of one third of the Thomas Christians. In 1665, an Antiochian Jacobite Prelate named Gregoriose (known in Malabar as Patriarch of Jerusalem) arrived in Malabar on the invitation of Mar Thoma I to validate his episcopacy. Through him, Mar Thoma I established relations with the Jacobite Church of Syria. More than 90 per cent of the Thomas Christians were Northists. Approximately 30 per cent of the Northists and the parishes of Ittithomman Cassanar of Kallissery among the Southists embraced the Jacobite faction of Mar Thoma I and the vast majority remained as Romo Syrian Catholics. Thus, the St. Thomas Christians of Malabar, who agitated to preserve their identity and autonomy, finally drifted into a schism dividing them, for the first time in their history, into two factions the *Pazhaya Koottukar* (the Old Loyalists) owing their allegiance to the Holy See of Rome and the other known as *Puthenkoottukar* (the Neo Loyalists) owing their allegiance to the Jacobite Patriarch of Antioch. This paved the path for the introduction of the Antiochian liturgy in India.

Aftermath of the Split

It is relevant and interesting to know the consequential whereabouts of the parties involved in the schism, viz. the Catholic faction, the Portuguese Padroado, Mar Ahtallah *(in absentia)* and the Jacobite faction.

(a) The Catholic Faction (*The pazhaya koottukar*)

At this juncture, the Congregation of Propaganda sent a few Carmelites to Malabar with instructions to choose a native co-adjutor to Alexander. They chose one Raphael Figueredo Salgado, a Portuguese born in India. The attempts to win over

Mar Thoma I and his followers did not succeed because of this appointment. When Salgado started working independent of the bishop, Mar Alexander objected and the Holy See suspended Salgado. Mar Alexander died in 1687. No Portuguese resident bishop was there in Malabar at that time. The Dutch did not allow any Carmelite missionary. Hence, the Catholic faction of the Church was left without an administrator for 17 years.

In the 18th century, there were appointees of Propaganda Fide for the Vicariate of Malabar designated as 'Vicar Apostolic' and appointees of Padroado for the Archdiocese of Cranganore designated as 'Archbishop' as detailed below, with resultant dual control.

Vicariate of Malabar (*Propaganda*)

Anjelo Francis (1700-1712), John Baptist Morteo (1712-1750), Florence of Jesus of Nazareth (1751-1773), Francis de Sales (1775-1779), Charles of St. Conrad (Admr. 1779-1783), Aloysius Mary (1784-1802).

Archdiocese of Cranganore (*Padroado*)

John Rebeiro (1701-1716), Antonio Pimenta (1716-1752), John Luis Vosconcellos (1753-1756), Salvador dos Reis (1756-1777), Two Administrators (1779-1782), Mar Joseph Kariattil (1782-1786), Thomas Paremakkal (Admr. 1786-1799), Ribammar (1799-1800) and George Sankurickal (1800-1801). Among them, Mar Joseph Kariattil, Thomas Paremakkal and George Sankurickal were natives. Mar Kariattil died on his way from Rome to Malabar and hence not taken charge.[12] They all had their residences at Puthenchira.

In the nineteenth century, there were no notable developments, except the establishment of a religious Congregation in 1831, at present named as CMI Congregation. The Padroado appointed only Administrators in the 19th century except in 1821-23. Rome discontinued Padroado in 1838. In the same year, Pope Gregory XVI suppressed the Archbishopric of Cranganore and the Bishopric of Cochin. All the faithful, both Syrians and Latinites, were brought under the Verapoly Vicar Apostolic of Malabar with jurisdiction extending from Mangalore to Kollam. The Portuguese authorities did not submit to these decisions of the Holy See resulting in a schism in the Padroado. The bulk of the Syrian Christians came under the Vicariate of Verapoly, which extended from Bharatappuzha River in the North to Pamba River in the South. The Sees of Cranganore and Cochin were revived in 1863. But, Cranganore was again suppressed in 1886 when Pope Leo XIII constituted the Indian hierarchy with Verapoly as one of the Archdioceses.

The Vicars Apostolic of Verapoly in the 19th century were:

Raymond (1803-1816), Peter Alcanatra (Admr. 1816-1831), Francis Xavier (1831-1844), Ludovic (1844-1855), Benardine of St. Teresa (1859-1868), Leonard St. Luis (1868-1877) and Marcellinus of St. Teresa (1877-1887 as co-adjutor with special charge of Syrians).

The Syrians were discontented for being under the Latin Carmelites, leading to several turbulent events. This opened the eyes of Rome. Two extraordinary Visitors were appointed to study and suggest solutions. In 1887, two Vicariates Apostolic were created exclusively for the Syrians, one at Trichur and the other at Kottayam with Adolf Medlycott (an English Prelate) at Trichur and Charles Lavigne (a French Prelate) at Kottayam. In 1896, those Vicariates were reorganized into three Vicariates, Changanachery, Ernakulam and Trichur with three native Prelates, Mathew Makil, Aloysius Pazhayaparambil and John Menachery respectively. In 1911, the Holy See created the Kottayam Vicariate exclusively for the Southists. In 1923, the Syro-Malabar Hierarchy was created with Ernakulam as the Metropolitan See exclusively for the St. Thomas Christians.

Another notable development in the latter half of the 19th century was the arrival of two Chaldean Syrian Prelates in Malabar, one Rokos in 1861 and another Mellus in 1874 claiming as representatives of the Catholic Patriarch Joseph IV Audo of Chaldea. They tried to wean away the Syrians from the rule of Latin Prelates with some initial success. This led to a series of confrontations. Finally Rokos was expelled. It is seen that he later worked for one year as the head of the Surai (Chaldean) Church in Trichur, which had no bishop from 1815 to 1860. Mellus also is seen to have worked as the head of the Surais from 1874-1882. He linked the Surai Church (The Church of the East) to the Nestorian Patriarchate of Chaldea.

(A note on the origin of this church known as 'the Church of the East' is given separately.)

(b) The Portuguese (*Padroado*)

Misfortune struck the Portuguese repeatedly. With the appearance of other European powers like Dutch, England, France etc. in the Indian Seas, the Portuguese failed to withstand the might and onslaught of those powers. The Arabs also revenged their defeat by crushing the Portuguese and chasing them from Muscat, one of the Portuguese strongholds on the eastern coast of Persia.

The St. Thomas Christians, by the Slant cross Oath of 1653, severed their relations with the Latin bishops. Holland occupied Malabar in 1663 and drove away the foreign missionaries. Padroado became weak and almost sterile by the establishment of the Congregation of Propaganda Fide by Pope Gregory XV. In 1769, Pope Clement suppressed the Society of Jesus (Jesuits). In 1838 Pope Gregory XVI withdrew the Padroado and suppressed the Metropolitan See of Cranganore. A new ecclesiastical unit named 'Vicariate Apostolic of Malabar' was erected and the Carmelites were entrusted with its administration. In short, whatever the Portuguese gained in the sixteenth century were lost one by one. At home, Spain took over the reign of Portugal. During the Napoleanic period, Portugal remained under the Protectorate of England. In India the Portuguese were confined to Goa and some small territories like Daman and Diu where they continued the brutal persecution and allied atrocities under the label of Inquisition.

When India became independent, the French handed over to the Government of India the territories of Pondicherry, Karaikal and Mahe in their occupation without waiting for any bargaining and bade goodbye to the government and to the people of India and returned to France with dignity. On the other hand, when the Government of India demanded the handing over of the territories, the Portuguese were dilly-dallying with claims for compensation and other lame excuses. They vacated only in 1961 when the Indian armed forces seized and annexed those territories, and that also by giving room for an accusation that they robbed India of gold and many other valuables.

But no one can deny that the Portuguese had done a lot of good things for India. They have built a lot of churches, seminaries, schools, colleges, hospitals, charitable institutions, printing press, publication houses and so on. They are the people who brought to India, pineapple, coffee, rubber, cashew, tobacco, groundnut etc. Universal education, abolition of slavery, prohibition of child marriages etc. are the social reforms introduced by the Portuguese. All those good works were nullified by their conduct. Their exit was, by any yardstick, ignoble and undignified. The imprint they left behind in the Indian mind was one of contempt and hatred, whereas France and England are still held in high esteem.

(c) Mar Ahtallah and His Whereabouts

The St. Thomas Christian Revolt of 1653 was not an incipient one. It was the culmination of the unrest and discontent among the St. Thomas Christians brewing up from the early half of the 16th century. The immediate provocation for the revolt happened to be the question of Ahtallah's identity, either answered wrongly or unanswered. Either the St. Thomas Christians who led the revolt or the Archbishop's party who ventured to suppress or defeat the rebels never cared to verify the bonafides of the claims of the man for whom they were mutually fighting. No man of reckoning in both camps had ever seen or contacted Mar Ahtallah personally. The most ludicrous aspect of this episode is that the identity of Mar Ahtallah remained a mystery for both the warring groups, not only at the time of the revolt, but also even after the Slant Cross Oath.

The available records show that Ahtallah was a long-bearded man of 62, Arabic and Syriac speaking, wearing the robes of a Syrian Prelate and claiming as ex-Archbishop of Damascus. According to his own admission, while he was

Archbishop of Damascus, he went to Rome and on return from Rome, he saw an usurper bishop (a youngster) occupying his chair. Mafia men robbed him of all his possessions at Damascus. Fr. Joseph of St. Mary (Sebastiani) OCD, one of the Apostolic Commissaries reported to the Congregation at Rome on Mar Ahtallah as follows: "The said Bishop had been to Rome for sometime, but after he returned to Aleppo, he was not welcome among the Jacobites, and so he passed on to the countries of Malabar; so have I learned from the Patriarch of the said Jacobites or Syrians." From some missionaries Fr. Sebastiani also knew that "Bishop Ahtallah, a Jacobite heretic, caught by the Portuguese and taken to Europe", had later died in Paris. When the ship (supposed to be) with Mar Ahtallah on board anchored at Cochin, no one was permitted to meet him. This paved the way for the circulation of a rumour that the Portuguese had thrown Mar Ahtallah into the Sea. Actually, this baseless rumour was the immediate provocation that enraged the crowd to indulge in vandalism culminating in the oath, which accidentally resulted later in the severance of the age-old relations with the Universal Church by a faction of the St. Thomas Christians.

Later, another news spread that Mar Ahtallah was led to Goa and handed over to the Goan Inquisition. No one knew as to what happened to him after being handed over to the Inquisition. This confusion led the people to suspect the execution of Mar Ahtallah at the hands of the Inquisition.

The officially approved version of the Goan authorities shows that Mar Ahtallah boarded the ship 'Nosa Senhora da Graca' from Goa and reached Lisbon on July 14, 1653. Msgr. Frescilla, the Archbishop of Myra, who came to Goa for some other purpose, also boarded the same ship.

Dr. Jacob Kollaparambil after due research, endorses the third version, that Mar Ahtallah proceeded to Rome Via Portugal as correct.

Mar Ahtallah, by his courteous behaviour, cultivated the friendship and confidence of Archbishop Frescilla. At Lisbon, it was Archbishop Frescilla who introduced Mar Ahtallah as

Patriarch of Antioch and helped to create a good impression about Mar Ahtallah. The King of Portugal decided to send Mar Ahtallah to Rome, overruling the arguments of Fr. Antonio Velloso, the representative of Archbishop Garcia. Archbishop Frescilla, who had some other mission at Rome, accompanied Mar Ahtallah to Rome. *En route*, they halted at Paris to meet the Apostolic Nuncio in Paris. The Archbishop recommended the case of Mar Ahtallah to the Nuncio and he, in turn, recommended the case to the Propaganda Congregation in Rome. An extract of the letter is given below:

> "He recommended to me a man who says that he was made Patriarch by the Patriarch of Antioch and who claims to have faculties to make four Patriarchs. He is very old and sick. He says that he wants to come to Rome, and it is hoped that the queen (Annie d'Austria) will give him money for the journey."[13]

In February 1654, Archbishop Frescilla fell ill due to congestion in the chest and died on March 10th. Apostolic Nuncio reported the death and burial of Archbishop Frescilla to Rome. In the letter, Nuncio mentioned the cause of death as the administration of a medicine prepared with antimony.

While reporting the death of Archbishop Frescilla to the Propaganda Congregation, St. Vincent De Paul made mention of Mar Ahtallah in the following words, "There remains in this city a good old man of eighty years, a foreigner, who was lodging with the late Monsignor Archbishop of Myra. They say that he is the Patriarch of Antioch. Be that as it may, he is alone and has no mark of prelacy. I would have persuaded him to return in the company of some religious going to his country, but his age and infirmities do not permit him."[14]

Sixteen days after the death of Frescilla, Mar Ahtallah also passed away (March 26, 1654) and was buried in the Jerusalem chapel of the Cordeliena Church. A noting in the death register reads as follows:

"On March 26, 1654, the most illustrious and the Most Reverend Lord John (sic), Patriarch of Antioch, whom the Most Reverend Archbishop of Myra was conducting to Rome, died. He was buried with his Patriarchal dress in a grave at the Jerusalem chapel. His pastoral staff, which is an Indian cane, is kept in the sacristy of the monastery."

Dr. Jacob Kollaparambil concludes his research in the following words:

"In reality, however, as is abundantly shown in these chapters, Mar Ahtallah, though a Catholic, did not have a canonical mission from Rome for the Church of Malabar. What he really claimed was the authority of an Oriental Patriarch on his own, or of a Maphrian by reason of an appointment by the Syrian Patriarch."

"Hence, it can be safely said that the improper reaction of the Portuguese to Mar Ahtallah's arrival in India, coupled with the misunderstanding of the St. Thomas Christians about the source of Mar Ahtallah's canonical mission, had been responsible for the outbreak of the revolution. After the revolution, the St. Thomas Christians were never satisfactorily informed of Mar Ahtallah's identity. Historians' conjectures served only to confuse the matter further. The documents brought to light in this study do dispel the many uncertainties that had shrouded the person of Mar Ahtallah and his mission. If such misunderstandings prompted the people to drastic steps, which in the course of time led some of them farther away from the right path, it may be hoped that the clarification of the truth now will impel the truth-seekers to retrace their steps."[15]

(d) The Non-Catholic Faction (*The Puthenkoottukar*)

Whatever be the deficiencies, the St. Thomas Church in India was, from the days of its origin, a cohesive community till 1653. They took part in the Slant cross Oath almost unanimously. It was the haste with which the Archdeacon got himself consecrated as bishop at the hands of the Jacobite Prelate, whether fact or fiction, that repulsed a fair chunk of the St. Thomas Christians away from him. This incident drove the Archdeacon (Mar Thoma I) and his followers into the lap of the Syrian Jacobite Church owing allegiance to the Jacobite Patriarch of Antioch. A byproduct of this shifting of loyalty was the change-over from the Chaldean (East) Syrian liturgy to the Antiochean (West) Syrian liturgy. An analysis of the course of events lead us to doubt whether the ambition of the Archdeacon to become a bishop at any cost was the underlying factor, that precipitated the events leading to a schism. On scrutiny of the balance-sheet of the entire happenings, we see that all the partners had gains under some counts and incurred losses under some other counts.

The Catholic faction gained relief from the yoke of the Padroado bishops and the Jesuits, without rupturing their communion with the Holy See of Rome. But, they had to continue under the Latin bishops till 1896 (another 243 years) to redress their grievances.

The Portuguese succeeded in building up a strong Latin Church in India. But the Dutch expelled them from the entire Malabar by 1663. Pope Gregory XVI unarmed them in 1838 by withdrawing the Padroado rights. Goa, the last straw in their hands, was also lost later, forcing a retreat from the entire Indian subcontinent.

The Archdeacon accomplished what he desired, by becoming the Metropolitan of India. His followers obtained a native bishop. The price paid for that gain was heavy and exorbitant. They on their own volition, knowingly or unknowingly, walked out of the universal Church. A new liturgy (Antiochean) was also thrust upon them.

The chequered history of the Jacobite Church in Malankara, involving a series of never-ending litigations and schisms, follows.

FOOTNOTES

1. John Pallathu, OCD (Fr.), *The Christian Church in Portugal Age*, p. 52.
2. Xavier Koodapuzha (Dr.), *Christianity in India*, p. 86.
3. Jacob Kollaparambil (Dr.), *The St. Thomas Christian Revolution 1653*, Index Item 1, p. 274.
4. *Ibid.*, pp. 16-17.
5. *Ibid.*, p. 7, Para. 4.
6. Xavier Koodapuzha (Dr.), *Christianity in India*, p. 91.

7. *Ibid.*, pp. 92-94.
8. Jacob Kollaparambil (Dr.), *The St. Thomas Christian Revolution 1653*, p. 108.
9. *Ibid.*, pp. 140-47.
10. David Daniel, *The Orthodox Church of India*, p. 56.
11. Cardinal Tisserant, *Eastern Christianity*, p. 82.
12. George Menachery, *The St. Thomas Christian Encyclopaedia of India*, p. 50.
13. Jacob Kollaparambil (Dr.), *The St. Thomas Christian Revolution 1653*, p. 175, Para. 3.
14. *Ibid.*, p. 175, Para. 5.
15. *Ibid.*, pp. 215-16.

The Jacobite Church in India

(Schisms and Litigations Galore)

22

Mar Thoma I, after claiming rectification of the defects in his episcopal ordination at the hands of the Jacobite Prelate Mar Gregorios, was comfortably in the saddle as Metropolitan of the St. Thomas Christians, though his following comprised only less than one third of the St. Thomas Christian community. Even after polarization at the hierarchical level and the division into two distinct camps, the Thomas Christians at the grass-roots level maintained their fraternal relations and fellowship nurtured over centuries. They found no difficulty in sharing the same Church building and appurtenances for their liturgical celebrations. Both camps genuinely aspired for unity and made sincere efforts at different levels for reconciliation. But, their efforts ended fruitless for one reason or other. Mar Thoma's consecration at the hands of a Jacobite Prelate, that tantamount to acceptance of Jacobitism, closed all avenues for reconciliation. The Catholic Church was not prepared to open the doors of the Church once closed due to the voluntary exit of the Archdeacon, later confirmed by himself with the acceptance of the heretic Jacobitism.

Mar Thoma VI (later Mar Dionysius I) made several attempts for unity. Kariattil Joseph Malpan (Malpan means Professor) and Paremakkal Thoma Kathanar (Kathanar means priest), two distinguished priests in the Catholic faction were deputed to Rome with a reconciliation mission. They met Pope in 1778, but the Pope declined the proposals of Mar Dionysius I. The Holy See consecrated Joseph Malpan as Bishop and sent him back to Malankara. En route return journey, Bishop Kariattil passed away at Goa. Thus, the mission failed.

Leaders of both factions assembled thrice in 1791 and 1792 at Chengannur and Kayamkulam and held discussions on the ways and means to achieve unity. But, the meetings ended in a stalemate.

In 1799, Mar Dionysius I reconciled with the Catholic Church. He celebrated mass at the Thathampally (Alleppey) Catholic Church, but retraced after six months, on finding his proposals not acceptable to the Holy See.

The advent of Jacobite Church in India marked a new dawn in the history of the St. Thomas Christians. Many historians expressed doubt as to whether Mar Thoma I had ever been consecrated by Mar Gregorios. Prof. George Menachery in his book *The St. Thomas Christian Encyclopaedia of India* observed as follows:

"At his request (read 'his' as 'Archdeacon's) Mar Gregorios, the Jacobite Metropolitan of Jerusalem arrived in Malabar in 1665. From this time onwards, we see the influence of Jacobitism on the ascendant among the dissidents till they completely succumbed to it and took the Syro-Antiochean Rite. It is not certain whether Mar Thoma I was ever given episcopal consecration. Mar Thoma I was followed by Mar Thoma II, III, IV and V, none of whom, according to many, received episcopal consecration. In 1751, the Dutch brought three Jacobite bishops to consecrate Mar Thoma V, but they refused to consecrate him. Later, they consecrated Mar Thoma VI."[1]

Mar Gregorios was a very shrewd person. He succeeded in creating an impression among the followers of the Archdeacon that he had come to Malabar to protect and save them. He celebrated the sacraments in the Antiochean (West Syrian) liturgy, but he never insisted on an abrupt change-over from the Chaldean (East Syrian) liturgy to the Antiochean (West Syrian) liturgy. The transition was a gradual process without giving room for any resentment on the part of the priests or the faithful. Even now, this change is not complete. Several Chaldean Syriac words are found in the Antiochean liturgy now in vogue in India.

At the hierarchical level, the *Puthenkoor* faction headed by bishops with title 'Mar Thoma' changed the title of Bishops from 1772 onwards as 'Mar Dionysius' as suggested by the Patriarch of Antioch. A chronology of the bishops of the *Puthenkoor* community upto 1934 is given below with remarks on the main developments in their periods.

	Bishop	Remarks
1.	Mar Thoma I (1653-1670)	Died in 1670.
2.	Mar Thoma II (1670-1686)	Died in 1686.
3.	Mar Thoma III (1686-1688)	His reign was very short, barely two years.
4.	Mar Thoma IV (1688-1728)	Arrival of one Gabriel, a Nestorian bishop in 1708. To counter the influence of Nestorianism, Mar Thoma IV out manoeuvred Gabriel by consecrating his own nephew as successor with title Mar Thoma V. Gabriel was later expelled from the country.
5.	Mar Thoma V (1729-1765)	In 1751, the Dutch brought Baselios Mar Sakrullah, Catholicos of Mosul, Bishop Mar Gregoriose and one Ramban Mar Juhanon to Malankara. They refused to consecrate Mar Thoma V.
6.	Mar Thoma VI (1765-1808)	(Title changed as Mar Dionysius I) Made several attempts for reunion, but failed. The Malabar independent church of Anjoor (Thozhiyoor) came into existence (Please see separate notes on this church). Consequent on the attack of Tipu Sultan of Mysore State, the headquarters of the Malankara Church was shifted from Angamaly to Kottayam in 1789.
7.	Mar Thoma VII (1808-1809)	Very short period. Deposited the Trust Fund in the British East India Company. This amount known as *Vattippanam* (interest money) was the subject of a series of litigations on the identity of the person entitled

	to draw the interest accrued on the deposit.
8. Mar Thoma VIII (1809-1815)	His consecration was called in question. Agitation led by Pulikott Joseph Ramban on the validity of Mar Thoma's episcopal ordination. This entailed in the discontinuance of the hereditary succession of the Pakalomattom family.
9. Mar Thoma IX	Pulikkottu Joseph Ramban ordained as bishop in 1815 with title Dionysius II was in the saddle. Mar Thoma IX held no office. He retired and lived as a monk at Kadamattom.
10. Pulikkottu Mar Dionysius II (1815-1817)	Accepted interest of the Trust Fund and completed the Old Seminary at Kottayam.
11. Punnathra Mar Dionysius III (1817-1825)	A peaceful period. Emphasis on educational institutions in the parishes.
12. Cheppattu Mar Dionysius IV (1825-1846)	Severance of relations with the Anglican Missionaries. Handed over charge in 1846 to Mar Koorilos, deputed by the Patriarch of Antioch. Mar Koorilos in charge from 1846 to 1866.
13. Pulikkottu Mar Dionysius V (1866-1909)	In 1866, the Patriarch ordained Pulikkottu Joseph Ramban (Grand nephew of P. Dionysius II) as Dionysius V. Two Reformist bishops Mathews Mar Athanasius and Thomas Mar Athanasius came to the scene. (Please see separate notes on the Mar Thoma Church.)
14. Vattasseril Mar Dionysius VI (1909-1934)	Patriarch Mar Abdullah excommunicated him. Abdul Messiah, the deposed Patriarch of Antioch invalidated the excommunication. In his period, a Catholicate was created for the Malankara Church. In 1912, Bishop Mar Paulose Murimuttathil was consecrated as the first Catholicos of the East.

Later history is under the Catholicoses as below:

Mar Baselios Paulos	– 1912-1913	Catholicos I
Mar Baselios Geevarghese I	– 1925-1928	Catholicos II
Mar Baselios Geevarghese II	– 1929-1964	Catholicos III
Mar Baselios Augen	– 1964-1975	Catholicos IV
Mar Baselios Mar Thoma Mathews I	– 1975-1991	Catholicos V
Mar Baselios Mar Thoma Mathews II	– 1991-2006	Catholicos VI

After the death of Mar Dionysius VI in 1934, the offices of the Malankara Metropolitan and the Catholicos were vested in one person.

Collaboration with the Anglican Church

In 1795, the English displaced the Dutch from Cochin. The State of Travancore also came under their sway. The English East India Company appointed a British Resident for Travancore and Cochin. The first two Residents, Col. Macaulay and Col. Monroe were anxious to help the local Christians. The Church Missionary Society (C.M.S.) under the patronage of the Church of England extended their gospel work to India, mainly at Calcutta and Madras. In Malankara, the missionaries of the CMS joined the Theological Seminary at Kottayam. They were engaged in educating the clergy under training and preaching gospel in the Syrian Christian parishes. Thus, a regular contact between the Malankara Church and the Church of England came into being. A synod of the Malankara Church held in 1818 at Mavelikara decided to promote close collaboration between the Anglican missionaries and the *Puthenkoor* community. Later, it was observed that the CMS missionaries who voluntarily offered their services to help the Malabar Church were undermining the basic faith and ecclesial patrimony of the St. Thomas Church in Malabar, resulting in the gradual alienation of the members of the Malankara Church. It was then estimated that 6000 members of the Puthenkoor community embraced the Anglican Church. Then only the community woke up to the reality and seriousness of the situation. Realizing that the continuance of the Anglican missionaries would be detrimental to the ecclesial patrimony of the Malankara Church, Mar Dionysius IV convoked a Synod of the Church in 1836 at

Mavelikara to find out a solution to the problem. The Synod decided to put a stop to the collaboration with the Anglicans, including the efforts to correct the liturgical texts. This decision of the Synod displeased not only the English missionaries, but also a section of the *Puthenkoor* community inclined towards the Protestant ideologies propagated by the missionaries. Palakunnathu Abraham Malpan of Maramon and Kaithayil Geevarghese Malpan of Kottayam, who were teachers in the Old Seminary along with the Anglican missionaries, poured oil into the fire by aggravating the anti-church feelings. This tussle later snowballed into another schism in the Puthenkoor community culminating in the exit of a sizeable chunk of the community to join either the CMS Church or the Reform party that later became the Marthoma Syrian Church.

(For further details, please see separate notes under the head 'The Mar Thoma Syrian church'.)

In this context, Mar Dionysius IV felt the urgency of fostering closer relations with Antioch to withstand the ideological onslaught of the Reformists. The Patriarch of Antioch, who had information from other sources on the developments in the Malabar Church, deputed one Bishop Mar Koorilos to make an assessment of the situation and to initiate appropriate action deemed necessary. Koorilos reached Malabar in 1846. Mar Dionysius IV, who found himself unequal to the task of confronting the Reformists enjoying political support, handed over charge of the hierarchy in 1846 to Mar Koorilos and retired. Thus, Mar Koorilos became the Metropolitan from 1846 to 1866.

In 1863, Patriarch Moran Mar Yakoub ordained Malpan Joseph Pulikkottil (the grand nephew of Mar Dionysius II), proposed by Mar Koorilos as the man of the hour, as bishop with title Dionysius V to succeed Mar Koorilos. Though Mar Dionysius V after ordination returned to Malabar, he was unable to take charge as Malankara Metropolitan, as Mathews Mar Athanasios, the Reformist bishop was holding the office under the orders of the Civil Court (details regarding the arrival of Reformist bishops Mathews Mar Athanasios and Thomas Mar Athanasios are given separately under the heading

'The Marthoma Syrian Church'). When the attempts of Mar Dionysius V failed to dislodge the reformist bishop, he invited the Patriarch to visit Malabar. In response to this invitation, Patriarch Peter III came to Malabar. En route, the Patriarch visited the Archbishop of the Anglican Church at Calcutta and discussed the issue with him. In 1876, the Patriarch convened a Synod of the Church at Mulanthuruthy.

The Synod of Mulanthuruthy (1876)

The Synod was presided over by the Patriarch. The Synod condemned the Reformist bishops who abstained from the Synod. The *Puthenkoor* community officially accepted the jurisdictional authority of the Patriarch and thereby became a part of the Antiochean Jacobite hierarchical structure. Armed by this authority, the Patriarch divided the *Puthenkoor* community into seven Episcopal Sees and appointed six new bishops. It was a departure from the traditional set up and conventional practices of the Church. Mar Dionysius V silently acceded to all the decisions of the Patriarch, as he was more concerned with his primary aim of arresting the process of Anglicanisation and the dislodging of the reformists. In the litigation that followed, the Royal Court of Final Appeal pronounced the historical judgment in 1889 vindicating the stand of Mar Dionysius V that reads as below:

"The Appellant's (Thomas Mar Athanasios) possession of the properties of the Church and its appurtenances and the assumption of the office of the Metropolitan have been wrongful since the death of Mar Athanasios (Mathews) and that the Appellant should, therefore, surrender the insignia and office of Metropolitan of the Malankara Syrian Orthodox Church and give up possession of all properties and moneys pertaining thereto which he now holds to the Respondent."[2]

The judgment upheld and established the following facts:

Recognition of the Patriarch of Antioch as the spiritual head of the Malankara Syrian Christian Community.

A person consecrated either by the Patriarch or by his authorised delegate shall alone be entitled to become a Metropolitan of the Church in Malabar.

A native Syrian Christian of Malabar accepted by the community alone can hold the office of the Metropolitan of the Malankara Church.

The Patriarch or his foreign delegate shall have no authority for the internal administration of the temporalities of the Malankara Church.

The Malankara Church shall be an independent Church with regard to the administiration of the temporal affairs of the Church.

The privilege to send *Mooron* (Holy oil) from time to time to the Malabar Church shall vest with the Patriarch.

The judgment strengthened the hands of Mar Dionysius to achieve his aims. But, its long-term repercussions were felt only later. The cumulative effects of the Mulanthuruthy Synod, the Mavelikara Synod of 1836 and the Royal Court judgment were:

The Anglican missionaries severed their relations with the Malankara Church, started their independent mission work and established the first congregation of the Church Missionary Society at Mallappally.

Mar Athanasios also severed his relations with the Malankara Church and established a separate independent church later known as the Mar Thoma Syrian Church.

The Patriarch claimed authority over the temporalities of the Church.

The Aftermath of the Mulanthuruthy Synod

The alliance of the Puthenkoor community with the Syrian Jacobite Patriarch of Antioch was helpful to solve the problem of Anglicanisation. But, the side-effects of the truce posed other grave questions. Patriarch Mar Abdullah demanded his pound of flesh. He raised the issue of the powers of the Patriarch over the Malankara Jacobite Church. He pointed out that his powers were not confined to the spiritual side only, but extended to all the areas of ecclesiastical administration as well. The Malankara Metropolitan Vattasseril Mar Dionysius VI, an astute man of a different calibre, was not in a mood to yield to such exaggerated claims. On finding Mar Dionysius VI not amenable to the demand, Patriarch Abdullah personally came to Malabar and convened a Synod on Nov. 25, 1909 at Kottayam. In the Synod, the Patriarch demanded written authority for him over the temporalities of the Malabar Church. The proposal failed to gain acceptance by the Synod. Thereupon, the Patriarch manoeuvred to earn more support by offering episcopal ordination to more people with the hope of obtaining registered deeds granting him authority over the temporalities. Mar Koorilos and Mar Severiose were ordained bishops after receiving documents as dictated by him. But later, the Civil Court invalidated the documents for lack of concurrence of the Malankara Christian Association.

The Catholicate for Bishop's Party

The scheming Malankara Metropolitan Mar Dionysius VI found a way out to circumvent the problem of Abdullah's demands for temporal powers. He proposed the establishment of a Catholicate for the Malankara Church, which would automatically bring forth more autonomy for the Church. The Metropolitan summoned a meeting of the Church representatives on Sept. 20, 1910 at Kottayam. The Assembly supported the Metropolitan's proposals and opposed the claim of authority of the Patriarch over the temporalities of the Church. The enraged Patriarch reacted by excommunicating Mar Dionysius VI in 1911. Simultaneously, the Patriarch installed Mar Severiose as the head of the Sudhist community in the *Puthenkoor* faction and elevated Mar Koorilos as the Metropolitan of the Malankara Jacobite Church. These developments divided the *Puthenkoor* community into two factions – the third schism – one supporting the Patriarch, known as the *Patriarchal* party and the other supporting the Malankara Metropolitan Mar Dionysius VI, known as the Bishop's party.

The Bishop's party argued that the excommunication was invalid as it was against the original Nomocanon of Bar Hebraeus, according to which the Patriarch cannot condemn a bishop without the consent of the Synod of bishops. But, this argument could not withstand the tests of law and facts in the light of a spurious copy of this Canon earlier filed as exhibit in the Royal Court in the suit against Mathews Mar Athanasios to prove that the consent of the Synod of the bishops was not required for condemnation of bishops. The installation of Mar Koorilos as Metropolitan was also objected to by the Bishop's party. At last, it was concluded that speeding up the consecration of Catholicos alone was the only solution. To accomplish this aim, the Bishop's Party ingeniously devised a short-circuit procedure to bypass Mar Abdullah. The Bishop's party approached Mar Abdul Messiah II, the deposed predecessor of Mar Abdullah, who willingly agreed to come to Malabar and consecrate the new Catholicos. As promised, Mar Abdul Messiah came to Cochin on June 13, 1912. He declared invalid the penal sanctions imposed on Mar Dionysius VI by the Patriarch Mar Abdullah. He also issued a circular explaining the background of his acceptance of the invitation to consecrate the Catholicos of the Malabar Jacobite Church. On the official request of the Malankara Christian Association, Mar Abdul Messiah as chief celebrant and Mar Dionysius VI and Mar Gregoriose as co-celebrants, consecrated Mar Paulose Murimuttathil as *Maphrian* or Catholicos of the Malankara Jacobite church in India on September 17, 1912. This was followed by the consecration of three other bishops on the basis of the *Staticon* (the letter of authorization granted to a bishop) issued by Mar Abdul Messiah. These consecrations led to a series of litigations in the civil courts. The hitherto Bishop's party thereby became the Catholicos party. The creation of the office of 'Catholicos', equal in rank and dignity of a Patriarch made the Bishop's party an autonomous Church free from the yoke of the Antiochian Patriarch. But, in the eyes of the law, the label 'Jacobite' caused some incongruities. Therefore, in the course of time, the Catholicos party changed the name of their church as 'Malankara Orthodox Syrian Church', substituting the word 'Orthodox' (indicative of an indigenous flavour) for the word 'Jacobite'. The Patriarch's party followed suit by changing their name as 'Malankara Syrian Orthodox Church', prefixing the word 'Syrian' to Orthodox as against suffixing by the former.

As we have already seen, Paulose Mar Koorilos became the Malankara Metropolitan of the *Patriarch party* (1911-17). He led the litigation against Mar Dionysius VI. One Sliba Mar Osthathios from Antioch (1909-30) assisted Paulose Mar Koorilos in the litigation. There were four other bishops for the Patriarch party; Geevarghese Mar Gregoriose (Angamaly, Niranam and Thumpamon), Paulos Mar Severios (Kochi). Paulos Mar Philexinos (Kandanad, Kottayam and Kollam), Abraham Mar Clemis (Knanaya) and Mar Juliose (Delegate of the Patriarch). The suit for Vattippanam was decided by the High Court in favour of the Bishop's party. The appeals on the property claims, right of succession, canonical set up, validity of penal sanctions etc., were also decided by the Supreme Court of India on September 12, 1958 in favour of the Bishop's party.

Reconciliation

Both parties realised the futility of the strenuous process of litigation and the fact that court verdicts cannot bring about a lasting peace. The leaders of the parties discussed and decided to accept each other and to work together as One Church. The Patriarch of Antioch endorsed their decision. On December 16, 1958, the bishops of both groups and Mar Julius, the Patriarchal delegate sat together and exchanged letters of mutual acceptance.

But, unfortunately, the accord did not last long. Disbelief and longstanding mutual alienation resulted in mutual accusations of breach of trust. The Patriarchal Party's sentiments were wounded by the statements like 'See of St. Thomas', 'Catholicos of the East', 'Head of the Malankara Church' etc. used by the Catholicos party. Another grievance of the Patriarch party was that they were being sidelined in the general affairs of the Church. Both camps also raised accusations of non-co-operation. In 1960, the bishops of the Patriarchal Party assembled at Manarcadu Church protested against the policies of the Catholicate and gave shape to an organisation named 'Antiochean Syrian Movement'. By 1961, the movement gained strength and raised two accusations against the Catholicos party as below:

> Patriarch accepted the Catholicos party unconditionally, whereas the Catholicos party accepted the Patriarch's party only conditionally, subject to their Constitution.
>
> The use of the title 'His Holiness' by the Catholicos would mean equality than subordination to the Patriarch.

In reply, the Catholicos party explained their standpoint as under:

> The Antiochean Patriarch can be invited for the installation of the Catholicos, provided the former is elected with the co-operation of the Malankara Church.
>
> Any accusation against the Catholicos has to be dealt with by the Malankara Synod. The Patriarch can preside over it, if he is invited to do so.
>
> The Malankara Church will acknowledge only those Patriarchs who were elected with their co-operation.

A repetition of the earlier polarisation was brooding up. The Patriarch of Antioch subsequently stated that he was unable to accept the Constitution of the Malankara Church on the following grounds:

> The Catholicos party is claiming a kind of secession from the Antiochian Syrian Jacobite Church by adopting the position of a 'sister Church'.
>
> A body in which the laity had the majority passed the Constitution of the Orthodox Church.
>
> The claim of the use of the title 'See of Thomas' is not constitutional.
>
> The establishment of the Catholicate by Mar Abdul Messiah was invalid as he had no authority to do it.

As the supporters of the Patriarch were not a negligible section, the Patriarch was invited to visit Kerala and reach reconciliation. The Patriarch accepted the invitation, reached Malabar and installed Augen Mar Timotheos as the Catholicos of the East on May 22, 1964 as a sign of accord and reconciliation. An impression of restoration of peace was again created. But the spirit of reconciliation soon vanished.

Catholicos for Patriarch's Party

In 1970, Mathews Mar Athanasios was chosen as successor to the Catholicos Augen Mar Timotheos. The use of the title *See of St. Thomas* provoked Patriarch to the extent of challenging even the *priesthood* of St.Thomas and the *See of St. Thomas*. In response to this challenge, the Catholicos asserted that

- The Malankara Church is an autonomous church and the Antiochian Church is only a 'sister Church'.
- The Catholicos of the East occupies the *See of St. Thomas*.
- There is no need of a Patriarchal Delegate in the Malankara Church.

'The Malankara Jacobite Syrian Christian Association' formed in 1972 submitted a memorandum to the episcopal Synod containing the points mentioned below:

- The Malankara Church and the Antiochian Jacobite Church are not mere sister churches.
- The claim of 'See of Thomas' is an innovation.
- The omission of commemoration of the Patriarch of Antioch in ordination ceremonies is not legitimate.
- The omission of condemnation of Pope Leo of Rome is also not legitimate.
- The true faith is not fully taught in the seminary at Kottayam.
- Professors in Seminaries hold Protestant views and doctrines.
- The affiliation to the Serampore College is not proper.
- The presence of the Antiochian delegate is necessary.
- The *tithe* (ecclesiastical tax) should be given to the Patriarch.
- There are heretical teachings in Sunday school textbooks.[3]

The conflict became widespread in the course of time. The denial of Visa to the Patriarchal delegate led to protests and demonstrations. The episcopal ordination of Kadavil Paulos Mar Athanasios without consulting the Catholicos or the

Synod led to open conflicts. On January 13, 1974, the Patriarch demanded explanation from the Catholicos on the following charges:

- The basis on the claim of the 'See of Thomas'.
- The Patriarch is the supreme head of the Syrian Church. Why the statement that the Catholicos is equal to the Patriarch.
- Being a part of the Syrian Church, why they say that they are an independent church called 'Indian Orthodox Church' and that the Catholicos is its head.
- There is no 'See of St. Thomas'.
- Why the Patriarchal delegate was forced to leave India.
- Why the relation with the Antiochean Church is only that of a sister church.
- The Patriarch as well as the Catholicos (Orthodox Syrian) enjoys the right to ordain bishops. But, they should be acceptable to the people.
- The Catholicos should not try to extend his authority over those churches, which follow the Patriarch.
- The Knanaya (Sudhist) community is not fully autonomous. It is part of the Malankara Church. The Catholicos (Orthodox Syrian) can extend his authority over only those who accept him.
- Historically, it is not correct to state that Apostle St. Thomas founded the Orthodox Syrian Church.

On February 24, 1974, the Patriarch ordained two more bishops, Thomas Mar Athanasios and Geevarghese Mar Gregorios.

The Catholicos gave the following reply to the Patriarch:

- Malankara Syrian Church is autocephalous.
- The Patriarch is trying to destroy the autonomy of this church.
- The delegate gave ordinations without permission.
- The Patriarch ordained bishops without permission.

- Patriarch has no right to demand explanation from the Catholicos.
- The Patriarch has disqualified himself from the authority by violating the constitution of the Church.

Similar war of words between the two factions continued for long. Allegations and counter-allegations vitiated the atmosphere. The Church has become an object of derision and ignominy. In 1974, the Catholicos filed a suit against the Patriarch's party. Moreover, they ordained five bishops. Patriarch's Party ordained two more bishops. In 1975, the Patriarch convened a Universal Synod at Damascus. The Synod excommunicated Catholicos and his bishops. The Patriarch ordained Paulos Mar Philexinose as the Catholicos of the East for the Malankara Syrian Orthodox Church.

The Supreme Court of India declared the final verdict on February 5, 1997 directing both factions to officially acknowledge and obey the Constitution of 1934 and to open the path for a reconciliation in which the Patriarch is given a unique spiritual authority over the Malankara Orthodox Church.

Both parties failed to realise that the division is a counter-witness to the gospel of Jesus Christ. Unending litigations helped only to impoverish the Church. Rancour and rivalry continued to reign over them even today. May God enlighten them.

When both parties were fully engaged in litigation and squabbles, another schism – the fourth in the series – occurred in 1930 whereby two bishops with a sizeable following under the leadership of Bishop Mar Ivanios embraced the Catholic Church. This is known in history as the Reunion Movement. (Please see separate notes on this Movement.) Altogether there had been four schisms and a subschism ever since the inception of the Jacobite Church in India in 1665.

The Present Position

With the erection of the Catholicate in 1912 at Kottayam, the Patriarch's party and the Bishop's party have become two distinct hierarchical entities. This division resulted in a series of litigations on the claims and counter-claims over the ecclesiastical properties. After the death of Mar Dionysius VI in 1934, the Malankara Association assembled at Kottayam took the following decisions:

Chose Catholicos Baselios Geevarghese II as Malankara Metropolitan. (This practice of one person holding the offices of 'Catholicos' and 'Malankara Metropolitan' is continued till date.)

The Church officially approved a Constitution for the Church.

The Church assumed the name 'Orthodox Church'.

The Patriarch's party in 1935 elected Paulose Mar Athanasios as Malankara Metropolitan. Later, the Patriarch ordained Paulose Mar Philexinose as 'Catholicos of the East'. In the confused situation of litigations, reliable statistics on these churches are not available.

Ecumenical Developments

Consequent on the Ecumenical Movement initiated in the 20th century, the Vatican II and the World Council of Churches encouraged a positive attitude towards fostering closer relations between churches. This had its impact on the churches in India. The Malankara Orthodox Syrian Catholicos and the Syrian Orthodox Patriarch of Antioch have already entered into separate dialogue with the Catholic Church. Separate commissions were also set up by both the churches for dialogue with the ten-member Commission of the Catholic Church constituted under the auspices of the Pontifical council for Promoting Christian unity. A common agreement on Christology has already been signed in 1984 between the Syrian Patriarch of Antioch and Pope John Paul II. A similar agreement has been signed between the Malankara Orthodox Syrian Church and Rome. A joint commission for dialogue was constituted in 1988 and dialogue on other points of disagreement is also in progress.

In 1947, the Synod of the Malankara Orthodox Syrian Church canonised Chathuruthy Mar Gregoriose, the only Saint in this Church. The Saint's tomb at Parumala (near Tiruvalla) is today a pilgrim centre.

In the administrative structure of both these churches, constitutional bodies of elected representatives of the laity and the priests play decisive roles. These assemblies give a democratic character in administration, provide a forum for the faithful to ventilate their grievances and aspirations and also to equip the hierarchy with requisite feedback enabling judicious decisions.

Separate notes on the schisms are given below:

1. The Independent Syrian Church of Malabar (Thozhiyoor/ Anjoor)

The history of this church traces its origin in a Syrian bishop Mar Ivanios, who visited Malankara from 1685 to 1694 and occasionally stayed at Mulanthuruthy to teach Syriac and to train the deacons. Among the students, the Bishop identified two youngsters, one Abraham and his younger brother Geevarghese, the sons of one Abraham of the Kattumangattu family, who were regular and disciplined in attendance and proficient in studies. Impressed by the dedication and exemplary character of the boys, Mar Ivanios ordained them first as deacons and later as priests. After becoming priests, they led ascetic lives in a small *Dayara* (monastery) near a place called Vettickal. Mar Ivanios passed away in 1694. In 1751, one Baselios Mar Sakrallah, the Syrian Catholicos of Mosul arrived in Malankara, accompanied by Bishop Mar Gregorios of Jerusalem, one Ramban and two deacons. The Catholicos built a Church at Mattanchery and stayed there. He was in the lookout of an efficient teacher in Syriac to teach the deacons. The choice naturally fell on Fr. Abraham Kattumangatt. The devotion and saintly life of Fr. Abraham very much impressed the Catholicos. Mar Baselios took the initiative to ordain Fr. Abraham as Ramban (monk-the Order preceding ordination as bishop) at the *Eliseema* Church at Mattanchery. Later, the parishioners of Cochin area assembled at Kandanadu unanimously appealed to Mar Gregorios of Jerusalem to consecrate Kattumangattu Ramban as bishop. Heeding to the aspirations of the faithful, Mar Gregorios consecrated *Kattumangattu* Abraham Ramban as bishop with title 'Mar Koorilos' and handed over to the new bishop the cross, the staff, the tiara and the holy oil (*Mooron*) brought from Antioch. Later, Mar Gregorios, in the last days of his life, bequeathed his assets and properties also to Mar Koorilos. The King of Perumpadappu (Cochin) granted to Mar Koorilos the documents of authority (*Theettooram*) over the Christian churches in the northern parts of Cochin.

The news of ordination of Mar Koorilos reached the ears of Mar Dionysius I. He took the consecration of a bishop without his concurrence as a challenge to his authority. Apprehending possible threat to his position, Mar Dionysius I moved swiftly to thwart all attempts to challenge his authority. With the help of the *Sarvadikaryakar* (chief minister) of Travancore, Mar Dionysius succeeded to persuade the King of Cochin to withdraw the *Theettooram*. On withdrawal of authority by the King, the despondent Mar Koorilos shifted his residence to a monastery (*Dayara*) at Karingasra and led the life of a monk, where he was, for all practical purposes, a prisoner with no freedom to move about. Later, he shifted his residence to a hutment monastery built at Thavanal, a valley in between two hillocks in the forest area. Bishop Chathuruthy Mar Gregorios (later St. Gregorios of Parumala), who was then residing in the Mulanthuruthy Church, used to visit Mar Koorilos at Thavanal. Finding the miserable life at Thavanal, Mar Gregorios promised help to construct a monastery building. Before the promise materialised, Mar Koorilos, along with his brother Fr. Geevarghese, fearing threat to their lives, proceeded to Malabar, outside the jurisdiction of the King of Cochin. En route, they halted at Anjoor in a temporary hut (this hut is at present a shrine). A Muslim landlord, who received a miraculous favour at the hands of Mar Koorilos in healing his son from rabies, donated a piece of land at Thozhiyoor (outside the Cochin State) for the construction of a church. With the liberal help of the local people, a church was built at the donated site at Thozhiyoor, which is now the Cathedral of the Thozhiyoor Church. Mar Koorilos breathed his last in 1802. His brother Geevarghese, consecrated by Abraham Mar Koorilos before his death, succeeded with the title Geevarghese Mar Koorilos II.

Though this Church originated due to an accidental schism in the *Puthenkoor* faction, they followed, without deviation or distortion, the faith and practices of the mother church. Fourteen bishops succeeded the founder Abraham Mar Koorilos I. Out of them, two passed away before assuming charge and one embraced the Catholic Church. The history of this church reveals that they had all along aspired for reunion. Two serious attempts they initiated for reconciliation with the Jacobite faction were foiled by the vested interests in the Jacobite Church. But, despite the hostile attitude of the Jacobites, this Church maintained cordial relations not only with the Jacobite Church, but also with the Marthoma Church and offered help to those churches in times of crises. When the possibility of a rupture occurred in the Apostolic line of succession of bishops in the Jacobite Church, Bishop Kidangan Skaria Mar Philexinos of the Thozhiyoor Church rescued them by consecrating three bishops, one after another in a row; Mar Dionysius II, Mar Dionysius III and Mar Dionysius IV. Similarly, when Thomas Mar Athanasios of the Marthoma Church died without a successor, Maliakal Joseph Mar Athanasios and his suffragan Geevarghese Mar Koorilos of the Thozhiyoor Church consecrated Titus I as Mar Thoma Metropolitan in 1893. Both the Jacobite Church and the Mar Thoma Church reciprocated by consecrating bishops in Thozhiyoor Church whenever that church faced similar situations. At one point of time, on the request of the British Resident Col. Munroe, one of the Thozhiyoor bishops acted even as Metropolitan of the Jacobite Church for one year.

This Church enjoyed clear apostolic succession till 1856 through the Antiochian patrimony. But, the subsequent bishops lost this pipeline succession. Then, Mar Koorilos of Syria, who was holding the post of Malankara Metropolitan, made an attempt to consecrate a person of his choice as bishop of the Thozhiyoor Church. This led to a dispute resulting in a civil suit. In 1863, the Madras High Court disposed of the Appeal declaring the independence of the Thozhiyoor Church. Thereafter, this Church is known as 'the Independent Syrian Church of Malabar', Thozhiyoor/Anjoor, with one bishop, seven or eight priests and membership around 5000. The blemish in ordination of Panakkal Mar Koorilos in 1856 still remains unerased. The existence of two Churches with the same faith, practices and liturgy is an affront to entire Christianity.

2. The Mar Thoma Syrian Church

In the eighteenth century, the British East India Company was in the process of establishing their political domination in India. Utilising the Company's presence, the Anglican Church missionaries came forward to spread the Anglican Church in India by establishing mission centres. At first, they concentrated in Calcutta and Madras. Later, they came into contact with the *Puthenkoor* faction of the St. Thomas Christians in Malankara. In the Synod at Mavelikkara in 1818, the Puthenkoor community officially approved a policy of closer collaboration with the Anglican missionaries. But, within two decades, the relations became strained and another Synod at Mavelikara in 1836 put an end to the alliance. Abraham Malpan of Maramon and Kaithayil Geevarghese Malpan of Kottayam, professors in the Old Seminary along with the missionaries, became committed to the Reformist ideas of the missionaries and assumed leadership of a Reform movement.

Abraham Malpan never intended to establish a separate reformed Church. He aimed at introducing the reforms in the Church in which he was member. But he was fully conscious that reforms could be introduced in an episcopal Church only with the support of the bishops and that the Jacobite bishops were generally of a reactionary frame of mind hostile to radical changes in their conventional faith and practices. Abraham Malpan, with astute farsightedness, devised a strategy to circumvent the roadblock and to bring in persons favourably disposed towards reforms at the higher echelons of the Church hierarchy. He deputed his nephew, Deacon Mathew, to Murdeen in Syria, the then headquarters of the Jacobite church. The deacon stayed with the Patriarch of Antioch for one year, earned the confidence and goodwill of the Patriarch, got himself ordained as priest, Ramban and finally as bishop with title 'Mathews Mar Athanasios' and returned to Malankara in 1843. On arrival, he claimed the chair of the Malankara Metropolitan. At this stage, Abraham Malpan passed away in 1845, at 49.

Cheppattu Mar Dionysius IV, the then Malankara Metropolitan visualised a conflict in the community, as an after-effect of the new development. He was convinced of the wisdom in leaning heavily on the Antiochean Patriarch to avert the impending catastrophe. He apprised the Patriarch of the gravity of the new developments in the Malankara Church. The Patriarch responded by deputing a Syrian Bishop Mar Koorilos to Malankara with mandate to take appropriate steps to tackle the crisis. Mar Koorilos arrived in India in 1846. On his arrival, Mar Dionysius IV stepped out after handing over charge of the hierarchy to Mar Koorilos. It was a calculated step aimed at ensuring greater freedom to Mar Koorilos to prudently handle the situation. Thus, the Syrian Prelate Mar Koorilos became the Malankara Metropolitan in 1846. Under the influence of the British officers and the missionaries, the Government by Royal Proclamation recognised Mathews Mar Athanasius as Malankara Metropolitan. In 1865, the Patriarch ordained Mar Dionysius V. As a sequel to the action of the Patriarch, Mathews Mar Athanasios, jointly with the Bishop of Thozhiyoor, consecrated Thomas, the son of Abraham Malpan, as bishop with title 'Thomas Mar Athanasios', in 1868.

Mathews Mar Athanasios was bent upon renewal of the Jacobite Church, but only with selective acceptance of Protestant ideologies. But circumstances forced him to do away with few age-old venerable traditions of the Church, which resulted in a stir in the community. In the confused situation, Patriarch Peter III personally came to Malabar in 1875 and convened a Synod at Mulanthuruthy in 1876. The Synod condemned both Mathews Mar Athanasios and Thomas Mar Athanasios for abstaining from the Synod. The Patriarch divided the Malankara Church into seven dioceses and consecrated six new bishops for the new dioceses. This unprecedented action of the Patriarch strengthened the Church. In the meantime, the Government withdrew its recognition to Mathews Mar Athanasios. In

1877, Thomas Mar Athanasios was appointed successor to Mathews Mar Athanasios. This resulted in another litigation.

In 1889, the Royal Court of Final Appeal decreed against Thomas Mar Athanasios on grounds of lack of authorisation of the Syrian Jacobite Patriarch for his consecration. Consequent on the court verdict, Thomas Mar Athanasios left the Old Seminary, where he was residing. Thereafter, a series of suits arose on the rights over various churches and properties. The Reform Party won Maramon and Kozhenchery churches by court decisions and Kottarakara Church without contest. Both groups shared five churches for worship on alternate Sundays.

The Mar Thoma Evangelistic Association was founded in 1889. Thomas Mar Athanasios passed away in 1893 without a successor. Mar Koorilos of the Thozhiyoor Church and his Suffragan Mar Athanasios jointly consecrated a new bishop, another son of Abraham Malpan, with title 'Titus I Mar Thoma'. By strengthening the evangelisation efforts, the membership of the community has grown by leaps and bounds. But, in litigations, properties were being lost one after another. Bishop Titus I consecrated his nephew as bishop in 1899 with the title 'Titus II'. He continued as suffragan till the death of Titus I. Later, after evaluating the pros and cons of the then prevailing situation, the Reform Party found that it would be prudent to establish a separate Church with a separate nomenclature for identity. Accordingly, the Reform Party accepted the name 'Mar Thoma Syrian Church', during the period of Titus II Mar Thoma. This was the second schism in the Jacobite Church and the first schism based on dogma and practices.

In the initial period, there was practically only one bishop in the Church. In 1917, Titus II consecrated Abraham Mar Thoma as suffragan bishop. Mar Titus II consecrated two more bishops in 1939 (1937?). Consequent on the growth of the Church, more dioceses were erected and more bishops were necessitated. Three bishops in 1953, two in 1975, one each in 1980 and 1989 and three in 1993 were ordained.

Faith

Very often, the Mar Thoma Church authorities described their Church as a bridge Church situated in between the traditional mainline Churches and the Reformed Churches. In the realm of dogma, the Mar Thoma Church weeded out some of the dogmas not found acceptable and selectively accepted some others that reconciled with their vision, as listed below:

Accepted Doctrines

1. Holy Trinity and Triune God.
2. Jesus Christ is full God and full man and saviour.
3. The Nicene Creed.
4. Sacrament of baptism including child baptism.
5. Salvation by faith in Jesus Christ.
6. Bible with 66 books alone the foundation of the Church.
7. Holy Order (priesthood) and three-tier hierarchical structure with bishop, priest and deacon.
8. Episcopacy with apostolic succession.
9. Holy Mass (Holy Eucharist) with Holy Communion in both species.
10. No mass in the absence of communicants.
11. Marriage for clergy.
12. Public penance.
13. Anointing the sick.
14. Lent and fast.

Doctrines not Accepted

1. Transubstantiation.
2. Prayer and mass for the dead.
3. Canonisation.
4. Intercession of Saints and Holy Mary.
5. Images and relics.
6. Term 'Mother of God'.

7. Devotion to Mary.
8. Auricular confession.

Chronology of the Metropolitans of the Church

1. Mathews Mar Athanasios Mar Thoma – 1843-1877
2. Thomas Mar Athanasios Mar Thoma – 1877-1893
3. Titus I Mar Thoma – 1893-1910
4. Titus II Mar Thoma – 1910-1944
5. Dr. Abraham Mar Thoma – 1944-1947
6. Dr. Yuhanon Mar Thoma – 1947-1976
7. Dr. Alexander Mar Thoma – 1976-2000
8. Dr. Philipose Mar Chrisostom Mar Thoma – 2000[4]

Note: During the period of the first two Metropolitans in the above list, legally there was no Marthoma Church.

When Abraham Malpan was alive, he had a large following of laity and priests favouring reforms, but it had no collective form or forum. After the exit of Thomas Mar Athanasios from the Jacobite Church, the reformists became an identifiably cohesive community outside the Jacobite Church, labelled as 'Reform Party'. Thence onwards, we see an unbelievably fantastic growth for the reform party, not only in membership, but also in multifarious areas. With the acceptance of the name 'Mar Thoma Syrian Church', the developments gathered further momentum resulting in an *espirit de corps* and growth in diverse directions aimed at spiritual revival and acquisition of inevitable temporalities. In the areas of number of priests, parishes, churches, bishops, evangelisation, education, charity, hospitals, printing and publishing, revision of liturgy, introduction of mother tongue in worship, Youth and Ladies organisations, a constitutional framework for the Church, membership in the World Council of Churches, co-operation with the Church of South India (C.S.I.) and the Church of North India (C.N.I.), mission centres outside Kerala, department of Sacred Music, training in evangelism, Church Government consisting of Synod and assembly of laity and priests, Maramon Convention etc., the Church made great strides forward.

Today, the Mar Thoma Church with headquarters at Tiruvalla, following the Antiochean liturgy, has become a full-fledged autonomous Church, with nine dioceses inside and outside India, nine bishops, more than 8,75,000 members in 1,14,470 families and all infrastructural facilities, is poised on tiptoe for a quantum leap forward.[5] The Indian Christian Directory shows the number of dioceses as 11 and population 9,00,000. This figure is likely to be more later and therefore correct.

In the areas of charity and elementary education, the performance of this Church is highly appreciable.

Many factors contributed for this phenomenal growth. Among them, we can notice: (i) the instinct for survival, (ii) the zeal of new converts, (iii) attraction of the reform ideologies, (iv) freedom from the burden of too much rituals and festivals, (v) dedication of the evangelists, (vi) shift from ritual-oriented Christianity to life-oriented Christianity, (vii) evangelisation crossing the frontiers of caste, language and geography, (viii) lack of racial or other discrimination within the Church, (ix) efficient co-ordination and management at the top level and so on.

Compared to the enthusiasm and achievements in the early decades, of late, the Mar Thoma Church is seen to be in the grip of some sort of inertia, lethargy and complacency, a common feature noticed in all human endeavours.

Another aspect noted is that the Church has not yet promulgated a definite doctrine of faith on the real presence of Christ in the Eucharist. Transubstantiation (change of substance from bread and wine to the body and blood of Christ) already stands rejected. Western Reformists have advanced several alternate theories in this respect – objective presence termed 'Consubstantiation' by Martin Luther, 'Memorial presence of Christ' by Calvin, 'presence of Christ seen through the eyes of faith' advanced by Wycliff and so on. The Catholic theologians have recently coined another term 'Transignification' to define the 'Real presence of Christ in the Eucharist'. The ambiguity in this vital doctrine of faith has to be set right at the earliest. (This was a serious issue in the suit 'K.N. Daniel *vs* Mar Thoma Syrian Church'.)

Similar is the case with 'monasticism'. Some initiatives were made, but appreciable progress is not visible. In these days of turmoil in the sphere of religions in India and the emergence of new ideologies like 'Hindutva', 'Cultural Nationalism', 'Inculturation' etc., monasticism has greater significance and attraction.

Another area where adequate importance seems to have not been given by the Church is the spiritual formation and renewal of individual members through spiritual exercises like introspection, recollection, penance, retreats, meditation, counselling, adoration etc. In this age of widening gap between preaching and practice and waning spirituality, no amount of efforts shall be excessive or superfluous in this area.

The most prominent elements in reformation were:

Return to the gospel message of salvation by faith in Jesus Christ.

Cleansing of wrong ways of life.

Taking up responsibilities to be witnesses of Jesus Christ to others.

All these centred on the study of the 'Word of God'.[6]

Unfortunately, this Church faced a schism in 1961, the notes on which follow:

2(a). The St. Thomas Evangelical Church of India

In 1953, the Representative General Assembly of the Mar Thoma Church chose three candidates for episcopal ordination. A controversy arose in the Church on the eligibility of one of the candidates chosen by the General Assembly. Despite protests, the Church ordained all the three chosen by the Assembly as bishops. The head of the dissidents was one K.N. Daniel, a pioneer lay leader of the Reformation, who has done yeoman service to the Church in the past. After the ordination, Mr. K.N. Daniel filed a civil suit in the District Court seeking the issuance of a prohibitory order against Dr. Yuhanon Mar Thoma Metropolitan. The charge levelled against the Metropolitan was that the Church under his leadership was drifting away from the reform ideals and that the Jacobite practices, once abhorred, were being allowed re-entry through the backdoor. After long five years of litigation, the Supreme Court of India dismissed the petition with costs.

When the litigation was progressing, the official camp made several efforts for reconciliation, but all efforts miserably failed due to the adamant attitude of the dissidents. Even 30 years before the ordination issue of 1953, there was a dispute in the Church on the doctrine of 'real presence of Christ in the Eucharist' resulting in a lot of bad blood between the rebels and the officialdom in the Church.

After the judgment of the Supreme Court in 1960, fourteen priests resigned their membership in the Mar Thoma Church and identified themselves with the priests defected earlier at the beginning of the dispute. The Church and the Metropolitan were equally adamant on their standpoint. The rift finally reached its inevitable logical conclusion by the inauguration of a separate Church by the dissidents named the "St. Thomas Evangelical Church of India" on 26th January 1961. After the formal inauguration, the priests ordained two among them – Rev. K.N. Oommen and Rev. John Varghese – as bishops by the imposition of hands by the priests present there. Initially they had five or six parishes and a good number of sympathizers in several other parishes. In the course of time, they established few more parishes.

Dr. Yuhanon Mar Thoma in his book *The Christian Church in India and the Concise History of the Mar Thoma Church* (Mal.) has narrated in detail the circumstances that led to the schism. According to the Metropolitan, three priests later returned to the mother church and two others joined the Pentecostal churches. The Metropolitan has also alleged that one Karl Mac Intaire, the founder of the Council of International churches in America (a defector from the World Council of Churches) was largely instrumental in the establishment of a new church by the dissidents.[7] Today, this Church has one bishop and more than twenty-five priests. In the growth of this Church, nothing remarkable has so far been noticed, worth mentioning.

As this schism took place in the Marthoma Church, already a schismatic Church, this is treated as a subschism and numbered as 2(a) as above.

3. Division in the Jacobite Church in India into Malankara Syrian Orthodox and Malankara Orthodox Syrian Churches

This schism has a long history of litigations in civil courts extending nearly 150 years with intermittent reconciliations and disruptions. All these finally led to a division in to two churches with parallel names, parallel heads, parallel constitutions and parallel hierarchies, but with uniform faith and practices. The strife started within the Jacobite Church, but ended with no Jacobite Church in India, a remarkable paradox in history – No winner, no loser – the Jacobite Church alone disappeared. (Please see detailed notes under title "Jacobite Church in India".)

4. The Reunion Movement and the Syro Malankara Catholic Church

The Slant Cross Oath of 1653 was the collective expression of the protest of the St. Thomas Christians against the religious colonialism practised by the Portuguese Padroado and the Jesuits. The Archdeacon, whose authority was till then confined to the temporal affairs of the Church, by a 'fake ordination' as bishop with title Mar Thoma I, extended his authority to the spiritual affairs of the Church. This led to wide resentment in the community. A vast majority of Thomas Christians were averse to accept the 'fake ordination', which tantamount to alienation from the mother church. This resulted in the division of the community into two factions, the Old Loyalists known as *Pazhayakoottukar* and the Neo Loyalists known as *Puthenkoottukar* owing their allegiance to the Archdeacon.

Mar Thoma I, fully conscious of the canonical defects in his ordination, longed for reconciliation with the Catholic Church to get the defects rectified. He wrote to the Carmelite bishop Sebastiani, the Vicar Apostolic of the Malabar Vicariate under the Propaganda Fide. His offer was not acceptable to Bishop Sebastiani. The opinions of the Church historians do not concur as to whether Mar Thoma I had ever got rectified the defects in his ordination. Ever since, we notice a series of attempts on the part of the successors of Mar Thoma I for reunion. Mar Thoma IV wrote to Pope Clement XI with the signatures of 12 priests and 29 parish representatives. But, no reply came from Rome. Mar Thoma V wrote to Pope Benedict XIV on August 16, 1748. Though Benedict XIV was a Pope not in favour of introducing Latin practices in the Eastern Churches, there was no response from the Holy See. As we have already seen, Mar Thoma VI (Dionysius I) made several attempts including the delegation of Kariattil and Paremakkal to Rome, agreement with Mathoo Tharakan etc., but Rome turned a deaf ear towards all these attempts. Cheppattu Mar Dionysius IV made intensive efforts for reunion. Mar Pulikott Dionysius V supported the moves initiated by the *Jathaikya Sanghom*, sponsored by Nidheerikal Mani Kathanar. The Vicars Apostolic of the Malabar Vicariate, not favourable to such moves, even admonished Fr. Nidheerikal for initiating the move.

Independent efforts made by Catholic bishop Mar Mathew Makil and Mar Alexander Choolaparambil with the active support of Bishop Mar Severios of the Puthenkoor Knanaya community also ended in vain. The Catholic Church, reputed for rigorous enforcement of discipline in the Church, had no soft corner or leniency towards the schismatics in the Malabar Church and hence stuck on adamantly to its characteristic rigidity.

The never-ending litigations with intermittent ups and downs put the community in a precarious position. Besides impoverishment, wastage of energy and mental strain, the community became an object of mockery and ignominy. The creation of the Catholicate, a parallel centre of power and authority further aggravated the strained relations with the Antiochean Church. Any sort of alliance or collaboration with the Reformed churches was unthinkable as the faith, traditions and practices of the community were incompatible with the Reformation ideologies. The Catholic Church was not favourably disposed towards reconciliation. In these circumstances, what is the way to get out of this desperate situation? This was the puzzling question confronted by each member of the community. In the case of a successful reconciliation with the Catholic Church, the only demand to be complied with would be the reacceptance of the papal authority. As regards faith, liturgy, episcopacy, practices etc. no alteration would be required. As such, the consensus of opinion was in favour of one more attempt for reunion with the Catholic Church as the only acceptable option.

In this context, an episcopal gathering of the *Puthenkoor* faction was held at Parumala on November 1, 1926 to examine the prospects of attempting another effort for reunion with the Catholic Church. The participants were Mar Basselios Geevarghese Catholicos (1925-28), Geevarghese Mar Gregorios (1912-29) and Geevarghese Mar Ivanios of Bethany (1925-30). Mar Ivanios was authorised to follow up the matter, with Rome.

In the first letter to the Holy See, Mar Ivanios requested for:

(i) the right to preserve the existing liturgical and other traditions,

(ii) the permission to continue the Synodal system and the bishops, and

(iii) the Catholic communion.

Rome conceded the first demand for preserving liturgical and other traditions, but insisted on obligatory celibacy for priests. The demand for Synodal system and the title 'Catholicos' were not favoured. Mar Ivanios wrote again on the Synodal System, but there was no response. In the light of the reply, the Catholicos retraced his steps. A 'wait and watch' policy was visible in the approach of Rome, in all the letters.

The Reunion of 1930 at Kollam

Finally, Mar Ivanios along with his auxiliary bishop Mar Theophilos, one representative of the clergy, a deacon and a layman reunited with the Catholic Church on September 20, 1930 at the Bishop's House chapel at Kollam before Most Rev. Aloysius Maria Benziger, Bishop of Kollam. Bishops

Lawrence Pereira of Kottar and Mar James Kalachery of Changanachery were present. Here, it is worth mentioning to note that out of ten attempts, one after another in a series, for reunion, the efforts of Mar Ivanios alone became fruitful, though not fully. Mar Ivanios was a scholar and a visionary, who was instrumental in introducing two innovative programmes in the Jacobite Church before reunion: (i) Monasticism, and (ii) streamlining of Catechism. Later, many others including the entire sisters of Bethany and many from the Order of the Imitation of Christ followed them. In June 1932, Pope Pius XI established the Syro Malankara hierarchy, directly under the Holy See, with Mar Ivanios as Metropolitan Archbishop and Mar Theophilos as suffragan bishop of Tiruvalla diocese. Subsequently, Rome clarified that there is no objection in admitting married clergy in their existing status and that married deacons can be ordained as priests, both subject to verification of their antecedents such as baptism, ordination, moral life etc. Resultantly, several married priests of the Catholicos faction embraced the Syro Malankara Church along with a substantial number of their followers and relatives. In the course of time, three bishops, (i) Valakuzhy Joseph Mar Severios of the Catholicate faction, (ii) Thomas Mar Dioscoros of the Sudhist Jacobite faction, and (iii) Poulose Mar Philexinos of the Thozhiyoor Church reunited with the Syro Malankara Catholic Church.

When there was dearth of priests in the early decades, the Syro Malabar Church extended their helping hands by deputing very many eminent priests in their Church and by sending boys to the Minor Seminaries of the Malankara Church for training as future priests. They also extended their moral, liturgical and social support and co-operation whenever necessitated. The growth of the Syro Malankara Church, in the first five decades of its inception, was remarkably impressive on all counts. Four more dioceses, viz.: Bathery, Marthandom, Mavelikara and Muvattupuzha were established to accelerate the tempo of growth.

A very significant turning point in the history of the Syro Malankara Church is the establishment of a Malankara Major

Seminary at Trivandrum for the formation of their own clergy wedded to preserve their venerable heritage and ecumenical vocation. The Eastern Churches that enter into communion with Rome generally express a grievance that they lose their tradition and identity by latinisation. In recent centuries, the Universal Church is veering around the tenet 'Unity does not mean uniformity and that unity in diversity is beauty.' Vatican II has underscored this tenet and declared it in unequivocal terms. "The Eastern Catholic Churches preserving the unity of faith and the unique divine constitution of the Universal Church, enjoy their own discipline, their own liturgical usage and their own theological and spiritual heritage."

The consolidated Statistical Statement of the Syro Malankara Church as at present is given below:

1.	Major Archbishop	–	1
2.	Archbishop	–	1
3.	Bishops	–	8
4.	Eparchial priests	–	511
5.	Religious priests	–	121
6.	Religious Brothers	–	40
7.	Major Seminarians	–	256
8.	Minor Seminarians	–	189
9.	Religious Sisters:		
	(a) Sisters of the Imitation of Christ	–	807
	(b) Daughters of Mary	–	836
	(c) Others	–	271
10.	Malankara Catholic Population	–	410000
11.	Parishes and Mission Stations	–	914
12.	Institutions:		
	Major Seminary	–	1
	Minor Seminary	–	7
	Pastoral Centres	–	8
	Priests Home	–	6
	Medical College	–	1
	Engineering College	–	1

Nursing College	–	1
Teachers' Training Colleges	–	2
Arts and Science Colleges	–	7
Teachers' Training Schools	–	20
Technical Institutes	–	8
Para Medical Schools	–	4
Higher Secondary Schools	–	25
High Schools	–	53
Upper Primary Schools	–	53
Lower Primary Schools	–	193
Nursery Schools	–	136
Boarding Houses	–	40
Orphanages	–	11
Dalit Hostels	–	2
Hospitals and Health Centres	–	40
Homes for the Aged	–	13
Rehabilitation Centres	–	8
Printing Press	–	7
Book Stalls	–	4
Publications	–	8[8]

In the Post-Vatican II scenario, the Syro Malankara Catholic Church has a major role to play in the realm of ecumenism, especially in view of the fact that most of the non-Catholic St. Thomas Christians follow the Antiochean liturgy. A meaningful role conducive to reconciliation depends largely on its fidelity to the venerable heritage of the Church. A church unfaithful to its heritage would be a misfit or an anachronism in the area of ecumenism. Let the Syro Malankara Church gather strength and vitality to become a pioneer in the emerging era of ecumenism, consistent with its legitimate diversity in liturgy, spirituality, discipline, traditions and theology.

(A step by step narrative of the events leading to the change-over from Chaldean to Antiochean liturgy and the interaction between Mar Ivanios and the Holy See on Reunion are available in the Book in English 'Syro Malankara Church' by Most Rev. Cyril Mar Basselios Metropolitan and its translation in Malayalam by Fr. Sylvester Kanjiramukalil, OIC.)*

In February 2005, Pope John Paul II elevated the Syro Malankara Hierarchy to the dignity of a Major Archiepiscopal Church with a Synod under a Major Archbishop.

After the sorrowful demise of Moran Cyril Mor Basselios, Major Archbishop and head of the Syro Malankara hierarchy, Moran Mar Basselios Cleemis, Archbishop of Thiruvalla was elevated to the dignity of His Beatitude Major Archbishop and head of the Syro Malakara hierarchy on 5th March 2007.

5. The Church of the East – Trichur

The title given above is the official name of an independent Church with headquarters at Trichur having a following of 15,000, at present. This Church is also known under different other names such as 'Surai Church', ' Chaldean Syrian Church', 'Nestorian Church', 'Assyrian Church of the East', 'Babylonian Church' etc.

Origin of the Church

As regards the origin of this church, the reliable tradition is that the King of Cochin, generally known as *Sakthan Thampuran* (the mighty King), in 1696 AD rehabilitated 52 Christian families at Trichur, picked up from different parts of the Cochin State, with a view to build a commercial town. As the criterion for selection of the families was efficiency to do business, we are not sure of the denomination of Christianity from which they were chosen. It seems reasonable to presume that they belonged to the St. Thomas Syrian Christian community as they followed the Chaldean Syriac liturgy (the liturgy then prevailing among the Thomas Christians) and that the Christian inhabitants in Trichur and surrounding areas in

* *Sources*: 1. Xavier Koodapuzha (Dr.), *Christianity in India.*
2. Most Rev. Cyril Mar Basselios, Syro Malankara Church.

that period of time were predominantly St. Thomas Christians. As those resettled families had no church in the vicinity for worship, the King gifted a piece of land and timber for building a Church. The settlers built the Church on the gifted land, dedicated it to Virgin Mary and named the Church as *Vyakulamathavin Valiapally* (Big Church of Our Lady of Dolours). The *Theettooram* (the royal Grant) of the King in favour of Iso Joseph (Jesus S/o Joseph) is still available in the archives of the Church. The problem of worship was solved and things went on peacefully. The later development of Trichur town as a commercial centre justified the attempts of the King.

Faith and Practices

This Church accepts the Nicene Creed without the later additions of *Filioque* and *Theotokos*. They follow the ancient Chaldean Syriac liturgy of Adai and Mari with the anaphora of Theodore of Mapsuestia and Nestorius. Blessed Virgin Mary is addressed only as 'Mother of Christ' and not as 'Mother of God'. Auricular confession is not practised. Communion in both species is insisted. Leavened bread is compulsory for Holy Eucharist. Lent for 50 days, 25 days prior to Christmas, 15 days prior to the death of Virgin Mary and 3 days in memory of the Fast of Ninavites are observed with strict abstinence. Episcopal system is followed in administration with compulsory celibacy for bishops and permission for marriage for priests, even after ordination. The Julian calendar is followed. Images and Relics are forbidden.

The chronological history of the heads of this church is as below:

From 1815-1860	No bishops.
From 1861-1882	Bishops Rokos and Mellus.
From 1882-1908	Bishops Abdiso and Augustine.
From 1908-1972	Nestorian bishops.

In the first period with no bishops, Archdeacon Abraham of Palai and his successor Joseph Cor Episcopa ruled from 1815-1830 and 1830-1849 respectively. During the succeeding

ST. THOMAS CHRISTIANS IN INDIA – PRESENT POSITION

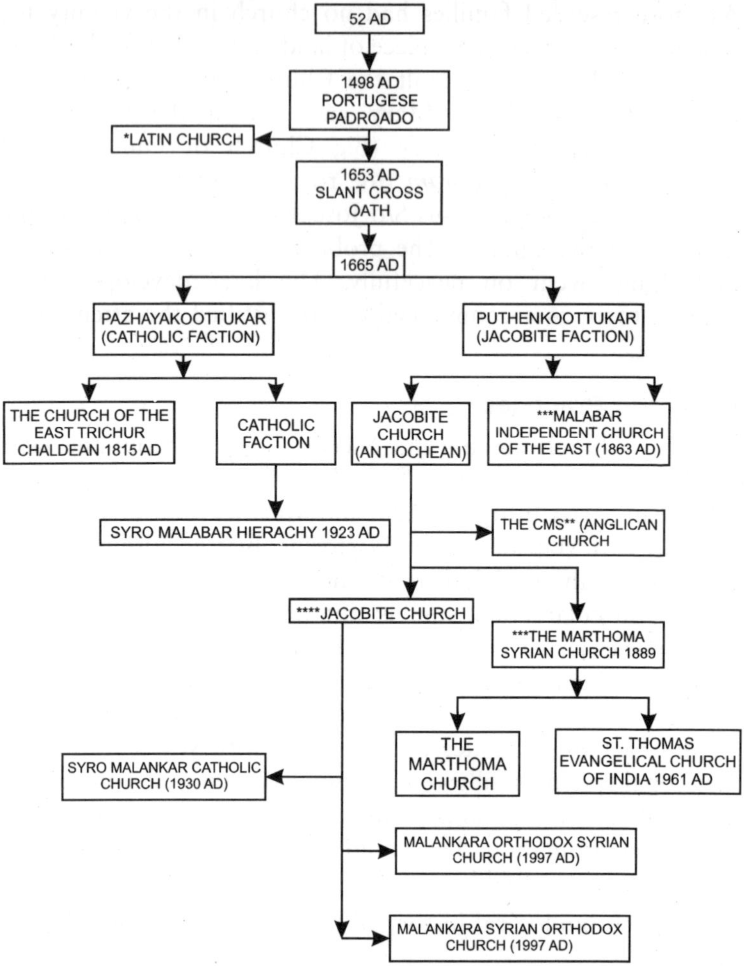

* The exit to the Latin Church was not the result of a schism or collective action.

** The exit to the Anglican Church was due to personal preference for Reform Ideology.

*** The years 1863 and 1889 given against the Malabar Independent Church and the Mar Thomas Syrian Church are based on final judgments of the Madras High Court and the Travancore Royal Court respectively.

**** A vertical split in the Jacobite Church occurred when that Church forsook the name Jacobite Church. Both parties changed their eleven years from 1849-1860, this Church was under the administration of one Denha Bariona who was deputed to Malabar by the Catholic Chaldean Patriarch, Nicholas Zeyl.

The Chaldean East Syrian Church

Please see the chronology of Bishops given on page 391. A Catholic Bishop, Mar Elias Mellus reached Malabar in 1874. With the strong support of the Syro Malabar Church, he continued up to 1882. In the litigation that ensued, the Mellusian faction won the civil suit. In 1908, a Persian Bishop called Timotheos Mar Abhimelek was welcomed by the dissidents. After the death of Mar Abhimelek in 1945, one Fr. Konikara Poulose governed them as administrator till 1949. After a vacancy of three years, Patriarch Mar Simon sent Bishop Mar Thoma Dharmo to Trichur. He formulated a constitution of the community which resulted in a conflict. In 1968, Mar Thoma Dharmo returned to Baghdad and became a rival Patriarch. There were a series of attempts for reconciliation. Finally, a conciliation was arrived at on 13th Nov. 1995 deciding the Bishops to share leadership by rotation. This is the arrangement now in vogue in this Church.

In the early stages itself, groupism emerged in this Church leading to litigations. One speciality of this small Church is that it is behind none in the matter of litigations. Besides Trichur, this church has parishes in Ernakulam, Cochin and Madras. It is ludicrous to note that bishops of Catholic, Nestorian and Chaldean Churches have ruled this church at one time or other.[9]

(A chart showing the present position of the St. Thomas Christians in India is shown on page 392.)

---

name for legal advantages in litigations. Consequently, each group independently named their church in 1997 AD as (1) Malankara Orthodox Syrian Church and (2) Malankara Syrian Orthodox Church. The Jacobite Church which existed for several centuries undortunately sank into oblivion in Malabar. The two entries in the Church thus occurred.

FOOTNOTES

1. George Menachery (Prof.), *The St. Thomas Christian Encyclopaedia of India*, p. 54.
2. Xavier Koodapuzha (Dr.), *Christianity in India*, pp. 140-41.
3. *Ibid.*, pp. 145-49.
4. Mathew, K.V. (Dr.), *The Faith and Practices of Marthoma Church*, p. 8.
5. Alexander Marthoma Metropolitan (Dr.), *The Marthoma Church – Heritage and Mission*, p. 107.
6. *Ibid.*, p. 17.
7. Yuhanon Mar Thoma (Dr.), *The Christian Church in India and the Concise History of the Mar Thoma Church*, pp. 94-104.
8. *Statistics published in the Catholic Malankara Directory 2004.*
9. George Menachery, *St. Thomas Christian Encyclopaedia*, pp. 91-94.

The Latin Catholic Church in India

23

Introduction

The Latin Catholic Church first came to India in the sixteenth century through the Portuguese Padroado and in the seventeenth century through the Congregation of Propaganda Fide. At first, this Church spread in Malabar. Therefrom, it spread to Goa and the Western coast. St. Francis Xavier was instrumental in spreading this Church in the eastern coast of the peninsular India. As on today, the Latin Church is present in almost all States in India. The role of the Syro Malabar Church in this endeavour is not only significant, but also really commendable. The vast majority of the evangelists, priests, nuns and bishops in the initial period, who worked in almost all States in India, hailed from the St. Thomas Christians of Kerala.

Prior to the arrival of the Portuguese in India in 1498, many foreign missionaries visited India, either en route their journey to China, Tibet etc. or totally for mission work in India. John Monte Corvino (1292), Jordanus de Ceverac (1325-30), Odoric of Pordenone (1324) and John Marinjoli (1348) are few among them. They baptised many, either individually or collectively. Evidences show the stray presence of Christianity in the Western Coast of India from Surat to Cape Comorin in the Pre-Portuguese period. These isolated communities almost became extinct for want of proper organisational structure and follow up. In 1329, Pope John XXII established a diocese named *Columbum*. There is no evidence to identify *Columbum* with Kollam or any other place in India.

Latin Church in Kerala Region

Organised evangelisation under a well-planned strategy took place only after the arrival of the Portuguese in the Malabar coast, accompanied by adequate missionary personnel and equipped with the powers under the Padroado. In subsequent years, many St. Thomas Christians also embraced Latin Rite for personal reasons like conviction, convenience, personal preference etc. This resulted in an unofficial division in the Latin Rite, colloquially termed as *Ezhunoottikar* and *Anjoottikar*, probably to distinguish between the early converts from the upper classes and new converts from the lower classes. This distinction existed for long with prohibition for inter-marriages, but with the educational and economic advancement of the community, this distinction is gradually withering away. The establishment of the Padroado diocese at Goa and its later upgradation as Archdiocese with Cochin as suffragan diocese in 1557 gave a fillip to the growth of the Latin Church into a well-organised hierarchical entity.

At first, the Portuguese concentrated their mission work in Calicut, where Gama landed first. Later, when relations with the Zamorin (King) of Kozhikode became strained and resulted in the murder of three Franciscans, the missionaries fled to other areas like Cannanore, Cochin and Kollam. Cochin became the headquarters of the Portuguese Viceroy. The Dominicans, the Augustinians and the Jesuits joined hands with the Franciscans. Portuguese Governor Albuquerque (1509 to 1515) devised a great plan of encouraging Portuguese soldiers to marry native women to produce children so that the next generation would remain loyal to the Church. Financial assistance and other inducements were resorted to win people for baptism. The letters of the King of Cannanore show that the early baptisms were from the low castes (*Thiyas*, *Muccuva* slaves and vassals). On 20th December 1514, Pero Mascarenhas wrote to the King of Portugal stating that 6000 people were baptised in and around Cochin. At the beginning of the 17th century, the number of Catholics in and around Cochin became numerous, spread over several parishes and a Cathedral at Cochin. Vincenzo S. Catherina, a Carmelite missionary in

Viaggio alle Indies Orientali mentions about three categories of Christians; the Portuguese soldiers, *Mestici* (born of Portuguese soldiers in Indian women), and the unskilled workers. Arthingal parish, a few miles south of Cochin, became a centre of Latin community. In 1644, there were 30,000 families in the whole of Malabar. Among them, 14,700 were in Kollam under the Jesuits. At Verapoly, 300 people were baptised every year. The new converts were distributed among Latin parishes. The new gentile Christians were called "people who have the law". The Portuguese generally referred to the Christians as 'St. Thomas Christians' and 'our Christians'.

St. Francis Xavier gave a new dimension to the evangelisation efforts. He initially concentrated his attention in areas south of Kollam, particularly, the coastal areas south of Trivandrum up to the Cape Comorin. The results of his personal efforts were fantastic. Though his unparalleled triumph was in the eastern coast from Cape Comorin to Nagapattinam, it is no exaggeration to state that he baptised almost all the inhabitants in the coastal belt, excluding the upper class Hindus, irrespective of their castes. Perhaps, the number personally converted by him far exceeded the number converted by others in the remaining parts of Kerala (Please see separate notes on St. Francis Xavier). Paulinos of St. Bartholomew speaks about the socio-religious situation of the new Christian community as follows:

"I have already noted that the number of these new converts comes upto one hundred thousand and I add another thirty thousand in the vicinity of Cochin alone. They are called *Munducars* (people of white clothes) to distinguish them from *Topasi* who speak Malayalam and Portuguese and put on hats and pants without socks and shoes. All of them were protected by the Dutch company and belonged to the authority of the King of Cochin. To keep them in order and subjection, they had two captains, one for the *Munducars* and the other for the *Topasi* and these two captains direct and rule them and are responsible for them to their authorities in Cochin. They were of very rich families and in business and in wealth they surpassed the Christians of St. Thomas because they were agriculturists while the others were merchants of copra, of oil and of pepper. The Latin Christianity was a great supporter to the Dutch company in Cochin: ...Dutch rule."[1]

"According to the report of Carole de San Conrado, the Catholic Thomas Christians had 263 priests, 82,893 people, 49 parishes and 5 Oratories while the Latin had 29 priests, 40,989 people and 28 parishes and two Oratories."[2]

The historical background of the Archdiocese of Verapoly deserves special mention. Originally, *Verapoly Vicariate Apostolic* of Malabar was erected in 1659 as an interim caretaker arrangement, in the context of the Dutch opposition to the Padroado jurisdiction and to the Jesuits. When the Propaganda Fide established the Latin hierarchy of India in 1886, Verapoly became an Archiepiscopal See of the Latin Church in Kerala. But the Cochin Padroado diocese erected in 1557 continued as the suffragan diocese of the Padroado See of Goa up to 1950.

The establishment of the Latin hierarchy of India by Pope Leo XIII in 1886 served as a fillip for the fantastic growth of the Latin Church in Kerala. Today, we find a flourishing Latin community in Kerala with eleven dioceses divided into two provinces and a population near around fourteen hundred thousand. The details of the dioceses are as below:

Sl. No.	Name of diocese	Year of Est.	Remarks
1.	Cochin	1557	Suffragan of Goa till 1950.
2.	Verapoly(A)	1886	Vicariate Apostolic from 1659.
3.	Kollam	1886	Part of Indian Latin Hierarchy.
4.	Calicut	1923	Bifurcation of Mangalore diocese.
5.	Vijayapuram	1930	Bifurcation of Verapoly diocese.
6.	Kottar*	1930	Bifurcation of Kollam diocese.
7.	Trivandrum(A)	1937	Elevated as Archdiocese – 2005.
8.	Alleppey	1952	Bifurcation of Cochin diocese.
9.	Punalur	1985	Bifurcation of Kollam diocese.
10.	Kottappuram	1987	Carved out from Verapoly.
11.	Neyyattinkara	1996	Trivandrum bifurcated.
12.	Cannannore	1999	Calicut bifurcated.

(A) Represents Archdiocese.

* Kottar transferred to Tamilnadu in 1956 due to States Reorganisation.

The Latin Church in Goa

The Padroado was an agreement between the Pope and the Kings of Portugal and Spain for mutual assistance and help. The agreement invested the Kings with several ecclesiastical rights and privileges in lieu of their evangelisation efforts in the newly discovered territories. The King of Portugal, a staunch supporter of Pope with unflinching loyalty to the Church, complied with the terms and conditions of the agreement in letter and spirit. Portugal attempted all possible means (with their own finance) at their command to attain the goal. (Please see notes on Padroado in chapter 39 of Part Five.) The conquest of Goa was a precious catch from where they could spearhead a campaign to convert not only Goa, but also the surrounding areas. Wherever they got themselves established, they put up forts, churches and hospitals with the co-operation and support of *Misericordia*, a confraternity established in Lisbon in 1498 for undertaking charitable activities in the colonies abroad as means to foster conversions. In their over-enthusiasm, they committed several excesses, but the end result was not only encouraging but also surpassed all expectations. In the beginning of the 19th century, there were 10,000 Christians in Bombay, 4,000 in Golconda, 500 in Surat, 285 in Karwar and 50 in Pune.

The rulers in Goa created a Christian atmosphere by building churches and chapels. A policy of intolerance was evident. Francisco Paes, the high treasury official mentions about a strange policy called '*Rigour of Mercy*'.

"It was the conversion of the pagans which weighed heavily with the King, Our Lord... He was informed that many residents of the Goa Island had become Christians, but many still continued to profess the Hindu faith and to conduct their rites in the temple. On hearing this, the King ordered that all the existing temples of the gentiles be demolished, that no new temples be erected nor gentile rites be celebrated in his sovereign territory. With this '*Rigour of Mercy*' he wanted the extinction of gentile cult and the conversion of all gentiles to our faith."[3]

In tune with the directions of the King, all Hindu temples in the island were destroyed within one year. Some even erected crosses in the Hindu temples. Prisoners captured during wars in Gujarat, Konkan and even Arabia were baptised. Political and naval protection was another means employed effectively to attract people to Christianity. The Great plan of Governor Albuquerque, encouraging marriage of soldiers with native women, was most successfully and widely executed in Goa, though with its inherent abuses. The first provincial council of Goa projected the image of a medieval Western Christianity associated with the spirit of crusade and inquisition. The subsequent Goan councils of 1575, 1585 and 1592 toed the line of *cujus regio, ejus religio* (people of a nation should follow the religion of the ruler). From 1560 onwards, through the ministry of the Franciscans, a Christian community emerged in Bassein and its surroundings. Gradually, the peninsulas of Bardez, Salsette, Diu and Daman became centres of Christian influence. In 1556, a printing press was established in Goa. The fleets usually carried a number of missionaries to India. Material assistance was given to the new converts at the initial stages. But, they were asked to pay 'tithes' after ten years. The entire burden of supporting the missions was borne by the King of Portugal. They received no financial assistance from the Church.

In the early stages, various religious orders worked under the Padroado jurisdiction of their colonial masters. The Franciscans reached Goa in 1510. Jesuits came in 1542, Dominicans in 1548, Augustinians (1572), Carmelites (1612) and the Theatines in 1640. In 1557, Goa was made an Archdiocese with Cochin and Malaca as Suffragan dioceses. For the Churches of Padroado jurisdiction, Goan Archbishop was made the Primate of the East. Subsequently, Macao in China (1576), Funchal in Japan, Mylapore in India, Yanking and Peking in China and the Prelacy in Mozambique were erected suffragan to Goa. The decline of the Padroado paved the way for Propaganda jurisdiction. In 1886, the Goan See was made a *Patriarchate ad honorem* with the new suffragan diocese of Daman. In 1928, the Sees of Daman, Diu and Dadra and Nagar Haveli were suppressed and annexed to Goa. In

1950, Cochin and Mylapore were detached from Goa. After the Independence of India, Goa was annexed to India in 1961.

Blessed Joseph Vaz, the Apostle of Kanara and Ceylon and Venerable Angelo D'Souza hailed from the Church in Goa. Acknowledging the prominence of Goa, the headquarters of the Latin Bishops' Conference of India is now located in Goa. Goa spread their mission centres to other parts of India like Kanara and Fisheries Coast. The Mughul mission was a part of the Padroado jurisdiction. Jesuits reached Akbar's court from Goa and laid the foundation of the Church in Agra, Delhi, Patna and Lahore. In faith, dedication and efficiency, the Goan Christians were not behind their counterparts in other regions in India. A sizeable number of Christians in the surrounding areas of Goa like Kanara, Pune, Bombay etc. are of Goan origin. As such, the Goan Christians are entitled and destined to play a major role in the currently unfolding era of ecumenism in India.

Latin Church in Other Regions of India

Tamilnadu

Next to Kerala, Tamilnadu has the largest Catholic population in India. Though Mylapore is blessed with the tomb of St. Thomas, the early Christianity disappeared in the course of centuries. The present Catholic population traces its origin in the 16th century through the missionaries of Padroado, especially the Jesuits. The outstanding names in this respect are St. Francis Xavier, Robert De Nobilee and John de Britto, the martyr (commonly known as Arulanandar). The role of Joseph Beschi and James de Rossi, who popularised the Christian heritage in Tamilnadu, is also memorable. The suppression of the Society of Jesus in 1773 was a fatal blow to the missionary activities. Consequently, the Paris Society of Foreign Missions with headquarters at Pondicherry was entrusted with the Madurai mission. Due to the French Revolution, they failed to do anything substantial. On revocation of the suppression, the Jesuits were again entrusted with the Madurai mission in 1830. In 1846, Madurai was made a Vicariate Apostolic, but in 1887, it became Tiruchirappally diocese, suffragan to the Archdiocese of Bombay. St. Francis Xavier was the pioneer of the evangelisation process in Tamilnadu, especially the eastern coast from Cape Comorin to Nagapattinam. Robert De Nobilee is remembered as the champion of inculturation. (Please see separate notes on these two evangelists towards the end of the chapter.) John Britto consolidated the fruits of labour of his predecessors, but he became a martyr in his early age and was buried at Oriyoor in Tamilnadu. His relics were subsequently exhumed and transferred to Portugal.

The Church in Tamilnadu is a mixture of various castes, prominent among them being *Dalits* and *Nadars*. 35 per cent of the population of Kanyakumari District are Christians, either Catholics or Protestants. This community is, to a great extent, culturally integrated. Movement of the *Dalits* for liberation and equal status and dignity is a problem still remaining unsolved in many areas of Tamilnadu.

Today Tamilnadu has 17 Latin Catholic dioceses including the latest at Dindigul and Chengleput.

Region of Andhra Pradesh

The Telugu-speaking people constitute the State of Andhra Pradesh. Christianity reached Andhra through the Jesuit missionaries in Karnataka (1689) and Pondicherry (1705-1773). Today the Catholic Church in Andhra Pradesh is an ecclesiastical province headed by the Archdiocese of Hyderabad with eleven suffragan dioceses and a Catholic population of about 900,000, 1.45 per cent of the total population of the State. About 75 per cent of the Catholics are socially, economically and politically marginalised. *Dalit* Christians faced discrimination not only in the society at large, but also within the Church, as in Tamilnadu. This strange situation is diametrically opposed to the Christian concepts of equality, fraternity and communion. The presence of Andhra Church is significant in the field of institutions for healthcare, education and social welfare. The people appreciate these institutions for their discipline, efficiency, service and administration, but in the realm of spirituality and evangelisation, the contribution and appeal of the Church are minimal.

Bishop Gorantla Johannes in his work 'Catholic Mission in the Region of Andhra Pradesh' comments as follows:

> "Owing to its reputation as a dedicated and service-minded institution, the Church receives many invitations, especially from the non-Christians, to serve in different fields. Nevertheless, for many, there is nothing more special in the Church that merited attention except its good administration and set up. They observe that the Church could offer a good education and good social work, but not spiritual riches than what they already have."[4]

Christianity in Andhra appears foreign in its image. For the people, the Church stands for man-made goals. The absence of zeal among the indigenous clergy, acute caste problem in the Church, the alienation of the clerical leadership from the people, failure to assimilate with the culture, art, language etc. are the main handicaps faced by the Church in Andhra. The vision of the kingdom of God, as radical and integral revolution has not made any serious impact on the community inside or outside the Church. The Church seems to have come down to acquiesce and accommodate the caste system. Concrete and effective steps on the part of the Church are warranted to eradicate this anti-Christian menace at all costs. Unless and until this black spot is effaced, the future of the Church in Andhra is foredoomed to failure.

Karnataka Region

Karnataka State, the sixth largest State in India, is situated in between Rivers Cauvery and Godavari, with a population of 52.7 million (2001 Census), out of which Christians constitute only 0.77 million spread over in the Bangalore Archdiocese and six suffragan dioceses. Though Kannada is the official language of the State, several language groups like Konkini, Telegu, Tamil and Urdu are found there.

The origin of Christianity in Karnataka still remains obscure. By the 16th century, early Christianity disappeared when the Portuguese became masters of the Arabian Sea. The relations between the Portuguese and the Vijayanagar Empire were cordial, as Islam became the common enemy of both. The

Portuguese Viceroy Antago de Noronha (1564-68) captured the town of Mangalore and built a fort there. The Jesuits and the Dominicans were entrusted with the missionary work in the area. A majority of the Christians in Mangalore were those migrated from Goa. The new converts were only a minority. In 1722, there were 24,000 Catholics in Kanara according to a census conducted by the Archdiocese of Goa.

In 1652, Sivappa Nayak seized the Portuguese ports in the South and the foreigners were asked to quit from the captured areas. Under a subsequent treaty, Nayak allowed them to work in Kanara. Fr. Joseph Vaz (later Blessed), one of the Goan missionaries worked in Kanara and later went to Ceylon. Thus, the Christians in Kanara belonged to different castes such as *Brahmins, Charodis* (*Kshatrias and Vaisya castes mixed*), *Cudras and Gaudis* (local fishermen caste). Mysore mission came first in the series. The Christian community fell prey to the atrocious persecution of Tipu Sultan. He forcibly converted many to Islam. On one occasion, 80,000 Christians were taken as captives; but only 10,000 out of them returned. What happened to others, no one knows. The Protestant missionaries also worked in the area in the first half of the nineteenth century. The Vicariate of Mangalore was established in 1853. In 1879, the Holy See put Kanara under the care of the Jesuit province of Venice. Later, it became a diocese in 1887. In 1923, the diocese of Mangalore was divided and the Calicut diocese was formed for the areas in Malabar. At present, Mangalore has a Catholic population of 3,20,300. The areas in the diocese of Bangalore were earlier a part of Mysore diocese with its headquarters at Bangalore. In 1953, Bangalore was upgraded as an Archdiocese. In 1928, the two districts of Raichur and Gulbarga were detached from the diocese of Hyderabad and the new mission *Sui Juris* was created and in 1949 it was raised as the diocese of Bellary. The other dioceses later created were Chickmagaloor (1963), Karwar (1973) and Shimoga (1988). In 1941, the diocese of Mysore was reconstituted by annexing the district of Oottacamund and a part of Coimbatore district. Later, these areas were separated from Mysore and the Oottacamund diocese was created. Here, we note that the

Karnataka mission succeeded in laying the solid foundation of a Church in Karnataka State by the contributions of the dedicated missionaries who manned the mission.[5]

Bombay Region

The origin of the Christian mission in the Bombay region is associated with the Surat mission of the Mendicant monks from the Middle East. Jordanus de Severac and companions reached Surat and began mission work in the nearby areas, but few of them became martyrs at Thane, in the 14th century. Some early records show that they were buried in a Church dedicated to Apostle St. Thomas. In the sixteenth century, few Franciscan and Jesuit missionaries joined the mission. The services of a Franciscan missionary named Antonio De Porto remains outstandingly memorable in this respect. But, the decline of the Portuguese and the emergence of the Dutch and English powers altered the political scene.

In 1637, the Congregation of Propaganda Fide established the Vicariate Apostolic of Bijapur, outside the Padroado. This resulted in a friction between Padroado and Propaganda Fide as the Padroado viewed it as a rival claim encroaching upon their rights and hesitated to accept it. In 1665, the islands of Bombay were taken over by the British. The Vicar Apostolic of Bijapur was shifted to Karwar (1712-17) and later to Bombay in 1717 with title 'the Vicar Apostolic of the Great Mughul'. In 1720, four Padroado Churches (*Upper Mahim, Lower Mahim, Mazagon* and *Fort*) were transferred to the Vicar Apostolic of the Great Mughul. This resulted in 'double jurisdiction' in the Latin hierarchy. In the beginning of the nineteenth century, there were ten thousand Catholics in Bombay, mainly the descendants of the early converts in Bombay, Goa and Mangalore areas. Along with them, there were converts from the scheduled castes in Pune and scheduled tribes in Thane District. In addition to these, a large number of Christians migrated to Bombay from Gujarat, Tamilnadu, Kerala etc. in search of jobs. The Syro Malabar Catholics in Bombay at present come around one hundred thousand.

The presence of the Church in Bombay was conspicuously in the field of education. The Catholics in Bombay are generally identified with the English speaking community. The Marathi and Konkani speaking Catholics do not seem to enjoy all the facilities and advantages available for the English speaking section.

J.V. Velinkar S.J. observed in the 'Catholic Mission in the Region of Bombay' as follows:

"The Church's influence in society has not been commensurate with the number of its institutions. In the city, this could be accounted for by the alien cultural appearance, the Church is perceived to have. Most priests and nuns in Bombay and its surroundings speak English well, but Hindi and Marathi poorly. Consequently, the medium of communication with government officials and other personalities is in English. Their impact on the social, political and cultural life is minimal. Even in the Hindi films, Christian men are depicted as drunkards and Christian women as being of loose morals. In literary awards, names of Christians rarely figure."[6]

Most of the clergy are unable to speak Marathi and Hindi properly and hence their influence on the society at large is relatively poor.

J.V. Velinkar S.J. adds:

"The leadership of the bishops, priests, religious and laity leaves much to be desired. In the sphere of communication, generally they are not able to communicate with the other leaders and government except through the medium of English. Moreover, Christian leadership mainly rests in the Cardinal Archbishop, and it is he who speaks to the civil and political leaders as the respected representative of the Christians. No other leader is taken cognisance of in the region. Unless the Christians of this region become fluent in speaking Marathi, Konkani and Hindi, it will not be easy for them to establish deeper and more effective contact and rapport with the non-Christians and work towards common solutions at various levels and make their impact felt."[7]

The vision for the future is bright, provided the Church is prepared to identify with the people and their culture. The Church should never be identified as a clerical kingdom. The leadership is to build up the community with a profound sense of solidarity and co-responsibility.

The Gujarat Region

Geographically, Gujarat is situated as a passage between the Middle East and the Far East. Christianity also reached India through this passage. In the fourteenth century, there were churches dedicated to Apostle St. Thomas in Gujarat. Dominicans, Jesuits, Capuchins, Franciscans and Carmelites worked in this region. The Ahmedabad mission was started only in the last decade of the 19th century. In 1891, Gujarati Vankars working in the convent of the Daughters of the Cross in Bandhra in Bombay were baptised. In 1893, Bishop of Bombay deputed one Fr. Manuel Gomes to Gujarat for mission work. German Jesuits started working at Anand in 1894. The Anand Credit Co-operative Society founded in 1914 by Fr. Zurhausen became the backbone of the Christian community. Humanisation became the basis for Christianisation. The Jesuits of Aragon province of Spain took over this mission during World War I. In 1933, the Ahmedabad mission was separated from Bombay as a distinct unit.

The great famine of 1899-1900 provided the Church with an opportunity for humanitarian service to the poor. The missionary activities were begun in Bharuch, Surat, Valsad and the Dangs districts. In the seventies, the arrival of Carmelites of Mary Immaculate (CMI) in Saurashtra was a turning point in the missions. The Salesians (SDB), Divine Word (SVVD) and SFX Religious congregations strengthened the missions with emphasis on orthopaxy (integral development for the cause of justice, truth, equality and freedom). Some of the activities undertaken were 'Food for work', irrigation projects, loans of seeds, fertilizers, buffaloes, dairy co-operatives, training in farming, encouraging saving habits, income generating projects for women, literacy drive for women through *Mahila Mandals* (association of women), social forestry, health care, soil conservation, water-shed management, remedial education and so on.

A thought-provoking observation of a Dalit leader V.T. Rajasekhar is copied below:

"It has to be admitted that no body in India has done so much service to *Dalits* and Tribals as the Christians. Those who are afflicted by the cancer of caste – the upper caste people – are criticising conversions, not because they are interested in the welfare of the untouchables, but because such conversions will deprive them of free servants."[8]

Catholic institutions enjoy good reputation. Caste mentality deeply embedded in the minds of the people remains a threat to integral human development. Clericalism is another area that does not promote collective responsibility. It is another form of casteism. Clerical kingdom cannot be identified with God's Kingdom. Clerical monopoly of the ecclesiastical administration makes the people of God mere onlookers. So long as the Church accommodated these vices, it has nothing much to desire, especially in a community like Gujaratis, who are by very nature conservative, superstitious and casteist in both thinking and action.

Chotanagpur Region

Nearly 90 per cent of the people of Chotanagpur Santhal Pargana Region are tribals belonging to *Munda, Khariah* and *Oraon* communities among the tribals. Before conversion to Christianity, they belonged to a pagan religion, believing in a God whom they call *Ponomeshwar, Shingthonga* and *Dharmes*. They observed omens and taboos and traditional rituals to appease their god and the spirits. They were living peacefully in the mountainous forests without any interference from outside. In the 17th and 18th centuries, outsiders occupied their areas and demanded exorbitant taxes from them. This intrusion upset their social, economic and cultural life. They became strangers in their own lands. Their god failed to protect them. In this crisis situation, the Lutheran missionaries, who reached there in 1845 defended them from the intruders and attracted many to the Lutheran Church. They faced stiff opposition from the British. Eventually, the Lutherans withdrew from the area. The tribals felt betrayed by the missionaries. In this situation, one

Fr. Constant Lievens, a Belgian Jesuit missionary offered them leadership and hope. Fr. Lievens offered assistance to those who were prepared to accept Christianity on condition that the entire village should convert. He discouraged individual conversions, which may in the longrun disrupt their peace, harmony and cultural ethos. The result was unbelievable. People began to approach Lievens representing the whole village. He employed catechetical instructors to teach them on Christianity. Lievens reached Chotanagpur on March 18th, 1885. By 1892, the number baptised rose to 36,000, really a marvellous achievement.

Lievens was afflicted by tuberculosis. In 1892, he unwillingly returned to Belgium. He passed away in 1893 at Louvain. Along with the disappearance of Fr. Lievens, the missionaries withdrew from the scene. This caused disappointment among the community. There was none to help them to recover their dispossessed lands. The Congregation superiors realised their grievance. The arrival of Fr. John Baptist Hoffmann and his efficient leadership changed the situation. The Chotanagpur Tenancy Act of 1908 safeguarded the right of possession of lands in 400 villages. Partial proprietary rights were restored for another 800 villages. In 1909, Fr. Hoffman registered the 'Chotanagpur Catholic Mission Society'. In 1913, the 'Chotanagpur Catholic Co-operative Stores' was also registered. The missionary method was to liberate the people from the oppressors and restore human dignity to them. The contribution in the field of education qualified them socially, culturally and intellectually.

In 1927, the diocese of Ranchi was erected. It was upgraded as an Archdiocese in 1952. On July 2nd, 1962, Jamshedpur diocese was erected. After World War II, several other missionaries opted to work in Chotanagpur area. Today, the hapless tribals of yesteryears live with dignity and self-respect just like other citizens in India. The history of Chotanagpur mission is the history of emancipation of people from oppression and tyranny. The missionaries evangelised themselves before evangelising others. The Ranchi mission reveals the history of humanising the society as a means for preparation for evangelisation. Today, the Ranchi Province has one Archdiocese and the Archbishop of Ranchi is one among the Cardinals in India.

Fidelis de Sa in his 'Crisis in Chotanagpur' states as follows:

"The policy adopted by Lievens encouraged the feelings of solidarity and the large scale conversion of the villages. He even told the villagers that he wanted the entire village to come together or else he would accept no one. This may seem strange today, but the words were addressed to a different audience in a different age and in a different situation. Strange as it may seem to readers today, Lievens' move was well intended, and even prudent, especially if one keeps in mind the clan organisation of the *Mundas*. By coming over in entire families and entire villages, the *Mundas* could preserve their social organisation; besides preserving peace in the villages."[9]

Region of West Bengal

The present religious affiliations of the people in West Bengal are: Hindus 77 per cent, Muslims 21.5 per cent, Christians 0.65 per cent, Buddhists 0.3 per cent and others 0.6 per cent. The high percentage of Hindus shown above is due to the classification of tribals and Adivasis as Hindus. Bengali is the official language of the State spoken by 85.4 per cent of the population. Hindi, Santhali and Urdu are also spoken by a minor percentage of people, 6 per cent, 3 per cent and 2 per cent respectively. There is no trace of any early Christianity there. The history of Christianity starts only with the arrival of the Portuguese. The early missionaries were those who accompanied the Portuguese, the Dominicans and the Augustinians, who established themselves at Hoogly. With the arrival of the British, the Portuguese influence declined. This altogether changed the evangelisation scenario in favour of the English Protestants. The contributions of Keinander, William Carey and Duff had a lasting influence on the cultural and religious leadership of Bengal. An array of outstanding Hindu leaders emerged and came to the forefront. Among them, Raja Ram Mohan Roy, Rabindranath Tagore, K.C. Sen,

Sri Ramakrishna, Vivekananda and Bankim Chandra Chatterjee deserve special mention. In this period, we notice a Hindu Renaissance, not confined to Bengal alone, but all over India. The Congregation of Propaganda Fide sent English Jesuits to Bengal and erected the Vicariate of Calcutta in 1834. The main concentration of attention of the Jesuits was on the institutional infrastructure for educational and charitable services. Daughters of the Cross, Sisters of Cluny, Loretto Sisters, Little Sisters of the poor and Irish Christian Brothers were actively involved in the missionary field.

In the modern church in Bengal, the image of Mother Teresa and her 'Missionaries of Charity' had a very big positive impact. She represented and projected the real Christian image before the public that really touched the human hearts at large, resulting in the unconditional acceptance of the values for which she stood for. The miseries caused by the influx of refugees and other calamities offered plenty of opportunities for extending Christian charity to the suffering people. Fr. Constant Lievens produced marvellous results in his work among the tribals presenting the Christian Church as a liberative force from exploitation and unjust social structure. But, the identification of the Catholic mission with English education and dependence on foreign personnel had a negative impact on the indigenous image of Christianity in its authenticity.

The future prospects of the Church in Bengal depend on its ability to identify herself with the problems of the people and its capacity to become the voice of the voiceless and the defenders of the defenceless. The crop is ripe, but the trained harvesters are few.

Region of Orissa

Orissa is comparatively a small undeveloped State in India, rich in resources, but economically backward. The religious affiliations of the people show that 95.42 per cent are Hindus, 1.82 per cent Christians and 1.60 per cent Muslims. The non-Catholic Christians outnumber the Catholics. The Catholic Church has an ecclesiastical province headed by the Cuttack-Bhubaneswar Archdiocese with four suffragan dioceses, Balasore, Berhampur, Rourkela and Sambalpur.

The Padroado missionaries in Balasore first initiated the missionary activities. In 1908, the Gangpur mission came under the Jesuits. In 1948, the Divine Word missionaries took over the Gangpur mission. The Congregation of the Missions (C.M.) runs the common philosophate at Gopalpur. The Regional Theologate at Berhampur came under the Society of the Divine Word. This Church is very actively involved in the areas of education and Health Care.

The caste system is deeply rooted among the people. The *Dalits* endure discrimination both inside and outside the Church. Clericalism stands in the way of co-responsibility and hence hampers unity and harmony of the 'People of God'. A realistic and practical scheme for the integral development of the human being, planned and executed diligently by the Church seems the only solution to foster evangelisation.

Region of North-East India

The term North-East India refers to seven States – Assam, Nagaland, Meghalaya, Arunachal Pradesh, Mizoram, Tripura and Manipur – situated on the North and East of Bangladesh. The Christian population in these seven States together constitutes 12 per cent of the total Christian population in India. The Protestant missionaries arrived in these areas very early. The Catholics came only in 1891. The first Catholic missionaries were four German Salvadorians who were deputed for the pastoral care of the Catholics in the army. Being Germans, they were kept in confinement during World War I. In 1915, there were 5176 Catholics and 1700 Catechumens, who hailed from the *Khasi-Pnars* tribe working in the tea-gardens of the Brahmaputra Valley.

From 1915-1921, the Belgian Jesuits took over the mission from the Salvadorians. In 1922, a group of Salesians of Don Bosco arrived in the scene under the leadership of Fr. Louis Mathias, who was later appointed the Prefect Fr. Apostolic and the entire Assam Mission was put under the charge of the Salesians. In 1934, Mathias was ordained the first Bishop of Assam. When Bishop Mathias was transferred to Madras in 1936, the number of Catholics in the area was 50,000. In 1947, the missions were extended to new areas like Manipur, Nagaland and Mizoram. In 1951, the new Diocese of Dibrugarh was carved out of Upper Assam and the hill areas of Nagaland and Manipur. Gradually, the North-Eastern States together became a full-fledged Ecclesiastical Province with Shillong as the Archdiocese.

The first mission efforts in Meghalaya were concentrated among the *Khasi-Pnars* of the Jaintia Hills. Many subgroups among them are matrilineal in their social structure. Now, 25 per cent of the Catholics are tribals forming the bulk of the population of the Shillong Archdiocese. In Mizoram, a major section of Catholics hail from the Mizo group. The diocese of Kohima is basically a Naga Church. The diocese of Imphal is of the Manipuri Naga tribes. Translation of the Bible into the vernacular is one of the effective means for evangelisation. The Church is fully conscious of the necessity to share the responsibilities of evangelisation with the natives. Today the Church in the North-East is a fast growing Church with an appreciable number of vocations. Here, it is essential to present Christianity as a movement for integral development of humanity.

Region of Uttar Pradesh

The State of Uttar Pradesh has recently been divided into two States; Uttaranchal and Uttar Pradesh. As separate details of these States are not yet forthcoming, here we refer to the original Uttar Pradesh before division. It is the most populous State in India with many temples, shrines, sages, Rishis and several other Holy Places of Hindus like Gangotri, Rishikesh, Badrinath etc. situated in the high mountains in the North. The religious affiliations of Uttar Pradesh are classified as Hindus (83%), Muslims (15.9%), Christians (0.2%), Sikhs (0.4%), Buddhists (0.16%), Jains (0.1%) etc. The history of Christianity in the State starts only with the arrival of three Jesuits at Emperor Akbar's Court. The Agra mission was originally formed as a part of the Tibet mission of the Capuchins. In 1784, the Vicariate of Mughul was attached to the Prefecture Apostolic of Tibet. In 1820, the Prefecture Apostolic of Tibet-

Hindustan was constituted as the Vicariate Apostolic of Agra, the mother diocese of many other dioceses in North India.

At present, the Religious congregations in the field of education represent the Church in urban areas. Health and Hygiene are other areas of Christian presence. The recent surveys revealed the need for greater presence in rural areas. Co-operation, dialogue and common celebrations with non-Catholic Christians and non-Christians are seen more effective for creating a conducive atmosphere for evangelisation. Monastic way of life is also found more attractive. The existing seminary type formation of clergy is outdated. This has to be revamped and reoriented to suit the purpose at hand. Institutions may bring more commandability and reputation, but there is nothing much to be desired from them in the realms of spirituality and evangelisation. Armchair administration and management and bureaucratic approaches cannot attain the targeted results. Gospel values have to be upheld for being felt by the people, who are to be convinced of the values for which the Church stands for.

In 1886, Agra diocese was upgraded as Archdiocese with Allahabad as suffragan diocese. Today the number of suffragan dioceses has become nine, one outside UP, two Syro Malabar dioceses and six Latin dioceses.

Source: Xavier Koodapuzha (Dr.), *Christianity in India*, pp. 220-22.

Region of Madhya Pradesh

The State of Madhya Pradesh has also been bifurcated recently. Here, we deal with the original Madhya Pradesh before bifurcation, the biggest State in India with a population of 81.2 million (2001 Census). Out of this, the tribals and scheduled castes constitute one third of the population of the State with majority in 23 out of 45 civil districts.

The Catholic Church became involved in this area with the arrival of three Jesuits in the Court of Emperor Akbar. During the British rule, there were Catholics in the Army and Railway towns. Later, Catholics from Kerala, Mangalore and Goa migrated to this area in large numbers. The Chota Nagpur mission exerted much influence in areas bordering the Diocese of Raigarh and Ambikapur. The Capuchin missionaries began to work in the princely States of Jabuva and Barwani. The Divine Word missionaries took up the work of the Capuchins. Fransalians and Franciscan brothers of Mt. Poinsur developed a community of few thousand Catholics along the Narmada banks. Sisters of the St. Joseph of Chambery in 1894 opened a school at Khandwa. In 1928, the Norbertines reached Jabalpur. The Carmelites of Mary Immaculate began their work at Jagadalpur and Sagar. Missionary Society of St. Thomas at Ujjain and Vincentians at Satna also had done hard work. Several Women Religious Organisations of the Syro Malabar Church took up missionary activities in various dioceses of Madhya Pradesh. The ecclesial community of Madhya Pradesh is composed of Goans, Mangaloreans and Anglo-Indians, those in the cantonments and railway colonies and those from Kerala with traditional Catholic background. A planned strategy with central co-ordination and follow up is difficult as the militant Rashtriya Swayam Sevak Sangh (R.S.S.), the Viswa Hindu Parishad, Ram Rajya Parishad and Arya Samaj in Hinduism are opposed to missionary activities.

Madhya Pradesh is an ecclesiastical province headed by the Bhopal Archdiocese and ten suffragan dioceses, of which four are of the Syro Malabar Church.

The Dalit Liberation Movement

Casteism is a deep-rooted cancer in the socio-political body of India. Hinduism ascribes a divine origin for casteism. Segregation of people based on ethnic origin, race, caste, colour, religion, occupation etc. existed in India even in the prehistoric period. The Aryans who migrated to India from the Mesopotamian areas found caste discrimination advantageous to them to sustain their identity, vested interests and primacy. On becoming priests and rulers, the Aryans enacted laws for the strict maintenance of the system in a way beneficial to them. Consequently, a flexible and feeble segregation in the initial stages gradually acquired rigidity and harshness, supported by a legal framework. In the course of centuries, the practice became more and more inhuman with resultant vices like untouchability, apartheid, slavery, exploitation etc. The unkindest cut of all was the exclusion of a sizeable section of the people from the ladder of castes identified and labelled as forest dwellers, menial labourers, toiling masses, 'uncivilised' and so on. They had no rights whatsoever, not even the right to life. If at all they had a right, it was a right to work, as and when commanded, for the benefit of their masters in the upper castes, till death. To borrow a phrase of Earl Bertrand Russell, the outcastes in India could revolt against their oppressors 'only when the sheep could revolt against the shepherd'. In yesteryears, they were known as 'Harijans' (people of God – a name given by Gandhiji), 'Girijans', 'tribals', 'Adivasis' etc. Lately, all these groups are known by a common nomenclature 'Dalits'.

In 1947, when India became independent, the Indian Constitution provided a democratic Republic based on Universal Adult Suffrage. Resultantly, all on a sudden, all adult *Dalits* were armed with the weapon of 'vote'. The politicians enlightened them on the invaluable value of the vote. For the first time in history, the Indian *Dalits* became conscious of their rights; the mighty elephant, which had never seen its body in the past due to the screen-like ears, saw its body and realised its power and strength. The post-independence period witnesses and signifies this transition of the *Dalits* from misery and oppression to liberation. They aspire for an abrupt transition to a new social order. Any delay in this respect makes them impatient and restless at the slightest provocation, landing them in confrontations and quarrels in and out of place. This phenomenon is clearly visible in all walks of life in India at present.

Casteism now stands abolished in the country under the law; it lost its tooth and nail. The upper classes lost the rights and privileges they enjoyed for generations. Many of them are mentally unable to reconcile with the emerging scenario. Their perceptions and perspectives are still influenced by casteism. Both groups have their own justifications and grievances. Even slightest doubts on the intentions of the opposite camp would enrage and provoke violent reaction. Two warring groups, one to continue the rights and privileges enjoyed for long and the other to enforce the rights and privileges obtained, face each other. This is the picture outside the Church.

When Christianity started evangelisation work in India, their first option was to target the *Dalits* for obvious practical considerations. Firstly, they were the downtrodden and neglected part of the community requiring integral development. Secondly, they had no organised religion and as such a new religion with the ideals of equality, liberty and human dignity would find spontaneous acceptance. As expected by the evangelists, the Christian ideals were attractive to them as a means to cast away the stigma and subjugation attached to their life and to secure recognition in the mainstream of public life. More than spirituality and salvation, the *Dalits* were motivated to accept Christianity by their urge for liberation from shackles and aspirations for a life of dignity and self-respect. When discrimination outside the Church was experienced within the Church as well, the result was despair and impatience.

Instances of even local clergy aligning and lobbying on caste lines are not rare. This is the background of the *Dalit* Movements within the Church.

This is a general feature noticed, more or less, all over the Church in India. When the government denied to the Christian *Dalits* the rights and privileges granted to the Hindu *Dalits*, the situation became tense. Wherever the *Dalit* population, particularly in parishes or dioceses, is dominant, the situation, at times, assumes aggressive dimensions. Tamilnadu, Andhra, Orissa and Gujarat are the States worst affected by this menace. In Kanyakumari district of Tamilnadu, 70 per cent of the members of the Church are *Dalits*. This vexed problem remains a headache to the entire Church in India.

A uniform solution applicable to all areas is impracticable as the situation differs in each area. This vice germinated from the degeneration of spirituality. Hence, both temporal and spiritual solutions may be warranted. Let the Church collectively think over it with the seriousness it deserves.

St. Francis Xavier

No student of history of Christianity in India can bypass the unique contribution of St. Francis Xavier, who played the role of a pioneer in establishing the catholic missions in the East on a solid foundation. Born in Navarre in Spain in 1506, he was brought up in his childhood fully committed to the burning zeal for the salvation of all. He gradually associated himself with the religious renewal movement initiated by St. Ignatius Loyola. Later he became one of the seven founder-members of the "Society of Jesus" along with St. Loyola. After ordination to priesthood, he made his profession on August 15, 1534. The King of Portugal endowed Francis with the faculty of 'Apostolic Commissioner' (a privilege granted by Pope Alexander VI to the King) and 'unexpectedly' deputed him to the missions in the Far East. Accordingly, Francis Xavier reached Goa in 1542.

Even from the beginning of his mission, Francis Xavier was concerned with two aspects: (i) formation of those already baptised, and (ii) discipline among the religious and the clergy, especially those from Portugal. The crux of his mission was his sincere and firm belief that those who are not baptised 'will be lost'. He spent fifteen months at Fishery coast and baptised thousands in different places from Cape Comorin to Nagapattinam. Wherever he baptised, he took particular care to impart catechetical instructions to those baptised. For this purpose, he trained selected local people for the care of those baptised. His missionary vision was not confined to the Indian coasts alone. Many other countries were included in his agenda. From 1545 to 1548, he visited Malacca and Indonesia. He returned to India in 1548 and proceeded to Japan in 1549 with his Japanese convert Anjiro. After returning from Japan, his final journey in 1552 was to China. While he was waiting for an opportunity to enter China, he died at Sancian on 3rd December 1552 and was buried there. Later, his body was taken to Malacca and thence to Goa. Pope Gregory XV canonised him in 1622.

He introduced a popular method for catechetical instructions. Children and adults were separately taught prayers.

Wherever he moved, he appointed catechists in those centres for education in the local languages and Christian formation. In 1552, he was made Provincial of the Society of Jesus in India and the East. He was a strict disciplinarian against immorality and idolatry. He never hesitated to take action against even his own compatriots whose practical life was a mockery of their own religion. As a disciplinarian with overall responsibility for the entire missions, he took strong decisions including the expulsion of members from the Society of Jesus. Anglican historian C. Bruce Firth said that he can be compared only with St. Paul.[10]

Francis Xavier was not an isolated missionary. He was a pioneer with solid vision, untiring energy, unshakeable faith, burning zeal and whole-hearted dedication, a combination of all the virtues of a missionary.[11]

Robert De Nobilee

Robert De Nobilee was an Italian Jesuit missionary, genealogically attached to the Royal family of Italy deputed to India by his Provincial Laerzio to study the missionary situation in India. He chose Madurai in Tamilnadu, the centre of Dravidian culture in India, for his mission work and studies. He discovered that Christianity spread by the Western missionaries was something looked down with contempt by the cultured section of the Indians. J. Thehekkedath in his work 'History of Christianity in India' observed as follows:

"De Nobilee found out that the chief reason was the contempt which Indians in general had for the *Paranghis* or the Portuguese, who did not bathe frequently, who ate beef, drank liquor and communicated freely with persons of the most despised castes. The *Paranghis* were considered to be on par with the untouchables and outcastes of India. They were regarded as polluting, like the *Paraiahs*; and anyone who joined them or received baptism from them would straightaway lose all the titles of nobility and be covered with infamy for the rest of his life."[12]

Among the hundreds or thousands of Christian missionaries who came from the West to spread Christianity in India,

Robert de Nobilee conspicuously stood apart from others. While most of his contemporaries identified themselves with the interests of their Kings, the culture of their nations and the transplanting of Western Christianity lock, stock and barrel, Robert Nobilee was impressed by the great cultural heritage of India. He discovered that the easy path to the hearts of the cultured Indians was assimilation with their cultural ethos. While the mission policy of others was colonial in its nature and character, while the methods they adopted were conquest, power and superiority, while the approach they accepted was marked by intolerance, domination and triumphalism, Robert De Nobilee chose a solitary path of his own. He followed a policy of fraternity, a method of interaction and dialogue and an approach of asceticism and inculturation, in sharp contrast with the colonial approach. He studied Sanskrit, learnt the Indian *Vedas*, entered into discourses and dialogues with Indian scholars and presented Christianity before the Indian, not as an alien religion, but as the *Satya Veda* (True knowledge) in the place of the lost Indian *Vedas*. To gain acceptance among the Indians, he became a true Indian ascetic not in appearance but in body, mind and spirit. He claimed that he was not a *Paranghi,* but Roman of the Raja caste and a *Sanyasi* (monk) who came to teach the spiritual law. The unique contribution of De Nobilee was his penetrating insights in discovering the spiritual treasures and the cultural heritage of India. He arrived at the conclusion that the only way to win the hearts, respect and esteem of the Indians was inculturation. He disassociated himself from his fellow-Jesuits, exchanged his black cassocks for *Kavi* robes and his leather shoes for wooden sandals. He retired to mud-walled hut with a small chapel and established himself as a *Guru.* He obtained the services of a *Brahmin* cook and followed a strict vegetarian diet with one meal a day. His simplicity, austerity, life of prayer etc. had great impact on the orthodox Hindus. He wore the cord, hair tuft, sandal paste, wooden sandals for shoes and the practices of customary bathing, vegetarianism, hutment asceticism and so on.

The Portuguese attempts to bring up, through unethical means, a hybrid population loyal to their colonial masters flopped in penetrating into the Indian minds. The caste Hindus who constituted the main body of the Hindu Society were kept out of the targets of the missionaries. The sublime teachings of Jesus Christ and the values upheld by Christianity were acceptable to the high caste Hindus. But, the Indians abhorred the lifestyles of the European missionaries and their new converts. In general, the Indians had a contempt for the *Paranghis*, a term used to cover the Portuguese and also those Europeans who toed the Portuguese line.

"The unique contribution of Robert De Nobilee in India is his penetrating insights in discovering the spiritual treasures and cultural heritage of India. He courageously endured the stress and strain to resist the colonial imperialism resulting from superiority complex and arbitrariness to impose the Western practices and traditions on the new missions in India."[13]

De Nobilee met with strong opposition to his methods from his own superiors and fellow missionaries. His Provincial Peso, Fr. Fernandez, S.J., Visitor Limenta and the Bishop of Cochin vehemently opposed his style of functioning. In 1612, he was even prohibited from giving baptism. This prohibition continued till 1616. Several Hindus and even his new converts were instigated against him. In 1619, a discussion held at Goa helped to clarify some of the issues. But, the matter was referred to Rome for a final decision. In 1623, Rome clarified that the high caste converts could retain their external symbols of nobility, without Hindu ceremonies. This was a partial vindication of the position of De Nobilee. He stood steadfast on his commitment and vision.

Later, De Nobilee extended his activities to Dharmapuri, Gingee and Northern regions to concentrate his apostolate among the *Adi Dravidas* and the *Cudras*. Fr. Balthasar De Casta and Fr. Manuel Alvarez helped him. His work among the Cudra caste assumed the character of a movement with remarkable success. A survey in 1644 revealed the number of converts in Tiruchirappally alone as 4183. In 1645, he was transferred to Jaffna in Ceylon. But Nobilee was growing old with declining health and becoming almost blind. Therefore, he returned from Jaffna, spent his last years in Mylapore and died on January 16, 1656, after a successful and innovative career.

He formulated a theology of inculturation specially suited for the Tamilnadu context. He fully overhauled the existing missionary style to introduce Christianity as a religion that upholds spiritual values and at the same time respecting the religious and cultural heritage of India – a harmonious blending of intellect and culture. He had to endure long-sufferings for a noble cause, but lived up to his high ideals of asceticism with success.

A letter of his Provincial Laerzio to the Jesuit general dated December 13, 1608 is reproduced below:

"Next in order the better to win the respect and esteem of this people, he buried himself in a mysterious solitude never going out of his house, admitting visitors only with extreme reserve. For the true means attracting these people is to excite their curiosity. Fr. Robert charmed everybody by his conversation, the stories and passages from Indian authors which he quotes from memory, and by a great number of verses of his own composition, which he partly sings and partly recites with exquisite delicacy and distinction."[14]

"Much talk is there on the importance of inculturation, but very little is done in bearing witness to a life of simplicity and asceticism widely respected and appreciated by the people of India. Evangelical zeal, genuine human concern and Christian charity will alone qualify the missionary to bear lasting fruits in the Indian missions. Robert de Nobilee has been a shining example and source of inspiration to the future generations of India."[15]

FOOTNOTES

1. PPLM 54-55, *Paulinus S. Bartholomew, Viaggio Alle Indie Orientali*, Roma, 1796, p. 143.
2. *Ibid.*, PPLM, p. 58.
3. Xavier Koodapuzha (Dr.), *Christianity in India*, p. 175.
4. Bishop Gorantla Johannes, *Catholic Mission in the Region of Andhra Pradesh*, New Delhi, 1995, p. 101.
5. Xavier Koodapuzha (Dr.), *Christianity in India*, pp. 202-04.

6. J.V. Velinkar S.J., *Catholic Mission in the Region of Bombay*, AKMD, p. 153.
7. *Ibid.*, p. 155.
8. Rajasekhar, V.T., *Dalit Voice*, Sept. 1984, p. 3 - AKMD, p. 164.
9. Fidelis de Sa, *Crisis in Chotanagpur*, Bangalore, 1975, p. 134. *Source:* Xavier Koodapuzha (Dr.), *Christianity in India*, pp. 226-28.
10. Cyril Bruce Firth, *An Introduction to Indian Church History*, 1983.
11. Xavier Koodapuzha (Dr.), *Christianity of India*, pp. 176-78.
12. Thekkedathu, J., *History of Christianity in India*, p. 212.
13. Xavier Koodapuzha (Dr.), *Christianity in India*, p. 184.
14. Thekkedathu, J., *History of Christianity in India*, p. 213.
15. Xavier Koodapuzha (Dr.), *Christianity in India*, p. 188.

Protestant Christianity in India

24

Introduction

In the sixteenth century, a revolt protesting against the faith and practices in the Christian Church took place in Europe. The *raison d'être* for the protest was the radical questions of faith raised by various European Reformers like Martin Luther, John Calvin, Ulrich Swingly, Wycliff and others. This revolt, known in history as 'Reformation Movement', resulted in an almost vertical division in the Church in Europe, till then holding a compact and united face, into two distinct entities, the Catholic Church and the Protestant Churches. By the eighteenth century, this division had its impact in the European colonies in America, Australia and the Afro-Asian countries including India. The Reformers generally focused on certain radical questions on faith of the Christian Church. The cardinal principles of alternative faith developed and accepted unanimously by the Reformists were:

1. The Bible is the supreme foundation of the Christian Church,
2. Justification by faith in Jesus Christ alone, and
3. Universal Priesthood for all believers.

Several other doctrines of faith were also involved in the reformation, but many of them failed to gain unanimous acceptance. To avoid division within their kingdoms, the monarchs in Europe, both Catholics and Protestants, arrived at a compromise formula known as '*Cujus Regio*, *ejus religio*' (religion of the ruler is the religion of the people). This formula reflected in the religion in each kingdom, in various degrees, in Europe and automatically had its impact in their respective colonies abroad. Resultantly, all the colonies had to heed to the will of their colonial masters in Europe. In practice, the Church in the colonies, to all intents and purposes, reflected the image of the divided Christianity in Europe. (Please see notes on the Reformation Movement available in Part Five – Chapter 32.)

The Latin Catholic Church spread in India and other European colonies under the auspices of the Kings of Portugal and Spain, who were empowered in this behalf by the Popes under the Padroado agreement. Toeing the line of the Catholics, the Protestant movement also devised a mechanism by forming an alliance of England, Holland and the Scandinavian countries. Accordingly, the Dutch settled at Pulicat near Madras and Nagapatnam, the British concentrated at Masulipatnam, Madras, Cuddalore and Calcutta. The Danes settled at Tranquebar (Tharangampady) in Tanjore district. The French chose Pondicherry for Catholic missionary work. The Portuguese were pioneers in the Western Coast of India. The Protestant missionaries opted the Eastern Coast. To animate and co-ordinate the mission work, the Reformists registered two societies, the 'Society for Promoting Christian Knowledge' (SPCK) in 1698 and another 'Society for Propagating the Gospel' (SPG) in 1701. These societies provided the Indian missions with financial support and ecclesiastical guidance.

The English East India Company

The English East India Company was registered in England, just like any other commercial company, aimed at trade and profit. The attitude of the Company was not favourable to the foreign missionaries. In fact, the Protestant missionaries followed the respective flags of their nations. In India, there was a saying that whenever a Protestant Church originated in Europe or America (a usual practice), a pocket edition or miniature of that Church would appear in India within days or weeks. Even allowing a margin for exaggeration, the truth behind the saying is more or less correct. Everyday a particular denomination of the Protestants takes shape in some corner of the World and a stereotype of that denomination is likely to emerge in India, sooner or later.

The East India Company had a practice of appointing Chaplains solely for the pastoral care of their own people. But, the Catholic Church followed the practice of mission work in other countries and among other peoples. The Protestants gradually followed suit resulting in an awakening among them. After the new charter of 1813, the company began facilitating the imparting of education. Gradually, the Church Mission Society (CMS) became more involved in the Indian missions. From 1833 onwards, more missionaries came to India from Europe and USA as detailed below:

Mission	Place of Arrival	Year
1. Basel Mission	South Canara	1834
2. Gossner's Evangelical Lutheran Mission	Bihar	1839
3. Leipzig Lutheran Mission	Tranquebar (Tharangampady)	1841
4. American Board	Bombay Ahmednagar	1813 1831
5. Madurai Mission	Madurai	1834
6. American Presbyterians	Punjab United Province	1834 1836
7. American Baptists	Andhra and Assam	1836
8. American Lutherans	Northern Circars and Andhra	1842[1]

In 1858, the British Parliament took over the administration of India from the East India Company. This facilitated not only to overcome the hostility of the East India Company but also for the devolution of greater freedom and more powers to those at the lower echelons of the mission in touch with ground realities. Later, due to the vicissitudes of history, political authority, hierarchical development, growth of missionary zeal in England etc., the Anglican Church in India became more powerful than the other Protestant Churches. Anglicanism gradually replaced Lutheranism.

Missionary Methods

(i) The Translation of the Bible into Local Languages and its Diffusion

The pioneers of this fruitful method were the Tranquebar Mission (Danish-Halle mission) under the leadership of Bartholomew Zeigenbalg and Plutschau of the Halle University Mission. The contributions of Marshman, William Ward, James Hough and others were also highly significant in this line. Though their initial translations were not upto the mark, their efforts provided the foothold for future improvements.

(ii) Establishment of Educational Institutions

This proved very effective to closely interact with people and enlighten them on the ideals of Christianity. Literacy ensured social progress, liberation from superstitions, scope for employment, desire for learning, cultural progress and so on. Anderson and Braithwait took the initiative to start the Madras Christian College in 1837. To promote literacy, dictionaries in native languages linked with foreign languages were compiled and published. This fostered assimilation with world culture. The contact with the ancient Christian communities in Kerala through the efforts of British Residents, Col. Macaulay and Col. Munroe, paved the way for the arrival of many enlightened missionaries like Rev. Thomas Norton (1816), Joseph Fen (1818), Benjamin Baily (1816), Henry Backer (1819) and others. Their contributions in the field of education were outstandingly memorable. The C.M.S. College and Press at Kottayam (Kerala) are the fruits of their labour.

(iii) Spreading of Christian Literature

The spreading of Christian literature translated into regional languages complemented the literacy drive initiated earlier by the missionaries. This enabled them to present Jesus Christ and Christianity in the proper perspective, Jesus as the Redeemer of the oppressed and exploited millions and Christianity as the ray of hope for liberation to the downtrodden, neglected and the toiling masses of all nations without discrimination. This awakened the people at the lower strata of the society, who spontaneously and positively responded to the call of the missionaries.

(iv) Evangelisation through Home Missions

The Zenana Missionary Society started in 1880 proved very effective and successful in the evangelisation of families. The role of Ramabai, a *Brahmin* convert proved very helpful in this respect.

(v) Integral Development of the Oppressed and Depressed Classes

This produced positive results not only in the welfare of the neglected poor but also in accelerating evangelisation. Hence, the missionaries concentrated more attention among the people in the lower strata. A vast majority of those baptised in those days belonged to this category.

(vi) Health Care

The Protestant missionaries played an active role in the field of health care. Vellore, Nellore, Guntur, Bareilly etc. point out their success.

1. The Lutheran Evangelical Missions in India

Among the many denominations of the Reformist Churches, the first one to establish in India was the Lutheran Church. The Pietist Movement in Germany (particularly in the Halle University), the Pre-Methodist awakening in England, Royal Danish sense of Christian responsibility, widespread evangelisation zeal created by the Reformists in Western Europe and the presence of existing Danish mission at Tranquebar contributed for the establishment of the Tranquebar (Tharangampady) Mission in the erstwhile Thanjavur Kingdom of South India.

(i) The Tranquebar Mission (Danish Halle Mission)

King Ferdinand IV of Denmark took the initiative to start a mission at Tranquebar. He sponsored the endeavour, financed the project from his own pocket, contacted the Leipzig Mission of Germany and deputed two eminent German evangelists to India. Accordingly, Bartholomew Zeigenbalg, a pioneer in

Dravidology accompanied by Plutschau landed at Tranquebar in 1706. They managed to enlist the support and co-operation of several eminent natives like Rajanaickan (a Catechist). Aaron (the first Tamilian to receive ordination), Sathyanathan (a pastor in Tirunelveli District), Vedanayagom Shastry (a Tamil poet), J.P. Fabricius of Madras and many others. One C.F. Schwartz (the teacher of the King of Thanjavur), who joined the mission accelerated the tempo of progress of the mission and enhanced the number of converts from 350 to 4000 through his strenuous efforts during a long span of forty-eight years. Thus, the Tranquebar mission, active in Thanjavur kingdom, expanded its areas of activity to Madras, Tiruchirappally, Cuddalore etc.

In the early stages, the attitude of the Danish officials in Thanjavur was not favourable to the missionaries. They created several obstacles, including wrongful confinement of missionaries. But, the Royal Danish mission and the Society for Propagation of the Gospel favoured and encouraged the missionaries. Therefore, they engaged themselves in the propagation of faith through translation, printing and publication of *Bible* and other Christian literature, discourses and correspondence with the non-Christians, establishment of schools and orphanages and so on. They succeeded in their efforts to establish a Church dedicated to the Gospel and rooted in the Indian culture. But, due to the impact of European enlightenment, Napoleanic Wars, political difficulties in India etc., the Tranquebar Church declined by the end of the eighteenth century. This led to the termination of the Royal Danish Mission in the early decades of the 19th century.

(ii) The Tamil Evangelical Lutheran Church

The seeds sown by the Tranquebar Mission were not lost altogether. The first heir of the Tranquebar Mission was the Society for the Propagation of the Gospel that incorporated most of the existing congregations in the Anglican Church, in 1825. But, many congregations in and around Tranquebar remained Lutheran. They joined together, resumed and reconstructed their Church. In 1971, this Church had 70,992 baptised members in 72 pastorates, besides a Diaspora church in Rangoon. In the area of education, their achievements were impressive with 168 elementary schools, 8 high schools, two training schools, one college and two schools for the blind supplemented by homes for children and hostels. In the Health Care area also, this Church was very active with significant results.

(iii) The India Evangelical Lutheran Church

The second offshoot of the Leipzig Mission took shape in 1894, when few missionaries shifted their allegiance to the Lutheran Church due to doctrinal differences with the American Missions. Radio evangelism, the Voice of the Gospel, the highly developed theological education (Concordia Seminary at Nagercoil), Translation of the Book of Concord into Tamil and Malayalam etc. were some of the innovative methodology adopted by this Church. In 1969, this Church had 39,448 baptised members.

(iv) The Andhra Evangelical Lutheran Church

The pioneer instrumental in the establishment of this Church was an enthusiastic American missionary of German birth, Dr. J.C.F. Heyer, who turned to Guntur in Andhra from his mission in Tamilnadu. This Church followed the Lutheran Confession in a moderate way. One speciality noticed in this Church was that a number of *Sudras* joined the Church; they formed 2 per cent of the membership. In 1944, this Church became autonomous and an Indian national, Dr. E. Prakasam was elected President. They had a network of excellent schools. In 1960, elementary schools were surrendered to the government. Andhra Christian College at Guntur, Andhra Christian Theological College at Rajamundhry, the Kugler Hospital at Guntur etc. still remain prestigious institutions of this Church. In 1969, the membership of this church was 2,81,055 in addition to 96,060 communicant members spread over 2125 congregations. A number of academic and technical institutions, hospitals etc. were also run by this Church.

(v) The South Andhra Lutheran Church

The American Lutheran Church supported this Church. They concentrated their attention in Nellore and Chittoor districts. Its baptised membership approximates 15,000 in 33 congregations. (Reliable statistics are not available.)

(vi) The Arcot Evangelical Lutheran Church

The Leipzig Mission venture in Tamilnadu became the starting point of a 'casteless' Church. In 1968, this Church had 18,367 baptised members in 19 pastorates.

(vii) The Jeypore Evangelical Lutheran Church

The missionaries crossed the hills in Andhra and reached the southern tip of Orissa around Jeypore in 1884. During and after World War I, the American and Denmark missions came to their help. They converted many from the upper class Hindus and the *Dalits* of the 'Dambas' tribe. In 1971, this mission had a membership of 53,324 in 702 congregations.

(viii) The Gossner Evangelical Lutheran Church

In 1845, J.E. Gossner, the Revival teacher in Berlin deputed four missionaries to India. They chose Ranchi and Chotanagpur as their mission fields. By the second half of the 19th century, this Church surpassed all other Lutheran Churches in India in growth and strength. Despite persecution and heavy losses to the Anglican and Catholic Churches and the uprising of the landless Sardars during the Political Revolt in 1857, the Lutheran Church increased its number of converts, from the *Uraons*, *Mundas* and some other linguistic minorities, to one hundred thousand in 1914. The development of Ranchi into a major industrial area made the Gossner Evangelical Lutheran Church alive to the social and spiritual problems of an urban society. By 1970, the membership of this church grew to 2,57,611 baptised members in 1228 congregations, an enviable growth on all counts.

(ix) The Northern Evangelical Lutheran Church

In 1867, two Scandinavians, one Norwegian and one Danish missionary left the service in the Gossner mission and began to preach among the Santals in the Santal Parganas

District of Bihar and established the 'Indian Home Missions to the Santals'. The Northern Evangelical Lutheran Church replaced the Evangelical Lutheran Church in N.E. India and the Ebenezer Lutheran Church. This Church later started the mission work in Nepal also. By 1970, this Church has grown to 42,069 baptised members, 7 High Schools, 4 Hospitals, 1 School each for Nursing and the blind, 2 Leprosy Homes, 1 Agricultural School, tea estate, Printing press and the Santhal Theological Seminary, Benagaria.

(x) The Evangelical Lutheran Church in Madhya Pradesh

The Evangelical Lutheran Missionary Society, Stockholm took up the mission in the districts of Bhopal, Shadol, Sarguja and Narasingpur of Madhya Pradesh in 1877. In 1971, this Church had 6275 baptised members.

Out of the ten Churches mentioned above, the most successful were the Andhra Mission and the Ranchi and Chotanagpur Mission. A major conference of the five missions in South India was held at Kodaikanal in 1905. All India level Conferences were later held at Guntur, Rajamundhry, Guntur and Madras in 1908, 1912, 1921 and 1925-26 respectively. The Danish Pathan Mission in Pakistan was added in 1941 to the Indian Missions and a Federation of the Evangelical Lutheran Churches in India was founded in 1966 with a membership of 0.775 million.[2] (The latest reliable figures of this church are not available.)

2. The Baptist Churches in India

"The third largest concentration of the Baptist Churches in the world (after USA and U.S.S.R.) is found in the crescent along the shores of the Bay of Bengal extending from Andhra Pradesh through Orissa, Bengal, Assam, Meghalaya, Nagaland, Tripura, Manipur down to South-Eastern Burma. Three-fourths of the two million Baptists of this region live in India, belonging to six thousand local congregations.

At the centre of this crescent lies Serampore, where the history of Baptists in India began nearly 180 years ago. The work of William Carey, the first Baptist missionary and his associates in the Serampore mission had an impact far beyond the limits of their denomination, so much so that Carey is frequently called the Father of the Protestant Missions (though he was not the first Protestant missionary). The first Indian Baptist, Krishna Pal, was baptised in the Hoogly River at Serampore in 1800. In the following twenty-two years he ministered not only in Calcutta and other parts of Bengal but also, for a time, among the Khasi people of Meghalaya. The early Baptists of Bengal are noted for their strong opposition to castes (though they opposed the giving of new names at the time of baptism). Various efforts for social reform, the establishment of the Serampore College and the publication of portions of the *Bible* in more than thirty-five languages were undertaken by the Serampore mission. During the first fifty years of its existence, the Serampore mission was entirely self-supporting."[3]

Though this Church had a promising beginning in Bengal, it did not achieve a proportionate growth or expansion in Bengal. A '*Madiga*' named Periah initiated an independent mass movement for the spread of the Baptist Church in Andhra Pradesh with marvellous results. In the 20th century, remarkable expansion of Baptists in Andhra and Orissa is noticed, but the major expansion was in the North Eastern States (Assam, Meghalaya, Nagaland, Manipur and Tripura). Baptists were the Christians first permitted to undertake mission work in Tripura State, where their main gains were among the tribals. The Baptist Churches in India are mutually related through a Baptist Union of India that provided nothing more than occasional meetings. They maintained a number of medical and educational institutions, including five Theological Colleges in Assam, Bengal, Orissa and Andhra. The Serampore College became one of ecumenical character. The Baptist Churches are actively involved in the National Christian Councils of India. One group among the Baptist Churches celebrates Sabhat on Saturday instead of Sunday and therefore known as 'Seventh Day Baptists'.

3. The Methodist Churches

John Wesley, an Anglican priest, is the founder of this Church, approved by England in 1794. They followed the teachings of John Calvin. The founder gave shape to a liturgy of his own. The Methodist missionaries reached India in 1956. At present, their membership in India is six hundred thousand under six bishops. The Methodists in South India are now part of the Church of South India (CSI) and those in North India are partially members of the CNI (The Church of North India). (Details about these unions follow.)

A Joint Ecumenical Commission of the Catholic and protestant churches was set up in 1966 between the Catholic and the Methodist churches. Dialogue on episcopacy, priesthood, sacraments, Petrine ministry etc. is in progress under the auspices of the Commission.

4. The Salvation Army

The Salvation Army given shape to in England in 1867 'conquered' India in 1882. They have no bishops or sacraments or churches. Songs, prayer, preaching and philanthropic activities form their lifestyle. They believe in 'Eleven Canons of Faith'. The teaching of the Army is that the life of the members itself is a sacrament and hence no other sacraments are required. Instead of baptism, they march below their flag of red, yellow and blue colours. In India, they have a membership of five hundred thousand, out of which one hundred thousand are in Kerala spread over in 500 centres. The Salvation Army in India is divided into six regions, Madras, Delhi, North-East, South-West and West.

The first Salvation Army Hospital was started in India in Nagercoil in 1900. Today, they run 9 Hospitals, 4 Dispensaries, 147 Primary Schools and 7 high and secondary schools. In 1906, to help the millions of handloom weavers, Capt. Prem Das (Maxwell) invented a fast loom and an improved warping machine. In 1908, the Salvation Army was invited by the U.P. Government to solve the problem of 'criminals among the tribals'. The experiment was successful not only in U.P. but also in Punjab, Madras, Bengal, Orissa etc. At the invitation of the Bombay Municipality, the Salvation Army in 1920 handled the problem of rehabilitation of beggars. The Salvation Army combines a fervent, joyous and religious faith with a practical worldwide social service network.

5. The Presbyterian Church

The followers of John Calvin, a French lay theologian, are known as Presbyterians. Calvin, with the assistance of his collaborator William Paul, systematised the Protestant teachings and published his book ' Institutes'. John Knox propagated this system in Scotland. Later, it spread to England, Holland and South Africa. Presbyters are the heads of the Congregations in this church. There is no episcopacy. Calvin did not accept the real presence of Christ in the Eucharist. This Church spread mainly in the North-East India with a membership of 4,50,000 at present.

6. The Anglican Church

As we have already seen, the Church of England, during the period of King Henry VIII, severed its relations with Rome and became an independent Church. Due to the national character of this Church, it was later known as the Anglican Church. During the period of monarchs Edward VI and Queen Elizabeth, this Church accepted most of the Protestant ideals. It spread to India during the British Rule. They built Churches all over India for the ecclesiastical needs of British officers and soldiers in India. In the meantime, the Church Missionary Society, the London Missionary Society and the Basel Missions started their own independent churches under the protectorate of the Anglican Church. All these churches work under the guidance of the Lambeth Conference.

7. The CMS Church in India (Travancore-Cochin CMS Diocese)

This church originated in the Central Kerala diocese of the C.S.I. Church, as the result of an agitation within the diocese under the leadership of Fr. Stephen, the parish priest of Enathu, who obtained episcopal ordination at the hands of an Orthodox Bishop named James Parkendise in 1966. The reason for the agitation was the denial of adequate representation and recognition for the converts from the lower classes. Due to internal conflicts and litigations, this community now stands divided into different groups. Bishop Stephen Vattappara, the son of Bishop Stephen claims that he is the moderator of four dioceses, Haryana, Delhi, Amritsar and Dehra Dun. Though Fr. Stephen was motivated by the desire to obtain a greater share of the welfare projects, the ultimate result of his movement was disappointing.

8. The Pentecostal Churches

The term 'Pentecostal' is very loosely applied to all churches upholding reformist traditions that charismatic gifts experienced on the day of Pentecost are still operative. Basically, all Pentecostals believe:

The *Bible* is God-inspired scripture.

Simplicity in worship.

The Christ will visibly return to earth.

Holiness of life.

Believer's baptism.

Individual believers as well as the Church shall be filled with and led by the Holy Spirit.[4]

The Pentecostal churches are congregational with no organisational set up above the congregation. This Church is growing very rapidly all over India. There are eight Ministerial Training schools in India at present with one college at Bangalore running a five-year course. The Revival Church among them deny the doctrine of Trinity, though all other Pentecostals accept the doctrine.

9. The Mennonite Brothren Church in India

The Mennonite Church Conference of North America sent few missionaries to India after 1899. They evangelised the Telegu people in Hyderabad and its suburban areas. Within a decade, another group of Mennonite Missionaries joined them. They spread the Good News of Redemption through Jesus Christ among the Telegu people. The mission field embraced a population of several millions living in over 2000 villages. By 1958, the live membership of the Mennonite Brothren Church of India had grown to 20,000 with a communicant constituency of one hundred thousand.

In 1958, a change in the administrative set up was necessitated. The Church conference in North America transferred the administrative responsibility of the Church entirely to the India Mennonite Brothren Christians. A constitution was formulated and accepted in 1959. Thence onwards, we see fantastic growth for this Church among people of all classes, castes and occupations. Even from 1900, this Church turned its attention to education. During the one hundred and five years of history of this Church, the educational ministry developed a system of organised schools ranging from primary schools to a seminary Training Centre at Shamshabad. Along with this, the Church turned its attention to 'Health Care'. The Church started Clinics and Dispensaries and two hospitals. Another area where they concentrated their attention was publications. A publishing and printing house was established at Mahboobnagar. Utilising modern technological advances, they initiated radio evangelism and correspondence courses. Within a span of little over one century, the Andhra Mennonite Brothren Church brought hundreds of faithful into its fold and now it is poised to bring many more hundreds in the years to come.

10. The Society of Religious Friends (Quakers)

This Church originated in England. In the early stages itself, it spread to North America and Europe. In India, there are about five hundred members, mainly in the rural districts of Madhya Pradesh, many of whose ancestors came into the society through the humanitarian work undertaken during the famine of 1897-99.

11. The Church of South India (CSI)

The Lambeth Conference of 1888 proposed a union of the churches based on four points noted below, came to be known as the 'Lambeth Quadrilateral' (Please see detailed notes on Lambeth Conference – Chapter 39 of Part Five):

(a) The Holy Scriptures of the Old and the New Testaments contain all things necessary for salvation.

(b) The Apostles' Creed and the Nicene Creed.

(c) The two Sacraments ordained by Christ Himself, Baptism and the Lord's Supper.

(d) The historic episcopate, locally adapted (Report of the Joint Committee on Union 1925).

A Joint Union Negotiations Committee was formed for negotiations.

The Lambeth Conference also issued a statement, which reads: "We believe that the Union is the will of God, even as our Lord prayed that we might all be one that the World might believe. We face together the titanic task of the winning of India for Christ – one fifth of the human race. And yet confronted by such an overwhelming responsibility, we find ourselves rendered weak and relatively impotent by unhappy divisions – divisions for which we were not responsible."[5]

Bengt Sundkler in his book *The Church of South India – The Movement Towards Union – 1910/1947* narrated in detail, step by step, the events and words ultimately led to the Union of churches. *Inter alia,* he cites two reasons for the initiative taken by the Indian Christians for Union "while these were some of the main organisations which tended to bring the European missionaries in South India together, one might well ask what were the general reasons why the Indian Christians themselves should begin to consider union. Singled out here are two of these reasons, one socio-economic, the other political."[6]

The inauguration of the Church of South India was the result of 47 years of negotiations among the uniting churches, namely, the Anglican Church, the Methodist Church and the South India United Church (SIUC). The SIUC itself was a federal – type union of churches coming under all the three systems of administration, episcopal, presbyterian and congregational. This concern, which led to the first World Missionary Conference at Edinburgh in 1910, was also the concern that produced the SIUC (South India United Church).

In 1900, the Presbyterian Churches of Scotland united together under a common name 'The United Free Church of Scotland'. In 1901, there was a similar development in India under the name 'The South India United Church'. It was an inspiration for the congregational churches. They followed suit and formed a union among them known as 'Madurai District' in 1905. The federations of the Presbyterian and Congregational churches initiated a dialogue in 1907. In 1908, they formed an alliance known as 'South India United Church'. It was the expression of the aspirations for unity and the first stepping-stone to the ultimate union of all churches in India. In 1919, the Anglican Church represented by Bishop Assariah and Dr. Sherwood Reddy entered into a dialogue with the S.I.U.C. at Tranquebar. It led to the acceptance of a common manifesto known as *Tranquebar Manifesto*. It was agreed in the manifesto that the prospective union of churches should imbibe the characteristics of the three types of churches, Presbyterian, Congregational and Episcopal. They also accepted all the four points setforth in the Lambeth Quadrilateral.

In 1940, the constituent churches officially accepted a common formula of union. The General Council of the SIUC accepted the formula. The Anglican Church agreed in 1947. The long process of dialogue and reconciliation happily concluded on September 27, 1947 with the inauguration of the 'Church of South India' by Bishop C.K. Jacob at the St. George Cathedral Madras. The South Indian Protestant churches thus accomplished the second step of union.

In 1989, the CSI Church had 22 dioceses including Sri Lanka as described below:

Karnatak	-	3
Kerala	-	4
Tamilnadu	-	9
Andhra	-	5
Sri Lanka	-	1
Total	-	22

According to available statistics, the Church of South India has 25,55,000 members, 1228 parishes, 1214 ministers and 8715 congregations.[7]

The CSI does not regard it as a final union. They look forward to a Union at all India level embracing all non-Catholic Churches within its fold. The CSI, at the instance of its Synod, sent invitations to all non-Catholic churches for dialogue. The CSI-Lutheran theological discussions continued from 1948 to 1959. The dialogue has resulted in the drafting of a constitution for a United Church.

In the meanwhile, the CSI has established a relationship of Inter-communion with the Mar Thoma Church in Kerala and the Church of North India, that came into being in 1970.

The presence of non-episcopal ordained ministers in CSI strained its relations with the Anglican Church. Though the CSI scheme was approved by the Lambeth conference in 1930 itself, the Conference held in 1948 adopted a position not favouring communion with the CSI. From the days of its inception, the CSI is a member of the World Council of Churches. As matters stand at present, the CSI is a member of the World Methodist Council and the World Alliance of Reformed Churches. It now looks forward for a union with the Church of North India (CNI).[8]

12. The Church of North India (CNI)

The plan of Union of Churches in North India found expression in the Edinburgh Conference of 1910 and the Tranquebar Manifesto of 1919. Various Presbyterian and Congregational Churches in North India came together in 1924 to form the United Church of North India. The Weslyan Methodist Church desired to convene a Round Table Conference to discuss the possibility of a wider union. Accordingly, a Round Table Conference was convened at Lucknow in 1929. The Australian Methodist Church, the Weslyian Methodist Church, the Methodist Episcopal Church and the UCNI participated in the Conference. The Anglican Church attended as a visitor. The Conference, after discussing various doctrinal issues, resolved to continue Round Table Conferences and emphasised the necessity of creating public opinion and the desirability of promoting fraternal intercourse between the Churches.

The next Round Table Conference was held at Delhi in 1930. The representatives of the Brothren Church and the Society of Friends attended the conference, in addition to the earlier participants. United Presbyterian Mission of the Punjab and two delegates from the Joint Committee on Union in South India attended as visitors. An All India Conference on Church Union was held at Nagpur in 1931 under the chairmanship of Bishop Azariah of Dornakal. Five representatives of North India and four of South India attended. The third Round Table Conference was held at Lucknow in 1937. Some of the churches that attended the previous Conference dropped out. The negotiations were continued by the United Church of North India with the Methodist Episcopal Church and the Baptists, around a Plan for Union. The Plan avoided any commitment to the Episcopate. From 1940, the Baptists withdrew, for a time, from the Round Table. A revised edition of the Plan was published in 1954. The Plan of Union was reviewed twice and finally accepted on the lines of the scheme accepted by the Church of South India.

The inauguration of the Church of North India took place on 29th November 1970 at Nagpur. Today, this Church has 19 dioceses representing different traditions and covering a membership round about six hundred thousand. As being a United Church and a Unifying Church, the Church of North India is committed to work for a wider Union with other churches in North India and therefrom to proceed to the inauguration of a Church of India.

Conclusion

The history of the Evangelical missions in India developed in the beginning of the eighteenth century from the evangelical awakening of Protestantism, first in Europe and later in America. Lutheran Pietists set the tone, Wesley Revival provided the necessary dynamism and William Carey's Baptist Missionary Society laid the foundation and structure of the mission. It began with the arrival of Bartholomew Ziegenbalg and Henry Plutschau at Tranquebar in 1706. Schwartz provided the required momentum. When he died in 1798, a Church with a membership of 20,000 was in place. William Carey arrived in 1793. He inaugurated a new era of awakening in the Protestant missions in India. The Serampore Trio consisting of Carey, Marshman and Ward translated the *Bible*, promoted humanitarian reforms, preached, printed and taught the gospel and founded a Christian College. Others followed the tracks cleared by the Baptists. In 1798 the London Missionary Society started their mission in South India.

In the 19th century, missionaries from Britain, America and Europe came for service in India representing their respective missions, societies and churches, as below:

British

Church Missionary Society	– 1813
Weslian Methodist Missionary Society	– 1819
General Baptist Missionary Society	– 1821
Church of Scotland	– 1829
Plymouth Brethren	– 1833
Welsh Calvinistic Methodists	– 1840
Irish Presbyterians	– 1841
Free Church of Scotland	– 1843

American

American Board of Commissioners	– 1812
American Presbyterians	– 1833
American Baptists	– 1835
Dutch Reformed Church of America	– 1836
Methodist Episcopal Church	– 1856

European

Basel Mission	– 1818
Gossner Mission	– 1839
Leipzig Missionary Society	– 1840
Berlin Missionary Society	– 1842
North German Missionary Society	– 1843
Swedish Lutherans	
Moravian Brothren	

These missions confronted several problems in India, cultural and linguistic diversities, caste, traditional religions, famine, poverty and the hostility of the East India Company. The War of 1857 ended the rule of the East India Company. This brought forth a more favourable atmosphere for the missions and facilitated the expansion of the Church Missionary Society and more Anglican dioceses. The nineteenth century witnessed the arrival of more Indian missionaries in the field of missions. In the period between 1914 and 1975, the number of missionaries increased and the Protestant Christian community doubled. Nationalism, World War II and Independence brought radical changes in the Indian scenario. India had the largest missionary force in the world. But, now their number has declined from an earlier figure of 5682 to about 3600 in 1970. In some areas like Nagaland, Arunachal, Tripura etc., foreigners are not permitted to enter. Radical Hindus try to reconvert Christians. Derogatory remarks and reports are made against missionaries. Anti-conversion laws are being enacted in some States. The future growth of the Christian Church in India is in the hands of the Indian Christians and their Church.

Ecumenism and Missiology

William Carey first initiated the Ecumenical movement during his evangelical missions in India. He urged the holding of a World Missionary Conference at Cape of Good Hope in 1810 and at regular intervals thereafter. Though his proposal was not carried through, missionaries of various organisations did meet regularly at Calcutta. Similar gatherings were held in Bombay and Madras. From 1872 onwards, All India-level gatherings are held regularly. An All India Conference held at Madras in 1902 became the model for the Edinburgh Missionary Conference in 1910 from which originated the International Missionary Council, the World Conciliary Council and other similar agencies. Such gatherings can provide interaction among various churches and mutual understanding, which can pave the way for ultimate union of churches.

Missiology

William Carey's 'Enquiry' was a missiological treatise. The Central theme of the thesis was tested and put into practice by Carey himself when he started his mission in India. Recently, J.W. Pickett and D.A. Mc Gavran developed this idea, with particular reference to the Indian context.

The theologians of the Catholic Church, more recently, are developing the practicability of this idea in the area of ecumenical thinking.[9]

FOOTNOTES

1. Xavier Koodapuzha, *Christianity in India*, pp. 247-48.
2. George Menachery (Prof.), *The St. Thomas Christian Encyclopaedia*, Vol. I, pp. 65-68.
3. *Ibid.*, Vol. I, p. 69.
4. *Ibid.*, Vol. I, p. 76.
5. *Ibid.*, Vol. I, p. 76.
6. Bengt Sundkler, *The Church of South India, The Movement Towards Union 1910/1947*, p. 30.
7. Xavier Koodapuzha (Dr.), *Christianity in India*, pp. 253-55.
8. George Menachery (Prof.), *The St. Thomas Christian Encyclopaedia*, Vol. I, p. 77.
9. *Ibid.*, Vol. I, pp. 78-79.